Superheroes Smash
the Box Office

Superheroes Smash the Box Office

A Cinema History from the Serials to 21st Century Blockbusters

SHAWN CONNER

McFarland & Company, Inc., Publishers
Jefferson, North Carolina

This book has undergone peer review.

LIBRARY OF CONGRESS CATALOGUING-IN-PUBLICATION DATA

Names: Conner, Shawn, author.
Title: Superheroes smash the box office : a cinema history from the serials to 21st century blockbusters / Shawn Conner.
Description: Jefferson, North Carolina : McFarland & Company, Inc., Publishers, 2023. | Includes bibliographical references and index.
Identifiers: LCCN 2023028586 | ISBN 9781476676661 (paperback : acid free paper) ∞ | ISBN 9781476650111 (ebook)
Subjects: LCSH: Superhero films—History and criticism. | LCGFT: Film criticism.
Classification: LCC PN1995.9.S76 C66 2023 | DDC 791.43/6527—dc23/eng/20230620
LC record available at https://lccn.loc.gov/2023028586

BRITISH LIBRARY CATALOGUING DATA ARE AVAILABLE

ISBN (print) 978-1-4766-7666-1
ISBN (ebook) 978-1-4766-5011-1

© 2023 Shawn Conner. All rights reserved

No part of this book may be reproduced or transmitted in any form or by any means, electronic or mechanical, including photocopying or recording, or by any information storage and retrieval system, without permission in writing from the publisher.

Front cover images © 2023 Shutterstock

Printed in the United States of America

*McFarland & Company, Inc., Publishers
Box 611, Jefferson, North Carolina 28640
www.mcfarlandpub.com*

To Louise, who loved Heath Ledger as the Joker … and couldn't believe that the Suicide Squad was a thing.

"Vengeance is mine."
Howard the Duck (1986)

Table of Contents

Introduction	1
Chapter I: It's a Bird, It's a Plane, It's … a Serial	3
1941–1958: *Adventures of Captain Marvel, Batman, Captain America, Superman, Batman and Robin, Atom Man vs. Superman, Superman and the Mole-Men*	
Chapter II: Biff! Bam! and, of Course, Pow!	12
1966–1968: *Batman*	
Chapter III: Hulk Fights a Bear	20
1970s, Pt. 1: *Wonder Woman, The Incredible Hulk, The Amazing Spider-Man, Dr. Strange, Captain America*	
Chapter IV: This Looks Like a Job for Two European Film Producers	30
1970s, Pt. 2: *Superman: The Movie*	
Chapter V: Marvel Gets Its Wish	36
1981–1987: *Superman II, Superman III, Supergirl, Howard the Duck, Superman IV*	
Chapter VI: How One Batfan's Dedication Transformed the Movie Industry	46
1989: *Batman*	
Chapter VII: In the Shadow of the Bat	53
1990–1992: *TMNT, Dick Tracy, Darkman, The Rocketeer, Batman Returns*	
Chapter VIII: Marvel's Woes, and a Dark Horse Enters the Race	60
1990–1995: *The Punisher, Captain America, Fantastic Four, The Crow, The Mask, Tank Girl*	
Chapter IX: Batnipplegate, and Marvel Scores a Hit	69
1995–1999: *Batman Forever, Batman & Robin, Spawn, Steel, Blade*	
Chapter X: Born That Way	79
2000–2002: *X-Men, Spider-Man*	

Table of Contents

Chapter XI: Hulk Throws a Tank — 86
2003–2005: *Daredevil, X2: X-Men United, Hulk, Hellboy, The Punisher, Spider-Man 2, Catwoman, Elektra*

Chapter XII: Batman Begins, Superman Returns and the Silver Surfer Rises — 96
2005–2007: *Batman Begins, Fantastic Four, Superman Returns, X-Men: The Last Stand, Ghost Rider, Spider-Man 3, Fantastic Four: Rise of the Silver Surfer*

Chapter XIII: The Year Marvel Broke — 106
2008: *Iron Man, The Incredible Hulk, The Dark Knight*

Chapter XIV: Summer of the Superhero (and a Winter of Discontent) — 113
2008: *The Dark Knight, The Punisher: War Zone, The Spirit*

Chapter XV: Alternate Histories — 118
2009–2011: *Watchmen, X-Men Origins: Wolverine, Kick-Ass, Thor, X-Men: First Class, The Dark Knight Rises, Captain America: The First Avenger*

Chapter XVI: Avengers Assembled — 129
2012–2013: *The Avengers, The Amazing Spider-Man, The Dark Knight Rises, Dredd, Iron Man 3, Superman Returns, The Wolverine, Thor: The Dark World*

Chapter XVII: A Raccoon and a Tree Walk into a Bar — 137
2014: *Captain America: The Winter Soldier, The Amazing Spider-Man 2, X-Men: Days of Future Past, Guardians of the Galaxy*

Chapter XVIII: High Hopes — 142
2015: *Avengers: Age of Ultron, Ant-Man, Fantastic Four*

Chapter XIX: Ask Not for Whom Dawns the Justice — 147
2016: *Deadpool, Batman v Superman: Dawn of Justice, Captain America: Civil War, X-Men: Apocalypse*

Chapter XX: Let the Amazons Have Some — 157
2017: *Logan, Guardians of the Galaxy Vol. 2, Wonder Woman, Spider-Man: Homecoming, Thor: Ragnarok, Justice League*

Chapter XXI: Peak Superhero — 167
2018: *Black Panther, Avengers: Infinity War, Deadpool 2, Ant-Man and the Wasp, Venom, Aquaman*

Chapter XXII: Endgame — 174
2019: *Glass, Captain Marvel, Shazam!, Hellboy, Fast Color, Avengers: Endgame, Brightburn, X-Men: Dark Phoenix, Spider-Man: Far from Home, Joker*

Chapter XXIII: After the Snap 180

    2020–2021: *Birds of Prey (and the Fantabulous Emancipation of One Harley Quinn), Wonder Woman 1984, Zach Snyder's Justice League, The Suicide Squad, Venom: Let There Be Carnage, The New Mutants, Black Widow, Shang-Chi and the Ten Rings, The Eternals, Spider-Man: No Way Home*

Epilogue 189
Chapter Notes 191
Bibliography 207
Index 225

Acknowledgments

I would like to extend my thanks to all the family and friends who made this book possible, who stood by me and in some cases went the extra distance and watched some of these things with me—my mom and my dad, Marie Laura and Neil Conner, my uncle Leo Paquette, my cousin Ken Paquette, as well as Robyn Hanson and Noémie Pratt-Ryan. I couldn't have gotten to the end of some of these movies without you. Also, thanks to my uncle Morley Conner, who instilled in me a lifelong love of reading, especially pulp fiction.

To all the comics creators whose work I grew up reading and still enjoy to this day, thank you. My imagination is richer for it, even if my bank account isn't.

Introduction

We live in a world dreamt up in the 1960s by middle-aged men on deadline to entertain 12-year-old boys.

As of this writing, four of the ten highest-earning movies are superhero films. In 2016 and 2017, the costume-and-cape brigade accounted for half of the year's ten top-grossing films in the international market; in 2018, 2019 and 2021, they accounted for four. Collectively, superhero flicks have made various studios billions of dollars and have become the predominant genre at movie houses and the measure of the state of filmmaking in the cultural conversation. They've changed the way we watch films and the way we talk and think about them, the way we tell stories and what we expect from them. They have changed business practices at film studios, TV production houses and networks.

And they've made comic books, graphic novels and the people who create them cool. The basement-dwelling, acne-ridden teen writing angry letters-to-the-editor about the Invisible Woman's latest hairstyle or demanding specifics about Wolverine's healing ability has been replaced, or at least joined, by the beautiful people dropping names like Jack Kirby, Steve Ditko and Modok on TV talk shows.

Studios now court once-derided fandom with Easter eggs, convention panels and four-hour director's cuts. Drugstore fantasies once regarded as nothing more than a way to sell cereal are now "canon" and harvested for fan-service. Superhero movies are *The Revenge of the Nerds* writ large on an IMAX screen, with Dolby sound.

We've been living in this world so long—almost two decades—that it's tempting to think that this condition was inevitable. But talk to any comic book fan of a certain vintage, like this author, and you are sure to hear the same mix of disbelief, awe and, yes, even wary satisfaction at the rise of the superhero movie to the top of the pop-culture heap.

For those of us who came of age in the seventies and eighties, live-action superhero offerings were mostly disappointing. Sure, the first couple of Superman movies were exciting. But before that, Batman, Wonder Woman, the Hulk and others barely survived the transition to TV, and after *Superman II* came the four-ring death-knell of *Superman 3*, *Howard the Duck*, *Supergirl* and *Superman IV: The Quest for Peace*. Yes, 1989's *Batman* was (arguably) a step in the right direction, and *Batman Returns* was, um, different. But then came *Batman Forever* and *Batman and Robin*.

And then, in 2000, with the release of *X-Men*, everything changed.

This book traces the origins of the current superhero movie–dominated cultural landscape, from the earliest serials to today's box-office record-setters. Some of the reasons for the genre's progress and popularity are obvious, some less so; some of the names familiar, others unsung. One thing's certain: There were many times that the species could have gone the way of the dodo bird, as per one DC Comics editor's take on Batman's prospects for movie stardom.

In covering this history, I have—for the sake of both my sanity and the reader's—restricted my scope to live-action American movies. Foreign films, animated features and TV series are absent or mentioned only in passing, with a few exceptions; for instance, there was no avoiding the mid-sixties *Batman* TV series, which perhaps was more influential than any other live-action comic-book adaptation on how the public perceived comic books in general and superheroes in particular.

As for my method, I've pieced together this history through books, articles, editorials, audio commentaries, podcasts, reviews and the movies and comics themselves. Inevitably in a book that sums up eight decades of moviemaking in fewer than 300 pages, some titles are going to be barely touched on or absent altogether. To those disappointed at the exclusion of a meaningful exegesis on *Ghost Rider: Spirit of Vengeance*, I can only say, in the words of *Batman & Robin* director Joel Schumacher (RIP): "I'm sorry."

So welcome, dear reader, to this history of superhero movies. Whether you're a casual viewer or a diehard fan, I hope that you will find much to surprise and astonish in the pages to follow.

Chapter 1

It's a Bird, It's a Plane, It's … a Serial

"Bob Kane asked, 'Where's the Batmobile?' I said, 'You're leaning on it.'"
—someone on the set of *Batman* (1943)[1]

"By now the sun had set, leaving the sky a haunting shade of mauve, when suddenly we saw a towering forest of oil derricks etched against the afterglow. 'Ooh,' we said to each other, 'isn't this strange? It feels just like being in another world!'"
—Patricia Ellsworth Wilson, daughter of Whitney Ellsworth, co-writer of the first live-action superhero feature, *Superman and the Mole-Men* (1951)[2]

The first superhero to soar onto the big screen should have been, and almost was, Superman.

Created in the mid-thirties by young Cleveland-based comics and science fiction fans Jerry Siegel and Joe Shuster, the strongman in tights and cape was an immediate sensation upon his 1938 debut. The comic book format was only a couple of years old at that point; the earliest examples were collections of newspaper strips. In 1935, National Allied Publications became the first publisher to print original material, and a few years later commissioned a Superman story from Siegel and Shuster.

Superman was the first modern superhero as we think of them. Some other contenders include Lee Falk's the Phantom, who debuted in newspaper strips in 1936, wore a costume and hid his identity. But the Phantom had no superpowers—unlike Popeye, who gained super-strength through consumption of cans full of spinach. The sailor man debuted in 1929. But, again, not exactly a superhero as we've come to think of them.

Comics may have been in their infancy, but serials were in their golden age. Depression-era audiences was ready for escapist fare, and these black-and-white shorts delivered spies, G-men, detectives, space explorers, jungle kings, jungle queens and femmes fatale in weekly installments, 20 minutes at a time, with cliffhanger endings. They were included in kid-enticing Saturday afternoon packages of newsreels, cartoons and features. By the time Superman debuted on newsstands in *Action Comics* #1, producers were already mining the funny pages for material and drafting the characters Ace Drummond, Dick Tracy, Secret Agent X-9 and Jungle Jim for the big screen.

Three studios were responsible for the bulk of the serials. Republic was the most action- and special effects–oriented; Columbia, which often subcontracted its serials to outside producers, had a reputation for cheapness. Universal was known for casting name actors and for making one of the classics of the form, 1936's *Flash Gordon*.

Recognizing the popularity of National's costumed do-gooder, Republic and Columbia bid on the film rights in late 1939. Columbia offered more money but was reluctant to give in to the publisher's demands, which included script approval. Universal stepped in, but Republic matched their bid and offered to pay for a National rep to act as a consultant. Republic and National came to an agreement but the publisher let the contract deadline pass and signed over the rights to Paramount.[3] The studio—perhaps wisely—opted to go the animation route, and between 1941 and '43 bankrolled 17 Superman adventures. The first nine, by Max and Dave Fleischer, are gorgeous, bespoke cartoons of the era.

Seeing an opening, Fawcett Comics approached Republic with the idea of a serial based on its own super-powered crimefighter, Captain Marvel. Created by writer Bill Parker, a Princeton grad who had worked on various Fawcett mags, and Fawcett staff artist C.C. Beck, Captain Marvel was a red-and-yellow-suited hero with the powers of Solomon, Hercules, Atlas, Zeus, Achilles and Mercury. His alter ego was 12-year-old orphan Billy Batson, who is granted the ability to change into the fully grown superhero by a New York subway-dwelling wizard named Shazam, the same word Billy uses to make his transformation.

All Fawcett asked in return for film rights was that Republic use the character's name in the title, give the publisher screen credit, and release the serial as part of its 1940–41 slate.[4] Republic used the carte blanche to take liberties with the superhero, though not as many as it and other studios would with other comic book properties.

The first live-action superhero, Republic's 1941 Captain Marvel (played by Tom Tyler, center, in *Adventures of Captain Marvel*, with two unidentified actors) is also "the most homicidal berserker superhero of cinema" according to Quentin Tarantino. Republic Pictures/Paramount.

Chapter I. It's a Bird, It's a Plane, It's ... a Serial

Released in 1941, the 12-part *Adventures of Captain Marvel* begins in Siam (Thailand), where Billy Batson has accompanied a group of archaeologists investigating an ancient tomb. When the rest of the expedition ignores warnings from the locals and enters a sealed crypt, Billy hangs back. The wizard Shazam appears and, impressed by the boy's moral rectitude, grants him the ability to transform into Captain Marvel. After Captain Marvel saves Billy's friends from angry villagers, the Americans leave, bringing with them an ancient artifact they found in the tomb: the Golden Scorpion. When the device's quartz lenses are aligned, it unleashes a powerful energy ray. Once back in the U.S., the archaeologists divide the lenses amongst themselves to prevent anyone from using the Golden Scorpion for nefarious purposes. A hooded villain, unimaginatively calling himself the Scorpion, begins killing the explorers for the pieces. Billy and his friends, but mostly Captain Marvel, stop him.

Considered by serial historians to be one of Republic's better offerings, the 1941 release is the first live-action superhero *anything*. It has the origin, dual identity, costume, superpowers and villain (though not superpowered himself) that were already standard tropes in the comics and would become the same in movies and on TV.

Which is not to say that the serial is faithful to the comics. Supporting characters like Captain Marvel's mortal enemy Doctor Sivana, are ignored. For plot's sake, the origin is set in Southeast Asia instead of New York. Billy, barely in his teens in the comics, is played by 25-year-old Frank Coghlan, Jr. Although Fawcett's version of the hero wasn't averse to using guns on occasion, Republic's villain-tossing, machine-gunning Captain Marvel is, in the words of Quentin Tarantino, "the most homicidal berserker superhero of cinema."[5]

At least Tom Tyler, in the title role, cuts an impressive figure; if press materials at the time are to be believed, he was a six-time consecutive world weightlifting champion. And the fight scenes are impressive, and plentiful. It's been said of William Witney, who co-directed with John English, that he never came across a scene that he didn't think could be improved by a fistfight.

For the flight scenes, the studio's in-house effects experts Howard and Theodore Lydecker used a *papier mâché* dummy on wires against real backgrounds, and filmed the costumed Tyler against fake ones. Stuntman Dave Sharpe provided the on-camera takeoffs and landings. Though the dummy is stiff and not entirely convincing, the effects wouldn't be improved upon for nearly four decades.

Superman may have been a more obvious choice, but story-wise Captain Marvel turned out to be the ideal hero for the serial format. Whenever Billy finds himself or his friends in a jam—every 20 minutes or so—all he has to do is say the magic word and, well, Shazam!

One of the stranger aspects of *Adventures of Captain Marvel* is the unquestioning nature of the population at seeing a man in a red Centurion-style outfit and cape flying above the streets of Los Angeles. "We'll get Captain Marvel!" is a frequent refrain heard once the action comes to the U.S. No doubt it just seemed easier to the filmmakers to position him as an everyday part of life, the same way that bystanders treated a man dressed like a bat in the next superhero serial, 1943's *Batman*.

Debuting in a 1939 issue of *Detective Comics*, Batman was another runaway hit for Superman publisher National. (Batman appeared under the imprint of Detective Comics, which gave DC its initials; both *Action Comics* and Detective were owned by National.) Creators Bob Kane and Bill Finger originally envisioned their cowled vigilante as a gun-toting, sometimes brutal dispenser of justice; a year into his career, DC softened his image by introducing his kid sidekick, Robin.

This time Columbia nabbed the rights, and the studio took no chances that it might sully its reputation for wallet-tightening. From its ill-fitting costumes to the nondescript convertible that serves as the Batmobile, *Batman* cuts every corner it can, and then some.

And forget about an origin story or colorful bad guys like Joker, Penguin and Catwoman. When *Batman* starts, Batman and Robin are already established Gotham City crimefighters, just part of the scenery in the daily lives of the citizens. The villain is Dr. Daka, a secret agent of the Japanese Imperial Government. Daka's need for the city's supply of radium for his radium gun fuels the serial's 15 chapters and about a dozen poorly choreographed donnybrooks between the heroes and the villain's band of low-rent thugs. According to Lewis Wilson, who played Batman, studio execs were so embarrassed that they "rented other facilities for us so we wouldn't be seen on the main lot."[6]

Directed by B-movie and Western vet Lambert Hillyer, the serial plods along to its own Bat-drum. The Massachusetts-bred Wilson's Batman has a Boston accent and sports a cowl with comically long, pointy ears and weirdly shaped eyeholes. The costume prompted comics writer Grant Morrison to later comment, "If Lewis Wilson's bizarre appearance inspired any terror at all in the criminal classes, it was surely that

Douglas Croft (left) and Lewis Wilson (right) boast the distinction of playing the first live-action Batman and Robin in Columbia's 1943 serial *Batman*. J. Carroll Naish (center) plays the fiendish Dr. Daka. Columbia Pictures.

Chapter I. It's a Bird, It's a Plane, It's … a Serial

instinctual dread engendered by the close proximity of the mentally ill, immensely rich, and unstoppably violent."[7] The serial plays up the image of Batman alter ego Bruce Wayne as an indolent millionaire playboy; socialite Linda Page (Winnipeg-born Shawn Smith, stage name Shirley Patterson, a former Southern California archery champion and Miss California 1940) seems to exist only to give him a hard time about his "easy" life. If she only knew! Sixteen-year-old Douglas Croft is the right age for the Boy Wonder, even if his tsunami of curly hair was decidedly off-canon.

Linda Page had appeared in a few early issues of *Batman*. But for some reason, the serial-makers replaced Commissioner Gordon with their own cop, Police Captain Arnold. J. Carrol Naish, who earned an Academy Award nomination for Best Supporting Actor for Columbia's *Sahara* that same year, plays the string-tie-wearing Daka, a racist caricature if ever there was one. Not that the comics were above that sort of thing, especially in the patriotic fervor of the times.

Even less faithful to its source than *Captain Marvel*, *Batman* nonetheless inspired DC to pick up a few ideas for the growing Batman mythos. The Batcave—known here as "the Bat's Cave"—debuts here, and comics artists altered Bruce Wayne's butler Alfred to look more like the serial's lean and proper live-action version (played by William Austin). The serial also influenced the sixties TV series, though to what extent is debatable. And that series became a huge influence not only on how the world came to see the Caped Crusader but also superheroes and comic books.

How well 1943's *Batman* did is difficult to say. The studio billed it as a "Super Serial" and rolled out a publicity campaign equivalent to a feature film. Blogger Ian Smith has said that it was the studio's largest-scale serial to date.[8] It might be impossible to say for sure. When Columbia moved from Hollywood to Burbank in 1972, nearly all of the studio's records and files were destroyed.[9]

The next superhero to fall victim to the serial system was Captain America. Writer-artist Joe Simon and artist Jack Kirby (born Jacob Kurtzberg) collaborated on the character as a response to the growing Nazi threat in Europe and the U.S.'s reluctance to get involved. The superhero debuted in 1941 in his own title, with a now iconic cover that left no doubt where his creators stood: It depicts Captain America socking Hitler on the jaw.

Captain Marvel and *Batman* took liberties with their source material, but they had nothing on *Captain America*. In Simon and Kirby's original conception, the hero is Steve Rogers, a young man deemed 4F by the Army. Determined to do his part, he volunteers to take an experimental super-soldier serum and, after the experiment, goes overseas to fight the Nazis. In the Republic version, he is Grant Gardner, district attorney by day and puncher of thugs, also by day. Like Columbia's Batman, the Republic Cap is already an established crimefighter known to police, law-abiding citizens and bad guys alike. There is no super-soldier serum or superpowers. Instead of a shield, the hero—played by Dick Purcell—uses a gun. With its stars and stripes, his costume faintly resembles the comic version, but without flourishes like helmet wings and buccaneer boots. Instead of Nazis, he faces the Scarab and his "thermodynamic vibration engine"—or "vibrator," as it's often called.

Had the script originally been intended for another character entirely? That's what some historians believe—that it had been rewritten from a vehicle for another Fawcett Comics character, Mr. Scarlet, or as a sequel to Republic's 1940 serial *Mysterious Doctor Satan*, itself originally scripted as a Superman serial. Whatever the reason for the serial's off-roading, *Captain America* publisher Timely was not pleased. After viewing the first chapter, the company fired off a letter to the studio. Republic shrugged off the complaints.[10]

Other than how much it diverges from its source material, the 15-chapter 1944 effort is notable mostly for its elaborate fight scenes and veteran movie actor Lionel Atwill's performance as the Scarab. "Never has a monocle been used more expertly than Atwill's ability to adjust it for dramatic effect," wrote historian Geoff Mayer.[11] The directors were Elmer Clifton and *Captain Marvel*'s John English, the writers a stable of serial vets; a couple of them had already worked on *Captain Marvel*. Before *Captain America*'s release, Dick Purcell died after collapsing in the locker room of a Los Angeles country club. "The strain of his vigorous assignment had taxed his heart too heavily," speculated historian Raymond William Stedman.[12] The actor was 35. *Captain America* exceeded its $182k budget by $40k.

Historically, the serial marked the cinematic debut of a Marvel character, since Timely eventually morphed into what we know today as the publisher of Spider-Man, X-Men and the Hulk. It was also the last superhero serial for four years. Then, in 1948, Superman finally soared onto the silver screen.

By then, the character been leaping tall buildings in a single bound for ten years. His popularity had led not just to the Paramount animated shorts but to a newspaper comic strip (the original goal of his young creators), a top-rated radio show and a novel. He was so popular that National had set up a company, Superman Inc., to handle licensing for its top asset.

After securing the rights, Columbia hired Sam Katzman to produce and Spencer Gordon Bennet and Thomas Carr to direct. All were serial vets; like Rudolph C. Flothow, who produced *Batman*, Katzman had a reputation for keeping both eyes on the bottom line.

The production marked the first time that the role of a character in superhero tights was coveted. Unlike the studio's *Batman*, where cast and crew hid on back lots away from the eyes of mainstream Hollywood, *Superman* was a high-profile production. Then again, the man who ended up in the role of Superman and his mild-mannered alter ego Clark Kent thought the whole thing was nothing more than a publicity stunt.

"I didn't think you could ever put Superman on film," said Kirk Alyn.[13] As if to confirm the former vaudevillian's belief, Columbia claimed in the credits that the "real" Superman was playing himself.

Noel Neill, the daughter of a newspaper editor and a stage dancer, played Lois Lane, the *Daily Planet*'s star reporter and Superman–Clark Kent's love interest. "I tried to look like her," said Neill, "but that's about all we did for any in-depth study. We didn't have time. We did a lot of exteriors and a lot of chases, and it was almost like a Western with the hero in long underwear."[14]

The serial's five-man writing team took elements from various media. Details of Superman's origin—depicted in the first episode—came from a 1942 novel by George Lowther, a writer on the radio show *The Adventures of Superman*. Publisher Perry White, photographer Jimmy Olsen, kryptonite and the line "This looks like job for Superman!" came from the radio show. Lois dated all the way back to *Action Comics* #1.

Following the origin, the remaining serial installments focus on Clark's arrival in Metropolis and Superman's tussle with the Spider Lady, a blonde crime boss who dresses like a singer at the Copacabana, over a "relativity reducer ray." The Spider Lady is played by Carol Forman, who specialized in serial villainesses like the Black Widow (no relation to Marvel's) and Queen Khana. For flying effects, directors Bennet and Carr used animation, already a step down from 1941's *Adventures of Captain Marvel* (although different only in degrees from 2006's *Superman Returns*).

The introductory episode came to theaters in early 1948. The Saturday afternoon crowd ate it up, and *Superman* grossed more than $1 million from a budget of $350k, making it the most financially successful serial in history.[15]

The following year, Columbia released *Batman and Robin*. The new serial, for all intents and purposes a reboot, featured a different cast, different director, different writers and a different producer, *Superman*'s Sam Katzman. But the results were still not enough to elicit fear in the hearts of evildoers.

This time, Robert Lowery played Batman. Johnny Duncan, a 27-year-old swing dancer and actor, was Robin. Commissioner Gordon makes his first on-screen appearance, as does photographer Vicki Vale. Vicki had first appeared in the comics just a year previous; Bob Kane said that he based her on Marilyn Monroe. (The Batman co-creator claimed that he had met Monroe at the wrap party for the first *Batman* serial and again when he came to Hollywood for the second. However, Monroe would have been 17 years old in 1943 and didn't make her film debut until four years later. Also—a *Batman* serial wrap party?) The Bat-Signal also makes its live-action debut. But the villain is, again, an original creation: the Wizard, a hooded nut who has invented a remote-control device that can direct vehicles from up to 50 miles away. Holy traffic jam, Batman!

It was another cheapie production. The Wizard hangs out in a cave that bears a remarkable similarity to the Batcave because ... it *is* the Batcave. The Batmobile is a 1949 Mercury convertible. Lowery's Batsuit was even more ill-fitting and ill-conceived than Wilson's, with a cowl sprouting devil's horns instead of bat-ears and a normal belt instead of a utility belt. "The damn ears would start flopping like a dog's, so they had to put Scotch tape on them," said Duncan, who wore a dime store mask to hide his identity from criminal masterminds. "Every day we had to put new Scotch tape on those ears, sometimes three or four times a day."[16] Both heroes keep their costumes in a filing cabinet.

Batman and Robin does not appear to have set the box office on fire.

The following year, Columbia released *Atom Man vs. Superman*. The sequel saw the return of the first's cast as well as director Spencer Gordon Bennet and scripters Joseph F. Poland, George H. Plympton and Royal K. Cole (all four also worked on *Batman and Robin*). The "Atom Man" of the title is infamous Superman baddie Lex Luthor, known here only as "Luthor." His appearance marked the first live-action incarnation of a comic-book villain. He is played by Lyle Talbot, fresh off his role as Commissioner Gordon in *Batman and Robin*. The serial presents the rivalry between Superman and Luthor as a given.

The effects show more imagination than those of the first. Bennet still uses animation for the flying scenes, but he also turned the camera on its side to film Alyn standing with his arms raised in front of a cyclorama (a panoramic image on a curved screen) while a wind machine and smoke pot provided additional effects. When Luthor uses another device to send Superman to what the villain calls "the Empty Doom," a forerunner to the Phantom Zone, Superman is seen in double-exposure against a backdrop of planets and stars. By most accounts, the 1950 serial was a financial success.

Television was now entering millions of homes, and National saw the writing on the screen. In 1951—two months after the last Superman radio episode aired—the publisher announced that it would produce a *Superman* TV series.[17]

Jack Leibowitz, National's second-in-command to owner Harry Donenfeld, hired Robert Maxwell to steer the series. Maxwell had been a producer, writer and director on the radio show. The two decided to make a feature first, figuring that National could recoup some of the budget at the box office while teasing the series, and then break up the longer piece into two half-hour episodes.

Maxwell approached Whitney Ellsworth to pen the script. A DC editor and writer who had taken over the Superman newspaper strip after original scribe Jerry Siegel was drafted, Ellsworth had also acted as a consultant on the Fleischer cartoons and the Batman and Superman serials,[18] and worked with Maxwell on the Superman radio show.

Credits list Barney A. Sarecky as producer, though the extent of his involvement is unclear. Lee "Roll 'em" Sholem, so nicknamed due to his speed and efficiency, was hired to direct. At some point, someone decided that the series would not feature the stars of the Superman serials. According to Noel Neill, neither she nor Kirk Alyn were told about the series.[19] Instead, National hired George Reeves and Phyllis Coates.

Reeves beat out over 200 applicants. "He *looked* like Superman, with that jaw of his," said Thomas Carr, who had co-directed the first serial and was hired to work on the series.[20]

The Iowa-born actor was a 37-year-old former boxer whose credits included a brief role in *Gone with the Wind*. His career was in a downturn when series producer Bernard Luber, a former colleague, mentioned the opportunity. The actor was reluctantly agreed, figuring the series would never get off the ground.

In the fall of 1951, independent distributor Lippert Pictures released *Superman and the Mole-Men*. The first live-action superhero movie, the $275k black-and-white effort clocks in at barely an hour.

The story involves an invasion of subterranean Mole-Men on the Midwest American town of Silsby. In fact, the strangers are simply concerned about the effects on their home of oil-drilling, but the appearance of four bald little people with bizarre facial hair panics the residents. Clark Kent and Lois Lane are in town, on assignment for the *Daily Planet* to cover the drilling of the world's deepest oil well. Superman stops the town's residents from attacking the pint-size eco-warriors with pitchforks and torches. Written by Ellsworth and Maxwell, it's the kind of morality play that would later inform series like *The Twilight Zone* and *Star Trek* and presents the hero as Siegel had originally envisioned him, a warrior for just causes.

Adventures of Superman debuted a year later, in September 1952. Maxwell produced the first year's shows, but he ran afoul of National and the show's sponsor Kellogg's. Reportedly, the publisher and cereal-maker wanted a more kid-friendly series; Maxwell's plots often involved kidnapping, murder and suicide. Too, comics publishers were starting to feel heat from some quarters. Though his infamous book *Seduction of the Innocent* would not be published until 1954, child psychologist Fredric Wertham had begun suggesting a link between the increasingly explicit medium and juvenile delinquency. So, for the second season, Ellsworth took over. (The change may also have been a matter of money, as Maxwell reportedly went over budget.[21])

There was a new Lois for the second season: Coates, concerned about being typecast as well as with Reeves' on-set drinking, according to Larry Tye,[22] left the show. Noel Neill slipped back into the reporter's shoes for the remainder of the series' run. Sixty years later, she and Kirk Alyn were remembered by the makers of 1978's *Superman*, who cast the two as Lois Lane's parents.

Adventures of Superman's ratings peaked in 1956 with Season Four when it was ranked sixth among syndicated series.[23] The numbers were still strong enough in 1958, following the sixth season, for Ellsworth and ABC (the series had moved to the network from syndication) to start planning additional episodes.

Then, in October of that year, John Hamilton, the show's Perry White, died of heart failure at 71. Less than a year later, Reeves himself was dead at 45, of a gunshot wound. To the LAPD, it was an open-and-shut suicide, with a motive: Reeves was frustrated at being typecast as Superman. But some believed that the actor, who had directed three recent episodes and was apparently hoping to direct more, was murdered. Rumors emerged of a love triangle with a studio-connected former mistress, Toni Mannix, and Leonore Lemmon. According to Tye, Lemmon was "famous for being the only woman ever tossed out of the Stork Club for fist-fighting."[24]

A 1996 book, *Hollywood Kryptonite: The Bulldog, the Lady, and the Death of Superman* tried to tie up loose ends. A decade after its publication, the movie *Hollywoodland* took up the case, with future Batman Ben Affleck as Reeves.

With the death of its star, *Adventures of Superman* had nowhere to go. "We realized of course that they were not going to do any more *Superman* because of what happened to George," Neill said. "Every agent that had a muscleman would drag him in and Ellsworth would say 'no, no, no.'"[25]

Instead, Ellsworth tried to get two other series going, producing pilots for both. In 1958's *The Adventures of Superpup*, human actors in dog masks portray Bark Bent, Pamela Poodle and other canine counterparts of the *Superman* cast. (This really happened.) A few years later, *The Adventures of Superboy* featured young versions of Superman-Clark and the first live-action appearance of Lana Lang, a supporting character from the comics. Twelve more scripts were written but never shot.

Adventures of Superman ran for 104 episodes, half in color. Many viewers regard the Season Two episode "Panic in the Sky" as a highlight. In it, an amnesiac Clark forgets that he's Superman as a meteor hurtles towards Earth.

The show continued to run in syndication, influencing future generations of viewers—including Ilya Salkind, the son of a European film producer.

Chapter II

Biff! Bam! and, of Course, Pow!

> "I bought a bunch of comics of various vintages, and when I read these things I thought they must be out of their minds. It was all so juvenile. Then, a very simple idea, and that was to overdo it. If you overdid it, I thought, it would appeal to adults but also appear stimulating to kids."
> —*Batman '66* producer William Dozier[1]

> "This wasn't my Batman! Hell, my parents were laughing at the show. Laughing at Batman!"
> —comic book writer (and Batman fan) Chuck Dixon[2]

TV's *Batman* was a pop-art explosion in the living rooms of America. After its January 1966 premiere, the show entered the Top 10 in ratings, increased circulation of *Batman* comics and sparked the first wave of Batmania. It was lightning in a bottle. It was, to quote Cole Porter, too hot not to cool down.

That it made it onto the air in the first place, and in the form it did, is a minor miracle.

According to producer William Dozier, the show began with a general concept: ABC wanted to inject more action into its primetime lineup using a comic-book or comic-strip character. Research led to the Caped Crusader only after execs realized that rights to the more popular properties, Superman and Dick Tracy, were tied up.[3]

Another theory holds that it was all East Coast ABC executive Yale Udoff's idea. "Udoff came in and said, 'We ought to do Batman,'" Edgar Scherick, ABC's head of programming, told author Bob Garcia. "We threw him out of the office, but he persisted and we decided to look into it."[4]

In his book *American Comics*, Jeremy Dauber wrote that an ABC exec had seen the original serial at the Playboy Mansion in Chicago, and quoted Dozier via historian Les Daniels: "The bunnies and Hugh Hefner and his friends were laughing and screaming and hissing the villain. It was all very campy."[5]

A repackaged version of the original 1943 serial did make the rounds of college campuses and rep theaters. But the four and a half-hour *An Evening with Batman and Robin*, as Columbia called it, seems to have begun circulating in 1965, when the TV series would already have been in production. Nevertheless, the series does borrow several signatures from the serial, including hidden Batpoles connecting to the Batcave, fight scenes that border on slapstick and cliffhanger endings. As for the *Playboy* magazine connection, other reports state that the serial played Chicago's Playboy Club, not the Playboy Mansion. The more likely scenario is that it enjoyed a run at the city's Playboy Theatre, a rep house unaffiliated with the Hefner brand and known for eclectic programming.[6]

At any rate, ABC handed *Batman* to Dozier. A former literary agent, he began his TV career as a writer before becoming a producer. A fan of serious drama, he had no truck with juvenilia like comic books. He made no bones about this in various anecdotes handed down through the years.

Lorenzo Semple, Jr., was a writer who had worked with Dozier on a failed TV spinoff of popular fictional detective Charlie Chan. "As we sat in the garden of that splendid caravanserai, sipping cool sangria, Bill pulled something from the inner pocket of his jacket," Semple recalled of a meeting with the producer in Madrid, where the scribe was living at the time. "For those who never had the privilege of knowing him, Bill Dozier was one sophisticated gent. 'This,' he said, with a look of humiliation bordering on shame, 'is what ABC has given us.'" It was a copy of a Batman comic.[7]

To be fair to Dozier, Batman had seen better days. For years, publisher National, which had become known as DC, had allowed editor Jack Schiff and his stable of writers and artists to dump the world's greatest detective into increasingly absurd plots. Each month, readers were treated to stories about a Zebra Batman or a Mer-Batman and characters like Bat-Mite and Ace the Bathound. Things had only begun turning around for the flagship character in 1964, when new editor Julius Schwartz instructed writer John Broome and artist Carmine Infantino to give Batman a new look and lose the silliness.

Comics historian Arlen Schumer suggests that much of the TV series' DNA may have come from a chance selection of comics that, in 1965, Dozier picked up at an airport on his way to discuss producing the series with ABC. These included the '65 *Giant Batman Annual*, which featured reprints of 1950s stories of "Batman and Robin's Most Fantastic Foes," with appearances by the Penguin, Catwoman, Mr. Freeze and the Joker, and an issue of Batman's regular title, *Batman* #171, "Remarkable Ruse of the Riddler."[8]

That the character was undergoing a transformation, however cosmetic, was lost on the dynamic duo sipping sangria in Spain. With just the older books to go on, they—well, someone—cracked the approach.

"After a day or so, the fairly obvious idea—it seems obvious now, at least—was to make [the show] so square and so serious and so cliché-ridden and so overdone, and yet do it with a certain elegance and style that it would be funny," Dozier told the Canadian Broadcasting Corporation early in the show's run. "That it would be so corny and so bad that it would be funny. That appealed to me. And I began to enjoy it."[9]

"At the risk of pretending to Minerva-like wisdom, I must tell it like it happened: The TV show concept virtually exploded in my sangria-enhanced brain, full-blown," Semple recalled in 2008. "Bill asked me what I was thinking. I replied it was a really terrific idea—trust me and fly back home to Los Angeles, and I would write it. Trust me."[10]

Dozier's company Greenway Productions worked with 20th Century–Fox's television arm to develop the show. Semple came on as story editor and wrote the pilot, selecting the Riddler for the inaugural villain. He may have been inspired by the bad guy's provocations in a spring 1965 issue of *Batman*, which marked the Prince of Puzzler's first appearance since 1948. Alfred, Commissioner Gordon and Aunt Harriet were written in from the comics, but Miles O'Hara, an Irish police chief given to say "begorra" at the drop of a shamrock, was an original addition. Wanting seasoned pros for the roles, Dozier cast veteran actors Frank Gorshin, Alan Napier, Neil Hamilton, Madge Blake and Stafford Repp in those roles.

This was not a time when thespians were begging for the chance to play second fiddle to a lead in tights. Recalled Napier, who had worked with John Gielgud and Orson Welles and was the first to be cast,[11] "My agent rang up and said, 'I think you are going to play on *Batman*.' I said, 'What is *Batman*?' He said, 'Don't you read the comics?' I said,

'No, never.' He said, 'I think you are going to be Batman's butler.' I said, 'How do I know I want to be Batman's butler?' It was the most ridiculous thing I had ever heard of. He said, 'It may be worth over $100,000.' So I said I was Batman's butler."[12]

But who would don the cowl? Eventually it came down to Lyle Waggoner, a TV regular, and Adam West. A native of Walla Walla, Washington, West had been in Hollywood for six years, working mainly in supporting roles.

"I had him come in and read the first script, and he had an immediate and very intelligent insight into what we were trying to do," Dozier told CBC. "He grasped the duality of this thing immediately. He would have to play it very straight and very square to have it come through as humor." West's deadpan reading of some of the most ridiculous lines in the history of broadcast television—a high bar indeed—would prove to be among the most memorable aspects of the show.

The producer found his Robin in Burton Gervais, aka Burt Ward. The 19-year-old was working in real estate and taking acting classes at UCLA. "He had never done anything before," Dozier said. "Someone told him we were looking for young actors so he got some obscure agent to bring him in and the moment he walked into this office I knew he was Robin. He had this 'Gee-whiz-Mr.-Dozier' approach right off the bat that couldn't be duplicated."[13]

The third-rated (out of three networks) ABC was either confident or desperate enough to order several episodes before Dozier and his crew even finished shooting the pilot. 20th Century–Fox invested hundreds of thousands of dollars on the Batcave (an estimated $800k) and props like the Batmobile. (For the latter, which would become one of the most iconic vehicles ever created, Dozier gave car customizer George Barris a budget of $15k and a timeline of three weeks.)

So a lot was riding on the comic book hero's caped shoulders when ABC had a test screening. It was a disaster.

"They had the lowest rating that night of anything they had ever tested at the preview theater!" recalled Dozier.[14] (According to one source, the network also broadcast a poorly received early version of what would become the first episode, "Hey Diddle Riddle," the previous fall.)[15]

Nevertheless, the network went ahead. When it aired the first two episodes—ABC had decided to broadcast the series twice a week, on consecutive Wednesday and Thursday evenings—on January 12 and 13, 1966, both garnered Top 10 ratings. At the time, the sitcoms *Bewitched*, *The Andy Griffith Show*, *Gomer Pyle*, *The Dick Van Dyke Show* and *The Lucy Show* ruled the Top 10.

Viewers of that small-screen debut witnessed something far different from anything else on TV: Dozier's distinctive narration; Neal Hefti's earworm of a theme over an animated title sequence; the Batcave, with its own nuclear generator and Bat-computer; the ingenious Batmobile; Frank Gorshin's Riddler, giggling maniacally in a skintight Kelly-green outfit festooned with question marks; Adam West's stoic Batman, walking into a nightclub like he just bought the place—and doing "the Batusi"; and all presented in retina-scorching colors for the kids and littered with knowing nods and winks for the grown-ups. Not all the show's signatures were yet in place: The crooked (or "Dutch") camera angles for the criminals' lairs, the celebrity cameos during the heroes' ascents up sides of buildings, and Dozier's outro "Same Bat-time, same Bat-channel" would all come later. But there was still plenty to spark conversation around the watercooler and on the playground. Overnight, *Batman* became must-see TV.

Chapter II. Biff! Bam! and, of Course, Pow!

Reviews were tentatively positive. *The New York Times* offered a prescient, if tortured, take:

> Bob Kane's heroes of the comic strip came to television last night as real-life people, and it looks as if the American Broadcasting Company has something going for it. The show was amusing in spots, though the avant-campists might contend it really wasn't bad enough to be excellent.... The true test for Batman won't be this week or next, but in a couple of months when the novelty of his cape and expertise wears off.[16]

The *Los Angeles Times*' Don Page wrote:

> If the aim had been satire, *Batman* would be hanging by its feet as a critical flop. But producer William Dozier wisely brought Batman to television as a live comic book and ABC probably has its biggest hit in many seasons.... [West and Ward] are flattering reproductions of cartoonist Bob Kane's paper heroes. Everyone in the cast overplays his part, particularly West, who delivers his comic book cliches with solemnity. Ward is suitably juvenile as the over-eager Robin.[17]

In the following months, one in three households tuned in to the new series. In total, 34 episodes aired in the first season, which ended in May. Semple, author of several first-season episodes, had trouble finding writers who understood the arch tone. "They either made it too silly, or they didn't get the humour of it properly," he said. "I wrote Bat-notes, as I called them, which I would give to the writers to give samples of the type of humor it was meant to be."[18]

Batman and Robin were the ostensible attractions, but people also tuned in to see that week's villain. Besides Gorshin as the Riddler, Dozier cast other well-known actors

Julie Newmar's Catwoman shares a milkshake with Adam West's Batman in an episode of the 1966–67 *Batman* TV series. The show appealed to adults and kids, although some comics readers cried foul. Greenway Productions/20th Century–Fox Television/Disney Platform Distribution/Warner Bros. Home Entertainment (home video rights).

like Burgess Meredith as the Penguin and Cesar Romero as the Joker. As Catwoman, Tony Award–winning stage actress Julie Newmar was squeezed into a skin-tight black outfit that was decidedly racier than the dowdy purple dress and green cape of the comics version. It seems that sex appeal was very much on the show's producers' minds. "Let's remember we must work dames into these scripts, both for Batman and Robin, wherever feasible," Dozier wrote in a note to Semple.[19]

Semple and his writers also came up with their own gimmicky adversaries, including Zelda the Great, the Bookworm and King Tut. All were played by actors recognizable to TV and movie audiences of the time, including Anne Baxter, Roddy McDowall and Victor Buono.

A full-fledged Batmania took hold. *Life* put West as Batman on the cover. Bat-paraphernalia flooded and flew off store shelves. In June, Shea Stadium hosted a "Batman Concert" with West, Gorshin and seven rock'n'roll bands. (This didn't go over so well, however, with attendance of only around 3000. Some blamed the low turnout on a newspaper exposé of the promoter and hot weather.) Link Wray, Sun Ra (on a novelty album credited to "The Sensational Guitars of Dan & Dale"), the Ventures, the Standells and Al Hirt covered the theme song. Both West and Ward recorded singles; for his, Ward read excerpts from fan letters. Frank Zappa produced. Competing networks jumped on the superhero bandwagon, CBS with *Mr. Terrific*, about a gas station attendant who takes "power pills," and NBC with *Captain Nice*, about a super-powered police chemist. The latter was concocted by Buck Henry, co-creator of *Get Smart* and co-writer of *The Graduate*. Each lasted a season.

And 20th Century–Fox rushed a movie into production. Semple wrote the script, populating it with first-season villains Riddler, Joker, Penguin and Catwoman. The latter had to be recast, as Newmar bowed out due to a chronic back ailment.[20] Cast and crew had already begun filming when Dozier cast Lee Meriwether, a former Miss America who had used her contest winnings to take acting classes with Lee Strasberg.[21]

With a bigger budget came more toys—a Batboat, a Batcopter and a Batcycle (complete with sidecar for Robin). Nelson Riddle did the score. The studio added a new title sequence and Leslie H. Martinson, who had directed a couple of Season One episodes, turned the dial on the fight scenes to only faintly comical. Animated sound effects weren't used until the final battle, on the deck of the Penguin's submarine.

The plot is, of course, ridiculous, even by the standards of the TV show. After joining forces to form United Underworld, Penguin, Joker, Riddler and Catwoman do everything they can to lure Batman to them, while Batman and Robin do everything they can to find them, while each group is convinced they're outwitting the other (while everyone compliments themselves on how smart they are). The foul foursome think they have killed off the Dynamic Duo at least three times, twice with Polaris missiles. Bruce Wayne falls for a Russian journalist, Miss Kitka, whom only Mr. Magoo would mistake for someone other than Catwoman. They meet cute when, in the office of Commissioner Gordon, Batman gives the world's most perfunctory press conference.

With its hurried six-week production schedule, *Batman* was never going to be *Citizen Kane*. But it has two scenes that have memed their way into pop culture. In the first, a struggling Batman saves himself from a shark with his Bat Shark Repellant. In the other, he races around a pier while holding a hissing bomb over his head, trying to find an unpopulated spot to toss it. "Some days you just can't get rid of a bomb," he sighs.

Seeing the villains interact is another attraction, since this is the first and last time

Chapter II. Biff! Bam! and, of Course, Pow! 17

they appeared together. As one would hope, they annoy the hell out of each other. Of all villains, though, it's the Joker who is the voice of reason.

The second live-action superhero feature film, *Batman* premiered in Austin, home of Glastron, the company that built the Batboat. The movie made twice its budget back; according to historian Joel Eisner, it "was a hit worldwide."[22] On TV, however, the bloom was off the bat.

ABC had ordered 60 more episodes for Season Two. But the ratings began to fall; by the spring of 1967, they were lower than the Batmobile's center of gravity. Repetition had taken its toll and the plots had become formulaic. There were more episodes with Julie Newmar's Catwoman, but Gorshin sat the season out, apparently over a contract dispute. Instead of reaching into back issues for villains, the writers created more original bad guys. These included Egghead (Vincent Price), a man whose only personality trait is making puns with the word "egg"; Chandell (Liberace), a murderous pianist; and Shame (Cliff Robertson), a parody of the title character of the 1953 Western *Shane*. Someone was smoking those jazz cigarettes in the *Batman* writers' room.

"There is a delicate balance between comic or camp and suspense, and if you listen to the critics too much about the camp, you become totally comic and lose suspense," said Ellis St. Joseph, who wrote a Season 2 two-parter with Catwoman and Sandman (Michael Rennie). "I think that kids as well as grown-ups wanted a little suspense to go along with the comedy, but they had lost it."[23]

The second season featured the guest appearance of two more crimefighters heroes. At the time, Dozier was also producing—and narrating—*The Green Hornet*, another ABC series based on a masked vigilante from the thirties. The show starred Van Williams in the title role and introduced Bruce Lee, playing his sidekick Kato, to American audiences. In the *Batman* episodes "A Piece of the Action" and "Batman's Satisfaction," the dual dynamic duos team up against Colonel Gumm, a stamp fanatic, in what is the first live-action superhero crossover event. *The Green Hornet* lasted 26 episodes.

With the second season tanking, Dozier decided to break up the boy's club. A female superhero, he reasoned, would attract little girls and keep the dads watching. According to *Batman* artist Carmine Infantino, the producer called *Batman* comics editor Julius Schwartz and asked, since Catwoman was a hit, if they could create more female characters. "I came up with Batgirl, Poison Ivy and one I called the Grey Fox, which Julie didn't like as much," the artist said.[24]

The new Batgirl—there had been an earlier one, briefly, in 1961, called "Bat-Girl"—debuted in a late 1966 issue of *Detective Comics*, midway through the second season. Dozier added the character to the third season's cast and chose Yvonne Craig for the role. The Illinois native was a former ballet dancer who had played ingenues in various TV series and appeared in two Elvis films.

Craig hadn't seen the show when she met with the producer, but soon caught up. "I had never seen anything like it," she told the *Los Angeles Times*. "I didn't quite know what to think then, but now I love the show; there are so many fun things about it. It's wild and bizarre."[25]

Costumer Pat Barto dressed her in a sparkly purple-and-yellow costume that, like Catwoman's, was designed for maximum sex appeal. A door in Barbara's swingin' sixties bachelorette pad opened to a room housing her purple Batgirl motorcycle, which she rode down a ramp onto the mean streets of Gotham. The Dominoed Dare-Doll, as she was nicknamed, was added to the animated titles and received her own theme song: "Are you a chick who fell from outer space? Or are you real with a tender warm embrace?"

But it was a faded *Batman* that welcomed the eager 29-year-old Craig. ABC ordered only 26 episodes for the season and aired the show once a week. Each episode had to include speaking parts for 13 characters, including Bruce Wayne and Robin's alias, Dick Grayson, along with Batman and Robin, Commissioner Gordon and Chief O'Hara, Alfred, the villain, the villain's two henchmen, another female character, Batgirl and Batgirl's alter ego, Barbara Gordon. (Due to declining health, Madge Blake appeared as Aunt Harriet in only a few third season episodes.) This left little room for the writers to develop anything other than the thinnest of plots.

The studio, which had already traded the original animated fight scene sound effects for less-costly flash cards in the second season, cut back on other frills. Sets that had once been customized for the villain of the week gave way to criminal lairs that looked thrown together for an off-off–Broadway show.

Familiar rascals returned, including Gorshin's Riddler, Romero's Joker and Meredith's Penguin. But Julie Newmar left to do a movie. In a radical move for the times, the producers hired Eartha Kitt, a dancer-actress-singer of African-Cherokee descent, as the third season Catwoman.

"We felt it was a very provocative idea," producer Charles B. Fitzsimons said. "She was a cat woman before we ever cast her as Catwoman. She had a cat-like style. Her eyes were cat-like and her singing was like a meow. This came as a wonderful offbeat idea to do it with a black woman."[26]

Old Hollywood continued to leave its stamp, with Milton Berle, Ethel Merman and Rudy Vallee appearing as villains as uninspired as their names (Louie the Lilac, Lola Lasagna, Lord Marmaduke Ffogg). The series continued its downward slide. In the space of just two years, it slipped from #1 to as low as #48.[27] In January 1968, two years after its debut, ABC announced *Batman*'s cancellation.

There was some talk of taking the show to another network, but nothing came of it. "When it looked like we couldn't [get on another network] they came with a bulldozer and bulldozed the whole set—the Batcave and all of that," Craig said. "Then, two weeks later, NBC said, 'Listen, we'd like to take a shot at *Batman*, if you still have the set.' They didn't want to start from scratch and build them because the set was $800,000."[28] While it's fun to imagine where a fourth season might have led, ABC had likely taken the show as far as it could go.

The low ratings and cancellation stoked the popular perception of superheroes and comic books as, at best, a fad, and, at worst, kids' stuff. For the industry, it was a lesson in economics.

"It was a very expensive show to do because of all the special effects," Dozier said. "It became too expensive for the number of people watching it at the time—the right kind of people, the people who spend money on the sponsor's products."[29]

In the months that followed, West and Ward found themselves unable to get non-costumed work. Dozier tried and failed to get a pilot featuring another decades-old DC character, Wonder Woman, onto network TV. Craig continued to appear on various shows, including in an episode of *Star Trek* as the green-skinned Orion slave girl Marta.

In 1973, at the request of the U.S. Department of Labor Wage & Hour Division, Dozier got the band back together—well, Craig and Ward; Adam West declined—for a PSA promoting equal pay for women. West re-donned the cape and cowl in 1979 to appear, alongside Ward's Robin, Frank Gorshin's Riddler and several other DC heroes and villains, in the NBC-TV specials *Legends of the Superheroes: The Roast* and *Legends of the Superheroes: The Challenge*.

Over 20 years later, West and Ward starred in the TV special *Return to the Batcave*, an attempt to relive past glories. Catwomen Julie Newmar and Lee Meriwether and Lyle Waggoner, West's main rival for the role of Batman, guest starred. West and Ward eventually accepted their status as pop-culture icons on the convention circuit, and later provided voices for animated Batman series and movies.

Batman was one of Semple's last TV assignments; he went on to write or co-write the movies *Papillon*, *The Parallax View* and the final Sean Connery–James Bond outing, *Never Say Never Again*. "Every word of it was fun," Semple said of *Batman*. "I still feel it was among the best things I ever wrote, by a long shot."[30]

"There were elements in it that were miraculous," said Newmar, not overstating the case. "The casting of Batman and Robin was miraculous, and certain other characters were perfectly wonderful. People met for the first time, they put it on film, and, wham-bang, it was done. It was remarkable."[31]

The series lived on in syndication, where it became, in writer Glen Weldon's words, "a nerdy gateway drug; a first, dazzling weekday-afternoon introduction to the concept of superheroes in general and Batman in particular."[32]

"I was just out of my fucking mind over *Batman*," said filmmaker J.J. Abrams, who has worked on the *Star Trek* and *Star Wars* franchises. "I remember going into my first day of kindergarten and crying because I was so sad I was going to miss *Batman*. I remember saying the words to the teacher: 'Am I going to miss *Batman*?' and having the teacher say, 'Sorry, I can't understand you, honey—you're crying so hard.' And I was sobbing. I couldn't get a breath."[33]

"The show was everything to me," said writer Mark Waid, who has worked for both Marvel and DC. "Had I not loved it, had I not been encouraged by my father to watch it and read the comics, I'd be a CPA today."[34] Less auspiciously, the show's animated sound effects would provide fodder for decades of headlines for any comics-related story (i.e., "Biff! Bam! Kapow! Comics aren't just for kids anymore").

With syndication came vindication. Even fans who had decried the mockery of their hero came to realize that Batman contains multitudes, from Adam West's self-serious, slightly dim do-gooder to the later "dark" iterations. From 2013 to 2016, DC published a series based on the TV show's conceptions of the characters. In 2014, Warner Bros. finally released the series on DVD and Blu-ray, introducing what was now regarded as a classic to a new generation. Writer-editor Jim Beard has put together two (so far) anthologies of essays about the show.

But perhaps the show's most momentous legacy is the enmity it inspired in one of those early viewers who cried, "What have they done to my Batman?" He was a young comics fan in New Jersey named Michael Uslan, and he would change the movie industry.

Chapter III

Hulk Fights a Bear

> "[Frank Price, head of what was then Universal Television] told me they had acquired the rights to the Marvel Comics superheroes [and asked] which one did I want to do? I ran screaming from the room and said, 'None of them!'"
>
> —Kenneth Johnson, writer-director-producer,
> *The Incredible Hulk* TV series[1]

After the surprise success of *Batman*, producer William Dozier had an idea for a show based on DC's Wonder Woman.

Along with Batman and Superman, the Amazon was one of DC's longest-running characters. Instead of originating in a New York City comics sweatshop, however, she sprang from the imagination of psychologist William Moulton Marston. In 1940, as the comics industry was taking off, Marston spoke about the unfulfilled potential of the medium in an interview for *Family Circle*. (The interviewer was Olivia Byrne, his partner and former student, who lived in a polyamorous relationship with Marston and his wife Elizabeth.) Max Gaines, publisher of All-American Comics (a sibling to DC-National), read the remarks and offered Marston a job as an educational consultant. The East Coast shrink, who had briefly worked at Universal Studios and helped invent the polygraph, suggested a superheroine who combined "all the strength of a Superman plus all the allure of a good and beautiful woman."[2] Gaines gave him the go-ahead, and Wonder Woman, written by Marston and drawn in an art deco style by H.G. Peter, debuted in *All Star Comics* #8, December 1941.

For his take, Dozier envisioned a straight-up sitcom. He hired *Mad* magazine writers Larry Siegel and Stan Hart to write a pilot for what the producer was calling *Wonder Woman: Who's Afraid of Diana Prince*. (The popular 1966 film *Who's Afraid of Virginia Woolf?* was in theaters around this time.)

The surviving five-minute promo shows actress Ellie Wood Walker as Diana Prince, a young woman living with a nagging mom. Putting on a Wonder Woman outfit, Walker looks in the mirror and sees not herself in the costume but Linda Harrison. (Harrison later played Nova in two *Planet of the Apes* movies.) If you wanted to launch a comic book character on TV, this was one way not to do it.

Another was Douglas C. Cramer's approach. The head of 20th Century–Fox Television during *Batman*'s run, Cramer had started his own production company. After selling the idea of a *Wonder Woman* pilot to ABC, *Batman*'s former home, he contacted another *Batman* alumnus, writer Stanley Ralph Ross, and asked him to come up with a script. Ross declined; he was offended by the producer's choice for a lead, former tennis pro Cathy Lee Crosby. According to Ross,

I said, "She's wrong for the part." "What do you mean?" "She's blonde." "So what?" "Wonder Woman has dark hair." "What're you talking about?" "I'm a fan of Wonder Woman. I read the comic book. Wonder Woman has dark hair." "What's the difference?" [Cramer] wanted to do it modern, where she's involved with the CIA. I said, "The CIA are scumbags. They're terrible." He said, "That's the way we're doing it." I said, "Forget me."[3]

Cramer hired writer John D.F. Black and director Vincent McEveety, whose credits included episodes of *Star Trek*.

Crosby's hair color wasn't the only deviation from the comics. In the 75-minute pilot that aired in March 1974, Wonder Woman, aka Diana Prince, has no superpowers. Her costume, which she dons halfway through the show, looks like a modified tennis outfit. A secretary to Steve Trevor, the character's love interest in the comics, she is called "Dee" by her co-workers and "Wonder Woman" by the bad guys she has gone undercover to ferret out. The plot is pure TV-movie-of-the-week fluff—she's trying to retrieve codebooks stolen by a businessman played by seventies stalwart Ricardo Montalban.

The best that can be said about the pilot is that Crosby's Diana is a strong, confident woman who takes no b.s. from the condescending creeps around her. But few viewers who knew her from her comics incarnation would recognize Crosby's "Dee" as the classic DC hero.

Then again, a casual reader picking up an early seventies issue of *Wonder Woman* might not have recognized her either.

In 1968, following a decade of lackluster comics (and sales), DC traded Diana's trademark red-yellow-blue outfit and superpowers for mod pantsuits and martial arts. Instead of fighting supervillains, she karate-chopped gang members when not running her clothing store, Di Prince's Boutique. At the behest of Gloria Steinem, who put Wonder Woman in her original costume on the cover of the first issue of *Ms.* magazine in 1972, DC had just restored her to full-fledged superhero status when Cramer's effort aired.

The show came in fifth for the week. ABC ran it again later that year but didn't pick it up for a series. Cramer called Ross back. "How would you do it?" he asked.[4] Ross suggested returning the heroine to her World War II roots with powers intact and he wrote a story faithful to her origin.

This time, Cramer hired a brunette: A former Miss World USA from Arizona, 24-year-old Lynda Carter had auditioned for the original TV-movie. She had only a few episodic TV shows to her credit, so Cramer had to convince the network brass to take a chance on an unknown.[5]

For the telefilm, called *The New, Original Wonder Woman*, Academy Award–nominated costumer Donfeld designed an outfit in keeping with the character's classic look: a red bustier embossed with a gold eagle and star-spangled blue satin hot pants. The bow on the superhero package was a groovy theme song ("In your satin tights/Fighting for your rights") and cartoony intro—like *Batman*, but with more bondage, perhaps a tip of the whip to creator Marston's original, somewhat kinky, conception of the character.

In the 1975 pilot, Diana, princess of the Amazons, rescues Steve Trevor and brings him to "an uncharted island in the Devil's Triangle," aka Paradise Island. Diana's mom, the Queen of the Amazons, holds a tournament to determine which Amazon will take Steve back to the world of men. Diana competes and wins. Using her invisible plane, she flies the injured pilot to New York. There they unravel a Nazi plot to bomb an American airbase.

Airing six years after the final episode of *Batman*, *New, Original Wonder Woman* is a slightly more serious attempt to do a live-action superhero. When Diana walks down the street in full Wonder Woman regalia, passersby are suitably surprised. Adrift in a strange land, she must figure out practicalities like how to make money. People don't just wake up one day calling her "Wonder Woman"; she gets the name somewhat organically. And Carter plays the whole thing straight, espousing Wonder Woman talking points like "Women are the way of the future" without a trace of irony.

But with Cramer and Ross at the helm, the 75-minute pilot can't help but have some *Batman* DNA. Cramer and director Leonard J. Horn populate the cast with comic actors: Cloris Leachman (Diana's mom), Lyle Waggoner (Steve Trevor), Fannie Flagg and Red Buttons. Henry Gibson and Kenneth Mars ham it up shamelessly as two dim Nazi villains. Cheesy moments abound: The "athletic tournament" on Paradise Island looks like an outtake from *Emmanuelle Does Themyscira* and the return flight to the U.S. is set to a slinky saxophone theme.

The pilot did well enough in the ratings for the network to order two more one-hour episodes, then 11 more. Series writers inserted characters from the comics, including sidekick Etta Candy and villains Baroness Paula Von Gunther, a Gestapo agent; Fausta, aka the Nazi Wonder Woman; and Drusilla, Diana's younger sister. The latter was played by Debra Winger in one of her earliest roles.

ABC dithered over greenlighting a second season of the show, which was more expensive than average due to its period setting. CBS stepped in with an offer and production company Warner Bros. agreed. They rechristened the show *The New Adventures of Wonder Woman* and set it in the present. Seventies Diana was no longer a Navy yeoman petty officer first class—basically, Steve's secretary—but an agent with the Inter-Agency Defense Command, a CIA-type crimefighting organization. The show kept Waggoner, but since Wonder Woman is immortal and Steve Trevor was not (something that would prove to be a challenging plot point for future Wonder Woman handlers), he plays Steve Trevor, Jr., the fighter pilot's son.

CBS-Warners hired a new producer, Bruce (brother of actress Angela) Lansbury, a veteran of the series *The Wild Wild West* and *Mission: Impossible*. "They wanted a new flavor ... and I had a reputation for doing lots of wild stuff," Lansbury said.[6] He gave Diana a computer and a robot dog.

Miss World USA 1972 Lynda Carter made a lasting impression as Diana Prince, aka Wonder Woman, for one season on ABC and two on CBS, 1975–79. Warner Bros.

Anne Collins had sold a script to *Hawaii Five-O* and was just starting out in the industry when she got the word that *Wonder Woman* was looking for a woman to fill the position of story editor. "There were very, very few women writing action-type stuff, and that's what I preferred to do," Collins said.[7] She was also familiar with the character, having grown up with two older brothers who were comics readers.

Lansbury moved the show in a lighter direction. In one episode, comedian Martin Mull plays a mind-controlling pop star; in another, former Riddler Frank Gorshin is an evil toymaker. In the third season, the show jumps all the sharks: Wonder Woman takes up skateboarding, saves teen heartthrob Leif Garrett, goes undercover as an aspiring singer and, yes, fights a shark.

Cast and crew were still filming when they got wind that the third season would be the last. "There was no one [from the network] that came down," Carter said. "I think I heard it on the set from someone, 'The show got cancelled.' And I said, 'Hunh?'"[8] The show had fallen to number 60 (out of 114 shows).[9]

The cancellation marked the beginning of a long dry spell for live-action female superheroes. (*Isis*, a live-action Saturday morning series, predated *Wonder Woman*. It ended in 1976.) But by then, CBS had a few other super-irons in the fire, all from the other top mainstream comics publisher, Marvel.

The imprint had morphed out of Timely, taking its name from the latter's first comic, *Marvel Comics #1* (1939). The Marvel era officially began in 1961 with the publication of the first issue of *The Fantastic Four* and continued with a Big Bang of creativity that birthed character after character, including Spider-Man, the Hulk, Iron Man, Daredevil, the X-Men and many more future household names.

What differentiated Marvel from DC, still the industry's top dog, was, primarily, the idea of the flawed hero. Writer Stan Lee and artists like Jack Kirby and Steve Ditko created protagonists who worried about paying the rent, getting a date and catching a cold. Marvel also pioneered the idea of a shared universe, where characters crossed over into each other's books and new stories referred to past events in previous issues or neighboring titles. This innovation encouraged brand loyalty, a clubhouse mentality and more dimes dropped at the newsstand.

Marvel also began attracting older readers. It wasn't long after Lee noticed feedback from university students that he began speculating, mostly in the comics' letters pages, about seeing the characters in the movies. Mainstream media attention and the approbation of filmmakers like Federico Fellini—who, in 1965, visited the publisher's New York offices—and Alain Resnais further stoked Lee's ambitions. The middle-aged writer, who had been toiling away in the New York City publishing salt mines for over two decades, longed for mainstream acceptance.

Lee wouldn't see his dreams of a Marvel character on the big screen realized for another decade, though, and even then it was a mixed blessing. In the meantime, there was television.

Marvel's relationship with the boob tube began in 1966 with *The Marvel Super Heroes*. The cheaply made animated series featured Captain America, the Hulk, Iron Man, Thor and Sub-Mariner in segments using static images (many from the comics themselves) and moving mouths. It lasted four months. Then, from 1967 to 1970, Grantray-Lawrence Animation produced *Spider-Man*. Also made on a tight budget, the series introduced non–comics-reading kids not just to Marvel's bestselling character but also his rogues' gallery: the Scorpion, Dr. Octopus, the Lizard, Vulture, Electro, Rhino and Mysterio.

Spidey also became the first modern Marvel character to make the leap to live action. From 1974 to 1977, dancer and puppeteer Danny Seagren played a silent version in educational segments on the kids' show *The Electric Company*. In all, 32 of these "Spidey Super Stories" aired. Apparently Lee gave the producers the rights gratis, for the promotion and publicity. The move paid off in at least one considerable way: The show's head writer was Tom Whedon, father of Joss—the writer-director who, decades later, took the nascent Marvel Studios to new heights with the first *Avengers* movie.

Then primetime came calling. Around 1976, producer Daniel R. Goodman purchased the rights to Marvel's crown jewel and struck a deal with CBS to beam the web-slinger's adventures into American living rooms.

In September of the following year, the network aired the pilot. Simply called *Spider-Man*, it starred Nicholas Hammond (Friedrich von Trapp in *The Sound of Music*) as Peter Parker, an NYU grad student and part-time photographer who's bitten by a radioactive spider. The plot, in a script by seventies crime show vet Alvin Boretz, was unambitious movie-of-the-week stuff: Formerly upstanding citizens have begun committing crimes and the trail leads to the head of a "human potential" movement who is controlling the minds of his followers. No Electros here, folks.

Some supporting characters from the comics made the cut including doting Aunt May, fulminating *Daily Bugle* publisher J. Jonah Jameson (whose outrage is best expressed in the line, "[Parker's] been trying to get $46 out of me for two days!") and mellow city editor Robbie Robertson. The telefilm includes Peter's superhero origin but leaves out his crimefighting *raison d'être*, Uncle Ben.

Although it often resembles a police procedural, *Spider-Man* moves along at a brisk pace, aided by decent performances. The fight scenes are only a couple of cuts above those in *Batman* (or *New, Original Wonder Woman*) and are silent—this is a quip-less webhead—but the stunts, with stuntman Fred Waugh in costume and climbing up and down sides of buildings, are impressively vertiginous. Adding value, the stuntman jerry-rigged a camera mounted on his head for a bird's-eye view of his ascents.

The pilot did well in the ratings but poorly with the valued 18–49-year-old demographic. CBS ordered five episodes and dubbed the show *The Amazing Spider-Man*, in line with the hero's long-running comic book series. After placing the show with a former *Six Million Dollar Man* producer, CBS bought seven more episodes for the 1978–79 season. The network aired the series sporadically; its last two episodes, a two-parter filmed on location in Hong Kong, appeared in the summer, more than four months after the previous episode. By then, the company had pulled the plug on the too-pricey-for-primetime show.

"For the cast and crew, it was so frustrating," said Ellen Bry, who played second-season love interest Julie Masters. "We were like, 'Okay, what part of high ratings, good network share, doesn't CBS understand?' People were finding us. But it was almost like *Where's Waldo?* They would cart out a new episode every so often."[10]

One person who wasn't sad to see *The Amazing Spider-Man* end was co-creator Stan Lee. "It was so basic," said Lee, who served as a consultant. "It had none of the humor [of the comics]. It had none of the drama—none of the intense human relationships that we tried to put in."[11]

Legend has it that the death blow was prompted by a remark made to CBS president William Paley. "You've gone from the Tiffany Network to the Comic Book Network," an acquaintance told the network exec.[12] There was some truth to this. Besides Spidey, there was Wonder Woman, who was about to lose her show, but also more Marvel properties coming the network's way, all under the auspices of Universal Studios.

After Spider-Man, the Hulk was next to arrive. In 1962, after launching *The Fantastic Four* and *The Amazing Spider-Man*, Stan Lee and artist Jack Kirby created the super-strong giant with the mind of a temperamental child (a riff on *Dr. Jekyll and Mr. Hyde*): Milquetoast scientist Bruce Banner is unable to control his transformations into the destructive green (gray in his first appearances) behemoth following exposure to gamma radiation. The Hulk debuted in his own title in 1962, but Marvel cancelled the comic after six issues. After floating around in various other Marvel books for five yeras, including the anthology *Tales to Astonish*, he was granted his own solo title again in 1968.

To bring him to the small screen, Universal looked to the main TV action templates of the time: *The Six Million Dollar Man* and its distaff spinoff, *The Bionic Woman*. Kenneth Johnson had worked on both, so Frank Price, Universal's head of TV programming, asked the writer-director to oversee it. "Pass," said Johnson.[13]

But then he reconsidered. "I thought, 'Well—maybe there's a way to take a little Victor Hugo, a little Robert Louis Stevenson and this ridiculous premise called 'the Incredible Hulk' and turn it into something, if they allow me to do it as a psychological drama with real adult appeal and with strong, classy casting.' And they did!"[14]

Johnson, who was reading Hugo's *Les Misérables* at the time, figured that he could work the novel's conflict between Jean Valjean and his relentless pursuer, Police Inspector Javert into the show.

Lou Ferrigno was one of the first to discover the trials and tribulations of playing a superhero. As the Hulk in the seventies CBS-TV series, the Brooklyn-born bodybuilder spent hours in the makeup chair and wore green contact lenses and a wig made of yak hair. Universal Television.

Johnson's idea of classy casting began with Bill Bixby, the director's "first and only choice"[15] for Bruce Banner. As familiar to audiences as a pair of comfy slippers, Bixby had a TV CV that included *My Favorite Martian*, *The Courtship of Eddie's Father* and *The Magician*. For Banner's alter ego, Johnson decided on Brooklyn-born bodybuilder Lou Ferrigno. The 275-pound Ferrigno, who had taken up weightlifting after being bullied as a child for a speech impediment, turned green and mean via a fright-wig made of yak hair, contact lenses and body paint that took three hours to apply.

Johnson wrote the 90-minute pilot in a week.[16] He dropped the comic's supporting cast and created tabloid reporter Jack McGee to serve as Javert to Banner's Valjean, and changed the character's origin: Instead of being bombarded by gamma rays while trying to save a life, David Banner (Johnson deemed the alliterative Bruce Banner "too comic book-y"[17]) is a scientist who experiments with gamma radiation in an effort to enhance his strength after he fails to save his wife from a car crash.

There are a lot of shots of Banner's car in the *Incredible Hulk* pilot; it's a great show if you want to watch Bill Bixby change a tire in the rain. It's also very science-y, with Banner and fellow scientist Elaina (Susan Sullivan) spending a lot of time frowning in front of computer screens. Banner's inner turmoil is the focus—that, and McGee's attempts to unravel the mysterious goings-on—but it's the scientist's relationship with Elaina, and her fate, that gives some punch to the otherwise bland story.

As for the money shots—well, there are only three Hulk-outs, and only a little smashing. If anything, the scenes of transformation from man to monster (and back) prove that 40-plus years later, in-camera special effects hadn't advanced much from the 1931 version of *Dr. Jekyll and Mr. Hyde*. Another disappointment, at least for comics fans, was Johnson's decision to keep the Hulk silent instead of giving free rein to his ego-driven monosyllabic tirades, as the comics did.

The pilot gave pop culture one memorable line: "Don't make me angry," Banner tells McGee. "You wouldn't like me when I'm angry." He's no Mark Ruffalo, but Bixby sells it.

The second Hulk TV-movie, *Death in the Family*, is faster-paced, although a better title might be "Hulk vs. Bear" since that scene is all anyone remembers about it.

The two telemovies did well in the ratings, and CBS commissioned a weekly hour-long series. It became a Friday night hit.

Next came *Doctor Strange*. Making his comics debut in 1963, the same year as the Hulk, Doctor Strange was, like Spider-Man, a Stan Lee-Steve Ditko creation. His origin depicts him as Stephen Strange, an arrogant surgeon who, following a car accident, suffers the loss of the nerve endings in his fingers. Unable to perform surgery, Strange journeys to Tibet, where he comes under the guidance of the mysterious Ancient One.

At first, the good doctor suffered the publishing vicissitudes typical of a second-tier comics character. He spent his first five years battling interdimensional evil first in an anthology, then starred in his own title for just over a year before cancellation. The first half of the seventies saw him guest-starring in other titles until a series of head-shop-friendly stories by writer Steve Englehart and artist Frank Brunner returned him to front-rack position in the minds of Marvel readers. When Universal came calling, he was a few years into his own title once again.

The studio assigned Philip DeGuere, Jr., to manifest the Master of the Mystic Arts' occult world on TV. Like Johnson, writer-producer DeGuere had extensive TV credits, including the World War II-era series *Baa Baa Black Sheep* and a brief stint on *The Bionic Woman*.

As with Spider-Man, the doctor barely survived his transition from page to screen. For 1978's *Dr. Strange*, DeGuere streamlined the character's origin into a tale of one mage passing the mantle to a protégé. Instead of a surgeon, Stephen Strange is a psychiatrist. Instead of one of the character's crazier villains, like the galaxy-cloaked Eternity, the main bad guy is a mortal-looking witch, Morgan LeFay.

The story kicks in when Stephen attends a young woman who has been possessed by an evil entity. Thomas Lindmer, the current Sorcerer Supreme, tells Stephen that the girl needs more help than even seventies psychiatric advice can offer. After Lindmer convinces him that other dimensions exist, the doctor agrees to train in the mystic arts and battle LeFay and her boss the Nameless One.

To put it mildly, the telefilm has not held up as a triumph of comics-to-film adaptations. For one thing, the occult elements butt up against the hospital scenes. Like *Spider-Man*'s resemblance to *Starsky & Hutch*, CBS-Universal's *Dr. Strange* often looks like a typical seventies medical procedural. As Strange, porn-stashed Peter Hooten gives a dazed, off-in-the-dream-dimension performance.

On the plus side, Academy Award–winning English actor John Mills lends some class to the production as Lindmer, and Jessica Walter is a chilly witch fatale as LeFay. Strange's "manservant" Wong (Clyde Kusatsu) sports three-piece suits and speaks in an American accent rather than following the stereotype in the comics. Paul Chihara's score elevates some scenes into moaning distance of eerie, and at least one set is modeled after Steve Ditko's original interdimensional visions.

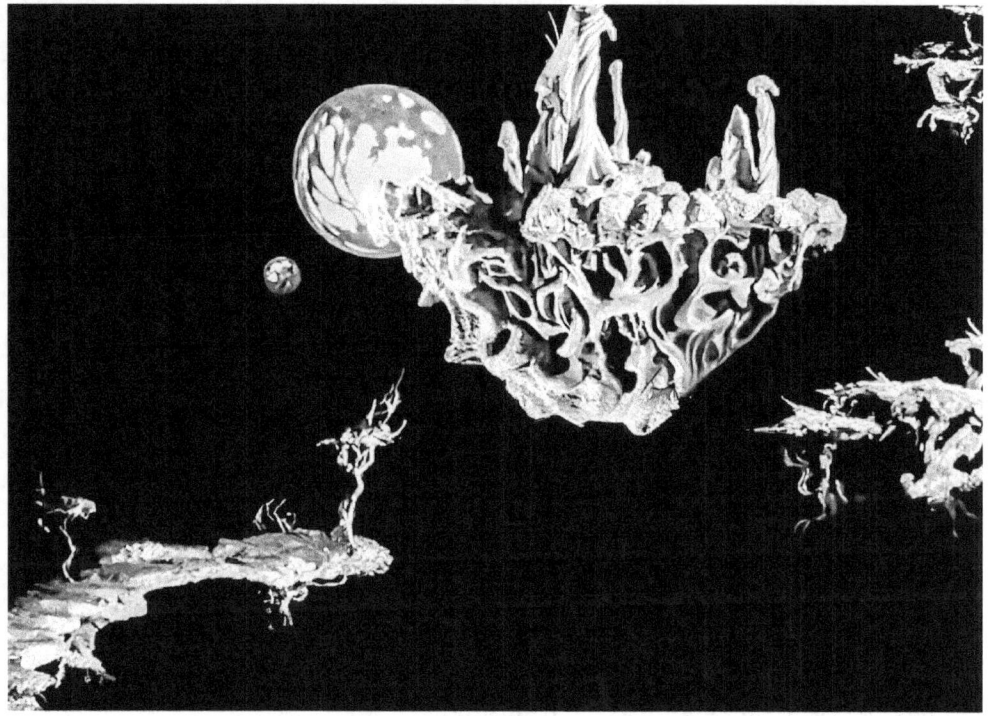

CBS's 1978 *Dr. Strange* TV-movie may be deeply flawed, but the set designers at least attempted to emulate the otherworldly dreamscapes of Marvel Comics artist Steve Ditko. Universal Television.

Up against a rerun of the mini-series *Roots*, *Dr. Strange* lost the ratings battle. Would Captain America, Timely's—and hence Marvel's—first superhero, fare any better?

Following the end of World War II, the character's popularity had waned until Timely cancelled his title. Then in 1963, Lee and Kirby thawed out the patriot for the first Avengers lineup. Five years later, he had his own title. By the time Universal came along, Kirby had returned to Marvel after a stint at DC and just completed a two-year victory lap on the *Captain America* title as both writer and penciller.

Little of what made the character tick made it into the two *Captain America* telefilms that aired, again on CBS, in 1979. Both suffered from the usual limitations of primetime network television and a less common one, a lead played by a former USC football player, Reb Brown.

The first movie, *Captain America*, aired in January. It's mostly origin stuff, and just as maladapted from the comic book version as CBS-Universal's other attempts, if not more so. Steve Rogers, an ex–Marine artist-drifter with a van, just wants to paint landscapes and portraits. An old friend of his late father's, Dr. Simon Mills, tracks him down to tell him that his dad had developed and experimented with the ultimate steroid, FLAG (Full Latent Ability Gain). It gave him incredible powers and earned him the nickname "Captain America." Mills convinces Steve to take up the cause and supplies him with a red, white and blue bodysuit, matching rocket-powered motorcycle (that launches out of the back of his van), and bullet-proof shield. Steve gets mixed up in an evil industrialist's plot to plunder a gold mine by blowing up Phoenix, Arizona.

As the square-jawed hero, Brown gives it the old college try, but he can't help but come across like an earnest chump. Asked by Mills, played by veteran character actor Len Birman, if he wants to "live a little longer," Brown's Steve answers, "Yeah, I guess so," as if he's just been asked if he wants to go for a beer after the game. Overall, the pace is slow, the dialogue risible and the action more like *The Six Thousand Dollar Man* than *The Six Million Dollar Man*. Heather Menzies, from the TV series *Logan's Run*, plays Mills' assistant.

Directed by Hungarian filmmaker Ivan Nagy, who went on to notoriety as a one-time boyfriend of Hollywood madam Heidi Fleiss, *Captain America: Death II Soon* is a much stronger effort. The sequel, which aired 11 months after the first, features more realistic action scenes, a cooler costume (according to Brown, it was changed after Marvel complained[18]), inventive camera angles and a more developed character: Steve now has a cat. The script is tighter, too, with venerable British actor Christopher Lee playing a terrorist planning to drop a gas that causes quick aging on Portland, Oregon, if he isn't paid a billion dollars. Based on the sequel, it's possible a TV show might have found its footing. Brown said that the network would have ordered more but Universal balked at Marvel's licensing fee. "[Marvel] wanted 50 grand an episode, and that nixed the deal."[19]

Following *Death II Soon*, the Hulk was the last superhero standing. CBS broadcast the final episodes of his series in the fall of 1981. In total, 80 hour-long episodes aired over four years, making it the longest-lasting attempt at a live-action superhero TV series up to that time. Johnson later said that he was surprised by the network's decision to cancel the show, as it scored well with women, men, teens and kids[20]—an early example of what is now known as a four-quadrant crowd-pleaser.

Throughout the series' run, the *Hulk* creator-showrunner stuck to his anti-comics stance. None of the supporting cast from the comics appeared, and instead of villains like the warty Abomination and the long-domed Leader, Johnson's Banner-Hulk encountered distressed strangers-of-the-week—a troubled rock star, a carnival mind-reader, etc.

The notable exception was the final season two-parter "The First," in which the Hulk meets an earlier version of himself, played by Dick Durock. Stuntman-actor Durock went on to semi-fame in the title role of a movie based on a DC character, Swamp Thing.

Except for ABC's *Greatest American Hero*, an original show created by TV guru Stephen J. Cannell, the cancellation of *The Incredible Hulk* marked the end of network TV's fling with primetime live-action superheroes, at least for the time being. The real superhero action had moved back to the big screen.

Chapter IV

This Looks Like a Job for Two European Film Producers

> "Nobody knew how to go about it. It was the blind leading the blind, all experimentation ... [but] somehow or other, we pulled it off."
> —Richard Donner, director, *Superman*[1]

By the end of the sixties, DC Comics was part of Kinney National Services, a conglomerate that included one of the world's oldest and most storied film studios: Warner Bros. The studio dated back to 1911. Over the decades it had released the first talkie, 1927's *The Jazz Singer*, as well as James Cagney gangster pictures, Busby Berkeley musicals and mid-century classics like *The Maltese Falcon*, *Casablanca*, *A Streetcar Named Desire* and *Rebel Without a Cause*. By the early seventies it was occasionally dipping its toes into genre films like George Lucas' science fiction debut *THX 1138*, Stanley Kubrick's *A Clockwork Orange* and the Charlton Heston sci-fi thriller *The Omega Man*.

When, in 1973, a trio of European film producers approached Warners about a *Superman* movie, the studio had no interest. Perhaps it was too soon after the spectacular flameout of the *Batman* TV series, and/or the cost of the special effects. Whatever the reason, the studio chiefs "absolutely didn't think it was worth it," said Ilya Salkind, one-half of a producing team with his father Alexander.[2]

Ilya had been on a Parisian stroll when a poster for a movie featuring the Spanish avenger Zorro caught his eye. Reminded of another hero, that night at dinner with his father he suggested that, for their next movie, they should do Superman. "Who?" Alexander asked.

Salkind the younger had discovered the DC character through comic books and the *Adventures of Superman* TV series in the fifties, while living in New York with his peripatetic parents.[3] Alexander was a second-generation filmmaker whose credits included the 1960 film *Austerlitz* and Orson Welles' 1962 version of Franz Kafka's *The Trial*. Berta Dominguez, Alexander's wife and Ilya's mother, was a Mexican-born poet and playwright.

The elder Salkind was intrigued by his son's suggestion and the two approached DC. But the publisher's proposed contract was "very complex," Ilya said, and included "these crazy controls on the character to a point that it became impossible to make a movie."[4]

The trio went to the top, perhaps to Ted Ashley, then head of Warner Communications. "And of course in two minutes, the deal was done."[5]

For $4 million ($6 million with renewable options), the Salkinds walked away with the key to the Fortress of Solitude: film and TV rights for 25 years not only to the world's most popular superhero but also his supporting cast, including humans, supervillains and relations.[6]

The Europeans began looking for talent and credibility, not necessarily in that order. They approached screenwriter William Goldman, but the Oscar winner (for 1969's *Butch Cassidy and the Sundance Kid*) "didn't feel it," Ilya said.[7] They considered Alfred Bester, a science fiction author who had written comics in the forties, including *Superman*, and whose wife Rolly was the first voice of Lois Lane in the forties radio series. Finally they landed Mario Puzo. Puzo, who had once toiled away in the same Manhattan magazine salt mines as Stan Lee, was the author of the bestselling 1969 novel *The Godfather* and screenwriter of its 1972 adaptation, the highest-grossing film up until that time. The Salkinds could parlay his name into investment money and media attention.

Puzo submitted a 500-page script that was, in the words of DC Comics artist-editor Carmine Infantino, "a dog."[8]

> The first story he wrote was about, some guys are trying to kill the Pope and Superman saves him. That's not a Superman story, what the hell are you guys doing? So I went upstairs and had a big fight about it. So they sent me out to the Coast and we sat in the Beverly Hills Hotel and we banged out Superman I and II, he, I and the Salkinds.[9]

Whatever his screenplay contributions, Infantino's name doesn't appear in the credits.

Next, Ilya brought on husband-and-wife team David and Leslie Newman and Robert Benton. David Newman and Benton had received Oscar nominations for their screenplay for Warners' *Bonnie and Clyde* (1967). They had also written the book for a campy 1966 Broadway musical based on Superman called *It's a Bird...It's a Plane...It's Superman*. The well-reviewed spoof closed after three and a half months.

The next big "gets" were Marlon Brando and Gene Hackman. Brando made headlines when he asked for, and received, $3 million and a cut of the gross for 12 days' work playing Superman's Kryptonian father Jor-El. Hackman was cast as Superman's arch-enemy Lex Luthor.

The search for a director led the Salkinds to Guy Hamilton. Hamilton had made a few James Bond films and so he was comfortable with big-budget action pictures. But when the Salkinds moved the production from Italy to England, the English director—a tax exile from his homeland—dropped out. Tom Mankiewicz, who was later hired to work on the script, said that the Salkinds moved the production from Italy because of the rising lira. Other reports say that Brando was persona non grata in the country following the release of the controversial *Last Tango in Paris*.

Ilya eventually hired director Richard Donner, whose movie *The Omen* was then topping the box office. Released in the summer of '76, the supernatural thriller featured well-crafted set-pieces like a public suicide by hanging and a decapitation via a glass pane. The Bronx-born Donner had grown up around movies—his grandfather owned a Brooklyn theater—and began directing episodic TV in the late fifties.

Donner called the script he was handed "a parody on a parody"[10]; Mankiewicz said, "It just went on forever. It was very campy."[11] The son of acclaimed screenwriter-director Joseph L. Mankiewicz, Tom too had worked on Bond films.

In a scene that seems to have originated with Puzo but survived multiple drafts, Superman sees a bald man that he thinks is his nemesis Lex Luthor. The man turns out to be *Kojak* actor Telly Savalas, who delivers his TV detective's signature line: "Who loves ya, baby?"

This was not the approach Donner wanted. The operating word for his big-budget superhero epic, he felt, should be "verisimilitude."

"We treated it as truth," he said. "And the minute you are unfaithful to the truth, to the dignity of the legend, the minute you screw around with it, or make fun of it, or parody it and make it into a spoof, then you destroy its innocence and honesty."[12]

Donner was given six months to prepare what would become the biggest-budgeted film in history before he had to start shooting Brando's scenes. And he had yet to find his leads.

For Superman and his alter ego Clark Kent, the Salkinds considered nearly every leading man in Hollywood, from Steve McQueen to Burt Reynolds to Jon Voight. Singer Neil Diamond put in his bid, and Ilya's wife's dentist came in for a screen test. After much cajoling from casting director Lynn Stalmaster, Donner and the Salkinds agreed to see an unknown stage actor, Christopher Reeve.

According to Reeve,

> I remember sitting in the dressing room with [actors] Bill [Hart] and Jeff [Daniels], saying, "You'll never believe what happened today. The phone rang. They are going to make a movie out of Superman." They said, "Which? Shaw's *Superman*? Or the one with the cape that goes 'Up, up, and away'?" We all had a good laugh. Movie? That sounds ridiculous, it would be stupid. Then I began to think: Well, at least I can read the script.[13]

Reeve read it, auditioned and got the role. For *Daily Planet* reporter Lois Lane, top actresses of the day, like Leslie Anne Warren, Anne Archer and Stockard Channing, tested with the Juilliard-educated 25-year-old. Finally, three days before the start of principal photography, Donner gave the role to Margot Kidder, a 29-year-old Canadian-American actress who had the most chemistry with her 25-year-old co-star.

"We came from similar backgrounds, and he looked like one of my brothers," Kidder said in 2016. "So the energy we had was one of brother and sister, which was often bickering, that took the place of romantic energy. No one noticed the difference one from the other—it worked. We didn't have to create a different reality."[14]

Principal photography began on schedule in March 1977. The shoot dragged on for month after month, and costs mounted—Donner was making two films, the first installment and its sequel, a strategy devised by the Salkinds for their *Three Musketeers* movies. Tension began mounting between the director and producers, particularly Pierre Spengler, a childhood friend of Ilya's who had worked with the father and son team. "As far as I was concerned, he didn't have any knowledge of producing a film like that," Donner said.[15]

According to Mankiewicz, who continued to work on the script during filming, the Salkinds were frustrated that the director was over-budget: "Donner kept saying, 'You keep telling me I'm over-budget. What is the budget?' Clearly they had promised their investors that they could make these films much cheaper than they were going to be."[16]

The Salkinds brought in an intermediary, Richard Lester. The English director, whose credits included the Beatles films *A Hard Day's Night* and *Help*, had his own issues with the producers; he had made both *Musketeers* films but only been paid for one. By sticking close, he figured, maybe he could hound the Salkinds into giving him the money that they owed him. According to Donner, Lester had successfully sued the Salkinds, but "each time he sued them in one country, they'd move to another."[17] Ilya hoped that Lester could move the production along. "[Donner] couldn't make up his mind on stuff," he said.[18]

The Salkinds and Spengler would have fired him, Donner said. "But by then,

Chapter IV. This Looks Like a Job for Two European Film Producers

Warners had gotten involved in distribution—and one thing they had was the right of director approval."[19]

Finally, after the studio pushed back its hoped-for summer 1978 release date, the Salkinds and/or Warners told Donner to just finish the first one and not worry about completing the sequel. He and Mankiewicz grafted what was meant to be the ending of the second movie onto the first, and Donner completed shooting in October 1978, 19 months from the start of principal photography and just weeks from the film's December 10 unveiling.

• • •

While anticipation grew for the first big-budget superhero movie, there was at least one man who wasn't excited but furious.

"I hope it super-bombs!" wrote Jerry Siegel in a 1975 press release.

Siegel had worked in comics until 1966 but was working as a clerk-typist in Los Angeles when he got wind of the multimillion-dollar movie being made out of the character he had co-created—and sold, with Joe Shuster, to National in 1938 for $130.

He sent his diatribe about the injustice of the situation to every news outlet he could think of, including a Long Beach paper called *Marina News*. The editor passed it along to Phil Yeh, a cartoonist and journalist who published a local arts paper called *Uncle Jam*. Said Yeh, "I recall that the press release was single-spaced and obviously from a man who had been wronged by a big company. As I read through the whole thing, which was several pages long, I too felt anger at this injustice to someone who had created Superman."[20]

Yeh published an interview with Siegel and the national press picked up the story. Neal Adams, a comics artist renowned for bringing a photorealist style to both Marvel and DC characters, joined forces with TV producer Robert Lipsyte and Association of American Editorial Cartoonists president (and Joker co-creator) Jerry Robinson. The trio harassed DC and its parent company into acknowledging Siegel and Joe Shuster as the men who had created Superman. Eventually, the company granted an annual pension of $20,000 (which was raised to $30,000 after the movie's release) to the two 64-year-olds.

"We were young kids," Siegel said in 1981 of selling off the rights for a pittance. "What did we know?"[21] As the credits came up on *Superman* in December 1978, their names appeared as the creators of the character.

• • •

Superman begins on the planet Krypton, where the High Council has gathered to banish a trio of criminals to the Phantom Zone. Scientist Jor-El warns the Council of the imminent explosion of the planet. They shut him down and so he places his newborn son Kal-El in a rocket and sends him to Earth. There, the infant is found and adopted by Jonathan and Martha Kent, a couple in rural Kansas. The newly christened Clark Kent gradually discovers his powers and eventually decides to move to the big city, Metropolis. He gets a job at the *Daily Planet* and begins saving lives as Superman.

The costumed hero's derring-do catches the attention of Lex Luthor, the self-proclaimed "greatest criminal mind the world has ever known." Luthor, who lives in the Metropolis subway system with his flunky Otis and his moll Miss Teschmacher, is planning to sink California with nuclear bombs, thereby increasing his real estate holdings. Figuring that the only thing standing in his way is Superman, the the criminal

For all of *Superman*'s (1978) special effects and headline-making star turns, a large part of the appeal of the first superhero blockbuster was the chemistry between Margot Kidder as Lois Lane and Christopher Reeve as the title character and his alter ego, nebbish Clark Kent. Warner Bros.

mastermind decides to kill the city's new savior. He stumbles upon Superman's weakness, kryptonite, and lures the hero to his hideout. A weakened Superman is saved by Miss Teschmacher when she realizes Luthor doesn't care that her mom is going to die in one of the missile attacks. (She lives in Hackensack, New Jersey, but Otis has incorrectly programmed one of the missiles.) Superman flies off to stop the missiles.

Primed by a viral marketing campaign based around the tagline "You'll believe a man can fly" and the recently released spectacles *Star Wars* and *Close Encounters of the Third Kind* audiences were ready for a big-screen comic-book fantasy. *Superman* opened at #1 and stayed there for 11 weeks.

Mainstream reviewers were mostly positive. "*Superman* is a pure delight, a wondrous combination of all the old-fashioned things we never really get tired of: adventure and romance, heroes and villains, earthshaking special effects, and—you know what else? Wit," wrote Roger Ebert.[22] "*Superman* is good, clean, simple-minded fun, though it's a movie whose limited appeal is built in," said the *New York Times*' Vincent Canby.[23]

For all of Donner's stated attempts at verisimilitude, the first big-budget live-action superhero feature film is not that far off from the boob-tube buffoonery of the *Batman* TV series. Villains Lex, Otis (Ned Beatty), and Miss Teschmacher (Valerie Perrine) are as cartoonish as Phineas Ffogg, Egghead, and Nora Clavicle. The friction between Reeve's earnest Superman and Kidder's salty Lois gives the movie its heart, but the contempt with which the seasoned reporter treats the cub is over-the-top cringe-y. And, even after millions in R&D and promises that "You'll believe a man can fly," the flying effects are only a notch above those in 1941's *Adventures of Captain Marvel*.

Today, *Superman* is regarded as a classic, perhaps because it captures a sense of wide-eyed wonder, innocence, and sincerity—in large part due to Reeve's performance—that would be impossible to replicate.

Interestingly, the film remains one of the few, if not the only superhero movie that

Chapter IV. This Looks Like a Job for Two European Film Producers

doesn't end with a big battle. Instead, the protagonist basically cleans up after a missile explodes and, in an ethically dubious use of his powers, turns back time to save his love.

This ending was, of course, the result of the shuffling of story elements from the proposed sequel, the thinking being that if the first movie tanked, then there would be no need for a second. But *Superman* set box office records and became the highest-grossing film of the year, ensuring a *Superman II*.

But Donner wouldn't be involved.

"I'd like to think I'm going to be [finishing up]," he told an interviewer in early 1979, just after *Superman*'s release. "I'd be very disappointed if I wasn't."[24]

In March, the Salkinds told Donner's agent that his client's services were no longer required.

Chapter V

Marvel Gets Its Wish

"I think that [Richard] Donner was emphasizing a kind of grandiose myth. There was an epic quality which isn't in my nature, so my work didn't really embrace that."
—Richard Lester, director, *Superman II* and *III*[1]

"It's a film about a duck from outer space. It's not supposed to be an existential experience."
—Gloria Katz, co-writer, *Howard the Duck* (1986)[2]

Superman opened the gate. But who, and what, would follow?

The obvious answer was *Superman II*. But a number of other comic book–related flicks crashed the party. Some of these, like *Hero at Large* and *Condorman*, were superhero films in name only; the former was a comedy with John Ritter as an Everyman who becomes a media sensation after foiling a crime while wearing a "Captain Avenger" outfit at the opening of a new movie. The latter was a spy caper that followed comic book writer-artist Woodrow "Woody" Wilkins and his attempts to craft a flying suit like that of his character Condorman.

Popeye was a different story. Based on the E.C. Segar character who debuted in 1929 in the comic strip "Thimble Theatre," the musical brought to life the irascible sailor with a penchant for spinach. Robert Altman directed a cast that included Robin Williams and Shelley Duvall, from a script by comic strip artist-writer Jules Feiffer, and with songs by Harry Nilsson. The ambitious 1980 effort was a flop, but it has its admirers.

Tights- and capes-wise, *Superman II* kicked off the decade. Directed by Richard Lester, and with a script mostly written by David and Leslie Newman, the second outing gave comics fans what the first movie hadn't: a big-screen, live-action super-battle.

The sequel begins with Lois Lane in another life-threatening situation. This time the Pulitzer Prize–hungry reporter is in Paris, up on the Eiffel Tower during a terrorist siege. Superman rescues her and hurls the terrorists' hydrogen bomb into space. It explodes, cracking open the Phantom Zone and unleashing the three Kryptonian villains exiled by Superman's father Jor-El before Krypton exploded.

Back in Metropolis, *Daily Planet* publisher Perry White sends Clark and Lois to Niagara Falls to work on a story about honeymoons. Lois risks her life to prove that Clark is Superman but Clark foils her plan. He then admits that he's Superman anyway. He flies her to his Arctic hideaway, the Fortress of Solitude. After they make love, he decides to give up his powers so he can lead a normal life. In a diner, he gets into an altercation with a trucker. The depowered Clark loses.

Meanwhile, in space, the escaped villains—General Zod, Ursa and Non—discover they have superpowers. They assault American astronauts on the moon before coming to Earth to wreak havoc. Once ensconced in the White House, they are visited by Lex Luthor, who promises to bring them the one threat to their domination of the planet—Superman—in return for Australia. Zod agrees. Lex and Miss Teschmacher take a hot air balloon to the Fortress and steal a crystal.

After seeing the devastation caused by Zod's crew, Clark returns to the Arctic and reverses the power-sapping process. In Metropolis, Superman fights Zod, Ursa and Non, then leads them back to the Fortress. He tricks them into losing their powers and tosses them down a ravine. Clark goes back to the diner and beats up the trucker.

For many, *Superman II* exceeded expectations. This was largely for two reasons: the villains, and the fight between Superman and his three equally superpowered nemeses, the first real cinematic attempt at capturing comic-book action.

Though dated now, the sequence is still impressive. And while Gene Hackman's Luthor is too comically egomaniacal to be much of a threat, Terence Stamp and Sarah Douglas as Zod and Ursa are gleefully evil. If it's true that a superhero film is only as good as its bad guy, or bad guys in this case, then the two English actors (Jack O'Halloran as the mute Non has little to do except look mean) make up for *Superman II*'s sins.

And these are many. Director Lester and scripters David and Leslie Newman mostly abandon Richard Donner's attempt to ground the first movie in some kind of realism. Clark is far too easily swayed to give up his powers, the fight with the trucker is ridiculous, Lex simply strolls into the Fortress of Solitude (after traveling to the Arctic in a hot air balloon, no less), and the super-battle is marred by an extended bit of sight gags caused by a blast of super-breath. The script also gives Superman contrived powers like a super-kiss that makes Lois forget his secret identity.

(From left) Sarah Douglas, Terence Stamp and Jack O'Halloran give the Man of Steel a worthy challenge as super-powered Kryptonians Ursa, Zod and Non in *Superman II* (1981). Warner Bros.

Some of the movie's more glaring flaws can be attributed to its stitched-together origins. The Newmans had to come up with a new beginning and ending since the latter was used in the original. Gene Hackman declined to return for reshoots, and Marlon Brando refused to let the Salkinds use any of his footage for the sequel. So Lester, hired after the Salkinds dismissed Donner, had to shoot around Hackman and add new scenes with Susannah York as Superman's mom Lara to provide the necessary exposition. For Lester to qualify as sole director, the Directors Guild required that he be responsible for at least half the movie's footage; although Donner had shot about 70 percent of the sequel during the original production, Lester used only about 30 percent. In 2006, Warner Bros. released *Superman II: The Donner Cut* on DVD with the restored footage.

In 1981, moviegoers greeted the theatrical release with open arms. Though it made less than the first, the Salkinds were keen to make a third. Ilya was already working on a treatment before the sequel's wide release when he saw Richard Pryor on *The Tonight Show*.

"What movies do you go to?" host Johnny Carson asked the comedian, on the show to promote his comedy *Bustin' Loose*.

"I wanna see *Superman II*," Pryor said. "Did you see *Superman I*? In this one—you remember the people in the glass? He goes and gets them and brings them back to Earth accidentally. There's four Supermans, one's a Superwoman. It's going to be good. The previews are great. You sit in the theater and just go, 'Yeah, Supe!'"[3]

That was enough for the producer. Salkind scrapped his treatment, which would have included Superman's cousin Supergirl, his long-running comics nemesis Brainiac, and the interdimensional pain-in-the-ass Mister Mxyzptlk, and rehired the Newmans to invent a scenario that would bring one of the country's most famous comedians together with the Man of Steel.

Richard Lester and Christopher Reeve returned, but Margot Kidder only showed up for a day or two of work; someone had decided that Superman needed a new love interest. Ilya pooh-poohed the notion that Kidder's role had been reduced due to the actress' bad-mouthing of the Salkinds over their treatment of Donner. "She didn't know the ifs and buts," Ilya said. "She's a good girl. She came back [on *III*] and nobody really forced her."[4]

Superman III was almost a franchise-killing disaster.

Pryor plays Gus Gorman, an unemployed doofus who, standing in line at a Metropolis unemployment office, discovers that he's a computer genius. His newfound abilities attract the attention of Ross Webster, a billionaire with a ski slope on the roof of his penthouse. Webster wants Gorman's help to corner the world's coffee supply and then its oil. To do this, Webster figures that he'll also have to put Superman out of commission.

At the *Daily Planet*, Perry White agrees to send Clark back to Smallville for his high school reunion. There, Clark reunites with his former classmate Lana Lang. While on a picnic with Lana, he agrees to talk his friend Superman into showing up for Lana's son's birthday. Superman arrives to find Smallville welcoming him with an event in the town square. Gus Gorman shows up in military garb, takes the stage, barks commands and hands Superman a piece of homemade kryptonite. Superman takes the kryptonite. But Gorman got the recipe wrong, and instead of weakening Superman, the mineral turns him evil. He grows a five o'clock shadow, gets drunk in a bar and sleeps with Webster's moll Lorelei Ambrosia after meeting her on the torch of the Statue of Liberty.

Chapter V. Marvel Gets Its Wish

In a cave in Utah, Webster and Gorman build a supercomputer. The villains, including Webster's sister Vera, decamp there. In a Metropolis junkyard, Superman splits in two—evil Superman, in costume, and good Superman, dressed as Clark. The two throw tires at each other. The "good" Superman wins.

Superman flies to the canyon in pursuit of Webster. The billionaire launches some bombs which Superman knocks out of the sky before tracking the villains to their lair. Webster uses his supercomputer to blast the hero with a kryptonite ray but Gorman intercedes. The supercomputer transforms Vera into a cyborg. Superman defeats the supercomputer and cyborg Vera. Back at *The Daily Planet*, Lois Lane compliments Clark on his story about his high school reunion.

Superman III is a grab-bag of terrible ideas. All traces of Donner's attempts at verisimilitude are gone, replaced by unfunny slapstick, cheap jokes and bad lines.

The movie begins with an elaborate series of sight gags caused by a bystander ogling Lorelei (New Zealand actress Pamela Stephenson). Webster (Robert Vaughn) calls Lorelei his "psychic nutritionist." Lorelei pretends to be a dumb blonde but, when no one's looking, reads Kant. Lana Lang refers to Metropolis as "the Big Apricot." While on the picnic, Clark accidentally eats dog food, which she has packed in plastic containers similar to those of the lunch food, as one does. Webster tells Gorman, "Colombia has two important crops," and mentions one, coffee, but not the other—an obvious allusion to cocaine, and as such an unsubtle reference to Pryor's well-publicized drug problems. (In 1980, the comedian set himself on fire while freebasing.) "Evil" Superman straightens out the Leaning Tower of Pisa. And what is it with Lester and hot air balloons? In *Superman II*, Lex takes one to the Arctic; here, Webster, Vera and Lorelei use one to get to their cave.

Amidst all this nonsense is one semi-inspired sequence: the showdown between Evil Superman and Good Superman. It's not well-thought-out, but it's comic-book-y enough to fire the imagination of a 12-year-old circa 1981.

Critics weren't as charitable as they had been for the Salkinds' first two ventures. An exception was *Vanity Fair*'s Stephen Schiff: "Like *Superman II*, this movie is ugly-looking, but in a cluttered, garish way that's strangely appropriate. It looks like a comic book, and Lester has seized upon the anything-goes cartoonishness to create a haywire comedy of absurdities and non sequiturs that matches the cuckoo rhythms of the screenplay."[5]

One of the more interesting notices came courtesy of Donald Barthelme. In the pages of *The New Yorker*, the *éminence grise* of American post-modern letters waxed poetic over Annette O'Toole, who plays Lana: "Freshness. Simplicity. American beauty. Believability. Directness. A certain sexual smolder not entirely disguised by ricky-tick Smallville couture."

After opening at #1, as the first two *Supermans* had, *III* tumbled. What should have been a shoo-in for one of the year's top-earners came in at 11th.

The Salkinds had already decided to change tack, at least temporarily. Before shooting began on *Superman III*, they announced production of a $30 million movie, *Supergirl*.

The superheroine debuted in a 1959 issue of *Action Comics* as Kara Zor-El, cousin to Kal-El (Superman) and a survivor of the explosion that destroyed Krypton. She guest-starred in various titles before getting her own in 1974 and again in 1982; both runs lasted a couple of years. In 1985, DC killed her off as part of its attempt to clean up its continuity with a cross-over event called Crisis on Infinite Earths.

The Salkinds, who had the rights to the character thanks to their original agreement with Warners, hired *Muppet Show* writer David Odell for the script and Jeannot Szwarc to direct. The French director had finished the troubled production that was *Jaws 2* (1978) and worked with Christopher Reeve on the 1980 time-travel romance *Somewhere in Time*.

For their Supergirl, the Salkinds, Szwarc and casting agent Lynn Stalmaster saw hundreds of young actresses. Alexander wanted a recognizable name, specifically Brooke Shields; Ilya wanted an unknown. They found Helen Slater, a 19-year-old graduate of New York's High School of Performing Arts. She had appeared in a series of TV commercials and a telefilm.

"We read every young girl you can imagine," Szwarc said. "We read in London, we read in L.A. We even read Demi Moore. Finally, we were in New York and [Slater] walked in. That was it. There was a close-up of her face on video, and she was so captivating. She was still in high school, she had done very little, but she really had something."[6]

The movie begins in Argo, a city that has survived the destruction of Krypton. Scientist Zaltar is in the midst of showing young Kara the Omegahedron, an energy source that powers the city, when he accidentally sends the object to Earth. Kara pursues the device and, once here, discovers she has superpowers. She goes undercover as Linda Lee, Midvale High student, as she hunts for the Omegahedron. Her search leads her to Selena, a witch who is using the alien power source for her own purposes. The two clash over the object as well as a local hunk, Ethan. Selena banishes Supergirl to the Phantom Zone, where she encounters Zaltar. The scientist gives her a pep talk and she breaks free, confronts Selena and returns the Omegahedron to Argo.

Slater is easily the best thing about the movie; she's a wide-eyed, earnest rock in a sea of absurdist camp. Faye Dunaway, who vamps it up as Selena, may be the second-best thing; it's unfair that she and Peter O'Toole, who plays Zaltar, both received Golden Raspberries for their efforts since Dunaway at least appears to have read the script. Brenda Vaccaro, who plays Selena's *Sex in the City*–type bud Bianca, and English comic actor Peter Cook as Selena's would-be swain Nigel, seem to be acting in different movies.

Marc McClure returns to his role as Jimmy Olsen from the *Superman* movies. Otherwise, little marks *Supergirl* as part of the franchise. Reeve, who purportedly agreed to make an appearance in the film before changing his mind, is seen only in a Superman poster hanging on the wall of a dorm room occupied by Lucy Lane, Lois' cousin (played by an enthusiastic Maureen Teefy).

Action-wise, *Supergirl* in a non-starter—our heroine fights a front-end loader and an invisible monster. And the belt-tightening that had begun with *Superman III* is even more apparent in this knockoff: When Kara falls to Earth, she lands in a lake, and a cardboard likeness emerges. Shots of her flying are set against stock footage of running horses. The sequence in which Kara discovers her new powers, however, features exceptional wirework and hints at a better movie lurking within the madness.

Supergirl opened at #1 and promptly disappeared from the moviegoing public's radar. This, along with the failure of the Salkinds' next film, *Santa Claus—The Movie* (directed by Szwarc and starring John Lithgow and Dudley Moore, scripted by David Newman), prompted the producers to start thinking about abandoning their once-golden goose.

Despite the failure of *Superman III* and *Supergirl*, DC Comics had at least claimed some big-screen turf. The same could not be said for its chief rival, Marvel. By the mid-eighties, the imprint whose figurehead, Stan Lee, most wanted feature film vindication didn't even have a character on Saturday morning TV, never mind in a movie. That, however, was about to change, though perhaps not in the way Lee, or anyone, would have wanted.

By the early seventies, many of the old pros who had made the company one of the world's most successful comic book publishers had retired or were running on fumes. The doors opened to young creators, many of whom had one foot in comics, the other in the counterculture. As well, the Comics Code Authority, that self-policing regulatory body formed in the wake of the funny book hysteria of 1954, had loosened its restrictions.

Out of this hookah-smoking milieu came the character who would become Marvel's first big-screen … something.

Steve Gerber was working as an ad copywriter in St. Louis when he started at Marvel. One of his first assignments was penning the adventures of Man-Thing, a mute swamp creature with glowing red eyes. The green, trunk-nosed monster came with the tagline "Whatever knows fear burns at the Man-Thing's touch!"

In a few panels in a 1973 Man-Thing story, Gerber and artist Val Mayerik introduced a wisecracking, cigar-smoking duck named Howard. A star was born. The misanthropic mallard graduated to backup features in *Giant-Size Man-Thing* (yes, it's a real title). In 1976, Marvel gave Howard his own title and, for 27 issues, Gerber used *Howard the Duck* as a soapbox to take jabs at politics, the economy, urban life, pop culture trends and comic books themselves—especially superheroes.

The book appealed to comics readers who were ready to move on from *The Invincible Iron Man* and *The Incredible Hulk*, or at least were game for something different. Howard also found an enthusiast in George Lucas, then a young director who had just made the 1973 nostalgia blast *American Graffiti* and was developing a movie called *Radioland Murders*. He showed an issue of *Howard* to his collaborators, Willard Huyck and Gloria Katz, Huyck's wife.

"He felt we would really like it because the sensibility in the comic book … is very similar to our own," said Katz. "So then we said, 'Let's make it into a movie.' But the rights were not available. Nor was there any technology available to make it into a movie."[7]

A few years later, she and Huyck again approached Marvel; according to Katz, the rights had reverted back to the publisher from Universal. (The studio may have picked them up in a package that included Doctor Strange, the Hulk and Captain America.)

Howard was in comic-book purgatory at the time, after been cancelled twice—in his regular-sized color comic, and then in a bi-monthly black-and-white magazine aimed at a more mature audience. This time, the publisher told the filmmakers to go ahead.

"Marvel was very nice and gave us a free option on it so that we could just run with it and try to develop it into a movie," said Katz.[8]

Lucas agreed to produce. The director, who after the first *Star Wars* trilogy could have talked a studio into financing a three-hour stop-motion biopic about Karl Marx, sold Universal on the idea. The trio's original thought was to do *Howard* as an animated film, but Universal wanted a live-action release for summer '86. Lucas, with the world's best special effects technicians at his disposal, was convinced it could be done. Huyck and Katz agreed. They considered puppets and CGI and finally agreed on a guy in a duck suit. In the end, two actors—a little person named Ed Gale and a 12-year-old boy—took turns in a costume with animatronic features controlled by a trio of puppeteers. A third actor provided the voice.

In developing their protagonist's look, Lucas, Katz and Huyck also had to deal with lawyers. "We went to very serious legal meetings at Disney about whether Howard the Duck was stealing his look from Donald Duck," Huyck said. "We put our models on the conference tables and all these lawyers would look at them. They'd say, 'Well, it still looks like Donald,' and we'd say, 'They're wearing different clothes.' They'd say, 'Can the bill be a little flatter or a little thicker?' They really got into it. We had to keep redesigning the duck."[9]

This caused delays. "We didn't have enough time," Katz said. "You wait for these executives to read the script, and every week that goes by will cost more in the long run. We were finally given a 'go' in May of '85 and the duck had not been built. We had to start shooting in October for a summer release."[10]

For the story, Huyck and Katz borrowed from the comics' origin, such as it was: Howard is plucked from his home planet Duckworld and deposited in Ohio, U.S.A. Originally, they weren't even going to explain his arrival.

"George's idea was to not have an origin story," Huyck said. "We had Howard as a private eye in Hawaii, and the audience would just have to accept that as normal, but the studio said, 'No, you have to explain how he got here.'"[11]

After landing in a Cleveland alley, brought to Earth via laser spectroscope (read: intergalactic portal), the alien fowl rescues a fledgling young rock star, Beverly Switzler, from thugs. The two hit it off and embark on a mission to return Howard home. But the laser spectroscope malfunctions, allowing an entity called the Dark Overlord to come to Earth and take possession of Walter Jenning, a scientist. The Overlord-Jenning kidnaps Beverly and takes her to the lab that houses the spectroscope. Howard and Beverly's friend Phil, a janitor with delusions of scientific grandeur, follows them to the lab, where Howard uses a neutron disintegrator on Jenning. Driven out of the scientist's body, the Dark Overlord assumes a monstrous form. Howard blasts him with the disintegrator, then destroys the spectroscope to prevent more Overlords from coming to Earth. Trapped on Earth, Howard becomes manager of Beverly's band, Cherry Bomb.

On August 1, 1986, *Howard the Duck* opened at #2 (behind *Aliens*). Reviewers roasted the duck, and in its second week, the movie dropped to #7 at the box office and continued its downward slide.

The movie was an ignominious beginning to Marvel's big-screen dreams. It wasn't just that the publisher's cinematic debut didn't feature one of its better-known creations, or that Howard wasn't even a superhero—he has no powers except a mastery of "quack fu"—but that *Howard the Duck* was such an obvious misfire. As heavy-handed as Gerber could be, the movie doesn't have a satirical bone in its animatronic body. It's simply an eighties-style summer blockbuster with duck puns, chase scenes, more duck puns, special effects (some of which, like the stop-motion monster at the end, are cool), rock music clichés, yet more duck puns, and someone—several someones—in a duck suit.

It was that last all-important element that came in for the most criticism. The studio kept its star under wraps until the film's release. Built to resemble the stump-billed latter-day comics incarnation, the movie Howard occupies the uncanny valley between cute and creepy. The Hollywood newcomer was awarded that year's Golden Raspberry for Worst New Star ("the six guys and gals in the duck suit"), one of seven nominations the movie received.

The movie itself became the butt of late-night talk-show jokes and, with an

Chapter V. Marvel Gets Its Wish

Universal kept the animatronic star of 1986's *Howard the Duck* under wraps until the movie's release. Universal Pictures.

estimated price tag of $52 million[12] ($132 million in 2022 dollars), a symbol of Hollywood excess. Rumors spread of an actual physical dust-up between Universal studio execs Sidney Sheinberg and Frank Price. The latter resigned soon after the movie's release, and *Variety* headlined a story about his ouster with "Duck Cooks Price's Goose."[13]

Howard does have its adherents, mostly among those who didn't know the comic books and weren't looking for anything more than the kind of summer popcorn flick that ends with the movie's theme (written by Thomas Dolby) played by Hollywood's idea of a New Wave band while its titular star duckwalks across the stage Chuck Berry–style.

Lea Thompson played Beverly alongside a supporting cast that included Tim Robbins and Jeffrey Jones. The actress said in 2016,

> So many people tell me they love the movie, sometimes with tears in their eyes. I see more of that in my real life, so when people are snotty about *Howard the Duck*, I just tell them that a lot of people really liked it, and that means more to me than people who want to try and make me feel embarrassed or bad about a movie I think I did good work in.
>
> It's cool that we're still talking about it after 30 years. That's pretty badass, as far as I'm concerned.[14]

Perhaps. But at the time, *Howard* was a blow to Marvel in particular and comic-book movies in general.

The next, and last, Christopher Reeve *Superman* effort did not improve their credibility. A year after *Supergirl*, the Salkinds sold their DC rights package to Cannon Film Group. Israeli producers Menahem Golan and Yoram Globus had bought the American studio–production company in 1979 after their success in the international market with exploitation flicks like the Hebrew-language sex comedy *Lemon Popsicle* (1978). Cannon began bankrolling B-movies such as *Enter the Ninja*, *Death Wish II* and *Last American Virgin* (a remake of *Lemon Popsicle*) and, to a lesser extent, artier fare such as Jean-Luc Godard's *King Lear*, Norman Mailer's *Tough Guys Don't Dance* and Barbet Schroeder's *Barfly*.

For Superman and friends, Golan and Globus paid $5 million,[15] roughly what the rights had cost the Salkinds in 1973 (and 38,461 times the amount National had paid Joe Shuster and Jerry Siegel in 1938). Cannon struck a deal with Warners to distribute and co-produce a new movie and even talked Reeve back into the cape for $5 million (20 times what he'd received for the first movie), funding for his passion project *Street Smart* and creative input.[16]

Reeve took the latter seriously. He wanted to do something on nuclear disarmament—against the advice of Tom Mankiewicz.

"Here are the rules," the *Superman I* and *II* creative consultant said he told the actor. "Don't ever get involved with something Superman could fix. He could disarm the world in 15 minutes. He doesn't have to go to the U.N. If he feels that strongly about it, he could get rid of all the missiles. Superman could feed the world if he wanted to. He could establish agricultural fields in outer space. Don't bring up things like that."[17]

Reeve may have heard him, but he didn't listen. Cannon signed off on the nuclear disarmament idea and hired scripters Mark Rosenthal and Lawrence Konner and director Sidney J. Furie. Rosenthal and Konner had written Helen Slater's 1985 follow-up to *Supergirl*, *The Legend of Billie Jean*; Furie's 1986 military action film *Iron Eagle* had been a box office success. Gene Hackman and Margot Kidder returned.

Kidder told the *Los Angeles Times* in early 1987, "The question was, 'Do you want to work in something you believe in, or do you want to quibble over what's supposedly your star price?' This is really a brave script, if we can pull it off. It's a vision of the world through a child's eyes, and it's a vision that makes more sense than our leaders."[18] By that time, though, Cannon had overextended itself with more than 30 movies in production and slashed the movie's budget from $36 million to $17 million. Most of that came out of the effects fund.

In the vision that rolled into theaters in the summer of '87, Superman tosses all of Earth's nuclear missiles into the sun. But, unbeknownst to our hero, Lex Luthor has planted some of the Kryptonian's DNA in one of the missiles. The result is the birth of a proto–Superman that Lex dubs "Nuclear Man." A criminal mastermind he may be, but a creative christener he is not.

Superman confronts Luthor, which leads to a fight between Lex's subservient creation and the superhero. During the brawl, which almost destroys the Statue of Liberty, Superman is infected with radiation sickness.

Meanwhile, ruthless financier David Warfield has bought *The Daily Planet* and replaced editor Perry White with his (Warfield's) daughter Lacy. Nuclear Man sees a picture of Lacy, is immediately smitten, and demands that she be brought to him.

Superman cures himself with an energy module that he found in the capsule that brought him to Earth and tricks Nuclear Man into an elevator where, blocked from the sun, he loses power. Superman flies the elevator car to the moon, but Nuclear Man revives. The two fight, and Nuclear Man pounds Superman into the moon, then flies to Earth and kidnaps Lacy. Superman pushes the moon out of its orbit to cause an eclipse, again weakening Nuclear Man, and rescues Lacy. Superman destroys Nuclear Man by tossing him into a nuclear reactor.

Yes, the movie is as ridiculous as it sounds—more, in fact, because the above doesn't mention the aerobics class Clark takes with Lacy (Mariel Hemingway), the double-date between Clark and Superman with Lacy and Lois, Lacy's ability to survive outer space in a pantsuit, or the wonderfully tacky special effects that resulted from the drastically reduced budget. Mark Pillow, a former Chippendales dancer, plays Nuclear Man.

When the movie bombed, Jon Cryer—who played Lex's nephew Lenny—was as disappointed as anyone. The actor called himself "Comic Con-fanboy-crazy" over the first *Superman*. Now he was in the Superman movie to end all Superman movies, and not in a good way.

"I'm so excited about the movie! When's it coming out?" Cryer later recalled asking Reeve. "And [Reeve] said [*takes a deep breath*], 'You need to know, it's an absolute mess. We had six months of flying work that we were supposed to shoot; they cut five months of it. They've thrown together an edit that barely makes sense.' And I was absolutely *devastated*, because I really wanted to be a part of bringing Superman back...."[19]

It would be nearly 20 years before Superman flew across movie screens again. More than a franchise-killing disaster, *Superman IV* almost destroyed the superhero movie genre. But some people just won't give up on a dream.

Chapter VI

How One Batfan's Dedication Transformed the Movie Industry

> "No longer portrayed as a pot-bellied caped clown, Batman has again become a vigilante who stalks criminals in the shadow of the night."
> —Michael Uslan, in a memo to producers Peter Guber and Jon Peters[1]

In the mid-1960s, when *Batman kapow!*ed its way into American living rooms, one of the series' outraged viewers was a young Michael Uslan.

"There was nobody in America more excited, waiting in more anticipation for it, and when it came on, I was both thrilled and horrified by what I was seeing," the New Jersey comics fan recalled.

"I was thrilled that Batman was on TV, the car was cool, everything was great, but then I realized that the whole world was laughing at Batman. He was being played as a joke. And that was [the world's] one and only reference point for Batman back then. And that kind of killed me."[2]

And so it was that Uslan, like Bruce Wayne, took a vow—to rehabilitate the Dark Knight's image in the eyes of the public.

Uslan was teaching the first accredited course in comics at Indiana University when he caught the attention of DC vice-president Sol Harrison. He was soon writing comics for the company while studying law, with a focus on copyright. In 1976, he took a job in the New York office of United Artists. There he met Benjamin Melniker, a former MGM studio exec who had brokered deals on pictures such as *Dr. Zhivago* and *2001: A Space Odyssey*. Melniker had never read a comic book in his life, but Uslan, with a fan's unbridled enthusiasm, won over the experienced negotiator. With Melniker backing him, the younger man approached DC's Harrison with his dream of making a Batman movie that would return the character to his shadowy roots.

"Don't waste your money," Harrison told him. "Find something else to do with it! Since he went off the air on TV, Batman is as dead as a dodo."[3]

Uslan pressed on. In October 1979, he and Melniker purchased the rights to Batman for the equivalent of what the Salkinds had paid for Superman ($5 million[4]) and formed BatFilm Productions. They took their idea to Warner Bros. but, as with Superman—and despite the success of the Salkinds' film—the studio had no interest in bringing one of the world's most iconic pop culture figures to movie theaters.

Warners wasn't alone.

"We were turned down by every CEO and every major studio in Hollywood," Uslan said. "I was told that I was crazy and this was one of the worst ideas they had ever heard.... They said, 'Michael, you're out of your mind' and that they can't do serious comic book films. 'We can't do dark superheroes,' they said, 'Nobody has ever made a movie based on an old TV series.'"[5]

Then Melniker suggested Casablanca Filmworks. The upstart had had success with the undersea thriller *The Deep* (1977) and the prison drama *Midnight Express* (1978), and Melniker knew one of their executives, Peter Guber. A former Columbia exec, Guber ran the studio along with Neil Bogart. Bogart ran Casablanca Records, the go-go disco label behind Donna Summer and Kiss.

Guber and Barry Beckerman, another decision-maker at Casablanca, loved Uslan's idea. And in July 1980, *Batman* became the first superhero movie to be announced at a comics convention when Uslan told fans at New York's Comic Art Convention "that the days of Pow! Zap! and Wham! are over. Our movie will *not* be about a superhero named 'Batman,' but about a superhero known as '*The* Batman.'"[6]

The nerd-whistle worked; the fans went wild.[7]

At the time, comic-book Batman was still years away from the full-scale rehabilitation that would result from two new entries to the canon, the 1986 limited-run series *The Dark Knight Returns* and the 1988 graphic novel *The Killing Joke*. But the seventies had seen a return to the character's early crimefighting form, with creative teams like Denny O'Neill–Neal Adams and Steve Englehart–Marshall Rogers putting some of the "dark" back into the Dark Knight and the detecting into *Detective Comics*.

The next step was finding a screenwriter. Turning to the James Bond brain trust, as had the Salkinds, Uslan and Melniker approached Richard Maibaum. Maibaum had worked on just about every Bond film since the franchise's 1961 inception. When that didn't work out, they hired Tom Mankiewicz, Richard Donner's script consultant on *Superman*.

In the meantime, the producers kept busy with other comic-book properties. They attempted to adapt two Marvel characters, Luke Cage and Doctor Strange, for TV[8] but had more success with DC's Swamp Thing. Created around the same time as Marvel's Man-Thing, Swamp Thing was a sentient creature with the mind of a scientist, Alec Holland, supposedly killed in a lab explosion. Melniker and Uslan hired horror maven Wes Craven to direct alow-budget eponymous feature based on the character. The 1982 B-movie made a small impression at theaters and a larger one in the burgeoning home video market.

Although it spawned a sequel, 1989's *Return of Swamp Thing*, and a 1990 USA Network TV series, its real legacy was prompting DC to resurrect the *Swamp Thing* comic book. This in turn led to the hiring of Alan Moore, a young British writer, for his first American assignment. Moore not only revitalized the series but, over the next couple of decades, contributed some of the most influential books in the medium's history, including the *Killing Joke* graphic novel and several titles that would be adapted to film: *Watchmen*, *The League of Extraordinary Gentlemen*, *V for Vendetta* and *From Hell*. Moore eventually distanced himself from all adaptations of his work and gave his royalties to his co-creators.

While Uslan and Melniker were producing *Swamp Thing* and working on other projects, their *Batman* enabler Peter Guber was making *Flashdance*. The movie was such a hit—earning over $200 million on a budget of $7 million—that Warner Bros. snatched up the producer and his new partner Jon Peters, a former hairdresser. Guber brought *Batman* with him and voilà, the Caped Crusader was back home.

But the movie still didn't have a director. Finally, in 1985, Guber and Peters' head of production Roger Birnbaum arranged a screening for Uslan of *Pee-wee's Big Adventure*, the first feature by a new director, Tim Burton. (According to show biz reporters Nancy Griffin and Kim Masters, another Warner exec, Bonni Lee, suggested Burton as director.[9]) Uslan, based on the East Coast, flew to L.A. to share his vision and favorite Batman comics.

"By the end of our third lunch, I had no doubt this was the director who could make an incredible film true to the integrity of the Batman," Uslan wrote in his book *The Boy Who Loved Batman*.[10]

But Burton was no comics reader. "Maybe I'm dyslexic," he told Bob Costas in 1992. "I could never tell which box to read…. I guess I grew up in the era where they got wordy and complicated. They weren't visual to me, they were more about words." He did like the TV show: "I remember running home to watch it." And he loved the character. "You just want to do something different with it."[11]

Burton rejected the Mankiewicz script, which he found too similar to *Superman*:

> It had the same light, jokey tone, and the story structure followed Wayne through childhood to his genesis as a crimefighter. I found it all rather disturbing because, while that route was probably fine in the case of Superman, there was absolutely no exploration or acknowledgment of the character's psychological structure and why he would dress up in a bat suit. In that respect, it was very much like the television series.[12]

Julie Hickson, the producer of two short films Burton made for Disney, wrote a treatment using some of his ideas. In March 1986, DC president Jenette Kahn asked writer Steve Englehart to help. After reading the existing scripts, Englehart saw what he thought the problem was. "[The screenwriters] couldn't resist sliding into comic-book movie shtick—making things funny that, if you actually thought about them, were much better serious. Easing the vibe rather than pressing it."[13]

Englehart turned in two treatments, one with the Batman, the Joker, Silver St. Cloud (a character he'd created during his Batman run in *Detective Comics*), the Penguin and Robin, as per the studio's request.

But the movie stalled again until Burton met Sam Hamm, a screenwriter who had read some of Mankiewicz's script and was enthusiastic about the movie. "I think the presumption was that this was sort of the last crack at a doomed project," said Hamm. He and the director "took that as a license to do what we wanted to do, which is to write a story about a guy who is obviously extremely fucked up and what happens to him as a result of it."[14]

On weekends, the duo hammered away at the script. During the week, Burton directed his follow-up to *Pee-wee's Big Adventure*, *Beetlejuice*.[15] When the horror-comedy opened to $8 million on its first weekend, Warner okayed a $35 million budget for *Batman*.

• • •

As early as his 1980 memo re: "The Batman," Michael Uslan knew who had to play the Joker.

Stanley Kubrick's *The Shining* was in movie theaters at the time, and Jack Nicholson's maniacal leer was everywhere.

Producer Jon Peters first mentioned the role to the bankable star while on the Boston set of 1987's *The Witches of Eastwick*.[16] But Nicholson needed convincing. He would be placing his trust in Burton, then 31, a director with only two features, both offbeat comedies, to his credit. And Nicholson would have to spend hours in a makeup chair to look like a clown.

Chapter VI. How One Batfan's Dedication Transformed the Movie Industry

Accounts vary, but the wooing of the actor may have included a horse-riding expedition at his Colorado ranch with Peters and Burton. According to Nancy Griffin and Kim Masters, the romancing of Jack also included a trip arranged by Peters on the private Warner Bros. jet to see the sets being built outside of London, at Pinewood Studios.[17] A $6 million paycheck, and a share of the box office and merchandising, accomplished what a private masseuse and a tour of English designer's Anton Furst's Art Deco vision of Gotham City couldn't.

Like the $3 million hiring of Marlon Brando for *Superman*, Nicholson's involvement instantly gave *Batman* a credibility that made up for his record-breaking price tag. But less than two weeks after the big get, Uslan was asked a question that felt like a betrayal of everything that, for the last decade-plus, he had been working towards. What, a Warner executive asked, did he think of Michael Keaton for Batman?

Not much—in fact, he was "apoplectic," he said in 2011. "I thought it was a joke, and it took them quite a while to convince me that they weren't kidding."[18]

Uslan had envisioned a square-jawed unknown *à la* Christopher Reeve, or at least someone who could bring the menace he felt the character needed, not *Mr. Mom*. The actor's slight, 5'10" frame was not the kind to strike fear into the hearts of Gotham's criminal underworld.

Burton, who worked with Keaton on *Beetlejuice*, argued that this was precisely *why* Keaton was perfect for the role. Who else but someone who isn't built like a pro wrestler would feel the need to dress like a bat to scare Gotham's criminal element? Also, they needed someone able to go eyebrow-to-eyebrow with Nicholson.

After a screening of *Clean and Sober*, a 1988 drama with Keaton as a real estate agent in recovery, Batman's protector came around. Other fans would need more convincing.

• • •

More pieces fell into place. Burton hired character actors Michael Gough and Pat Hingle to play Alfred and Commissioner Gordon. The role of Carl Grissom, a mobster who bosses around a pre–Joker Nicholson, went to tough-guy actor Jack Palance, and love interest Vicki Vale—last seen in the 1949 serial *Batman and Robin*—to Sean Young, who was known to movie fans for *Blade Runner* and *Wall Street*.

As script rewrites came in, Young became concerned that her role was shrinking. One day, halfway through a table-read of the script in front of Warner execs, "she made a comment like, 'I feel like I'm disappearing from the pages,'" recalled actor Robert Wuhl, hired to play Alexander Knox, a reporter for the *Gotham Globe*. "And then proceeded ... to read in a monosyllable, monotone voice. It sucked all the energy out of the room."[19]

At the last minute, Young injured her arm while she and Keaton practiced their horse-riding skills (for a scene that would eventually be cut).[20] The role went to Kim Basinger, a Hollywood "It Girl" for her roles in the last Sean Connery–James Bond film *Never Say Never Again* (with a script by *Batman* TV series story editor Lorenzo Semple, Jr.) and the S&M-lite *9½ Weeks*.

Robin was part of the script until he wasn't. "We could never get Robin in before the last third of the movie," Burton said. "By that time, we just wanted to get on with the story rather than introduce somebody else new in tights, simply because the comics lore dictated it."[21]

As the first day of principal photography approached, the producers still weren't satisfied with the script. Even after shooting commenced, it went through almost daily rewrites.

Some of the tensest on-set moments came during filming of the third act. Figuring that audiences wouldn't like the idea of younger man—Keaton was 38 at the time—beating up the 52-year-old Nicholson, Peters decided that, instead of a knock-down drag-out fight between the two, Batman would pursue the Joker to the top of a Gotham cathedral's bell tower.

Burton hated the idea, having no clue how the scene would end. "Here were Jack Nicholson and Kim Basinger walking up this cathedral, and halfway up Jack turns around and says, 'Why am I walking up all these stairs? Where am I going?'" Burton recalled. "I had to tell him that I didn't know." The director called it "the most frightening experience of my life."[22]

• • •

In November 1988, several weeks into filming, a story appeared in *The Wall Street Journal* with the headline "Batman Fans Fear the Joke's on Them."[23] The story noted that hundreds if not thousands of fans had written letters or signed petitions protesting Keaton's casting. A month later, Warner released a 90-second teaser of character intros, car chases, gunfire and the Batmobile. "Coming this summer," reads the end card as Nicholson laughs as though seeing his check for the first time.

If the intention was to redirect fans' energy, the strategy worked. People lined up just to see the trailer. Posters with only the bat symbol against a bronze oval and the release date further stoked enthusiasm. By the time *Batman* was released, Batmania V.2 was in full bloom. One apocryphal story has it that T-shirts with the bat design sold so quickly that licensees ran out of black material.

Such was the hype that the movie behind it didn't have to be good; it just had to be different. And *Batman* was certainly that.

As in the serials and the TV series before it, the movie begins with Batman already waging his one-man crusade against Gotham's underworld, headed by mob boss Carl Grissom and his second-in-command, Jack Napier. Napier is carrying on a dalliance with Carl's girlfriend, so Grissom sends his duplicitous crime bro on a fake mission to a chemical plant. Napier realizes he's been set up, but it's too late; Batman arrives. A fight between Batman and the hoodlum ends with Napier falling into a vat of chemicals.

At the *Gotham Globe*, reporter Alexander Knox and photojournalist Vicki Vale agree to work together to uncover the secrets of mysterious billionaire Bruce Wayne. They meet Bruce at a soirée at Wayne Manor. Vicki and Bruce make googly eyes at each other.

Jack emerges from his chemical bath disfigured and insane. He undergoes cosmetic surgery to make himself look even more like an evil clown, kills Grissom, and poisons several innocent Gothamites before taking over the local airwaves to announce his intention to give away $20 million at the upcoming Anniversary Festival, Gotham's bicentennial. Batman/Bruce smells a rat.

Then the Joker sees a picture of Vicki. He arranges a date with the blonde photojournalist at the Flugelheim Museum. At the museum, the Joker harasses Vicki, then dances to a Prince song (the Joker dances *a lot* in this movie) while defacing the museum's art collection, which consists of the most famous paintings in our (i.e., the real) world.

Bruce visits Vicki at her apartment to reveal his secret. Before he can confess that he's Batman, the Joker arrives to harass Vicki some more. He shoots Bruce. The bullet is deflected by a serving tray that the billionaire has hidden beneath his dinner jacket.

Chapter VI. How One Batfan's Dedication Transformed the Movie Industry 51

An hour or maybe a week later—*Batman* exists outside of time as we think of it—citizens gather at a major downtown Gotham intersection for the Anniversary Festival. Large balloons float overhead. The balloons are filled with the Joker's poison gas. Batman flies in low in his custom Batwing plane uses pincers at the front of the plane to cut the strings of the balloons. The balloons float harmlessly away. The hero makes a U-turn and strafes the town square with air-to-ground missiles and machine guns in an attempt to kill the Joker. Although he was able to use pincers at the front of his Batwing to cut the strings of balloons, Batman completely misses his target, who is garbed in a bright purple suit and is standing stock-still.

Batman then crashes the Batwing into the steps of a church. The Joker grabs Vicki and pulls her into the church. Batman, who is uninjured, pursues the two of them up several flights of stairs. How many flights is unclear, but when they reach the roof, the view is on a par with that of the Chrysler Building. Batman and the Joker fight. Everyone falls, but Batman and Vicki cling to the edge of the skyscraper church by their fingers while the bad guy plummets to his (supposed) death.

In the summer of 1989, *Batman* was *the* movie to see. It broke box-office records on its opening weekend. Reviews were mostly positive because, really, what could critics

The makers of 1989's *Batman* were worried that audiences wouldn't accept 38-year-old Michael Keaton (left) beating up 52-year-old Jack Nicholson. Warner Bros.

compare it to? What was it, even? The movie went on to rake in over $411 million, nearly a billion in 2022 cash. A soundtrack featuring songs written and recorded for the movie by Prince—who was on on the Warner Bros. record label—sold two million copies. Bat merch flew off the shelves.

Like *Superman*, the movie has grown in stature and is considered, by some, a classic. Viewed today, it's the film's most controversial aspect, Michael Keaton in the title role, that holds up as one of its strongest features. The other is Anton Furst's sets; Burton's most significant innovation was to create, with the designer, a claustrophobic, shadow-filled Gotham where the idea of a man dressing up as a bat to fight crime seems like a sensible response to the world.

Narratively, too, the movie exists in its own world, one of dream-logic spiked with Dada-esque nonsense. There is nothing to take seriously in *Batman*, yet it's the most serious treatment yet of a superhero.

The movie's dark tone has proven to be as influential, if not moreso, than the breezier approach of *Superman*. Moreso than any other attempt at a comic-book flick, *Batman* looks and feels like a real film, with A-list actors and high production values. Its success breathed new life into the catatonic superhero movie genre, and even reminded people that comic books still existed. And it restored the reputation of the hero who had been so resoundingly mocked two decades earlier.

For Michael Uslan, it was mission accomplished, and then some.

Chapter VII

In the Shadow of the Bat

"I'm everyone. I'm no one. Everywhere. Nowhere. Call me 'Darkman.'"
—Liam Neeson in *Darkman* (1990)

"It's great. The lights are coming up after *Batman Returns*, and it's like kids crying, people acting like they've been punched in the stomach, and like they've been mugged. Part of me relished that reaction, and part of me to this day is like, 'Oops.'"
—*Batman Returns* screenwriter Daniel Waters[1]

Even if *Batman* had never been made, we would still have had *Teenage Mutant Ninja Turtles* and *Dick Tracy*. Both were already in production when Burton's film was released.

The brainchild of Gary Propper, a professional surfer and manager of melon-bashing prop-comic Gallagher, and Kim Dawson, a Disney Channel producer, *Teenage Mutant Ninja Turtles* was based on a comic book series that came out of a mid-seventies retail innovation. The direct market was a network of stores that were dedicated to comics, thus levelling the playing field by allowing small, independent publishers to share rack space with the big guns, Marvel and DC, as well as other established imprints like Archie. Creatively, the proliferation of new publishers meant new artists, new writers and new characters.

The Turtles debuted in a 1984 self-published black-and-white comic. By the time of *Batman*'s release, Raphael, Michelangelo, Donatello and Leonardo, as they were called, were the stars of their own animated TV series, and Turtles action figures were selling by the truckload.

Propper and Dawson managed to wrest the rights from their creators, Kevin Eastman and Peter Laird. The New Hampshire comics fans agreed on condition of script approval. "Our biggest fear was that a movie would look like *Howard the Duck*," said Mark Freedman, their licensing agent.[2]

The producers began shopping their proposal around to studios. Their pitch, coming as it did post–*Howard* and pre–*Batman*, was met with the kind of reception one would expect for an obscure comic book property with a silly name. They joined forces with a sitcom writer, Bobby Herbeck, who pitched the idea to Golden Harvest. The Hong Kong–based studio, a specialist in martial arts films, agreed to finance the project. Herbeck then visited Laird and Eastman to come up with an acceptable screenplay idea.

"I thought, 'I'm there for a month, max.' Right?" Herbeck said. "I was wrong. It was six or eight weeks. Never saw two guys who disagreed so much. It got to the point where when I met with them, I could tell by their body language and their eyes. If Peter [Laird] was looking down at the floor, I would just go right into, 'What didn't you like, Peter?'"[3]

Herbeck borrowed elements from the comics and the animated series, pitting the Turtles against a group of bad ninjas, the Foot Clan, and included supporting characters like newswoman April O'Neil and vigilante Casey Jones. Steve Barron, a former camera assistant who had worked on the first *Superman* movie and made videos for Michael Jackson, A-ha and Madonna, directed, and Jim Henson's Creature Shop designed and made the costumes, a combination of foam rubber and animatronics.

A compendium of pizza jokes, a pre-adolescent's ideas of romance, and eighties ninja movie clichés, the $12 million movie sent shock waves through the movie industry when, in March 1990, it opened to the third biggest three-day weekend ever.[4]

Just three months later, while executives, critics and industry insiders were still asking what the hell just happened, a much more familiar hero arrived in theaters. Unlike the Turtles, he had name recognition, a decades-long history of multimedia crossovers, and backing by some of the biggest names in Hollywood. He never had a chance.

Dick Tracy debuted in newspaper funny pages in 1931. Chester Gould's pointy-chinned, squint-eyed detective quickly became famous for his trademark trench coat and fedora, gadgets like his wristwatch phone, and a rogues' gallery of grotesque villains. He also proved to be endlessly adaptable, generating a radio show, comic books, novels, serials, feature films, live-action TV shows and animated series.

Warren Beatty had long dreamed of an updated movie version. The Hollywood golden boy grew up reading the strip and worked on developing the film for years. In 1988, a year before *Batman*'s release, he convinced Touchstone, a division of Disney, to give him a budget of $25 million. Beatty hired the best talent his Rolodex could provide, including songwriter Stephen Sondheim, production designer Richard Sylbert and prosthetic makeup designers John Caglione, Jr., and Doug Drexler. All would go on to win Academy Awards for their work on *Dick Tracy*. He also lured A-list actors Al Pacino and Dustin Hoffman and, to help sell the idea of a Depression-era detective to the kids, a pop star, Madonna. *Top Gun–Turner and Hooch* writing team Jack Epps, Jr., and Jim Cash provided the script.

The plot consists of Dick Tracy trying to stop Big Boy Caprice's crime syndicate from taking over small businesses in a thirties-era city. Tracy becomes embroiled in mob politics while fending off the advances of Breathless Mahoney, a nightclub singer at Club Ritz, one of Big Boy's establishments. In the final act, Big Boy kidnaps Tracy's girlfriend Tess Trueheart. With the help of an orphan (known simply as The Kid) and Breathless, who has been helping Tracy disguised as The Blank, the detective rescues Tess. Big Boy falls to his death and Breathless dies of gunshot wounds.

Like *Batman*, *Dick Tracy* is ahead of its time in comic-book-y world-building. Intense primary colors, Depression-era sets and a parade of misshapen villains add up to a one-of-a-kind would-be franchise. The only thing missing is a compelling story and a hero to root for; Beatty is taciturn to the point of blandness. As the growling, mincing, lip-smacking Big Boy Caprice, Pacino commits grand theft blockbuster at every turn.

Dick Tracy opened to better reviews than *Teenage Mutant Ninja Turtles*. But this isn't saying much since critics (a) were old enough to recall Gould's strip and (b) were familiar with Beatty's work and (c) didn't know the Turtles and (d) didn't want to. When final numbers were tallied, it was clear which characters resonated with the public; at a cost of $13.5 million, *Teenage Mutant Ninja Turtles* made $202 million, while on a budget that rose to an estimated 46 to 50 million dollars, not including marketing and promotion, *Dick Tracy* made $162 million. Even Beatty's well-publicized Old Hollywood–style affair with Madonna wasn't enough to put young bums in seats.

Chapter VII. In the Shadow of the Bat

Studio execs viewed the film as a flop and traded *Howard-the-Duck*-style memos complaining about Hollywood excess. But enterprising producers wondered if any other Teenage Mutant Ninja Turtles—who would spawn a film franchise still in play today—were lurking out in the Wild West of independent comics publishing.

• • •

In 1990, comics writer Peter David published "The Perfect Super-Hero Film of All Time."[5] In the essay, he listed all the tropes found in a standard superhero comic and measured recent movies against the list. By his metrics, which included such qualifications as the Hero Must Utter His Name Near or at the End of His Origin, only one film ticked all the boxes: *Darkman*.

The movie grew out of director Sam Raimi's frustration at not being able to option the rights to the Shadow. A thirties pulp hero, the Shadow began as the host of a radio series sponsored by publishing house Street and Smith. He became popular enough for the publisher to hire Walter B. Gibson, a prolific author and professional magician, to write stories based on the character. Gibson gave the Shadow (a vigilante who operates clandestinely and has the ability "to cloud men's minds") a secret identity, millionaire playboy Lamont Cranston. Under the pen name Maxwell Grant, Gibson wrote 282 of 325 Shadow novels. As with Gould's Dick Tracy, the Shadow transitioned easily to multiple platforms, including feature films, a serial, comic strips, comic books and TV series. His tagline, "Who knows what evil lurks in the hearts of men? The Shadow knows!" entered the culture. He was a huge influence on Bob Kane and Bill Finger in their conception of Batman.

But Raimi, a Michigan native who broke into the film industry with his 1981 horror-comedy *The Evil Dead*, was stymied by rights-holder Universal. The studio had its own plans for the character, which wouldn't come to fruition until 1994 with the release of a big-budget film starring Alec Baldwin.

"So I thought, 'I'll make my own Shadow then. I'll call it *Darkman*, which is just an obvious Shadow ripoff," Raimi told *Collider* in 2007.[6] The success of *Batman* convinced Universal to greenlight the movie.[7]

Darkman, scripted by Raimi, his brother Ivan *et al.*, is a standard superhero origin story with a few horror-movie twists. Scientist Peyton Westlake is working on a new type of synthetic skin when his lawyer girlfriend Julie Hastings stumbles upon an illegal waterfront construction scheme. Mobsters break into Peyton's lab searching for an incriminating document. Led by the sadistic Robert Durant, the thugs kill Peyton's assistant, throw Peyton into a vat of chemicals, and blow up the lab.

The explosion tosses the scientist into the waters of the nearby bay. He emerges with enhanced strength and a high pain threshold but is disfigured and unable to control his emotions. After rebuilding his lab, he uses his synthetic skin formula to reconstruct his face. But the material only lasts a short time before it melts. To get revenge on Durant, he uses the skin to impersonate the mob boss and confuse the gang. Durant kidnaps Julie, and a final battle ensues high above the waterfront, in the frame of the troublesome development.

Like *Swamp Thing*, *Darkman* succeeds on its own B-movie terms, and often rises above its clichés thanks to performances by Liam Neeson, in one of his first lead roles, and Frances McDormand as Julie. As Durant, who collects fingers via a cigar-cutter, Larry Drake is such an outstanding villain that the producers brought him back for the 1995 direct-to-video sequel *Darkman II: The Return of Durant* (neither Neeson nor

Raimi were involved). A bravura helicopter chase scene and shoot-out and the vertiginous final waterfront showdown deliver the goods for action fans even if, as in *Batman*, the scene ends with lead characters dangling from great heights by their fingertips. The setting for the final confrontation also presages a similar high-rise climax in the little film *The Dark Knight*.

Darkman was the first original superhero movie by David's definition but, more importantly, it served as a calling card for its then 29-year-old director when Sony came calling about a much bigger superhero movie project.

Another director dipping his résumé into these waters was Joe Johnston. A former effects artist at George Lucas' Industrial Light & Magic, Johnston had won a collective Academy Award for his effects work on *Raiders of the Lost Ark* and was just coming off directing *Honey I Shrunk the Kids* when he read a collection of Dave Stevens' comic *The Rocketeer*. Attracted by its thirties setting and retro adventure style and art, he asked his agent to inquire about the rights. When Johnston found out that Disney had them, he offered to direct the adaptation despite "several confrontations" with the studio during the production of *Honey*. "I couldn't resist the idea of directing a picture based on Dave Stevens' graphic novel," Johnston said in 2017. "It was everything I'd been searching for up to that point."[8]

Coming out of the West Coast indie comics scene, Stevens' series was a beautifully drawn homage to serials like Republic's *King of the Rocket Men* (1949) and *Radar Men from the Moon* (1952). The hero was Cliff Secord, a stunt pilot who discovers a jetpack. Stevens' retro theme extended to the setting, a sunlit pre–World War II California, and Cliff's girlfriend Betty, a model whom Stevens based on fifties pin-up queen Bettie Page.

However, the latter detail didn't survive the transition to Disney. Once the studio took over, "Betty and anything else 'adult' went right out with the bathwater," Stevens said. "They really tried to shoehorn it into a kiddie property so they could sell toys. All they really wanted at the end of the day was the name."[9]

Stevens had originally given the rights to B-movie auteurs Paul De Meo and Danny Bilson, who had finally landed at Touchstone after nearly every other studio turned them down. The Disney offshoot was known for more adult fare, but studio head Jeffrey Katzenberg decided he wanted to release *The Rocketeer* under the family-friendly banner.

Johnston went to bat for the comic where he could, fighting to keep elements like the hero's helmet. Disney considered Bill Paxton and Vincent D'Onofrio for the lead, but the director wanted a relative unknown. Finally, after going so far as to bring in a staff writer for an audition, the studio agreed to the director's choice of Bill Campbell, an actor known for the TV series *Dynasty* and *Crime Story*.

The Rocketeer begins with Cliff wrecking his plane during a chase and finding a jet pack. With the aid of his mechanic pal Peevy, the pilot masters the new tech and together they try to keep it out of the hands of a group of Nazis. Neville Sinclair, a movie star who is secretly head of the group, and his henchman Lothar kidnap Cliff's girlfriend Jenny and try to escape on an airship. Aboard the airship, Cliff and Sinclair fight over the rocket pack. Neville escapes using the rocket pack, but not before Cliff sabotages it.

The movie opened at #4 in June 1991. Critical reception for the old-fashioned adventure film was mixed but generally positive. But *The Rocketeer* never had a chance to win over initial audience apathy; two weeks after it opened, *Terminator 2: Judgment Day* rendered obsolete every other action movie in the vicinity.

Chapter VII. In the Shadow of the Bat

But the film's thirties-by-way-of-the-nineties innocence has aged well, with new generations discovering its nostalgic charms and elaborate practical effects. Two decades later, a few of those fans tapped Johnston to make another superhero period piece, this one based on a much better-known character.

A whole year went by following *The Rocketeer*'s release before another superhero film reared its cowl. Released in June 1992, *Batman Returns* was everything that people hoped the sequel wouldn't be.

"I would read quotes from parents where they would say things like, 'Was it Warner Brothers' intention to make my kids cry?'" screenwriter Daniel Waters said. "The answer is that we actually just never thought about it."[10]

To say that *Batman Returns* was not what people were expecting is an understatement. Director Tim Burton had no interest in following up his 1989 blockbuster with something predictable or even related to its predecessor. "Tim made a big thing of saying 'Can we just pretend the first one doesn't exist? Let's just not even address it,'" Waters said.[11]

Batman scripter Sam Hamm had already written a screenplay for a sequel, but Burton had liked *Heathers*, a 1989 dark comedy set in a high school with a script by Waters. The writer swiftly realized that his task was not to please studio executives, DC Comics staff, the moviegoing public, Batman fans, his muse, or the PTA. "I felt like I was the Huntsman and Tim was the Prince, and that I had to go out into the forest every day and bring back something for the Prince," the writer said. "It felt less like a normal writing job and more like my job was simply to try and get Tim intrigued in what I was writing."[12]

Waters' hands were tied in one regard: the villains. The decision to use Catwoman and Penguin, two of the TV series' more popular bumblers, "was so set in stone by Warners that there was never even a conversation about it," Waters said. "Some Illuminati decision was made way before I was brought on."[13]

Burton cast sitcom star Danny DeVito as Oswald Cobblepot, aka the Penguin. Sean Young, who'd missed out on the Vicki Vale role in the first movie, lobbied for Catwoman; she reportedly tried to track down Burton on the Warner lot, but succeeded only in interrupting a meeting between Michael Keaton and a studio executive. She went on *The Joan Rivers Show* and, in a homemade Catwoman costume, proclaimed, "I am Catwoman!" The director gave Michelle Pfeiffer the part.

Burton wanted to stay in California, despite the hundreds of thousands that the studio had spent on storing the original's sets in England. Two of Hollywood's largest stages were set aside for filming. Anton Furst was unavailable, so the director hired his *Beetlejuice* collaborator Bo Welch to create sets like Gotham Plaza and Arctic World, the Penguin's home.

Waters burned through five drafts of the script, but Burton and the studio still weren't satisfied.[14] In July 1991, a month before filming was scheduled to begin, the producers hired screenwriter Wesley Strick to "normalize the movie a little bit," said Waters, paraphrasing Burton's producing partner, Denise Di Novi.[15]

Considering that *Batman Returns* makes the first movie look like a textbook example of linear storytelling, one has to wonder what a pre–Strick *Batman Returns* would have looked like. The film goes beyond dream-logic into a post-narrative funhouse of its own. Perhaps the simplest way to summarize the story is to note that Penguin and Catwoman team up to kill Batman. Also, Penguin runs for mayor of Gotham. Also, an evil industrialist named Max Shreck wants to build a power plant. Oh, and it's Christmas time.

Looking past the plot, the sequel is darker, in both content and look, than *Batman*. Penguin kills a cat (offscreen). Black goo oozes from the villain's mouth as he eats raw fish. Penguin kills Gotham's Ice Princess. Penguin and Catwoman threaten animals. Batman causes a three-car pile-up of Gotham City police cars that is surely fatal for one if not more of the officers (this is never mentioned or returned to). Batman blows up a circus strongman. And it's even more claustrophobic, as though the action takes place inside a snow globe designed by Edgar Allan Poe, Salvador Dali and Moe Howard. Faced with this heart of darkness, all critics could do was compare the movie favorably and/or unfavorably to *Batman*.

Parents, though—well, they had something to say.

"Simply put, *Batman Returns* is not a children's movie," wrote columnist Donna Britt in the *Washington Post*. Burton, she said, turned "kiddie favorites such as rubber duckies, clowns and circus fire-eaters into destroyers" and called Batman himself "robotically ruthless, exploding and setting folks on fire."[16] (Burton was originally going to go further but cut a couple of the more violent shots to get a PG rating.)[17]

Britt also complained about what she called "the 'subtle' sexual stuff, like when Penguin leers at Catwoman, 'Just the pussy I was looking for!' Or Catwoman's sartorial choices: whips, leather, vinyl."[18]

NBC's Faith Daniels devoted a segment of her talk show to the topic "Parents Against *Batman Returns*." The *Los Angeles Times* published letters from irate child-rearers. The *New York Times* ran an editorial that chastised McDonald's for

With its undertones (and overtones) of sex and violence, Tim Burton's *Batman Returns* (1992) was exactly what parents weren't waiting for. Pictured: Michael Keaton and Michelle Pfeiffer. Warner Bros.

promoting the film. A non-sectarian Christian organization protested the Happy Meals tie-in. "The objective of the (Happy Meal) program was to allow young people to experience the fun of Batman the character," a spokesperson for America's favorite fast-food purveyor said. "It was not designed to promote attendance at the movie. It was certainly not our intent to confuse parents or disappoint children."[19]

Whatever its merits, or lack of thereof—and *Returns* remains the most polarizing of all *Batman* movies—the final judgment came at the box office. Burton's spiked bonbon opened to the biggest weekend ever, smashing the record held by its predecessor. But the sequel went on to earn only a little more than half that of the first one, on twice the budget.

Addicted to easy-flowing Batcash, the studio that was initially reluctant to make a *Batman* movie now had to figure out how to keep the franchise from going further off the rails.

Chapter VIII

Marvel's Woes, and a Dark Horse Enters the Race

> "We bought it to burn it. The deal was we buy it, we burn the master so we can do it right."
> —Marvel executive Avi Arad on the Roger Corman–produced 1994 *Fantastic Four* movie[1]

In 1986, the year of *Howard the Duck*, New World Entertainment bought Marvel from the publisher's previous owner, Cadence Industries. The conglomerate's holdings included a movie studio, so Marvel now found itself in the same situation as DC had in the early seventies: sharing a parent company with access to means of movie production. But that didn't much help Marvel's big-screen ambitions.

When Boaz Yakin pitched a project based on a Marvel character to a New World exec, the suit "didn't know what the fuck the Punisher was."[2]

To be fair, the grimacing vigilante was known mostly to Marvel readers. The Punisher debuted in a 1974 issue of *The Amazing Spider-Man* and didn't get his own title until 1986. A former Marine and Vietnam vet named Frank Castle, he has no superpowers but many guns and a thirst for vengeance following the murder of his wife and son. (Creative teams, in comics and film, would change his background and origin as they saw fit, altering his government bona fides, number of family members killed, methods of their deaths, and identities of the killers.) The most obvious precedent was Charles Bronson's vigilante in 1974's *Death Wish*, but co-creator Gerry Conway has cited Don Pendleton's the Executioner, the star of a series of paperbacks, as inspiration.[3]

Yakin was a 21-year-old New York University graduate and comics fan who had only one other script on the go (*The Rookie*, which became a 1990 Clint Eastwood movie). He must have talked a good game because New World greenlit the project. Yakin wrote a script in ten days.[4]

The studio assigned Robert Mark Kamen, creator of Columbia's *Karate Kid* series, to produce, and Mark Goldblatt, film editor on *The Terminator*, to direct. They rewrote Yakin's screenplay, moving it further away from what the screenwriter felt was a faithful adaptation, to the point of dropping the character's signature skull shirt, about the only thing separating him from any other armed-to-the-teeth eighties action berserker.

As *The Punisher* begins, Frank is already in mid-career, with a body count of 125. While foiling a drug buy on the waterfront of an unspecified Pacific Northwest city, he gets caught up in a turf war between the local mob and the Yakuza. When Yakuza head Lady Tanaka kidnaps a bus-load full of Mafia kids mob boss Gianni Franco enlists the Punisher's help. After defeating Lady Tanaka and her goons, the Punisher is betrayed by

Chapter VIII. Marvel's Woes, and a Dark Horse Enters the Race

Franco. Frank kills the mob boss in front of his son, advising the boy not to follow in his father's footsteps.

As Frank, action star Dolph Lundgren gives a suitably dead-eyed performance. Louis Gossett, Jr., as a cop (and Frank's former partner) on the Punisher's trail and Barry Otto as an alcoholic former thespian add humanity and levity to the mayhem.

The Punisher received theatrical release in the fall of 1989 everywhere but the U.S. and Sweden, making it the second Marvel-based movie and the first R-rated superhero film. (This is using a definition of the term "superhero" that is loose but necessary, since a lack of superpowers would also disqualify Batman.) In early 1990, New World sold off most of its film and video holdings, and a year later Live Entertainment (now Lionsgate) released the movie on video, allowing home viewers and critics to see what they'd missed. Reviews tended towards the negative, but a *Time Out* writer described the thriller as "destructive, reprehensible, and marvellous fun."[5]

For Marvel, which had dozens of established superheroes at its disposal, seeing movies made out of relative newbies must have been a source of frustration. But things didn't get any better with adaptations of two of the publisher's flagship properties, Captain America and the Fantastic Four.

In 1984, while the Cannon Film Group was still flying high, they optioned the rights to Cap and Spider-Man. The company went so far as to take out ads in trade magazines trumpeting the upcoming productions. After the bottom fell out of the studio in the late eighties, co-founder Menahem Golan left, taking the rights to the two Marvel characters with him.[6]

With the options about to run out, director Albert Pyun "proposed a way to make the film on a budget and before the rights expiration date."[7] His credits included two late additions to the Cannon catalogue, *Alien from L.A.*, with model Kathy Ireland, and *Cyborg*, with Jean-Claude Van Damme. Golan accepted the proposal and Pyun hired Matt Salinger, son of J.D., for the lead. He was filming in Yugoslavia when the money ran out.

"My producer, Tom Karnowski, literally was told to travel to different countries with a suitcase to pick up cash," Pyun said. "It was a miracle the production didn't shut down and fall apart. So we just shot as fast as possible and used that momentum to finish the shoot."[8]

Pyun worked from a script by Stephen Tolkin, brother of author Michael Tolkin (*The Player*). His movie is the first to follow the character's origin, albeit liberally, and to feature Cap's mortal enemy, the Red Skull (actor Scott Paulin in prosthetics). But the movie's sincerity is undercut by production values, lower even than the 1979 TV movies, and an inexperienced lead (Salinger) who is only marginally more substantive in the role than footballer Reb Brown.

Like *The Punisher*, 1990's *Captain America* was destined for home video. Which is more than could be said for the next Marvel movie.

Two years after Cannon made off with Spider-Man and Captain America, German producer Bernd Eichinger optioned the rights to the Fantastic Four. The Fantastic Four was beloved by comics fans for launching the Marvel Universe, for the family-like dynamics between the four heroes—a brother and sister, a husband and wife (although that union came later), and a best friend—and as a showcase for a burst of mid-sixties creativity from Stan Lee and Jack Kirby unparalleled in comics history.

Eichinger's films included *Christiane F.*, about a teenage heroin addict, and *The*

Neverending Story. He reportedly paid $250,000 for the rights to the Fantastic Four[9]; Lee told some conventiongoers, "Our lawyers just gave away the rights."[10] Six years later, the producer was running out of time. The rights were about to revert back to Marvel, and Eichinger still hadn't found financing.

Enter Roger Corman. If anyone could get the movie made before the deadline, and with next-to-no cash, Eichinger figured, it was the king of the Bs. A Detroit native, Corman had studied English literature at Oxford, lived in Paris and worked various jobs in L.A. before producing his first movie, 1954's *Monster from the Ocean Floor*. He directed over 50 films and produced hundreds more, including cult classics *Death Race 2000*, *Piranha* and *Rock'n'Roll High School*. Corman had also co-founded New World Pictures, the studio that eventually became New World Entertainment (and Marvel's owner from 1986 to '89).

As his December 31, 1992, deadline approached, Eichinger contacted Corman. The German producer had a budget of $1,000,000. Corman huddled with his team. "They said, 'Yes, we think we can make it look pretty good,'" Corman recalled. "I said, 'It doesn't make any difference, we just have to start shooting.'"[11]

Eichinger wanted to commence right away; Corman suggested they put off filming until the last minute to better prepare. "Wouldn't that be too obvious?" Eichinger asked. "It's gonna be pretty obvious whether it's December 26 or 31," Corman said.[12] As director, the producer enlisted Oley Sassone, who had made *Bloodfist 3: Forced to Fight* for Corman. Sassone told an interviewer in 2015 that he was "thrilled" to get the assignment.[13]

A Corman writer, Craig J. Nevius, collaborated on the script with Kevin Rock (1993's *Warlock: The Armageddon*). An early draft "embodied early Fantastic Four," said Mark Sikes, the casting assistant. Sykes had worked in a comic book shop for years and was a collector.[14]

Sikes helped cast the Fantastic Four, including former Dallas Cowboys football player Michael Bailey Smith as Ben Grimm aka the Thing, the team's super-strong, brick-hided tough guy, and a former Miss Nebraska, Rebecca Staab, as Sue Storm, the Invisible Woman. Alex Hyde-White and Jay Underwood, bit players on various TV shows, came aboard as Reed Richards, aka Mr. Fantastic, who has the ability to stretch into impossible shapes, and Johnny Storm, aka the Human Torch, a variation on an early Timely (pre–Marvel) hero who can control fire and turn into flame. Joseph Culp, son of actor Robert Culp, was cast as the Fantastic Four's arch-nemesis Doctor Doom. Filming began on December 28. "I was cast on December 14," said Underwood. "So it was a fairly quick process."[15]

Most of the 21-day shoot took place in Venice, California. The budget was so tight that the cast wore their own clothes. "The dress I'm wearing in that scene where I'm Doom's princess?" said Kat Green, who played Ben Grimm's girlfriend Alicia Masters. "That's my mother's dress from like 1975!"[16]

Post-production was a guerrilla affair, with an effects house pitching in and Sassone cutting the film while making another movie.[17] David and Eric Wurst composed the music and hired a 40-piece orchestra out of their own pocket.[18]

Following filming, the actors toured comics conventions and a world premiere was announced for Minneapolis' Mall of America on January 19, 1994. And then Avi Arad shut it down.

Arad was an Israeli toymaker who, thanks to a merger between the toy company he

Chapter VIII. Marvel's Woes, and a Dark Horse Enters the Race

Producer Bernd Eichinger had a million-dollar budget and a looming deadline to make a movie out of Marvel's first superhero team, the Fantastic Four. It shows in the finished product, a 1994 film that Marvel executive Avi Arad paid to have buried. Pictured (from left): Carl Ciarfalio, Rebecca Staab, Alex Hyde-White, Jay Underwood. Constantin Film.

co-owned with Ike Perlmutter and Marvel, had a controlling interest in the publisher. In Stan Lee's words, Arad had "insinuated himself into the job"[19] of overseeing Marvel's properties.

Apparently, the overseer heard about the *Fantastic Four* movie by chance. While he was visiting Puerto Rico, someone noticed his Fantastic Four T-shirt: "Hey, are you excited about the movie?"[20] asked the fan. This was news to Arad, who returned to the U.S. and paid Corman one or two million dollars (reports vary) to bury the film.

Arad didn't like the idea of a cheap effort that would tarnish both the Marvel brand and what was potentially one of its most valuable properties. But bootleg copies soon began appearing on the convention circuit. The unreleased movie became a cult favorite, appreciated for the sincerity behind the project and the obvious effort to do right by the characters, whatever the limitations of the budget. Many of the beats and cast from the team's early years are represented, including the origin (stolen rocket, cosmic rays, unwanted powers), the tortured romance between beauty and beast (the Thing and blind sculptress Alicia), Doctor Doom and another baddie modeled after the first issue's villain the Mole Man, the Thing's oft-repeated and always ill-timed resignation from the team, the catchphrases "Flame on!" and "It's clobberin' time!," and even Reed and Sue's wedding (a landmark in the comics).

The no-budget effects are (unintentionally) hilarious. Reed's stretching arm is a long board in fabric with a glove attached, and the Torch is animated. Stuntman Carl Ciarfalio, shorter than Ben Grimm actor Michael Bailey Smith, wears a pebbly rubber costume as the Thing. And the Invisible Woman lives up to her name; Staab's Sue Storm barely registers, she has so little to do.

While *The Fantastic Four* has yet to see an official release, it is viewable on the internet. Those who are curious but have no desire to watch a murky VHS copy of a rushed, bargain basement superhero film on YouTube are advised to check out Marty Langford's 2015 documentary *Doomed! The Untold Story of Roger Corman's The Fantastic Four* for a taste of one of, if not the most punk-rock superhero movies ever made. Even Corman, a man whose oeuvre includes *Attack of the Crab Monsters*, called it "the strangest film production I've been involved with my entire life."[21]

If Marvel couldn't catch a break, independent publishers and creators were having a moment.

Based on a black-and-white comic by James O'Barr, 1994's *The Crow* was darker than Tim Burton's *Batman* not just in content but also in background.

O'Barr created *The Crow*, a series about a young man who rises from the dead after he and his girlfriend are killed by a street gang. A few years prior, O'Barr's partner was killed by a drunk driver. Eighteen at the time, O'Barr enlisted in the Marines. While serving, he began writing and drawing *The Crow*; eight years later, in 1989, Michigan-based Caliber published the first issue.

Science fiction author and Blue Öyster Cult lyricist John Shirley discovered the comic and brought the idea of a movie adaptation to producer Jeff Most. The two convinced O'Barr to sell them the rights. "Their enthusiasm convinced me that the film would be done correctly," the artist said.[22]

Shirley began working on the script and Most teamed with Edward R. Pressman, a producer whose credits included 1982's *Conan the Barbarian*. That movie was based on a pulp-era character, created by Robert E. Howard, who was popularized first via a series of sixties paperback reissues with vivid, visceral Frank Frazetta covers and then, beginning in 1970, by a Marvel comic book series.

Alex Proyas, an Australian music video director, was hired to direct. Most said that Proyas' "texturing and shading and shot design" was almost identical to that of O'Barr's comics. For his part, O'Barr cited as an inspiration Will Eisner, creator of the forties noir comic strip *The Spirit*, as well as gloomy British post-punk bands like the Cure and Joy Division.[23]

For their lead, the producers and Proyas decided on Brandon Lee. The son of martial arts star Bruce Lee (Kato in William Dozier's *The Green Hornet*), Brandon had already made a few low-budget martial arts and action films.

Proyas began filming in February 1993 in Wilmington, North Carolina. A few days before Lee's final scenes were to have been filmed, the actor was killed by a dummy cartridge in a prop gun.

Distributor Paramount dropped out a month later, but Proyas finished what he could and, with Pressman, restructured the film.[24] Miramax stepped in, contributing funds needed to complete the movie, and agreed to distribute.

Lee plays Eric Draven, a rock guitarist murdered by a street gang that also killed his fiancée. A year after his death, he is resurrected by a supernatural crow. Finding he has superpowers, including the ability to quickly heal, Eric kills members of the gang one by one. He returns to his grave but, after gang members kidnap his young friend Sarah, he re-emerges for a showdown with the bad guys.

The movie is largely faithful to the comic, even borrowing dialogue and fight

Chapter VIII. Marvel's Woes, and a Dark Horse Enters the Race 65

scenes, although it changes roles for some of the supporting characters. Reviewers inevitably compared the movie to Burton's *Batman* films, but *The Crow* is both more grounded and more generic, and steeped in the era's downbeat, nihilistic sensibility. Grunge and industrial acts dominate the soundtrack, which sold three million copies, even more than Prince's *Batman* album.

The R-rated (for violence) release didn't come close to earning as much as *Batman Returns*, but it did well enough in theaters, home video and cable to generate three sequels and a Canadian TV series. In an echo of the *Teenage Mutant Ninja Turtles* vs. *Dick Tracy* smackdown, *The Crow* did far better than the revival of an older, better-known hero, the Shadow.

Released two months after *The Crow*, *The Shadow* was the movie that Universal (and rights-holder/producer Martin Bregman) hadn't wanted Sam Raimi to make. Directorial duties went to Russell Mulcahy, whose credits included *Razorback*, an Australian horror film about a giant wild boar, and *Highlander*, a fantasy about immortal warriors. Mulcahy and screenwriter David Koepp set the action in late thirties New York, where the Shadow, aka Lamont Cranston (Alec Baldwin), encounters a Tibetan mystic (John Lone) with plans for world domination. Penelope Ann Miller plays Lamont's partner-in-crimefighting, socialite Margo Lane, and future superhero movie stalwart Ian McKellen makes an appearance. *The Shadow* received praise for its atmosphere, sets and effects (including early use of CGI) but the pulp-era mystery man couldn't compete with *The Lion King*, *Forrest Gump* and James Cameron's *True Lies*. Intended to kick-start a franchise à la *Batman*, *The Shadow* was instead put out to pasture.

The Shadow also couldn't compete with hipper fare like *The Mask*. Based on a series from Dark Horse, a Milwaukie, Oregon–based imprint, *The Mask* stars Jim Carrey as Stanley Ipkiss, an Edge City bank clerk who finds the titular object. Upon donning the accessory, he transforms into an ultra-confident zoot-suited prankster with cartoonish powers and a misshapen green head.

This was a breezier Mask than the revenge fantasy of the comics, where Stanley metes out justice upon those he feels wronged by. Comics-friendly New Line Cinema, which optioned the rights to *The Mask* a year before its success with *Teenage Mutant Ninja Turtles*, originally saw it as a horror movie but director Chuck Russell disagreed. "I didn't want this to be the next Freddy Krueger," said Russell, who had made *A Nightmare on Elm Street 3: Dream Warriors* for New Line. "I wanted the main character to be more like [a] Tex Avery [cartoon character]."[25] He hired Carrey, a Canadian comic who was breaking out in the sketch comedy series *In Living Color*, after seeing him do stand-up in L.A.

The Mask proved to be a perfect showcase not just for the comedian's unabashed mugging but also for rapidly improving digital effects. Carrey's performance and the Avery-ish CGI—the Mask's eyeballs telescoping out, Stanley spinning around like the Tasmanian Devil, Milo the dog turning into a canine version of the Mask—enlivens uninspired dialogue and a standard plot. The movie also marked the acting debut of 21-year-old Cameron Diaz as Tina, Stanley's crush.

A huge hit on its summer 1994 release, *The Mask* made 15 times its $23 million budget to become the most profitable comic book adaptation of all time, a record it held until 2019.[26] A 2005 sequel, *Son of the Mask*, bombed.

As *The Mask* opened, Dark Horse owner Mike Richardson signed with producer Lawrence Gordon to develop eight more of the publisher's properties.[27] None of those movies came to fruition, but three other Dark Horse titles were in the pipeline. The first to drop was *Timecop*, a typical nineties sci-fi action film about, as per the title, a time-traveling cop. Professional kickboxer turned actor Jean-Claude Van Damme starred. Released less than two months after *The Mask*, the $27 million "low-rent *Terminator*" (Roger Ebert[28]) opened at #1 and became one of the highest-grossing movies in Van Damme's's oeuvre. In 2010, *Timecop* landed on an *EW.com* list of 12 Underrated Movie Gems.[29]

The next film from the Dark Horse stable was *Tank Girl,* released in March '95. The movie's sassy heroine had debuted in *Deadline*, a British comics anthology. Created by a British art students Alan Martin and Jamie Hewlett, Tank Girl, aka Rebecca Buck, drives and thrives in a tank in a drought-ridden future Australia. Her boyfriend is a mutant kangaroo. The comic was marked by an anarchic spirit and slashy, punk-ish art, and Tank Girl herself swiftly gained popularity and became a symbol for the UK LGBTQ community. In 1991, Dark Horse began publishing her adventures in North America.

American director Rachel Talalay came across one of these issues and was immediately taken by Rebecca. "I just opened it and I'm like, 'Okay, this is me!' I was such a punk rocker and such a rebel—or at least a rebel in my own mind."[30]

A Yale-educated Baltimorean, Talalay had fallen in with filmmaker John Waters' crew before moving to L.A.[31] There, she produced a couple of *Nightmare on Elm Street* films and directed 1993's *Freddy's Dead: The Final Nightmare*. Talalay spent a year trying to convince *Deadline* publisher Tom Astor and *Tank Girl* creators Martin and Hewlett to let her option their baby.

"We sold them the rights thinking that the worst that could happen was that they would make some duff 'made for television' adaptation *à la The Incredible Hulk* or *Wonder Woman*," Martin said. "For which we didn't care. We thought it would be ironic, there would be some humor in it and everyone would appreciate it any way."[32]

After winning over the Brits, Talalay sold the idea to MGM/UA head Alan Ladd, Jr. The studio gave her a budget of $25 million, a little more than the budgets of *Timecop* and *The Mask*.

Just starting out in the business, writer Tedi Sarafian contributed an action-oriented script that Talalay passed on to Martin and Howlett to punch up. The studio encouraged an international search for the lead; according to the director, three future Spice Girls met at a London audition.[33] But Talalay found her Tank Girl in Lori Petty, an American actress who had starred in 1991's *Point Break* and 1992's *A League of Their Own*. "Lori just knew that she was Tank Girl," Talalay said. "There's a way that somebody comes in and you knew that they had to be part of this project, that their life was part of this project."[34]

Like the comic, the movie is set in a drought-ravaged Australia. Water & Power, run by the evil Kesslee, controls most of the remaining resources. In a raid on Tank Girl's settlement, which has its own well, W&P goons kill her boyfriend and capture the heroine. At the W&P compound, Kesslee tortures Tank Girl. Then Jet Girl, a mechanic, helps her escape. She and Jet Girl team up with a gang of mutant kangaroos called Rippers and overthrow the despot.

Released in March 1995, the movie fizzled: It brought in only one-fifth of its budget and received lukewarm, sometimes puzzled reviews. For years, Talalay was reluctant to talk about it, but when she did, she made it clear that the movie suffered from studio interference. "There was not one iota of this movie that John Calley understood," she said of the studio boss who had replaced Ladd during production.[35]

Among the new regime's required changes were the excision of a scene in Tank Girl's bedroom showing a wall of dildos. Talalay also said she had to fight for her choice of production designer (Catherine Hardwicke) and costume designer (Arianne Phillips); the latter had worked on *The Crow*. Hardwicke went on to direct *Twilight*. Academy Award–winning makeup artist Stan Winston took a cut in salary to work on the animatronic Rippers.[36]

Even without the dildos, *Tank Girl* got slapped with an R, a rating that director and star deemed sexist. "Because it was a female hero saying these things, we got an R rating and the R rating really really hurt us in terms of the box office," Talalay said.[37] According to Petty,

> The only reason being that I'm a female. That was it. There was no violent bloody murder, you know, there was blowing up stuff, but there was no nudity. I'd have been naked the whole damn movie if I knew it was going to be R! We thought it was going to be PG-13, and that's what we made. And they gave us an R because the only reason I could think of is that I was a woman, you know, ruling shit.[38]

The movie has since attained semi-cult status, prompted in part by Petty's unapologetically ass-kicking heroine, Winston's Rippers and a Courtney Love–curated soundtrack. Naomi Watts made her American film debut as Jet Girl and Malcolm McDowell dined out on his role as Kesslee.

"When I made *Tank Girl*, I truly believed that I would break the glass ceiling," Talalay said in 2017, after going on to a career as a TV director. "I just thought, I believe in this comic. It's so out there, it's so outrageous, it's so punk, it's so me. I said, this is my shot, and I'm going to go all out there, and you're either going to love it or you're going to hate it. I didn't care if it averaged out as a five, because I wanted it to be a one or a ten."[39]

Time has not been as kind to the next flick from the Dark Horse stable, which also featured a female lead but in a much more regressive fashion than *Tank Girl*. Based on a nine-issue series, *Barb Wire* stars Pamela Anderson Lee as a leather-corseted bartender slash bounty hunter in a future (2017) city called Steel Harbor. With a plot shamelessly recycled from *Casablanca*, the flick annoyed critics on multiple levels while failing to offer anything action-movie-bedraggled audiences hadn't seen before. A 2015 denofgeek.com reassessment tried, and failed, to find much nice to say about the B feature outside of the production design: "The sets are generally nicely detailed and make the film feel bigger than it is."[40]

The mid-nineties saw two other comic-book related movies of almost-note. One was *Judge Dredd* with Sylvester Stallone in the title role. Set in yet another dystopian future, the sci-fi actioner about a cop enforcing the law in Mega-City One was roundly dissed by the press, despised by the comic's creators, and sparsely attended by the public.

The following year, another ode to nostalgia appeared. Paramount's *The Phantom* stars Billy Zane in a movie based on Lee Falk's 1930s comic strip about a masked avenger whose identity and mission are handed down from generation to generation. Like *The Shadow*, it was a throwback adventure flick with supernatural elements, set in the late thirties on the jungle island of Bengalla as well as in New York. It received nominally better reviews—as of this writing, 41 percent on *Rotten Tomatoes* compared to *The Shadow*'s 34—but failed to break even at the box office.

Along with *Dick Tracy*, *The Rocketeer* and *The Shadow*, *The Phantom* further proved that modern audiences just weren't eager to see period pieces that seemed to scratch a Baby Boomer, or even pre–Boomer itch—unless, perhaps, it came with the name "Indiana Jones" attached. (Doc Savage, a pulp hero who debuted a few years after the Shadow, received B-movie treatment in a campy 1975 flick with former Tarzan Ron Ely in the title role and set to marching music by John Philip Sousa. It bombed.)

With more failures than successes, by the mid-nineties the superhero movie had more or less stalled in its development. What the genre needed was a big-budget film that was exciting, fun and new. What it got was *Batman Forever*.

Chapter IX

Batnipplegate, and Marvel Scores a Hit

> "I'm sorry."
> —Joel Schumacher, director of *Batman Forever* and *Batman & Robin*[1]

A year and a half before the release of the follow-up to *Batman Returns*, Joel Schumacher stood next to producer Peter MacGregor-Scott and Warner Bros. marketing executives and addressed about 200 licensees.

Don't worry, the director reassured them. The next movie in the franchise was going to be "a more adventurous, entertaining *Batman*."[2]

The New-York-born-and-raised Schumacher started out as a costume designer, then began writing scripts and directing. After a few turkeys, he scored with *St. Elmo's Fire* and *The Lost Boys*. When Warner Bros. approached him, he had just made the mad-as-hell Michael Douglas movie *Falling Down* and was filming *The Client*, a John Grisham legal thriller.

"They didn't say, 'Do you want to make a movie?'" Schumacher said. "It was very corporate. There was a seriousness to it, and it was kind of naïve on my part because I didn't quite realize I'd be involved in the licensing and marketing, the Kenner toys, the McDonald's, Walmart, Sears, you name it."[3]

According to Warner Bros. co-chair Robert Daly, the director would bring a "hip sensibility" to the franchise.[4]

Tim Burton, no longer involved except as a producer, approved Warner Bros.' decision. He also met with the studio's choice for screenwriters, Lee and Janet Scott Batchler. The husband-and-wife team, whose calling card was a spec script called *Smoke and Mirrors*, whispered the Batspeak the director wanted to hear, saying that "the key element to Batman is his duality," according to Janet. "And it's not just that Batman is Bruce Wayne. All the villains also have secret identities. Superman may be Clark Kent, but Lois Lane is always Lois Lane and Lex Luthor is always Lex Luthor. And when we said that, Tim just kinda went, 'Yes!' And at that point, we pretty much had the job."[5]

The Batchlers did their research, reading the first year of Batman's adventures, current issues and Frank Miller's disruptive *The Dark Knight Returns*. They also read academic papers psychoanalyzing the hero. This led to the creation of a new love interest, Chase Meridian, a psychiatrist who falls for both Batman and Bruce Wayne.

According to Janet Batchler, Warners insisted on two villains. Schumacher chose Two-Face, aka Harvey Dent, a district attorney who turns to a life of crime after a mobster disfigures one side of his face with acid. Following infrequent appearances during the forties and fifties, Two-Face became a recurring foe in the early seventies under the guidance of writer Denny O'Neil and artist Neal Adams.

The Riddler seemed like the obvious next choice, Batchler said. "You're trying to make a big, pop tentpole movie. And we said, 'Look, we can't be using an obscure villain. We need a villain that everybody knows. And the villains that people know are the Joker, Catwoman and the Riddler.' And they had already done the Joker and Catwoman."[6]

Schumacher wanted his *Client* star Tommy Lee Jones for Two-Face and settled on Jim Carrey for the Riddler after he couldn't get Robin Williams. The director also wanted Robin in the picture, and this time Batman's sidekick would stick. Schumacher gave the part to Chris O'Donnell, a 27-year-old actor who had been Golden Globe–nominated for his performance opposite Al Pacino in 1992's *Scent of a Woman*.

Michael Keaton was originally going to return as the lead but bowed out; in 2017 he said it was because of the script,[7] but a few years later, he blamed the direction in which Schumacher wanted to take the movie.[8] Val Kilmer, on a roll after *The Doors*, *Tombstone* and *True Romance*, agreed to suit up. In his self-produced 2021 documentary *Val*, the actor said he was so enthusiastic about playing Batman that he didn't bother to read the screenplay.[9]

Batman Forever begins with Batman confronting Two-Face, who has taken a hostage in a bank vault. Batman saves the hostage but the villain gets away. Meanwhile, at Wayne Enterprises, research scientist Edward Nygma is working on a machine that can manipulate people's brainwaves. Bruce Wayne deems it too dangerous. A senior Wayne exec fires Nygma, who in turn kills the man. Nygma now transforms himself into the Riddler.

When he begins receiving anonymous riddles Bruce consults Chase Meridian, a criminal psychologist who was at the scene of Two-Face's bank robbery. The two attend the circus. Two-Face appears and, certain that Batman is in the audience, demands that the Caped Crusader reveal his identity or he'll detonate a bomb. A trapeze act, the Flying Graysons, try to remove the bomb. Dick, the youngest, gets the bomb out of the tent but returns to find that Two-Face has killed his parents and brother by shooting their wires. Bruce takes Dick under his wing, which leads to Dick discovering Bruce's secret identity. Dick pleads with the older man to let him help fight crime.

The Riddler and Two-Face make a deal: If Two-Face funds the creation of a larger version of the Riddler's brainwave manipulator, aka the Box, the Riddler will learn Batman's true identity for Two-Face. At a party, the Riddler uses his prototype on Bruce and finds out he's Batman. Bruce decides to quit being Batman and settle down with Chase, but then the Riddler and Two-Face break into Wayne Manor, destroy the Batcave and kidnap the psychologist. Bruce comes out of his day-long retirement and accepts Dick as his partner. As Batman and Robin, they invade the villains' headquarters, save Chase and defeat the bad guys.

If nothing else, *Batman Forever* upheld the studio's end of the bargain with licensees, delivering a colorful, corny and family-friendly vehicle for selling ... Happy Meals. In Barbara Ling's sets, neon pinks and blues replace the blacks, blues and gunmetal grays of the earlier Gotham. Schumacher frames the bad guys with the same tilted angles as the TV series. Jones and Carrey compete to chew the scenery, leaving nothing on the table, or anything of the table. (Their best moment occurred offscreen, though. According to Carrey, one day during filming, he approached Jones while the actor was having lunch to ask if his co-star had a problem with him. "I cannot sanction your buffoonery," the livid Oscar winner told Carrey.)[10]

The action sequences are both more ambitious than anything in the first two

Chapter IX. Batnipplegate, and Marvel Scores a Hit

movies and completely gonzo, including one in which the Batmobile drives up the side of a building. That was not in the Batchlers' script, Janet said. "We have a philosophy on action sequences and that wouldn't have fit into it because nothing happens as a result of the action sequence. The plot is not changed because of it. It's just eye candy—very cool eye candy, but eye candy. Joel called us 'the logic police.' We would've been going, 'Excuse me? How does he get down?!'"[11] Akiva Goldsman, Schumacher's collaborator on *The Client*, also receives screenplay credit.

Similarities to the earlier franchise entries include the usual armchair psychoanalysis regarding duality, inevitable perhaps since Chase (Nicole Kidman) is a psychologist. And, although Schumacher shot some scenes on location in New York and Los Angeles, Gotham still feels as hermetically sealed as a biosphere.

Compared to Keaton, Kilmer brings little to the role(s). He later said that he was uncomfortable in costume:

> Whatever boyish excitement I had going in was crushed by the reality of the Batsuit. When you're in it, you can barely move and people have to help you stand up and sit down. You also can't hear anything and after a while people stop talking to you…. It was a struggle for me to get a performance past the suit and it was frustrating until I realized that my role in the film was just to show up and stand where I was told to.[12]

He wasn't the only one who hated the Batsuit. With costumer Bob Ringwood, Schumacher had designed a new version, complete with nipples. Fans went batshit. Even Tim Burton was not amused.

"[Back then] they went the other way," he said in 2022. "That's the funny thing about it. But then I was like, 'Wait a minute. Okay. Hold on a second here. You complain about me, I'm too weird, I'm too dark, and then you put nipples on the costume? Go fuck yourself.' Seriously. So yeah, I think that's why I didn't end up [doing a third film]."[13]

All of this was lost on the average moviegoer, who returned in droves for the zippy but empty *Batman Forever*. With no reason to change horses, Warner Bros. backed Schumacher and Goldsman for the next installment. Schumacher decided to add Batgirl.

"I didn't realize that there were so many young girls who were Batman fans, and as I looked around, I noticed that there weren't any teenage super heroines in our culture," Schumacher said. "Fortunately, Batgirl did exist."[14]

She did, and she was Barbara Gordon, Commissioner Gordon's daughter in the comics and in the TV series. Schumacher and Goldsman changed her identity to Barbara Wilson, Alfred's niece, and the director cast *Clueless* actress Alicia Silverstone.

Kilmer bailed to make *The Saint*, a reworking of an old Roger Moore TV series, and work with Marlon Brando on *The Island of Dr. Moreau*. George Clooney, working across the lot in the Warner Bros. co-production *ER*, stepped into the benippled Batsuit. Chris O'Donnell returned as Robin,

For villains, Schumacher and Goldsman went with a couple of lesser-knowns, Mr. Freeze and Poison Ivy. The former had been a frequent recidivist, played by three different actors on the TV series, but Poison Ivy was making her live-action debut. Warner okayed a $25 million paycheck, or about $100,000 per pun, for Arnold Schwarzenegger to play Freeze. Bane, a strongman in a luchador mask who relies on a supply of a serum called venom to maintain his freakishly wide physique, was added as Ivy's henchman. Freeze dated back to 1959 in the comics, Poison Ivy to 1966, Bane to 1993.

As in the previous movie, *Batman & Robin* opens with a villain in mid-crime. This

Joel Schumacher's *Batman & Robin* (1997) with (from left) Alicia Silverstone, George Clooney and Chris O'Donnell is considered one of *the* worst superhero movies. The nipples on the costumes didn't help. Warner Bros.

time it's Mr. Freeze, stealing a diamond from the Gotham Natural History Museum. Batman and Robin arrive, a fight ensues, Freeze escapes.

In Brazil, scientist Jason Woodrue tests a serum on a serial killer, turning him into a musclebound brute. Nerdy, awkward botanist Pamela Isley threatens to expose Woodrue so he wrecks her lab. Once she inhales toxins, the verdant seductress Poison Ivy is born.

Back in Gotham, Barbara Wilson arrives from England at Wayne Manor to visit her uncle Alfred. He announces that he's dying. Barbara takes a motorcycle out for a late-night ride and encounters a gang of angry street punks. Dick rescues her. At a Wayne fundraiser, Poison Ivy douses Batman and Robin with her pheromone spray. Mr. Freeze crashes the party but is defeated by Batman and Robin. He is immediately shipped off to Arkham Asylum where he is just as quickly freed by Ivy and Bane. In Freeze's headquarters, Ivy unplugs the cryogenic chamber holding Nora, Freeze's wife, and frames Batman for the murder. Batman and Robin argue over Ivy.

Meanwhile, Barbara hacks into the Bat Archives and finds the Batcave. A computer simulation of Alfred tells her that he "took the liberty to create something in your size." The newly costumed hero joins Batman and Robin at the Gotham Observatory, where they defeat Ivy and Freeze. We learn that Freeze's wife Nora is still alive, and Batman makes a deal with Freeze to cure Alfred.

If this sounds like the cartooniest Batman movie yet, it was. The Dynamic Duo's boots sprout ice-skating blades so they can fight Freeze's hockey-outfitted goons. Batman shows Robin his personalized "Gothcard," with the inscription "Good Thru: Forever." "Never leave the cave without it," he tells his sidekick. Silverstone is directionless in the ill-conceived Barbara Wilson–Batgirl role. (According to writer Glen Weldon,

Goldsman's original draft had Batgirl shouting "Pow!" and "Zap!" during her fight scenes.[15]) The logic police are again AWOL for the action scenes, not to mention the byzantine plot. Bane, one of the deadliest foes to bedevil Batman in the comics in decades, is wasted as Ivy's muscle.

Critics flayed the movie. "Like a wounded yeti, *Batman & Robin* drags itself through icicle-heavy sets, dry-ice fog and choking jungle vines, before dying in a frozen heap," wrote the *Washington Post*'s Desson Howe. "Unfortunately, that demise occurs about 20 minutes into the movie, which leaves you in the cold for approximately 106 minutes."[16]

Some appreciated the fun factor, such as it was. As Janet Maslin wrote in the *New York Times*, this was the first *Batman* to suggest "that somewhere in Gotham City there might be a Studio 54."[17] And, amidst the silliness, one moment stands out. As *Comics Alliance*'s Chris Sims has pointed out, a discussion between Bruce and Alfred shows "a better understanding of the [Batman] character than anything in the other three movies."[18] "Death and chance stole your parents," Michael Gough's Alfred tells Bruce. "You have done everything in your power to control the fates. For what is Batman if not an effort to master the chaos that sweeps our world? An attempt to control death itself?"

But that was 30 seconds of a two-hour-plus, 12-clown car pileup. Still, Schwarzenegger's star power and the eternal optimism of the early summer moviegoer took the movie to #1 on its opening (June 1997) weekend. But the public soon soured on the project and, on the following weekend, attendance nosedived by 63 percent.[19]

"They're saying I've made the worst film ever," Schumacher told his friend Woody Allen.

"That would be a real achievement," Allen replied. "You haven't even done that."[20]

A couple months later, Warner pulled the plug on a fifth installment. Batman was, once again, dead as a dodo.

• • •

While Warner Bros. schemed to get Batman back onto fast food cartons, one man stood against the forces of rampant commercialization of caped and masked comic book characters.

"There will be no *Spawn* coloring books," Todd McFarlane said. "No fucking *Spawn the Movie* toothpaste, okay? Let's keep some integrity for the content. Let's maintain some dignity here."[21] Strong words from a man with creative control over a film with a dwarf clown who emits green farts.

McFarlane was then a 31-year-old Canadian artist whose work on Marvel's *The Amazing Spider-Man* and *The Incredible Hulk* had catapulted sales of those titles into the stratosphere. At the height of his popularity, the first issue of a new Spider-Man title written and drawn by McFarlane sold 2.5 million copies.

Two years later, dissatisfied over the lack of creative control and rights at Marvel and DC, McFarlane led a revolt of seven comics artists and writers. They abandoned the mainstream and formed their own imprint, Image, a splashy, visuals-first-and-second comics publisher. The time was right for the new outfit; the comics industry was then going through a speculator-fueled boom. The bubble would eventually burst, sending Marvel into bankruptcy, but in the early nineties, comics that were deemed potential collector's items were selling in record numbers. When the first issue of McFarlane's *Spawn* sold 1.7 million copies[22] and became the highest-selling independent comic in history, Hollywood took notice.

The first to come calling was Columbia, but when the studio wouldn't grant McFarlane creative control, the artist sold the rights to New Line (*Teenage Mutant Ninja Turtles*, *The Mask*) for $1, veto power over director, cast and writer, and ownership of the film's merchandising.[23]

New Line hired, and McFarlane approved, a coterie of special effects artists for the adaptation: director Mark A.Z. Dippé, special visual effects supervisor Steve Williams and producer Clint Goldman were all former employees of Industrial Light & Magic, the special effects house founded by George Lucas. Alan B. McElroy (*Halloween 4: The Return of Michael Myers*) provided a script based on a story he devised with Dippé.

As in McFarlane's "Marilyn Mason goblin screech of a comic" (Grant Morrison), Al Simmons is a government assassin who is betrayed by his colleagues. After his murder, he awakens in Hell. He makes a deal with a demon named Malebolgia to serve as his soldier in exchange for the chance to see his wife Wanda again. Imbued with superpowers and given an elaborate, wallet-chain-inspired costume, he re-emerges on Earth where he's met by an obnoxious clown named Violator. Violator tells Al that he can see Wanda again if Al kills his former boss, Jason Wynne. What Violator doesn't tell Al is that killing Wynne will unleash a bioweapon that will kill everyone else on the planet.

Spawn came in second on its August 1997 opening. Laura Miller at salon.com summed up the critical consensus: "This movie sucks."[24] But *Spawn*, like *Teenage Mutant Ninja Turtles*, wasn't aimed at critics. Its intended audience of teenage boys helped the movie make back double its budget, which had risen from $20 million to $45 million due to additional special effects.

Most of these are dated now, particularly the Saturday morning cheese of the scenes set in Hell. But the FX team took cues from McFarlane's visual flair in animating Spawn's cape in a way that hadn't been seen before (and would be echoed in 2016, with Marvel's *Doctor Strange*). The soundtrack, which went to #7 on Billboard, features unique pairings like Sneaker Pimps with Marilyn Manson and Henry Rollins with Goldie.

The real star of the show, though, at least from an adolescent moviegoer's perspective, is John Leguizamo's Violator. The comedian's performance makes Danny DeVito's Penguin look like Mr. Rogers. Also along for the ride is Martin Sheen, whose presence gives the film a whiff of credibility.

Notably, Spawn's alter ego Al Simmons is played by Michael Jai White, making the actor the first Black lead in a big-budget superhero movie. But Spawn was by no means the first Black superhero on film.

Released 20 years earlier, *Abar, the First Black Superman* features the titular hero, granted psychic powers "of a divine origin," defending a Black family from their racist white neighbours. Louisiana-born African-American James Smalley, reportedly a pimp, wrote and produced *Abar*, which was rechristened *In Your Face* for home video. "The cast ... seems to be competing for whoever can give the stiffest, most incoherent line reading of the fantastically terrible script," wrote Aisha Harris at Slate.[25]

Following *Batman* and *Batman Returns*, two other Black superhero flicks appeared. In 1993, Robert Townsend followed up his 1987 hit *Hollywood Shuffle* with *Meteor Man*. Once again producing, writing and directing, Townsend stars as a Washington, D.C., schoolteacher who gains superpowers from a meteor. The following year, Daman Wayans played an inventor-turned-vigilante in *Blankman*.

Chapter IX. Batnipplegate, and Marvel Scores a Hit

As in *Abar*, the stakes in both are modest; the two heroes just want to clean up their neighborhoods. And both acknowledged the influence of the original *Batman* TV series. The former co-starred Frank Gorshin, the original Riddler, as a drug lord, and the latter's final fight scene used Dutch angles and animated sound effects (for example, "Wham!"). Wayans' character, who may be the first on-the-spectrum superhero, was a fan of the show, as was the writer-actor. "When I was a kid, I used to go bananas for *Batman*," he said. "Hearing the theme music was like hearing the bell on the Good Humor truck."[26] Neither film fared well at the box office or in reviews.

Spawn was followed by two more superhero movies with Black leads. One was another strike against DC, or would have been if anyone had cared enough to pay attention. The other threw a much-needed lifeline to Marvel.

The first was *Steel*. The character was the indirect result of a 1991 summit of DC writers and artists that led to the decision to kill Superman. The idea was to bring back the world's most popular superhero, but after exploring what his loss would mean, both in the comics and the real world. To DC's surprise, the stunt turned into a marketing bonanza, sparking mainstream press coverage and lineups at comic book stores for bagged copies of *Superman* #75, the key issue that speculators felt was sure to escalate in value. (In 2022, a copy could be had for $18 plus shipping.)

To fill the S-shaped void left by the Man of Steel's absence, DC created a host of new heroes. One was Steel, aka John Henry Irons, a weapons manufacturer for the army who makes a suit of armor to fight crime.

Music producer Quincy Jones was intrigued enough to option the rights to the African-American hero. "I have seven children and, as a parent, I'm really aware of the lack of role models for today's kids," he said. "It's really left a hole in the world, and I don't mean just for black kids. Their perspective on the future has changed for the worse, and I hate seeing young people who don't believe in the future. Steel ... represents a role model."[27]

Jones and his co-producers hired Kenneth Johnson, the man who had mainstreamed the Hulk, to write and direct. Johnson, who had created two popular sci-fi TV series, *V* and *Alien Nation* after the end of *The Incredible Hulk*, accepted the assignment with typical good humor.

"The comic itself was filled with these weapons that were blowing blood and brains on the wall," he said. "It was horrifying. I told [the studio] I couldn't do it like this. I'm not into that sort of ugly, ultra-violent stuff. So they said, 'No, no no, it has to be PG-13. Just take it and do whatever with it. Create weapons that don't make them splatter or something.'"[28]

But Johnson had more to worry about than weapons that didn't splatter. For their lead, Jones and his producing partner David Salzman had cast Shaquille O'Neal. The 7'1" Los Angeles Lakers starting center had made two movies, *Blue Chips* and *Kazaam*; as an actor, critics agreed, O'Neal was a great basketball player.

Steel dribbled into theaters in August 1997, shortly after *Spawn*. It begins with Irons testing weapons for the army. A soldier named Nathaniel Burke fires one of the weapons and it misfires, injuring Irons' friend Susan "Sparky" Sparks. Burke is dismissed from the army but procures some of the weapons and offers them to the highest bidder. Irons builds a suit of armor and takes to the streets of L.A. to stop the weapons sale. Sparky, confined to a wheelchair, helps him via computer monitor and communication devices. On the night of the auction for the weapons, Burke's thugs kidnap Sparky. Steel infiltrates the auction, is captured himself, then tricks Burke into returning his sonic cannon to him. Burke fires a laser at Steel but it bounces off his armor, killing Burke.

The well-intentioned but leaden movie was greeted with ambivalence by moviegoers and derision from critics. Many singled out the movie's star, whose wooden performance gives a bad name to the lumber industry. In his armor, O'Neal looks like a Rent-a-RoboCop. Groaners include "I'm gonna smoke you like a blunt" and, when Steel brandishes a weapon at some thugs, "It's Hammer time!" Annabeth Gish, who plays Sparky, received some positive notices for her role as Sparky.

Although Steel's origin was connected to Superman, the movie's only reference to the comics is a "Man of Steel" tattoo that Irons sports and a throwaway line: "You ain't Superman. And you sure ain't getting paid!"

Steel earned less than $2 million on a budget of $16 million. Johnson blamed marketing and a studio that wouldn't let him hire the actors he wanted.[29]

• • •

By 1998, Marvel—now Marvel Enterprises, which included the publishing imprint, a production arm called Marvel Studios, and Toy Biz—had survived high- and low-profile movie flops, an industry-wide recession, and bankruptcy. (For more on the latter, see Dan Raviv's 2002 book *Comic Wars: How Two Tycoons Battled Over the Marvel Comics Empire—And Both Lost*.) The publisher was due for some good luck.

Its rabbit's foot came in an unlikely form. Created by writer Marv Wolfman and artist Gene Colan, Blade was a half-human, half-vampire hybrid who hunted the undead. He debuted in a 1973 issue of Marvel's *Tomb of Dracula*, one of a flood of horror books that followed the relaxation of the Comics Code (the Church Lady of the industry) in the early seventies. The vampire hunter remained a supporting character until 1994, when he received his own (short-lived) title.

Still, people were interested in bringing him to the screen. In 1992, *Variety* reported that rapper LL Cool J was in talks to play the B-lister.[30]

Ernest Dickerson, who had made the giddy horror-action-comedy *Tales from the Crypt: Demon Knight*, brought the idea to New Line. Studio president Mike De Luca hired comic book fan and screenwriter David S. Goyer to write a script.

The Michigan-born and -raised Goyer sold his first screenplay in 1989 for what became the Jean-Claude Van Damme movie *Death Warrant*. His other credits included a 1996 *Crow* sequel, *The Crow: City of Angels*, and New Line's neo-noir sci-fi film *Dark City*.

"I heard that New Line wanted to make a lower-budget black superhero film," Goyer said in 2018. "At the time Marvel was in bankruptcy, and they'd already sold the rights to X-Men and Spider-Man and a few other things, and I knew they were thinking about Luke Cage, Black Panther.... I suggested Blade, as a trilogy. I remember I came in and said, 'I'm going to pitch you the *Star Wars* of black vampire films.'"[31] Later he admitted, "It sounded really cool but the truth is I had no idea what it meant."[32]

The 1992 *Variety* story reporting on a possible *Blade* movie mentions several other Marvel projects, including *Spider-Man*, with James Cameron attached; *Elektra*, with Oliver Stone; *Doctor Strange*, with Wes Craven; and *The Black Panther*, starring Wesley Snipes. But Snipes became frustrated at Columbia's lack of progress with a Black Panther movie and signed on for *Blade*.

Perhaps owing to the scathing reviews for Dickerson's 1996 buddy movie *Bulletproof*,

New Line turned to Stephen Norrington.³³ The Brit had worked in special effects before directing a 1994 low-budget movie called *Death Machine*. "It was well-shot and well-directed in terms of action," De Luca said. "Wesley wanted to do a take on Hong Kong action films and Hong Kong martial arts and that incorporated well into Blade's universe."³⁴

Four months before *Blade*'s August 1998 release, *Ain't It Cool News*—the emerging bellwether for upcoming comics-related projects—ran a positive review of a test screening. "*Blade* will be at the very least a cult hit. The movie succeeds on several levels. My friends and I were amazed that NONE of the following happened: 1. degenerate into a cheesy love story, 2. plot holes you could drive a semi through, 3. ridiculous bad guys, 4. completely illogical happenings."³⁵ (It's unclear if the reviewer saw an earlier test screening in which Blade faced off against an eight-story CGI blood monster. When they realized that audiences checked out at the lack of human connection, Goyer and Norrington changed the ending to a less CGI-packed showdown between Blade and bad guy Deacon Frost.)

"We knew we had something, but the issue was, could it cross over?" recalled producer Pete Frankfurt. "Would it be considered a horror movie, a black action movie like [Snipes' 1992 action film] *Passenger 57*? There were a lot of ways for this movie to get boxed in."³⁶ The R-rated film surprised everyone by opening at #1 and staying there for another weekend.

Set in Los Angeles, the brushed metal-looking action flick involves Blade's attempts to stop Deacon Frost from instigating a "vampire apocalypse." Blade is no reluctant hero; his self-appointed mission is to kill all vampires, whom he holds responsible for the death of his mother. Stephen Dorff, a charismatic young actor just coming off a couple of crime thrillers, plays Frost. Goyer envisioned the ambitious young vampire as "almost like a character from a Bret Easton Ellis novel."³⁷

Besides Blade, Frost is the only character carried over from the comics, although some other elements, like Blade's origin, stay true to the source. Other characters, like an aging vampire hunter (Kris Kristofferson) and hematologist/love interest Dr. Karen Jenson (N'Bushe Wright) were Goyer inventions.

Critics were unsure what to make of the movie. Was it a superhero flick? Horror? It bore the Marvel imprint but had more than enough blood and gross-out effects to satisfy casual horror fans and earn its R.

Audiences liked it enough to turn out in droves, making *Blade*

Blade (1998), starring Wesley Snipes as a vampire hunter, capped a decade of Black superhero movies. It also gave Marvel its first bona fide box-office hit, even if the publisher received only a fraction of the profits. New Line Cinema/Marvel Enterprises.

Marvel's first bona fide hit, even if the company, which co-produced, reportedly pocketed a mere $25,000 of the $45 million movie's $133 million in ticket sales.[38]

Its success was a relief to the comics publisher, whose big-screen aspirations had been stymied for decades by bad deals, low-budget fiascos and *Howard the Duck*. *Blade*'s success not only broke the Marvel movie jinx but showed that even a minor character from the publisher's catalogue could be turned into a marquee name. And if it could happen to Blade, what about one of the company's big names—Spider-Man, say? Or the X-Men?

Chapter X

Born That Way

"The toughest aspect of this to crack was creating believable human drama in such a fantastical scenario. What if [mutants] really existed? What if this phenomenon really happened?"
—Bryan Singer[1]

"The Marvel writers and Stan Lee gave you a good dose of anguish. And they also gave you some great girl-watching and great romance."
—Sam Raimi[2]

The Uncanny X-Men was one of the last titles created by Stan Lee and Jack Kirby in the early sixties. Lee later admitted that he had been running out of ideas for origins. "I couldn't have everybody bitten by a radioactive spider or exposed to a gamma ray explosion," he said. "And I took the cowardly way out. I said to myself, 'Why don't I just say they're mutants. They were born that way.'"[3]

The book never rose to the heights of top Marvel breadwinners like *Spider-Man*, the *Avengers* and the *Fantastic Four*, and the publisher cancelled it in 1970. Five years later, writer Len Wein and artist Dave Cockrum relaunched the X-Men with a new, more diverse lineup: the African American Storm, the Russian Colossus, the Canadian Wolverine, the German Nightcrawler. The comic quickly became a fan favorite and company bestseller, topping even *The Amazing Spider-Man*.

In 1992, the Fox Kids Network began airing *X-Men: The Animated Series*. This was thanks in part to the efforts of network head Margaret Loesch, who had worked on cartoons at Marvel Productions in the eighties. The West Coast studio arm of the New York publisher produced series based on Marvel characters but also on toys like G.I. Joe, the Transformers and My Little Pony.

Fox's *X-Men* became the top-rated kids' cartoon and sold 14 million action figures.[4] In 1993, the year that Marvel Entertainment merged with Toy Biz, the latter's Avi Arad brokered a deal with 20th Century–Fox and producer Lauren Shuler Donner to make an *X-Men* movie.

Others had expressed interest in the mutants. In the mid-eighties, producers approached Gerry Conway and Roy Thomas about writing a screenplay for a proposed feature. The Marvel scribes had drummed up the story for *Conan the Destroyer*, the 1983 sequel to *Conan the Barbarian*.

According to Conway, "I remember their [the producers'] attorney had apparently read Syd Fields' book on screenwriting [*Screenplay: The Foundations of Screenwriting*]—and he kept asking us things like, 'Where's your plot point A?' And we're like, 'What?'"[5] In 1989, Stan Lee and *X-Men* comics writer Chris Claremont discussed a Carolco Pictures adaptation with James Cameron producing and Kathryn Bigelow directing until, in a meeting, Cameron got distracted by the idea of a Spider-Man movie.[6]

Donner, whose résumé included the *Free Willy* franchise and *You've Got Mail*, didn't know from the X-Men, but she knew superhero movies, at least indirectly—she was married to *Superman* director Richard Donner.

The producer went through several screenwriters, including Andrew Kevin Walker (*Se7en*) and author/comics fan Michael Chabon. Then she hired a director, Bryan Singer, whose 1995 crime thriller *The Usual Suspects* had been a sleeper hit. "I had seen *The Usual Suspects*, and I needed a director who could handle multiple characters, had a visual style, could direct action—a whole thing unto itself—and could direct actors," she said in 2014.[7]

Singer said that he was attracted to the themes of prejudice and bigotry that had emerged in the comics. "I'm gay or bisexual, whatever, so that probably factored into [his decision to do the movie] a bit because mutancy is discovered at that age in puberty when you're different from your whole neighborhood and your family and you feel very isolated … and I wanted to get involved in action-adventure and this was an avenue to do it."[8]

A fan of Donner's *Superman*, Singer wanted to ground his movie in reality, adamantium claws, shapeshifting and all. He plowed through the animated series, scrapped the script he was given, and wrote a treatment with producer Tom DeSanto. One of the questions they faced was which characters to include, since many had passed through the team's ranks since its inception. They went with most of the lineup from the cartoon, including Cyclops, the team leader with laser beam eyes; Jean Grey, a telepath; Charles Xavier, aka Professor X, their benefactor and teacher; Storm, a weather goddess; Wolverine (Logan), a ruffian with retractable steel claws; and Rogue, a teenager who can absorb the power and lifeforce of others.

Singer hired David Hayter, a struggling actor who was answering phones for the director, to write the screenplay. Hayter knew the comics, but that was about all. He recalled, "They gave me plenty of time to consider the pressure, because the fact that I was working on an $80 million movie at Fox as my first writing job caused some consternation among the upper ranks. Everybody made it clear to me what was at stake and the various ways I would be destroyed if we didn't pull it off."[9]

Magneto, the X-Men's main nemesis from the comics, was the obvious choice for a villain. The filmmakers added Mystique, a blue-skinned shapeshifter, and Sabretooth, a furry giant with razor-sharp claws and fangs; both debuted in the late seventies in the comics. A fourth baddie, Toad, may have been a sop for fans: dating back to the early Lee-Kirby stories, his powers are super-agility and a prehensile tongue. To play up the prejudice angle, Singer and Hayter added an anti-mutant Senator.

The summer 2000 release announced itself as a different kind of superhero movie from its first frames and setting: a sheet-metal gray day in Auschwitz, circa 1944. As Nazis process Jews on their way into the death camp, a young boy watches as his parents are herded through a barbed-wire gate. Distraught, he uses his telekinetic powers to bend and twist the gate towards him before he is rifle-butted in the head by a German soldier.

Cut to present-day Meridian, Mississippi. A teenage boy and girl are in her room; their lips meet, and the boy turns pale and suddenly can't breathe. The girl, Marie, runs away from home and tracks another mutant, Logan, to northern Alberta. She convinces him to help her but, as they're driving south, they encounter Sabretooth. Cyclops and Storm arrive in time to help Logan (aka Wolverine) prevent Sabretooth from taking the girl and the two X-Men bring her and Logan to their Westchester, New York, headquarters, Xavier's School for Gifted Youngsters.

Meanwhile, U.S. lawmakers, under the leadership of Senator Robert Kelly, are trying to pass a Mutant Registration Act. For Magneto, now grown up from the boy in the concentration camp, the act reminds him a little too much of Nazi Germany. He comes up with a plan to use a device to mutate world leaders who are gathering at a summit on Ellis Island. To power the device, he needs Marie, aka Rogue. He and his Brotherhood of Mutants—Sabretooth, Mystique and Toad—capture the girl and take her to the Statue of Liberty where the mutant political reformer has set up his device. The X-Men fly to New York Harbor, destroy the device and free Rogue. They capture Magneto, but Mystique escapes.

The $75 million movie is modest by today's blockbuster superhero standards; it has a running time of just over 90 minutes, decent but unspectacular action scenes, and relatively low stakes. But from Singer's bold (some would say misguided) attempt to ground the movie in the darkest period of the 20th century to its sleek sci-fi look, state-of-the-art CGI and (gasp) linear storytelling, *X-Men* was unlike any other superhero movie that had come before.

The film packs a lot into its running time, too, introducing nearly a dozen characters and, with the exception of its early scenes of Magneto as a boy and Rogue at home, avoiding superfluous backstory and tired origin beats. As seasoned mutants Charles Xavier and Magneto, Patrick Stewart and Ian McKellen give gravitas to the film's

Bryan Singer's *X-Men* (2000), based on a Marvel Comics team, raised the genre to a new level of seriousness. From left: Patrick Stewart as Prof. Charles Xavier, Anna Paquin as Rogue, James Marsden as Cyclops, Shawn Ashmore as Iceman, Famke Janssen as Jean Grey, Halle Berry as Storm, and Hugh Jackman as Wolverine. 20th Century–Fox.

philosophical leanings, while the actors cast as the X-Men—Famke Janssen as Jean Grey, Anna Paquin as Rogue, Halle Berry as Storm and James Marsden as Cyclops—play it straight. The breakout performance is Hugh Jackman's as the conflicted Wolverine. Jackman was a last-minute replacement for Dougray Scott, who couldn't get away from the Australian set of a *Mission: Impossible 2*. His casting raised fan ire over his 6′2″ height (in the comics, Wolverine is perhaps 5′4″), but the cries of outrage soon sputtered to a halt.

Speaking of fans, the first superhero movie of the new millennium includes one of the first instances in a comic book adaptation of, if not fan service, then at least fan acknowledgment. "What did you expect? Yellow spandex?" Cyclops asks Wolverine as they suit up for the final battle, referencing the team's early costumes.

It didn't just please fans. A massive hit, *X-Men* demonstrated that an audience existed for superhero movies that didn't try to justify themselves with armchair psychology, winking irony or juvenile revenge fantasy.

"There was no template for it," Singer said in 2016. "Comic book movies had died, there was no concept of one as anything but camp."

Fox wasn't the only studio hitching its wagon to Marvel's star. In 1999, after a long and protracted dispute involving many studios, Sony bought the rights to Spider-Man. The deal (encompassing feature, sequel and TV rights to the webslinger and other characters appearing in *Spider-Man* comics) for from seven to ten million dollars (accounts vary), plus five percent of any movies' gross revenue and half the revenue from consumer products. (For $25 million, Sony could have bought rights to many more Marvel characters, including Iron Man, Thor and Black Panther, but they turned down the larger offer.)[10]

The studio was already developing a big-budget *Spider-Man* movie when Fox released *X-Men* in July 2000. In January, the studio announced its director: Sam Raimi. Raimi had pitched the studio in the fall of the previous year, proclaiming his fandom for the character, and mentioning that, when he was 12, his parents paid a local painter $30 to execute a large Spider-Man mural on his bedroom wall.

"[Raimi] came in and said, 'It's a soap opera about a boy who loves a girl, and that's what I want to focus on,'" producer Amy Pascal said. "[Sony CEO] John Calley and I just looked at each other and said, 'Well, that's the movie we want to make too.'"[11] (Calley, who had been head of MGM–United Artists when Rachel Talalay had made *Tank Girl*, had moved to Sony in 1996.)

By his own admission, Raimi was "absolutely terrified" at the prospect of bringing one of the most popular characters of all time to the big screen and working with a budget of $100 million to do so. (His highest-budgeted movie, at $50 million, was the 1999 sports drama *For Love of the Game*; *Darkman*, his attempt at an original superhero movie a decade earlier, was budgeted at $14 million.) According to Raimi, "They had a start date, the script was in not-great shape, and I had no idea how I was ever going to bring what I thought all the fans must have been expecting—this great aerial ballet, this graceful movement of Spider-Man swooping through the city of Manhattan, through the canyons. It had to be done with great grace and agility."[12] Raimi didn't preach verisimilitude, but he did want to approach the movie straight:

> For me, there was no joke. I don't want to be safe as a filmmaker saying, "I know this is goofy, but let's pretend it isn't." I never wanted to have that separation for me and the material or assume that the audience had it. There is no safe place. There's simply just

believing—believing that Peter Parker exists and investing wholly into his heart and matters of his soul. And sharing that drama with the audience.[13]

A script had been in development since 1985, when Cannon acquired the rights, and it had gone through many revisions and rewrites as Spider-Man swung from studio to studio; in 2002, just before the movie's release, the *Los Angeles Times* published an entire article trying to parse who wrote what.[14] After deciding to keep some elements from a treatment by James Cameron, Sony assigned franchise specialist David Koepp (*Jurassic Park, Indiana Jones, Mission: Impossible, The Shadow*) to the job.

"My big pitch was, it should take a really long time for Peter Parker to become Spider-Man," Koepp said. "He's not going to have the outfit on for 45 minutes, and that's okay. It's such a powerful origin story, we need to really stretch it out." He also proposed that Peter Parker, Spidey's alter ego, and his love interest, Mary Jane Watson from the comics, "end apart, because that's romantic."[15] In 2022, Koepp said that he "wrote more drafts of that script than I think any script I've done before or since.... It was hard work." He replaced classic Spidey foes Electro and Sandman (the villains in Cameron's treatment) with two other vintage foes, Doctor Octopus and the Green Goblin.[16] Although Koepp receives sole credit, at least two other writers, Scott Rosenberg and Alvin Sargent, contributed rewrites. Eventually, Doctor Octopus was dropped in favor of just the Goblin, a green-and-purple-costumed, pumpkin-bomb-tossing maniac on a jet-fueled glider.

As the production gathered steam, word got out that it was taking certain liberties with canon. In Cameron's treatment, Peter's ability to shoot webs is result of the spider-bite; in the comics, Peter, science nerd that he is, makes his own web-shooters and fluid. Perhaps thinking that this would be one suspension of disbelief too many, Raimi and Koepp kept Cameron's idea. Fans expressed their displeasure.

"I don't think that the fans thought I was the right person to direct Spider-Man in general," Raimi said. "And then the organic web shooters—when the fans found out I was going that way, they tried to have me removed from the picture."[17]

His casting choices were less controversial. *The Cider House Rules* was making waves when Raimi and Pascal began their search for Peter Parker, and they found him in that movie's 26-year-old star Tobey Maguire. For Mary Jane, they signed Kirsten Dunst, who had a breakout role as captain of a cheerleading squad in the 2000 comedy *Bring It On*. Willem Dafoe, who had two decades' worth of credits playing lead and supporting characters, good guys and bad, signed on for the role of Norman Osborn, the industrialist father of Peter's friend Harry who becomes the Green Goblin. Of his decision to take the role, Dafoe said that he wanted to work with Raimi and that he liked "this fairly new idea of making a film out of these comic book characters."[18]

As per screenwriter Koepp's conception of the story, *Spider-Man* take its time getting to the action.

High school student Peter Parker is visiting a Columbia University lab when he is bitten by a radioactive spider. The next day, he discovers he has enhanced strength and agility, and the abilities to sense danger, stick to walls and shoot webs from his wrists. After seeing an ad for an underground wrestling competition with a cash prize, he decides to use his newfound powers to win the jackpot and impress his high school crush, Mary Jane. But when he tries to collect his money the promoter refuses; a robber breaks in and Peter stands by while the criminal takes the cash. A few minutes later, Peter learns his uncle Ben has been killed by a carjacker and realizes that the killer was the criminal he let free. He vows to follow his uncle's counsel that "with great power comes great responsibility" and use his powers for good.

Norman Osborn, head of a company called Oscorp, tests a performance-enhancing formula on himself ("Risks are part of laboratory science!" he declares) in hopes of in hopes of securing a military contract. The formula drives him insane and he kills a technician. When the Oscorp board of directors fires Norman, he makes off with prototypes of a green exoskeleton and a rocket-powered glider.

Some time later, Manhattanites gather downtown for the World Unity Festival. Norman, in his Green Goblin armor, flies in on his glider and disintegrates the Oscorp board directors with a pumpkin-shaped bomb. Peter, photographing the event for his new employer *The Daily Bugle*, sees that the Goblin's actions have endangered Mary Jane. He strips down to his costume, saves the girl and chases off the bad guy. "We'll meet again, Spider-Man!" cackles the Goblin.

They do, when Spider-Man swings into a building on fire and finds the Goblin waiting for him. By greeting, Goblin punches Spider-Man in the face, then follows up this act of macro-aggression by suggesting they form a partnership. The hero rebuffs the Goblin and, angrier than ever, the villain flies off.

At a Thanksgiving dinner given by Harry, Norman figures out Spider-Man's alter ego and, hence, his weaknesses: the people Peter loves. As the Goblin, he scares Peter's Aunt May and kidnaps Mary Jane. Atop the Queensboro Bridge, he offers Spider-Man the choice: save Mary Jane or a tram car full of children. After saving both, Spider-Man

Romance, a component of Marvel's Spider-Man comics since the beginning, was something director Sam Raimi wanted for 2002's *Spider-Man*. Pictured: Tobey Maguire, Kirsten Dunst. Sony Pictures.

follows the Goblin to an abandoned building. In the ensuing showdown, the villain is killed by his own glider.

Corny, colorful, and with only a passing interest in reality, *Spider-Man* is a far different beast than *X-Men*. Spider-Man's origin is given its due and then some. (Rosemary Harris and Cliff Robertson play the thankless roles of Aunt May and Uncle Ben.) Tweaks include the substitution of a hipper-sounding "genetically modified" spider instead of the original's radioactive arachnid. (For early sixties Marvel, everything was about radioactivity.)

Maguire brings dewy-eyed vulnerability to Peter but he and Dunst don't exactly crackle together on-screen, though a scene in which an upside-down Spidey kisses Mary Jane immediately memed its way into the broader pop culture landscape. Spidey himself lacks the wisecracking energy he has in the comics. Comic relief is left to J.K. Simmons as Spidey-hating *Daily Bugle* publisher J. Jonah Jameson. But whatever was missing by way of quips was made up for by the John Dykstra–led CGI team's depictions of the hero in action. After ceding some control to the team, Raimi—a practical effects enthusiast and innovator—and his collaborators achieved the director's goal of putting a "great aerial ballet" on the screen. However, the final battle between hero and villain points to a potential pitfall of the genre: the difficulty of keeping the characters relatable when they're masked, and/or largely CGI.

Overall, though, *Spider-Man* impressed critics, delighted fans—once they'd gotten over those organic web-shooters—and broke box office records. *Blade* threw down the gauntlet, *X-Men* picked it up and *Spider-Man* ran with it. A new era had begun.

Chapter XI

Hulk Throws a Tank

> "I want the audience to have a taste of the Hulk; it's amoral, unconscious, primal—a very basic instinct. And when the action comes, [the audience] should be carried along by the emotions and enjoy the action along with the intense psychodrama."
>
> —Ang Lee[1]

With the Marvel brand suddenly hot, studios rifled through their files to see which rights to the publisher's characters might be collecting dust. New Regency came across Daredevil.

Created by Stan Lee and Golden Age artist Bill Everett at the tail end of Marvel's early sixties creative boom, Daredevil was a kind of second-rate Spider-Man. His real identity was Matt Murdoch, a defense attorney who, as a boy, was blinded by a radioactive substance that fell out of a truck. The substance enhanced his other senses as well as his strength and agility. After a mobster killed his father, a boxer named Battlin' Jack, Matt grew up to become a lawyer and a superhero in a bright red costume with horns with a tricked-out billy club for a weapon.

Like the X-Men and Doctor Strange, "The Man Without Fear," as he was billed, spent much of his early career as a minor leaguer, a status reflected in third-rate foes like Stilt-Man, Jester and the Owl. Then in the early eighties, he became the talk of the comics shops thanks to a take-no-prisoners approach by Frank Miller. The writer-artist, who would later reboot Batman with the 1986 mini-series *The Dark Knight Returns*, revitalized the *Daredevil* comic with noirish melodrama by way of ninja assassin–love interest Elektra, psychotic villains and surprisingly (for the time) graphic violence. In one issue, Elektra is impaled on one of her sai by another assassin, Bullseye.

A few years after Miller's run ended, Daredevil made his live-action debut: in *The Trial of the Incredible Hulk*, one of three late–1980s TV-movie spinoffs of the series, lawyer Matt Murdock (played by teen heartthrob Rex Smith) defends David Banner against charges of some typical Hulk-induced mayhem. He dons a black ninja-like outfit to help the Hulk fight crime boss Wilson Fisk, aka the Kingpin.

Nearly a decade later, 20th Century–Fox optioned the rights to the character, who then got shuffled off to Columbia and finally New Regency. In 2000, the studio, coming off back-to-back hits with *Fight Club* and *Big Momma's House*, hired Mark Steven Johnson to write and direct a *Daredevil* film. Johnson had helped out on a *Daredevil* script when the movie was at Columbia.

"I loved the character so much that I just wanted to give them my suggestions," said Johnson. "First and foremost, I'm a fan. I just want to see a great *Daredevil* movie."[2]

The director found a fellow traveler in his lead, Ben Affleck. According to the actor,

"I thought I had, I was pretty sure I had, and I then went back and made sure I had read every issue of *Daredevil* ever published. It was more about taking what I already knew and had been a fan of since I was a kid … and faithfully delivering that to the screen."[3] Affleck had made a career out of straddling the worlds of mainstream and indie filmmaking, appearing in box office gold like *Pearl Harbor* and *The Sum of All Fears* as well as low-budget pics written and directed by his pal (and comics fan) Kevin Smith.

With James Acheson, designer of Sony's Spider-Man outfit, Johnson worked to get the right red for the hero's costume. The director hired Hong Kong wirework specialist Cheung-Yan Yuen to help with the fight scenes and a consultant to help Affleck play Matt's blindness.

The movie begins with Daredevil's origin. Young Matt Murdock, growing up in New York's Hell's Kitchen, is bullied until the accident that leaves him blind but enhances his senses and strength. When the mob kills his father, a boxer and part-time enforcer, he decides to fight crime.

About 20 years later, he's a lawyer and costumed vigilante. When a judge frees a rapist, Matt, as Daredevil, chases the bad guy into a subway station and, in a fight on the platform, flips him onto the tracks, where he's hit by a train. The police and reporter Ben Urich arrive at the scene and discuss the rumors about a mysterious red-suited "urban legend." Urich tosses a match onto the subway platform and two large Ds light up.

The next day, Matt is having coffee with his law partner, Foggy Nelson. In walks a young woman. Matt is captivated by her scent. His advances are rebuffed but he follows her out onto the street and to a children's playground. He asks for her name but she refuses and they fight, doing flip-flops on the teeter-totter until they achieve mutual respect. Her name, she tells her blind acrobat stalker, is Elektra Natchios.

Later, in a bar, Daredevil beats up several patrons in an effort to find crime boss Wilson Fisk, aka the Kingpin, and the man responsible for his father's murder. In an unrelated matter, the Kingpin hires an assassin, Bullseye, to kill one of his lieutenants. The lieutenant happens to be Elektra's dad. Bullseye not only kills the man, he frames Daredevil for the murder. Elektra, now in her own red costume and out for revenge, attacks Daredevil. During a fight, she plunges one of her sai into his shoulder before Bullseye impales her on Daredevil's billy club. Daredevil, wounded, follows Bullseye into a church, where the latter uses the bells to overwhelm the hearing-enhanced hero. A police officer shoots Bullseye through the hands, and Daredevil throws the wounded assassin through a stained-glass window.

A battered but unbowed Daredevil manages to make it to the Kingpin's high-rise office. As the two fight, Kingpin unmasks Daredevil, revealing "the blind lawyer from Hell's Kitchen." Matt rallies himself and breaks both of Fisk's legs but stops himself from killing the villain. Soon after, Matt visits Elektra's grave, where he finds a necklace with her name written in Braille.

Coming after the sleek sci-fi modernism of *X-Men* and the pop fizz of *Spider-Man*, *Daredevil* was a step back into the Stygian depths of nineties movies like *The Crow* and *Blade*. The hero is shown popping pain pills, recovering in an isolation tank, and confessing to a priest. Gothic and religious imagery dominates. No watering hole is safe from the appearance of a sociopathic Irish assassin (Colin Farrell plays Bullseye with a brogue) or a vengeance-seeking vigilante; it sucks to be an after-work tippler in this Hell's Kitchen.

For good or ill, Johnson's *Daredevil* often pays homage to the comics, perhaps more than any other superhero movie up to that time. The "DD" initials that are set ablaze on the subway platform form the character's insignia. A shot of Daredevil clutching a cross is from a 1999 cover by Joe Quesada. The origin beats borrow from a 1993–94 Frank Miller–John Romita, Jr., run. Names of characters and buildings echo the names of various *Daredevil* writers and artists.

Story-wise, it's a compendium of clichés, including but not limited to: a fight in a church; a reporter on the trail of the hero; a party in which hero and villain, in their civilian identities, exchange their philosophies with barely concealed hostility; and a supposedly dead character revealed to still be alive at the end. *Daredevil* also follows the *Batman* formula of reverse-engineering the character's origin by tying Matt's father's death to the main villain, Kingpin (Michael Clarke Duncan). If it's true, as director Bryan Singer said, that "there was no blueprint" for what he was trying to do with *X-Men*, *Daredevil* cobbles one together from other movies.

Reviews were dismissive, but *Daredevil* was a hit. It opened at #1 on Valentine's Day 2003 and, though attendance dropped, it earned more than double its budget. Released a year later on DVD, an R-rated director's cut (which included a subplot involving rapper Coolio) received better notices.

Affleck later disavowed the movie—"I hate *Daredevil* so much," he said in 2016, as he was gearing up to play another cowled crusader—but Johnson remained proud of the effort. "I do like the look of *Daredevil* very much," he said in 2019. "We hadn't seen a superhero come home covered in scars, and chewing on pain pills, and it was kind of grim."

It has been argued[4] that *Daredevil*'s tone anticipated Christopher Nolan's take on Batman. But the movie can also be seen as the end of the nineties' string of grimdark comic-book heroes gritting their teeth through rainy back alleys. If nothing else, it's the first superhero movie with a mid-credits scene—one that lets viewers know that Bullseye—played with malevolent panache by Colin Farrell—is still alive and dangerous. And it's one of the first to debut a character, Elektra (Jennifer Garner), with the intention of spinning her off into her own feature.

Audiences hungry for more superhero action didn't have long to wait. Less than three months after *Daredevil*, *X2: X-Men United* landed in theatres. The opening weekend receipts had barely been counted when 20th Century–Fox put the sequel in play. Bryan Singer agreed to return, and the studio assigned David Hayter (*X-Men*) and Zak Penn (1993's Arnold Schwarzenegger vehicle *Last Action Hero*) to work on separate scripts.

New characters were added. On the hero side were Nightcrawler, a Germant mutant with blue-black skin, white face and prehensile tail, capable of transporting himself and others, leaving behind a malodorous stench of sulfur, and Colossus, a Russian who can transform his body into organic steel. On the villain side: Col. William Stryker, a mutant-hating human, and Yuriko Oyama aka Lady Deathstrike, a mutant with similar powers to Wolverine. MIA: Toad.

The action begins when a brainwashed Nightcrawler makes an unannounced appearance in the White House, freaking everyone out, especially William Stryker. The military scientist convinces the president that mutants pose a danger to humankind. Stryker and his forces raid Professor X's school and capture Charles, Cyclops and some students. Brotherhood of Mutants' Mystique discovers that Stryker is going to use a replica of Cerebro, Charles' mutant detection device, to kill every mutant in the world. She helps Magneto escape from his purpose-built plastic prison and they join the rest of the X-Men in a raid on

Stryker's base, an abandoned military installation in northern Alberta. They destroy Cerebro II and rescue the prisoners.

Smarter, faster and more confident than the first, *X2* impressed audiences, critics, and fans. It also surpassed *X-Men* at the box office and in accolades.

While Sony, New Regency, and Fox were profiting from their nineties Marvel deals, Universal was pursuing a feature film starring its seventies prize, the Hulk.

The studio had never given up on the big green behemoth. Following the TV series, it produced the aforementioned trio of TV-movies, *The Incredible Hulk Returns*, *The Trial of the Incredible Hulk* and *The Death of the Incredible Hulk*. All were made without the participation of series creator Kenneth Johnson but featured original leads Bill Bixby and Lou Ferrigno.

Two years after NBC aired the last of the trio, Universal began contemplating a *Hulk* movie.[5] According to Tad Friend in a 2003 *New Yorker* article, "Eight successive writers or teams of writers spent seven years trying to craft an *Incredible Hulk* screenplay that would satisfy [Universal]."[6] These included but were not limited to Michael France, writer of an unproduced *Fantastic Four* screenplay; Michael Tolkin, author of the novel-turned-movie *The Player* and brother of *Captain America* co-writer Stephen Tolkin; and *X-Men*'s David Hayter.

Finally, in the post–*X-Men*–*Spider-Man* frenzy, Universal gave the go-ahead to producers Gale Anne Hurd and Marvel Enterprises' Avi Arad. Hurd had started out at New World Pictures as executive assistant to Roger Corman and produced the James Cameron films *The Terminator*, *Aliens* and *The Abyss*.

The producers set out to find the person who could bring one of Marvel's best-known properties to the big screen in a marketplace suddenly starved for superheroes. "We knew that to do the Hulk, we couldn't use a shooter," said Arad. "It needed to be a character-based director."[7]

Ang Lee was known for literary arthouse fare like *Sense and Sensibility* and *The Ice Storm*. But the Taiwanese-born director had also made the well-received action flick *Crouching Tiger, Hidden Dragon* (2000). And he directed a 2001 BMW clip that ends with actor Clive Owen covering a nicked ear with a Band-Aid featuring a Jack Kirby image of the Hulk.

At this point, there was little question of going back to the green body-paint and yak hair of the seventies and eighties; this Hulk would be full CGI. In post-production, Lee donned the motion-capture suit to provide a blueprint for the movements of the jolly green giant, who was being animated by Industrial Light & Magic. To play Hulk's human alter ego (given back his original, "too-comic-book-y name" Bruce Banner), the director chose Eric Bana, an Australian actor whose breakout role was in 2001's *Black Hawk Down*.

Lee and his writing partner James Schamus decided to explore the underpinnings of Bruce Banner–The Hulk's rage, something that comics writers had begun to do in the mid-eighties. They also retconned his origin to include Bruce's father David who, in a fit of anger, accidentally murders his wife (and Bruce's mom) Edith. Lee also planted the idea that Bruce has inherited mutant DNA from his father. The movie, they decided, would simply be called *Hulk*.

Following the childhood flashback that opens the movie, *Hulk* skips ahead 30 years. Bruce is now a scientist researching nanomeds at Berkeley Lab when a colleague is trapped in a gamma ray spectrometer, or gammasphere. Bruce rescues him but is exposed to radiation himself. The radiation merges with his altered DNA. It is at this point that his father David, who has been working as a janitor at the lab, reintroduces himself to his son. A stressed-out Bruce Hulks out and destroys the lab. He wakes up at home, where he is found by Betty Ross, his ex-girlfriend, lab partner and daughter of the man about to become his worst enemy, Gen. Thaddeus "Thunderbolt" Ross. Gen. Ross interrogates Bruce and places him under house arrest. Glenn Talbot, who is with a private firm interested in Banner's research, shows up to needle the scientist, who is already in a bad state thanks to the interrogation and a phone call from his dad saying that he, David, has just sicced three mutated dogs on Betty. Bruce Hulks out, injures Talbot and bounces over to Betty's cabin. After saving her from the crazed canines, the Hulk falls asleep at the cabin. Gen. Ross arrives with the army and sedates and imprisons Bruce. Meanwhile, back at the lab, David Banner exposes himself to nanomeds and gamma radiation. His newfound powers include the ability to absorb different materials and electricity.

Bruce wakes up in an isolation tank in an underground army base. To get a tissue sample from the Hulk, Talbot provokes him into his transformation. Talbot gets the sample but enrages Banner, who turns into the Hulk and kills him, then wrecks the base and escapes. After fighting the army in the desert, the Hulk arrives in San Francisco, where Betty calms him down. Later, Ross stages a confrontation between father and son that escalates into a fight between their super-powered selves. The fight ends when Ross drops a bomb on both of them. Following the explosion, Bruce is shown working as a doctor in the Amazon rainforest.

Ang Lee's Hulk, as it is unofficially known, was the most serious film treatment of a superhero yet, and still one of the most daring. It's talky and science-y and the title hero doesn't appear until nearly 45 minutes in. The relationship between Bruce and Betty is, for the most part, mature and even believable. (Jennifer Connelly plays Betty, her second comic-book movie role after *The Rocketeer*.) The movie strains to give more basis for Bruce's anger and his transformation into a giant green rage-machine.

At the same time, Lee isn't shy about acknowledging the character's four-color roots. He uses comic sans for the opening credits and, in some scenes, split-screen images that mimic the panels of a comic-book page. Hulk even gets to wear his trademark purple pants and utter a line straight out of the comics: "Puny human!" And, though it takes a long time to get there, a sequence in which Hulk decimates the army in the desert is the most intense, sustained visualization of comic book–style action yet to be put on film.

But the combination of too much pseudoscience-y exposition and father issues and not enough smashing alienated audiences and critics. An easy film to admire but a hard one to love, *Hulk* opened to the sixteenth largest weekend in history before dropping in attendance by 70 percent.

The run of Marvel-based movies was interrupted by the arrival of another Dark Horse–derived property, *Hellboy*.

Created by writer-artist Mike Mignola, the character was a half-demon with a stone hand and a Howard the Duck–like penchant for cigars and wisecracks. Dark Horse began publishing a *Hellboy* series in 1994, and it was unlike anything else on the stands. Mignola filled the stories with macabre humor and supernatural and horror archetypes drawn in a highly stylized chiaroscuro style that cried out for cinematic adaptation.

Guillermo del Toro heard the call in 1997. There was just one catch: yes, the Mexican horror director wanted to make a *Hellboy* movie—but with Ron Perlman, an actor best known for TV, and his role in CBS's *Beauty and the Beast* (1987–90), as the lead.

"And you know studios, they don't want Ron Perlman; they want movie stars," said co-producer Lawrence Gordon. "So, we would go to studios, and they'd say, 'Wait a minute, can't you do it with X? Can't you do this with Y? Did you try so-and-so?'"[8] Gordon and producing partner Lloyd Levin were serial comic book–rights procurers; their other properties included *Mystery Men*, a Dark Horse superhero parody by Bob Burden that was adapted into a post–*Blade*, pre–*X-Men* movie, and Alan Moore's *Watchmen*. They also co-produced *The Rocketeer*.

Perlman too was skeptical. "That's a great idea, and God bless you, I love you for entertaining the idea, but it'll never happen," he told del Toro.[9]

Finally, Revolution Studios, an independent with a Sony distribution deal, greenlit a *Hellboy* movie—with Perlman as the lead—after del Toro's *Blade II* opened strong in March 2002. Borrowing story elements from the first *Hellboy* mini-series, "Seed of Destruction," del Toro wrote a screenplay from a treatment he co-authored with Britisher Pete Briggs.

Hellboy begins in 1944 on the coast of Scotland. Nazis in league with ancient Russian mystic Grigori Rasputin open a portal which will allow the Ogdru Jahad, an army of monsters, to bring about the apocalypse. With the help of occult specialist Prof. Bruttenholm, an Allied Forces battalion shuts down the interdimensional gateway, but not before a small, red, horned creature hops through. Bruttenholm wins over the baby demon with an American candy bar.

Sixty years later, two of the Nazis, Karl Kroenen and Ilsa Haupstein, revive Rasputin. The evil trio is determined to reopen the portal but need Hellboy's stone appendage. Employed by the Bureau for Paranormal Research and Defense (the B.P.R.D.), the arm's owner now lives in the Bureau's New Jersey headquarters with several cats. After Rasputin and his Nazi pals unleash a demon in a museum and kill Bruttenholm (Hellboy's surrogate father), Hellboy and the rest of the B.P.R.D.—telekinetic Liz Sherman and an amphibious Creature from the Black Lagoon–type named Abe Sapien—confront the bad guys in Russia and foil their plan to reopen the portal.

Reviewers regarded the stew of occult ideas, Lovecraftian horror, monster battles and B-movie romance clichés as a refreshing break from the emerging superhero narrative. Perlman's Hellboy is the Rick Blaine of the Underworld, pining in his cups after Selma Blair's Liz. Kroenen, a killing machine held together by a rubber suit, is a truly eerie creation, as is the decapitated head Hellboy lugs around during the third act. Doug Jones' Abe Sapien, a triumph of practical effects and creature design, is a gentile counterpart to the gruff protagonist. The storytelling, the mix of comedy and horror, and Perlman's gruff but lovable performance propelled *Hellboy* to #1 on its opening weekend.

A *Punisher* reboot was not received as warmly. Opening two weeks after del Toro's film, this version of the Marvel vigilante—again titled *The Punisher*—was the result of a 2000 agreement that gave Artisan Entertainment the rights to over a dozen Marvel characters. These ranged from veteran campaigners Ant-Man and Black Panther to newer operators like the mercenary Deadpool and Mort the Dead Teenager, the star of a four-issue 1994 mini-series.[10]

Artisan, which had its roots in the home video boom of the eighties, hired Gale Anne Hurd to co-produce with Marvel's Avi Arad. Thomas Jane, known for supporting roles and for playing Mickey Mantle in the 2001 baseball drama *61**, signed on after seeing *Punisher* comics artist Tim Bradstreet's photo-realistic conception of the character (which was similar in appearance to the actor). To direct, Hurd and Arad chose

Hurd's husband Jonathan Hensleigh, a former attorney who had worked on the screenplays for the action pictures *Die Hard with a Vengeance, The Rock* and *Con Air*. Artisan gave the first-time director a budget of $34 million, one of the largest in the studio's history but small potatoes in action and superhero movie terms. Hensleigh rewrote a script by Michael France, an early writer on Lee's *Hulk*, set in Florida. The director kept the location.

The reboot takes a step back from New World's 1989 version to deliver a Punisher origin. In this version, Frank Castle is a former FBI agent who loses not just his wife and son but other relations to mob violence. The murders take place at a family reunion, under the orders of crime boss Howard Saint following the death of Saint's son in an undercover operation with Frank. In retaliation for the retaliation, Frank goes after the mobster's wife and friends while Saint sends various goons to kill him.

As with the first *Punisher*, reviewers took a look at the crime scene and sniffed, "Nothing to see here, folks." Moviegoers moved along, while at least one corner of the fan press was outraged. "I LOATHE THIS FILM," wrote Harry Knowles at *Ain't It Cool News*. "This is everything that we've grown past in the last 6 years of Comic Book Cinema…. This is a complete disaster, a turd, a blight upon Marvel's good name. I prefer Corman's *Fantastic Four* to this, that at least had moments that make me happy."[11]

This begs the question, though: What would it take to make fans of the vigilante mass murderer happy? In their own way, both film adaptations had been true to the character. At least the '04 version restored his trademark skull T-shirt.

The Punisher marked a step forward for Marvel in one regard. As the studio's first release as an equity owner, the company had more of a say about how Frank was presented on screen than it had for its other heroes.[12] After years of watching others call the shots, Marvel's eyes were on the prize: making its own feature films and being in total control.

The studio was still in the passenger seat regarding Spider-Man, who returned to the big screen in Sony's summer 2004 sequel *Spider-Man 2*.

Reuniting director Sam Raimi with the original cast, the movie bucked superhero franchise trends by adding only one new villain. But he was a doozy; the classic baddie Dr. Otto Octavius, aka Doctor Octopus, a stocky, bespectacled nuclear physicist with a bowl cut. "Doc Ock" had been plaguing the web-head since his 1963 debut in *The Amazing Spider-Man* #3. When his four mechanical arms fuse to his body in a lab accident, he turns to crime. In the seventies, he almost married Aunt May.

For a script, Raimi engaged Michael Chabon, whose 2000 novel *The Amazing Adventures of Kavalier & Clay* was set in the mid-century New York comics industry (it won the Pulitzer Prize for fiction). The director's instructions, Chabon said, were to "make Peter the most miserable he has ever been."[13] The author receives a "Story by" credit; Hollywood vet Alvin Sargent, who worked on the first movie, is credited with the screenplay.

Things are not going well for Peter as the movie opens. He's easily distracted from his pizza-delivery job, his best friend Harry Osborn hates him, Aunt May is facing eviction, and he's broken up with Mary Jane. The latter, starring on Broadway in *The Importance of Being Earnest*, is engaged to the astronaut son of *Daily Bugle* publisher and sworn Spider-Man enemy J. Jonah Jameson.

Peter's only solace comes via attending science demonstrations like the one being conducted by his mentor, Dr. Octavius. The physicist has developed neural-linked mechanical tentacles to handle nuclear fusion material; he shows them off at Oscorp, the same private enterprise that previously gave rise to the Green Goblin, not that that should set off any warning bells. When a reactor destabilizes, the tentacles fuse to Octavius' torso and his wife is killed. After escaping from the hospital, the now unhinged Doc Ock goes on a crime spree to fund his experiments. One of his bank robberies happens to coincide with Aunt May and Peter's visit to the bank to request a loan. Peter suits up, Ock grabs May, Spidey saves her, and the mad scientist escapes.

Shortly after, Peter notices that he is losing his powers and decides to give up superheroing. Doc Ock makes a deal with Harry to get some tritium, a rare mineral, in exchange for killing Spider-Man. "Get to him through Parker," Harry tells Otto.

And so Dr. Octopus kidnaps Mary Jane, Peter's ex. Peter's powers return and he suits up to fight the tentacled menace atop a runaway elevated train. Otto captures Spidey, who is weakened from stopping the train, and delivers him to Harry. Harry discovers that Spider-Man is his friend Peter and lets him go. Spider-Man confronts Doctor Octopus at the mad scientist's secret lab as a nuclear reaction threatens New York. Otto sacrifices himself to stop his experiment. Peter reveals his identity to Mary Jane. Harry discovers a cache of Goblin equipment and Mary Jane abandons young astronaut Jameson at the altar to be with Peter.

With New York endangered, and with new and improved action sequences and the best big-screen supervillain since Terence Stamp's Zod, the sequel fulfilled expectations and beyond. As Doc Ock, English stage and screen actor Alfred Molina is a compelling and charismatic antagonist, with a glint of madness in his eyes. The fight on the el train is a *tour de force* of superhero action moviemaking and superior to anything in the first film. Throughout the film, Raimi and his writers sprinkle elements from the comics and Easter eggs, basically treats for the fans. The Peter-quits-being-Spidey subplot was a callback to a 1967 story, "Spider-Man No More!," down to a shot mimicking an iconic cover by artist John Romita. A busker performs the theme from the 1967 animated *Spider-Man* TV series and Dr. Curt Connors, the alter ego of another iconic Spidey villain, the Lizard, make a cameo appearance.

Another huge hit for Sony, *Spider-Man 2* also pumped up Marvel brand equity, overshadowing the flawed but profitable like *Daredevil* and *Hulk*. But where was the publisher's chief rival, DC, and its sister studio Warner Bros., during this gold rush?

In plain terms, the old-school studio—it dated back to 1903—just couldn't get its superhero movie shit together. While the Warner–DC alliance was having some success on TV with series both live-action (*Lois & Clark*, *Smallville*) and animated (*Superman*, *The New Batman Adventures*, *Justice League*), its feature film efforts had hit a wall. After *Superman IV* and *Batman & Robin* torpedoed their respective franchises, multiple attempts at rebooting both fell prey to bureaucracy and indecision. And so it was with great disappointment that those hoping for a DC renaissance at the movie house instead got *Catwoman*.

A solo Catwoman venture had been in the offing since the early nineties, when *Batman Returns* screenwriter Daniel Waters wrote a screenplay in which Michelle Pfeiffer returns as Selina Kyle. In the proposed film, Selina goes undercover in a fictional Las Vegas–style city and battles the three fascistic superheroes who rule the town.[14]

For various reasons, the movie never got off the ground. But producer Denise Di Novi, who had worked with Tim Burton on the first two *Batman* films, continued to pursue a stand-alone *Catwoman* film until, some time around 2003, Warner—unable to commit to a *Batman* or *Superman* reboot—finally greenlit the project with Halle Berry in the lead. To direct, the studio hired Pitof, who had made *Vidocq*, a 2001 supernatural mystery. At some point, the decision was made to create an entirely new Catwoman, one unrelated to the Selina Kyle of *Batman Returns* or the comics. "We had a real challenge with *Catwoman* because fans are very into being true to the comics," Di Novi said. "The challenge that we had is that there are 12 versions of her."[15] She wasn't exaggerating, much.

In 2004's *Catwoman*, Patience Phillips is a timid graphic designer at a cosmetics company who discovers the dangerous side effects of a new beauty product, Beau-line. Her boss tries to kill her, but she is revived by feral cats. Upon awakening, she finds that she has enhanced night vision and agility (i.e., the ability to land on all fours) and heightened senses. She is also more assertive; after donning a tight, skimpy black leather outfit, she shuts down the 24-hour party across the street, steals a motorcycle and tries to stop her former employers, a husband-and-wife team, George and Laurel Hedare, from peddling more Beau-line.

The result looks like a generic nineties psychological thriller version of a superhero movie. As Laurel Hedare, Sharon Stone embodies both the flick's thriller and camp aspects: "Somebody help, it's Catwoman, she's shot George!" she shouts at some cops, as though Catwoman is a household name.

Benjamin Bratt plays Tom Lone, a police detective who is pursuing Patience romantically and her alter ego professionally. At least Catwoman rescues him, and not vice versa. The movie ends in the most clichéd way possible, with Laurel falling to her death as Catwoman tries to save her.

Although set in a modern, very un–Gotham-like city (played by Los Angeles, Vancouver and Winnipeg) and ostensibly unrelated to Warner Bros. original Bat franchise, the movie lifts its origin beat for beat from *Batman Returns*, but fleshes it out with references to the Egyptian cat god Bast and the rare feline breed Mau, hints of previous incarnations of Catwomen, and a crazy cat lady. There's nothing as silly as *Batman Returns*' Selina trashing her apartment, but Patience eats tuna out of cans. She also responds to catnip and hates rain. Beau-line is an echo of Joker's Smylex in the 1989 *Batman*. "If you stop using it, your face disintegrates," Catwoman tells Tom.

The press piled on in a way not seen for a superhero movie since *Batman and Robin*. Lost in the furor were the film's finer points, like the interracial romance between Patience and Detective Lone, played by half–Peruvian Bratt, and the fact that it was the first superhero movie with a woman of color in the lead.

For her efforts, Berry was rewarded with that year's Golden Raspberry for Worst Actress. At the ceremony, and with her Oscar for 2001's *Monster's Ball* in hand, the actress thanked the studio, her manager and agent, fellow actors, the French director ("I didn't know what he was saying, I'm sure it showed in my performance") and the writers ("all 20 of them").[16]

The spinoff bomb preceded another with a female superhero lead, *Elektra*. Released in early 2005, the film saw the return of Jennifer Garner as the ninja assassin left for dead in 2003's *Daredevil*. Here she is revived by Stick, a blind sensei with the benevolent ninja organization the Chaste, using the ancient art of kimagure. Years later, after being exiled from the Chaste, the assassin agrees to a job only to accidentally befriend her targets, a father and daughter. Elektra realizes that the Hand, the evil opposite of the Chaste, is behind her hiring. Elektra protects the girl, Abby, and her dad against Hand leader Kirigi and his minions Tattoo, Stone and Typhoid. After nearly dying in a fight with Kirigi and his crew, Elektra is again revived by Stick. She realizes that Kirigi is the one who killed her mother and challenges him to a fight. In the final contretemps, she destroys Kirigi's minions, impales Kirigi and throws him down a well. She resurrects Abby, killed in the melee, using kimagure.

The New Regency/Horseshoe Bay/Marvel Studios co-production received glowing reviews—for the heroine's outfit, designed by Lisa Tomczeszyn (*Spider-Man*, *Daredevil*). "No question, the film's best special effect is Ms. Garner, especially when she's in costume," wrote the *New York Times*' Manohla Dargis.[17]

Outside of the outfit, the rest of the movie was derided as ponderous, muddled and predictable. Continuous flashbacks to Elektra's mother's death kill any momentum. Unintentionally funny moments include all of Typhoid's appearances; just when everyone—movie characters and viewers alike—have forgotten about her, there she is again. Terence Stamp, Zod in *Superman II*, gives the kind of old-pro performance as Stick that makes everyone else look like amateurs. The script, by *X2*'s Zac Penn et al., takes the convenient and conventional path of tying the character's origin-inducing traumatic incident—the death of her mom—to the main villain.

New Regency had given director Rob Bowman a budget of $43 million, half that of *Daredevil*, and a tight shooting schedule that revolved around Garner's prior commitment to the TV series *Alias*. "I knew going into the project … that we weren't going to be able to make *Spider-Man*," said Bowman, whose TV credits included dozens of *X-Files* and three prior features. "We didn't have the time to make *Spider-Man*. We didn't have the time to make *Daredevil*!"[18]

A couple of months after *Elektra*'s release, Marvel Studios head (along with Jerry Calabrese) Avi Arad admitted to investors that the studio had rushed the production. "We will never do that again," he promised.[19]

In 2022, the movie's *Rotten Tomatoes* approval rating was 11 percent, putting *Elektra* two points ahead of *Catwoman* and *Supergirl*. None of the three made money, and all were victims of indifference, cluelessness and/or mishandling. Ten years would pass before a studio was willing to bet on another female-led big-budget superhero movie.

Chapter XII

Batman Begins, Superman Returns and the Silver Surfer Rises

"I want to tell the origin with a certain degree of gravity, and in a more grounded way than what has been done before."
—Christopher Nolan, director, *Batman Begins*[1]

"It was of course required that his take be different. It wasn't the nonsense that our Gotham City was, where we could be buried by a giant ice cream cone."
—Adam West on *Batman Begins*[2]

Christopher Nolan had made three arty, well-received thrillers when Warner Bros. hired the British director to breathe life into the rotting corpse of movie Batman.

In his 45-minute pitch to the studio, he preached the Richard Donner–Bryan Singer gospel: verisimilitude. "What I wanted to do is make the audience believe in the reality of this character," Nolan said. "Batman is unique among superheroes in presenting that opportunity. He really is just a guy that does a lot of push-ups."[3]

Warner had been trying to reboot its former cash cow since *Batman & Robin*. In 1999, new president Alan Horn made getting a new *Batman* up on screens a priority. A 2001 merger between parent company Time-Warner and AOL may have added pressure for the studio to come up with a successful franchise.[4] By the time Nolan got involved, in 2003, Warner Bros. could heat a Batcave with scripts for abandoned projects. These included *Batman Unchained*, the aborted sequel to 1997's *Batman & Robin*; *Batman: DarKnight*; *Batman Beyond*, a live-action adaptation of the popular *Batman: The Animated Series*; *Batman: Year One*, a Darren Aronofsky-directed adaptation of Frank Miller's 1987 take on Batman's early days; and *Batman vs. Superman: Asylum*, a Wolfgang Peterson-directed showdown written by Andrew Kevin Walker with a rewrite by *Batman & Robin*'s Akiva Goldsman.[5]

After abandoning those efforts, Warner turned to Nolan and screenwriter David S. Goyer. At this point in his superhero movie-writing career, Goyer had penned three *Blade* movies (and directed the third, 2004's *Trinity*) as well as *The Crow* sequel *City of Angels* (1996). "By the time [Nolan] and I came along, [Warner Bros.] knew they had to do something radical," the writer said. "And they were kind of desperate. I just remember when I got the job, everyone was saying, both online and amongst my friends, 'Oh, that'll never get made.'"[6]

Nolan and Goyer developed a story that delved more deeply into the character's origin than any previous live-action version. Outside of a few references in dialogue and scenes of Bruce Wayne's parents getting gunned down, neither the TV series nor the previous movies explored the interval between the Waynes' deaths and the start of Bruce's crimefighting career. Even in the comics, the first Batman origin only ran two pages.

Chapter XII. Batman Begins, Superman Returns and the Silver Surfer Rises

Nolan's *Batman Begins* attempted to fill in the gap. As the movie begins, Bruce is a boy who falls into a well and is swarmed by bats. Not long after, he is attending the opera with his parents when they are gunned down.

Years later, his parents' killer is granted parole for testifying against mob boss Carmine Falcone. After confronting Falcone, Bruce realizes he's going to have to toughen up if he's going to clean up Gotham City. To train, he gets himself incarcerated in a Southeast Asian prison and beats up desperate, savage inmates. Impressed by his one-man fight club, a mysterious stranger named Ducard invites him to level up with a group of ninjas called the League of Shadows. Bruce realizes that the League has nefarious aims and sets fire to their mountaintop headquarters, but saves Ducard.

Back in the city, Bruce learns that he is no longer in control of Wayne Enterprises. In the basement of WE's business tower, he meets with Lucius Fox, a genius inventor-engineer who has sunk untold millions of Wayne funds into designing and building equipment for urban warfare. His R&D includes a tank-like vehicle, the Tumbler, and (nipple-less) body armor.

Batman begins, but the new crimefighter's mettle is tested by the Scarecrow, aka psychiatrist Jonathan Crane, and Ducard. Ducard, it turns out, is really Ra's al Ghul, leader of the League of Shadows. Crane and Ra's are conspiring to "watch Gotham tear itself apart through fear" by dumping the former's fear serum into Gotham's water supply and then, via a "microwave emitter," releasing the toxin into the air. In the finale, Batman destroys the gadget and fights Ra's on the Gotham monorail.

Nolan's take not only resuscitated the franchise but earned the superhero genre a seat at the adults' table. The $150 million movie was more expensive, more modern-looking, and more cinematic than any costumed adventure flick that had come before. And this *Batman* movie finally got out of Gotham; the location shots, such as a glacier in Iceland, give it an epic scope. Gotham itself looks like an actual contemporary city. Painstaking practical effects are favored over CGI shortcuts. An A-list cast, including Michael Caine and Morgan Freeman, read the comic book–level dialogue as though it was David Mamet. Liam Neeson's Ra's al Ghul is a standard villain, but Cillian Murphy's Scarecrow has a welcome weirdness. Gary Oldman is the first James Gordon who doesn't look like he's pushing retirement age. And, as Bruce Wayne–Batman, serious British thespian Christian Bale brings a new level of believability to the role(s).

For all its pretensions, though, *Batman Begins* is still a *Batman* movie, and is no less preposterous than its predecessors. Why does the League want to destroy Gotham? Because it's become corrupt. But outside of Falcone, the film offers little evidence of this. The supposed romance between Bale's Bruce and Katie Holmes' crusading attorney Rachel Dawes is chemistry-free and even thinner than the playboy's insta-affair with Vicki Vale in the 1989 *Batman*. And the master criminals' plan is as complicated and pulp-y as Dr. Daka's scheme to steal Gotham's radium supply in the 1943 *Batman* serial.

Still, Nolan's was the Batman that 21st-century audiences wanted, and Warner-DC needed. The movies had finally caught up with the comics, and the Caped Crusader had become the Dark Knight.

• • •

After Spider-Man and the X-Men, the Fantastic Four was one of the properties that Marvel and its fans most wanted to see realized on the big screen. Nostalgia for the team that inaugurated the Marvel Universe was one reason, but so were the comics' cosmic scope and the team's family dynamics. There had already been a *Fantastic Four* movie—Roger Corman's 1994 attempt—but that had been made on a shoestring and never released.

After crushing that low-budget effort, Marvel Studios' Avi Arad and rights-holder Bernd Eichinger took the property to Fox. The movie went through several directors, including Peyton Reed. Reed, who was coming off 2000's *Bring It On* with Kirsten Dunst, proposed setting the movie in the sixties, the group's comic-book heyday, and ignoring the origin story completely. He spent a year developing the film before parting ways with the studio. "It felt like they sort of wanted to make a B-movie out of it," he said.[7]

Fox and Marvel hired Michael France (*Hulk*) to write a new script, and then Mark Frost (*Twin Peaks*) for rewrites. Both, as kids, had been fans of the comic. "I felt that the script needed to go right back to the roots of the comic," Frost said. "You had to have fun with this movie; it wasn't a dark movie like *Hulk*. This wasn't the sturm und drang of Peter Parker, or the angst of Bruce Banner."[8] The writers faced some of the same challenges as Craig J. Nevius and Kevin Rock when they scripted the Corman version—updating the Cold War origin and integrating arch-nemesis Doctor Doom into said origin. Simon Kinberg, who was working on the third *X-Men* movie for Fox, also turned in a rewrite.

Fox producer Ralph Winter (*X-Men* and *X2*) and Marvel began meeting with directors. Tim Story got the job.

"Tim had done *Barbershop*, a movie we at Marvel were big fans of," said Kevin Feige, Arad's second-in-command at Marvel. "There were a lot of characters in that film.... You liked these characters, and you also felt that they were real characters, not caricatures. So when we heard Tim was a big fan of this comic series—he knows almost every issue inside out—we just couldn't wait to meet with him.... [H]e came in and talked about the people as if they were four real people."[9]

Casting was difficult, Story said. "We didn't want to just throw in every obvious movie star that you read on internet lists!" Finally, after going through "*so* many people,"[10] he and the producers decided on Chris Evans as Johnny Storm, aka the Human Torch; Ioan Gruffudd as Reed Richards, aka Mr. Fantastic; Jessica Alba as the Invisible Woman, aka Susan Storm; Mike Chiklis as Ben Grimm, aka the Thing; and Julian McMahon as Victor von Doom, aka Doctor Doom. Evans and Welsh actor Gruffudd were in the early stages of their movie careers, while Alba, Chiklis and McMahon were known to TV audiences for their series *Dark Angel* (co-created by James Cameron), *The Shield* and *Nip/Tuck*, respectively. Chiklis went after the role and then spent hours donning "60 pounds" of prosthetics to play the rockiest Fantastic Four member.

"I was very insistent," he said. "I really wanted it to be a costume because I felt that if it was just a CGI, that you'd lose the humanity."[11]

Story and his cast were still filming when, in the fall of 2004, another film about a bickering superhero family opened.

"It left us with a certain nervous energy," Arad said of Pixar's hugely successful *The Incredibles*. But, he added, "it was such a good movie that I felt it would only help."[12]

Rumors spread that Fox and Story changed their flick as a result, a claim that the director disputed.

"We changed about one percent of our movie due to *The Incredibles*," Story said after the movie's release. "We had a scene in the beginning where the Thing shakes a cat out of a tree and it was extremely similar to the scene in *The Incredibles* so we took it out, that was it."[13]

Chapter XII. Batman Begins, Superman Returns and the Silver Surfer Rises

The 2005, Marvel-approved version of *Fantastic Four* starred (from left) Jessica Alba, Ioan Gruffudd, future Captain America Chris Evans and (wearing 60 pounds of prosthetics) Michael Chiklis. 20th Century–Fox.

The 2005 *Fantastic Four* begins with Reed convincing his old college friend Victor von Doom, now a space entrepreneur, into letting him use his, von Doom's, space station to test the evolutionary effects of "a high-energy cosmic storm" on biological samples. The experiment goes wrong and Reed, his friend Ben Grimm, genetic researcher Susan Storm, her kid brother Johnny, and Victor are exposed to the storm. After returning to Earth, the five discover that they've changed in various ways: Johnny can control fire and "flame on," Reed can stretch his body into impossible shapes, Susan can become invisible, Ben has developed a rock-like hide and is incredibly strong, and Victor's skin is turning metallic. Except for Johnny, who uses his newfound powers to pick up girls, and Victor, who is nuts, all are dismayed at the changes wrought by the cosmic storm.

Reed, Sue, Johnny and Ben leave Victor's Rocky Mountain compound and return to New York. There, Reed and Sue, who had been dating Victor, rekindle their romance and Reed builds a machine to replicate the storm and reverse its effects. Victor uses Reed's machine to return Ben to his natural state and to complete his own transformation. He then kidnaps Reed and fires a missile at Reed's lab in the Baxter Building. Johnny reroutes the missile, Sue frees Reed, Ben uses the machine to return to Thing form, Johnny returns and together, on the streets of their hometown, the fighting foursome defeat Doom.

Like *X-Men*, the $100 million movie is, in retrospect, modest. Story plays up the family dynamics and character moments over the action; Johnny parties like a hip-hop star with his first platinum record, Reed tinkers with machines, Sue tries to keep the boys from fighting (and never becomes a damsel in distress) and the Thing is appropriately gruff and tortured. Like the X-Men, the Fantastic Four are not burdened with secret identities that drive contrived plot machinations. Doom wants only to destroy the team and win his lady back. World conquest, or even just the destruction of a New York borough, can wait. And the movie is barely more than 90 minutes.

Obviously made by people with affection for the source material, *Fantastic Four* wasn't quite the effects-studded, kick-ass cosmic adventure fans might have hoped for, but it was far from an embarrassment and did well enough for Fox to greenlight a sequel. Story became the first African-American to direct a major big-budget superhero movie.

Fox's next Marvel movie was far from modest. Released in May 2006, the $210 million *X-Men: The Last Stand*, or *X3*, was the most expensive film ever made at the time of its release. It combined two stories from the comics, one about a cure for mutancy and another in which Jean Grey, unable to control her powers, transforms into the destructive entity Dark Phoenix. The film also included a plethora of mutants new to movie audiences. The Beast, a scientist with super-strength and ape-like agility, and Angel, a winged rich kid, came from the comic's original sixties run. Kitty Pryde, who has the ability to phase through walls, was a late-seventies addition to the team. New villains were Juggernaut, who wears a stone helmet and crashes through walls, and Arclight, who generates shock waves. Nightcrawler, introduced in *X2*, is absent, gone the way of other one-offs, like Toad, but Professor X, Storm, Iceman, Rogue, Mystique and Colossus all have supporting roles. Cyclops is killed off early. Moira MacTaggert, a recurring scientist in the comics, makes a brief appearance. A glimpse of the head of a Sentinel, one of an army of giant mutant-destroying robots, and a scene in the Danger Room, the X-Men's training center, as well as blink-and-you'll-miss-them cameos by deep-cut mutants, are among early examples of superhero-movie fan service. The movie's most spectacular set-piece is a scene in which returning villain Magneto mentally moves the Golden Gate Bridge so that he and his cohort don't have to take a ferry to Alcatraz.

Bryan Singer, director of the first two, sat this one out. Brett Ratner, the man behind the *Rush Hour* action-comedy franchise, took over; Zak Penn (*X2*) and Simon Kinberg (*Fantastic Four*) contributed the script.

With an abundance of characters and subplots, *X3* generated mixed reviews and was generally considered a disappointment. The biggest complaints came from fans who were dismayed to see the Dark Phoenix Saga, one of Marvel's most famous storylines, playing second fiddle to another plot. But the movie went on to become the franchise's top earner, until it was unseated eight years later by a sequel to a reboot.

Less than two months after *Last Stand* opened, Warner released the movie for which Singer had left the X-franchise: *Superman Returns*.

Following his success on *X-Men*, Singer's interest had sparked the reboot into production. Since regaining the rights from the Salkinds in 1993, Warner Bros. had been considering various Superman film projects. Prior to Singer's involvement, the studio had been eyeing *Superman: Flyby*, a retelling of the hero's origin written by J.J. Abrams. But Singer, a fan of Richard Donner's original, had another take in mind, one in which Superman returns to Earth long after the events of *Superman II*, as though Gus Gorman, Lorelei Ambrosia and Nuclear Man never happened. Singer developed the story with screenwriters Michael Dougherty and Dan Harris, and cast an unknown, Brandon Routh, in the lead. The result was a mélange of homage, reboot and sequel.

The movie begins with the hero arriving back on Earth after five years in space,

Chapter XII. Batman Begins, Superman Returns and the Silver Surfer Rises

where he's been searching for remnants of his home planet Krypton. He reunites with his mom and, as Clark Kent, returns to work at *The Daily Planet*. Lois Lane, he learns, is now engaged to Richard White, reporter, seaplane pilot *and* nephew of *Daily Planet* publisher Perry White. And she has her Pulitzer!

Other things, though, have remained the same. Criminal mastermind Lex Luthor is still on the loose and scheming to get richer and more powerful through another outlandish real estate scheme, this one involving the theft and use of yet another Kryptonian crystal, one that will allow him to create his own continent. He has another moll, Kitty, whom he disdains nearly as much as he did Miss Teschmacher—perhaps more, considering that he puts her in mortal danger in a runaway car to distract Superman. Again, Lex decides that the only thing that stands between him and his plan is Superman. Again, he waltzes into Superman's Arctic fortress as though it were Macy's. Again, Superman saves Lois. And again. Again, Lois puts other lives in danger—including her own son's.

But the movie lacks the charm of the first, or even second *Superman*, and Singer's approach is disorienting. As Clark, Routh has Christopher Reeve's fumbling mannerisms down pat, and he looks the part of the superhero, but his performance is mainly a serviceable imitation. Twenty-three-year-old Kate Bosworth makes no sense as Lois, considering that the reporter has supposedly been pining over Superman for five years; Margot Kidder was 30 when she made the original. Bosworth also lacks Kidder's edge. A scene that tries to ape the original's rooftop patio rendezvous between Lois and Superman falls flat due to the leads' utter lack of chemistry. As Lex, Kevin Spacey is more menacing than Gene Hackman but lacks the actor's affable oiliness. For those who care about such things, i.e., fans, the movie commits the most egregious offense against canon yet by giving Superman and Lois a super-son.

Superman Returns does one thing really well, though. With its state-of-the-art CGI, the film honors and improves upon the sense of wonder from Donner's film. This Superman really does look like he can fly, and a scene in which he stops a plane from crashing into a baseball field by holding it up by its nose is a showstopper.

More moments like this might have saved the film, which failed to endear itself to moviegoers, critics or fans. Apparently, most people didn't miss Superman, or Donner's version, as much as Singer did. Or maybe they just wanted a better *Superman* movie.

While Warner Bros. was trying to relaunch its biggest DC properties, other studios were dipping into Marvel's second- and third-tier properties. Hence, Sony's *Ghost Rider*.

Created by Marvel editor-in-chief Roy Thomas, writer Gary Friedrich and artist Mike Ploog, Ghost Rider was a stunt-cyclist-turned-demon with a flaming skull for a head. His birth was a result of the time-honored comics tradition of jumping on any and every passing pop-culture trend and, in 1972, few fads were bigger than the stunts of real-life daredevil Evel Knievel.

At the behest of Marvel's Avi Arad, a Harley Davidson enthusiast, Sony okayed a movie version. The studio hired *Daredevil*'s Mark Steven Johnson to write and direct; Nicolas Cage, who had come close to playing Superman in a proposed *Superman Lives* movie (to be directed by Tim Burton) in the late nineties, was already in the driver's seat. "This character is absurd," said the actor, a comics fan who remembered buying the first issue of *Ghost Rider* when he was seven. "He's an absurdist character and I think that's a good thing because that gives me a chance to bring comedy to it as well."[14]

There was a script, by *Batman Begins*' David S. Goyer. Johnson set about making

Goyer's R-rated screenplay palatable to a general audience. He also wanted to stay true to the comic while simplifying the character's origin:

> *Ghost Rider* [the comic] has some great stories and an amazing look which is what attracted me to it, but it's also very flawed in some ways. The origin of it has been very mixed up and they keep trying to change it and update it and it got more and more confusing until no one knew what to make of it.... I have to make things simple so that people can understand what the hell is going on.[15]

Prior to the movie's release, the fan press got wind of some of the changes and responded in character, i.e., not well.

"That's their identity," Cage said. "You can't tell them to let it go. That's what gives them something to get excited about. Even if it means they don't want to get excited about the movie that makes them excited. They have to complain about something which is part of the fun of being a comic book fan. No, complain all you want and have it. Go see it and then complain some more if you want."[16]

Hitting theaters in February 2007, the horror-action-comedy begins with a flashback, establishing that the Ghost Rider has been around for centuries, meting out justice in various human guises. The latest is Johnny Blaze, a famous Knievel-esque stunt-rider who makes a deal with Mephistopheles to save his father, but things don't go quite as he'd hoped. Nonetheless, he must hold up his end by defeating Blackheart, the demon's son. With the help of three fallen angels, Blackheart is searching for a contract that will allow the bearer to unleash Hell on Earth. As Ghost Rider, Johnny defeats the angels and their leader and retrieves the contract. When he refuses to give the contract to Mephistopheles, the demon curses him to spend the rest of his life as the Ghost Rider.

"The film is a work of genius," wrote *Wired*'s Annalee Newitz, "full of burning skulls and 'Satanize my ride' cycles, while Nicolas Cage's Ghost Rider winningly exudes cheesiness mixed with full-bore fanboy zoom. This movie is stupid in the best possible way."[17] The review was titled "10 Reasons Why *Ghost Rider* Kicks Your Burning Ass."

But Newitz was an outlier, and most critics came up with many reasons why the movie did not kick their burning asses: cheesy dialogue, an uncharacteristically toned-down Cage, and the deal-with-the-Devil machinations of its plot. Nevertheless, moviegoers placed the movie at #1 for two weekends in a row, practically guaranteeing a sequel.

• • •

With a returning director and cast, and coming after what many regarded as the best superhero movie up until that time, *Spider-Man 3* was as burdened with responsibility as Peter Parker on one of Aunt May's worst days.

Following *Spider-Man 2*, Sam Raimi set to work on the screenplay with his brother Ivan and returning scripter Alvin Sargent. They brought back the Green Goblin, though this time with Norman's son Harry (James Franco) donning the costume, and added another baddie, Flint Marko, aka the Sandman. In the comics, Flint gains his powers after coming into contact with sand that has been irradiated by an experimental reactor.

As Avi Arad pointed out to the director, the Goblin and the Sandman were old-school villains. Why not, suggested Arad—who had left Marvel in 2006 but was still attached to the Spider-Man franchise as an independent producer—give some screentime to a more contemporary bad guy? And he had just the character in mind, an antihero who had started out as alien black goo: Venom. Raimi recalled the producer saying, "Sam, listen, you are so aware of all of these seventies villains, but you really need to incorporate Venom into this story because the fans really love Venom and don't be so selfish with villains that you know and love." And Raimi said, "Okay."[18]

The inky symbiote began inhabiting hosts in 1984, with Peter Parker as his first victim. Four years later, it took over reporter Eddie Brock. The creature eventually took on a personality of its own.

Spider-Man 3 wedges in all three villains—Sandman, the Goblin, and Venom— as well as a love triangle between Peter, Mary Jane and new girl Gwen Stacy. The latter, an early romantic interest from the comics, is a fellow student in Peter's physics class at Columbia. She's also the daughter of an NYPD captain, George Stacy.

Instead of putting Peter through the wringer, as in *Spider-Man 2*, the threequel begins with a contented hero about to propose to MJ. But things go wrong after MJ's opening night in a Broadway musical. In Central Park after the show, Peter and MJ are contemplating their future when a meteorite lands nearby. An inky black special effect gloms onto Peter's scooter. Soon after, Harry attacks Peter with new, improved Goblin tech, including pumpkin bombs. ("I hate those things," mutters Peter.) Harry is convinced that Spider-Man killed his father. After an airborne battle, Peter knocks Harry off his glider and onto the street below.

Meanwhile, petty criminal Flint Marko has escaped Rikers Island. He has a sick daughter whom he wants to help. But, running from the law, he winds up in a particle physics facility and falls into a sand pit that houses an experimental particle accelerator just as the facility scientists turn on the machine. Trapped in the pit, he survives "demolecularization" to find that he can now transform into and control sand.

At the hospital, Harry wakes up with amnesia. Then, in a downtown office tower, 62 stories above the street, an out-of-control crane smashes into the room where Peter's classmate Gwen is modeling. Spider-Man prevents her from falling to her death. At a public celebration, Spider-Man is awarded a key to the city for saving Gwen. Much to MJ's chagrin, the superhero repeats his patented upside-down kiss thing with the new girl. MJ is doubly unhappy because she received a bad review and the musical's producers have fired her.

Marko, in the form of a sandstorm, blows through the ceremony on his way to an armored truck. Spidey gives chase but Marko escapes. "Where do all these guys come from?" the hero wonders.

Capt. Stacy informs Aunt May and Peter that it was Flint who killed Ben Parker, and not the car-jacker Spidey apprehended after the murder. Later, Peter is at home in his apartment, lying in bed in his Spidey suit. The alien substance from the meteorite infects the suit, turning it black.

Newly Venomized, Spider-Man pursues Sandman into a subway tunnel and turns him into mud. Peter realizes that he is infected and that he is acting strangely. After deducing that loud sounds annoy his alien invader, Peter uses the church's bell to drive it out of him. Unfortunately, new Bugle photog Eddie Brock happens to be in the church at the same time, and Venom finds a new host.

The new Venom-Brock alliance teams up with a dried-off Sandman to defeat Spider-Man. The villains lure their enemy to a construction site where they're holding MJ hostage. Harry learns that Peter didn't kill his father and, as the Green Goblin, comes to Spider-Man's rescue. Harry sacrifices himself to save Peter; like his father, Harry is impaled by his glider. Peter defeats Venom-Brock and forgives Marko.

The movie excels in its action scenes and special effects, particularly the Sandman

CGI, and the black Spider-suit looks cool. Attentive fans could rejoice in hearing the theme from the sixties *Spider-Man* animated series played by a brass band and seeing Flint in his trademark black-and-green-striped T-shirt, a piece of attire that screams "ex-con on the run from the law" today as much as it did when the character first popped out of the Marvel sandbox. Dylan Baker makes his second appearance as Dr. Curt Connors, aka the Lizard.

In every other way, though, Raimi's third *Spider-Man* is a letdown. Overstuffed with villains and subplots, full of outrageous coincidences and Mack truck–sized plot holes, it's a cobweb in a windstorm. The troubled romance between Peter and MJ is forced, and Gwen (Bryce Dallas Howard) is never more than a plot device. Revealing that Marko is the "real" killer (until next time) of Uncle Ben is one visit to the origin well too many. Venom brings out the worst in its hosts, often to laughable effect. A sequence in which a Venom-ized Peter struts down Manhattan streets, performs a lewd, hip-thrusting dance outside of a clothing store, and then upstages MJ at the restaurant where she serves (and sings), is a love-it-or-hate-it sequence on a par with the playground pas de deux in *Daredevil*.

A May 2007 release, *Spider-Man 3* became the highest-grossing in the series.

But Raimi wasn't satisfied with the movie, and bowed out of a fourth after finding himself unable to crack a story that would justify it. That seemed to suit Sony; the studio had already decided that it was time for a reboot.

Where *Spider-Man 3* tried to modernize the franchise with a more recent villain, *Fantastic Four: The Rise of the Silver Surfer* continued to mine the wealth of sixties-era Marvel material. For the sequel to 2005's *Fantastic Four*, returning director Tim Story and the screenwriters—including the first movie's Mark Frost and *Simpsons* vet Don Payne—looked to two iconic storylines from the mid-sixties, the pinnacle period of Stan Lee and Jack Kirby's historic 100-issue run on the title.

"The Wedding of Sue and Reed" was a 1965 mega-event (in *Fantastic Four Annual* # 3) wherein just about every one of the Fantastic Four's supervillains crash the party. It was played mostly for laughs. Not so 1966's "The Galactus Trilogy," in which the quartet encounters planet-devouring entity Galactus and his herald, a silver alien who wields "the power cosmic" and cruises the spaceways on a surfboard while pondering the meaning of life, the vastness of the universe and the shortcomings of humanity. The Silver Surfer, as he was dubbed, captured readers' imaginations, and went on to guest-star in and headline various series over the decades.

In 2007's *Rise of the Silver Surfer*, Reed and Sue are about to tie the knot when a mysterious flying silver object threatens the wedding. Johnny pursues it and realizes it's humanoid, but the encounter destabilizes his powers.

In the European kingdom of Latveria, Victor von Doom tries to make a deal with the alien, but fails. Reed realizes that the alien is readying Earth for destruction. At the behest of the U.S. Army, the Fantastic Four agree to work with their old enemy to capture the new threat. They succeed and the army imprisons the silver-skinned being. Doom steals the prisoner's cosmic-powered surfboard, which is also the beacon for the herald's boss, Galactus. The Fantastic Four set the Surfer free and they corner Doom in Shanghai. Absorbing the powers of the entire team, Johnny defeats Doom. The Surfer regains control of his board, flies into Galactus and blows himself up, saving the planet. In Japan, Reed and Sue marry. In the final scene, the Surfer, floating in space, revives.

Like its predecessor, and unlike most superhero movies of the time (or since), *Rise*

Chapter XII. Batman Begins, Superman Returns and the Silver Surfer Rises

is a briskly paced adventure that clocks in at a reasonable 90 minutes. Story, the writers and the cast again try to capture the lighthearted tone of Lee and Kirby's work without getting too hung up on the superheroics. For special effects thrills, though, the early sequence in which the Human Torch pursues the Silver Surfer between New York skyscrapers was, as Grant Morrison writes, "a genuine triumph that, for the first time, came close to the purity of Jack Kirby's vision."[19] And the Surfer—Doug Jones (Abe Sapien in 2004's *Hellboy*) in a gray-silver motion-capture suit with a thick coating of CGI, with Laurence Fishburne adding the voice—is another visual triumph. The same cannot be said for Galactus, who is depicted as a cloud or, as one reddit user described the apocalyptic menace, "a space fart" (@KiraHead, 2019). But then, Kirby's original conception of a giant humanoid in a purple kilt and deer-antler helmet may not have worked on-screen either.

The sequel's fizziness was held against it. After the self-seriousness of Fox's *X-Men* movies and *Batman Begins* and the balance of action, comedy and romance in the first two *Spider-Man* movies, *Rise* turned off reviewers and moviegoers. The more expensive sequel earned less than its predecessor, and Fox filed the Fantastic Four under "Reboot—maybe?" It does bear the distinction, for whatever its worth, of being the last Marvel-based movie released before the Mother Ship began beaming its own transmissions down to planet Earth.

Chapter XIII

The Year Marvel Broke

> "We made choices and we believed in what we were doing. We didn't know with certainty what would work and what wouldn't work. If we were wrong, that would have been the end of it. [Marvel] could've been a one-off studio if it didn't work. But—in a way—we didn't have anything to lose at that point so it allowed us to just go with our instincts."
> —Marvel Studios president Kevin Feige[1]

In November 2005, Marvel Studios announced its first production: *Iron Man*.

"We didn't have Spider-Man," recalled the company's Kevin Feige. "We didn't have Fantastic Four. [We had] 'the B-list characters'—that was the *L.A. Times* or somebody's headline. I never really thought that because I knew that Iron Man was really cool and Hulk was, arguably, next to Spider-Man, the biggest character we had."[2]

Earlier in the year, when Marvel first announced it was going into the feature film business, Ol' Shellhead wasn't even on the original slate. Captain America, Doctor Strange and the Avengers were mentioned, as were other sixties-era characters Ant-Man, Black Panther, Hawkeye and Nick Fury, seventies martial arts hero Shang-Chi and two eighties-era teams, the duo Cloak and Dagger and the sibling quartet Power Pack. But when New Line's rights to Iron Man went up for grabs, Marvel pounced. "For the first time, with Iron Man at New Line, Marvel said, 'No, we're not extending,'" Feige said.[3] (Former studio head Avi Arad said in 2014 that he "had a very tough time getting Iron Man back from New Line, but we got it back. I always loved Iron Man."[4])

Iron Man debuted in a 1963 issue of Marvel's anthology title *Tales of Suspense*. As envisioned by Lee and Kirby, along with writer (and younger brother of Stan Lee, née Lieber) Larry Lieber and artist Don Heck, the superhero was a Cold War invention: an international playboy–arms dealer named Tony Stark who builds a hi-tech suit of armor to fight Commies and supervillains. Early adversaries included the Mandarin, a Yellow Peril caricature, as well as future heroes/Avengers Black Widow and Hawkeye. Iron Man was also a founding member of The Avengers. He received his own title in 1968, but was another Marvel also-ran until a 1979 storyline, "Demon in a Bottle," waxed his armor in readers' eyes; the storyline depicted the hero's struggle with alcoholism. Two more arcs in the mid-oughts, Warren Ellis and Adi Granov's "Extremis" and the multi-title crossover "Civil War," kicked him up a few notches in fan approval.

The studio's decision to make its own movies followed a deal with brokerage firm Merrill Lynch. Arad and Feige had grown frustrated watching others squander the company's IP in sub-par efforts like 2004's *The Punisher* and 2005's *Man-Thing*, both the result of Marvel's 15-character agreement with Artisan Entertainment in 2000. (The poorly reviewed *Man-Thing*, released in 2005, went straight to cable in the U.S., though it managed to scrape together $1 million in international markets.)

In return for a loan of $525 million, the company put up ten characters as collateral. Going forward, responsibility for glory or for thoroughly mucking things up would fall squarely on the shoulders of the now full-fledged production studio.

The move was "scary" for some of his colleagues, said Arad, then a co-head of the studio. "None of them was involved in entertainment, so they just were terrified of the idea."[5] At the time, Marvel Studios consisted of some offices in a Toy Biz subsidiary that made kites in Santa Monica and a few employees, including Arad and Kevin Feige.

Feige had been working as Lauren Shuler Donner's assistant on *X-Men* when Arad noticed the 27-year-old go-getter. "Sometimes I couldn't make it to set," Arad said. "I had to run a company, too, so I'd call him and say, 'What did you see there?' and he'd tell me, like, 'I think the hair is not right'.... I just knew he was a star."[6]

Feige, a USC film school grad and *Star Wars* fan, realized early on that there was gold to be mined in those thousands upon thousands of pages of Marvel comic books. He said in a 2014 profile, "I would hear people, other executives, struggling over a character point, or struggling over how to make a connection, or struggling over how to give even surface-level depth to an action scene or to a character. I'd be sitting there reading the comics going, 'Look at this. Just do this. This is incredible.'"[7]

The Merrill Lynch deal was put together by David Maisel, who was enlisted by Arad to join Marvel Studios as chief operating officer in 2003. Maisel had worked at Disney, which knew a thing or two about licensing and franchises. According to *The Hollywood Reporter*, Maisel met with Arad and Arad's partner Ike Perlmutter to convince them that Marvel could negotiate a better share than the five percent licensing fee it was getting from studios.[8]

Marvel could have launched with a movie starring a character who was more familiar to the public. Shortly after getting the rights to Iron Man, Maisel, Arad or both made a deal with Universal for the Hulk. Universal would retain the rights, but Marvel could make at least one Hulk movie and pay Universal to distribute. (Marvel had a six-picture distribution deal with Paramount.) This applied only to features where the Hulk was the central character, though; Marvel owed Universal nothing if he appeared in, say, an Avengers flick.

The company put both *Iron Man* and what would become *The Incredible Hulk* into production, but studio hearts were with the underdog. "We wanted to get Iron Man to work," Feige said. "We thought it could because of the character of Tony Stark, and because it was a mechanical suit. No super-powers. We loved the idea of a techno Tom Clancy hero."[9]

Five months into *Iron Man*, the studio committed to a director. Jon Favreau had written and starred in the 1996 indie feature *Swingers* and directed the 2003 hit *Elf*. Feige said, "I was so impressed with *Elf*, which could simply have been a silly comedy but had so much heart and depth to it. It has actually great action sequences in it."[10]

Favreau had also made the 2005 film *Zathura: A Space Adventure* which, though not a hit, mixed CGI, practical effects and motion-control models. And he was a familiar in the Marvel universe for his role as Matt Murdock's friend Franklin "Foggy" Nelson in 2003's *Daredevil*. Favreau enjoyed working on that movie and kept in touch with Arad. "Eventually he brought me in to talk about *The Incredible Hulk* and *Iron Man*. Hulk, to me, didn't have it. I loved the TV show growing up, but Ang Lee's film had been done not that many years before, and I didn't really trust CGI that much back then. Iron Man, however, seemed kind of cool.... Tony was a conflicted person, so it was an opportunity to tell a complex story."[11]

With Favreau's hiring came the addition of several others who would become instrumental in growing the studio, including editor Dan Lebental, executive producer Louis D'Esposito and production assistant Brad Winderbaum. In turn, Winderbaum brought in casting director Sarah Finn and visual effects producer Victoria Alonso.

Favreau took up the familiar cry of verisimilitude, although his watchword was "plausibility." He placed a sign with the word above his door "so that everybody who came in for a meeting would have to read that and remember that that was the tone of our film."[12]

Their leading man was as big a gamble as the titular hero: Robert Downey, Jr., had first tasted stardom in quintessentially eighties movies like *Less Than Zero*, based on a Bret Easton Ellis novel about dissolute L.A. rich kids. He had a breakout role as the title character in 1992's *Chaplin*, but the actor's ensuing and well-publicized struggle with substance abuse made him a risky proposition.

By the mid-2000s, however, he was on the redemption track. Favreau caught him in the well-received noir-comedy *Kiss Kiss Bang Bang*, written and directed by another comeback kid, Shane Black (*Lethal Weapon*). The performance, the actor said, was his "calling card to *Iron Man*."[13]

Downey fought for the role. He said in 2019,

> I took a meeting at Marvel. And then I was very pushy, to be honest, which is not really in my nature. But I just had a sneaking suspicion that I had nothing to lose. I decided to take it more seriously than I'd ever taken anything. I felt confident, and then I was told that the meeting went well but I wouldn't put too much on it, it's probably not going to go your way. I refused to let go of it.[14]

Getting approval for the hard-to-insure Downey was "the hardest and most important challenge that I faced," Favreau said. "Once Robert was cast, everything else was much easier relative to that because I knew I was going to have a good movie."[15]

For once, the fan community embraced a casting selection. "Brace yourselves for what happens when someone makes the right choice for once," wrote *Ain't It Cool News* contributor Moriarty. "I can't even express how much I love that choice."[16]

For some fans, the actor's well-documented problems were tailor-made for Tony the tippler. "[Stark] was built up and torn down many times," wrote Rob McWorley of comics2film.com. "I think when people heard Robert Downey was going to play the part, there was actually a big relief."[17]

Following Downey, Marvel recruited two more high-profile actors, Jeff Bridges as Obadiah Stane, Tony Stark's mentor, and Gwyneth Paltrow as Pepper Potts, Tony's long-suffering assistant and love interest. Attitudes about playing a foil to someone in tights and a cape (or armor in this case) had changed. Favreau said, "Fortunately, in my generation there's enough people who love Marvel that it doesn't just feel like what it must have felt like when Alec Guinness was offered Obi-Wan Kenobi, you know, and it was like, 'What is this?' Yeah, and you don't trust it until it's over."[18]

Previous producers and directors had mostly paid lip service to comics writers and artists, either through "consulting" gigs, on-screen acknowledgment or PR name-dropping. When New Line had Iron Man, the studio brought in three writers to talk on camera about the character. They were all screenwriters.[19] Favreau invited *Iron Man* comics writers and artists to the Playa Vista set during pre-production.

Chapter XIII. The Year Marvel Broke

Even the fans agreed that Robert Downey, Jr., was the right Iron Man for the debut offering from Marvel Studios in 2008. Marvel Studios.

"The fact that this brain trust was even created showed such intense respect for the character and its legacy," wrote Brian Michael Bendis on his message board. Bendis had been penning Iron Man's adventures with the Avengers since 2004. "A half hour into the meeting I was so happy to be in the room I was going to burst. Comic creators not being treated like the second class porn peddlars [sic] we used to be treated like but actual writers. It was very cool."[20] Feige later asked Bendis to help write the movie's post-credits scene—the first in what would become a Marvel signature.

Favreau took pains to capture the look of the comics, even returning to the character's original boxy armor for the movie's first act. For Tony's sleeker, more modern suits, he consulted fan-favorite *Iron Man* artist Adi Granov.

Still, as production loomed, something was wrong.

Early on, Marvel had hired Hawk Ostby and Mark Fergus (*Children of Men*) to write a parallel screenplay to one that was already in development. Commissioning two screenplays at a time was becoming commonplace for studios attempting to engineer blockbusters. According to Ostby, Favreau then "cherry-picked and built a script out of the two versions and that became the interim version."[21]

Toward the end of 2006, a few months before filming was to begin, the villain—an early and outdated foe from the comics called the Mandarin—had yet to be cast. Enthusiasm over the script was at a low ebb. A cost-cutting Maisel asked if they could drop the villain and, at a meeting in the new year, Favreau suggested making Stark Industries' second-in-command Obadiah Stane the bad guy.[22] Ostby and Fergus incorporated the change.

They continued writing as production began. "They had no script, man," Bridges said in 2009. "They had an outline. We would show up for big scenes every day and we wouldn't know what we were going to say. We would have to go into our trailer and work on this scene and call up writers on the phone, 'You got any ideas?' Meanwhile the crew is tapping their foot on the stage waiting for us to come on."[23]

"It's sort of the dirty secret about these superhero films that the script is unfortunately the last thing to get the proper attention," Favreau said.[24]

The actors, Downey in particular, improvised. One of his ad-libs was Tony Stark's last-minute confession, "I am Iron Man."[25] It stayed, even though (in the comics) Tony had maintained his secret identity for decades.

Against all odds—and they were considerable—the movie turned out better than anyone could have hoped. Despite its being the studio's first time at bat, despite the ragtag nature of the script, despite everything that could have gone wrong (and despite the things that did), *Iron Man* came together in a way that won over fans, critics and the public.

Tony Stark is on his way to a meeting with arms buyers in Afghanistan when he and his crew, including buddy Lieutenant Colonel James "Rhodey" Rhodes, are attacked. A bomb, one of Tony's own, explodes near him. He awakens in a cave with another prisoner, Dr. Ho Yinsen, who explains that he's placed an electromagnet next to Tony's heart to stop shrapnel from entering it. Ho explains that they have been captured by a thousand-year-old criminal organization, the Ten Rings. Raza, the gang's leader, demands that Tony build him a missile of the kind that Tony came to sell. Instead, Tony makes an "arc reactor" (via patented Stark tech) to power the electromagnet and a suit of armor and escapes, fighting off the Ten Rings before flying away and crashing the suit in the desert. Rhodey finds his friend and takes him home. After recovering, Tony announces that Stark Industries will no longer make and sell arms. Company manager Obadiah Stane warns him about the company's sinking IPO. "We're iron mongers, Tony," Obadiah reminds him.

Tony returns to the lab to refine his armor. Hearing that the Ten Rings is destroying Yinsen's home village, he flies back to Afghanistan to fight the terrorists. Meanwhile, Obadiah has been colluding with the Ten Rings, selling them arms in exchange for the remnants of Tony's first suit. Pepper figures out Obadiah's scheme but is too late to stop him from paralyzing her boss and removing the arc reactor from his chest. They save Tony by replacing it with the original prototype. Tony dons the Iron Man armor and confronts Stane in a battle over the Stark Industries building. Unable to defeat Stane and his more powerful armor, Tony instructs Pepper to overload the arc reactor that powers the building. The resulting electrical surge short-circuits Stane's suit. At another press conference, Tony announces that he is Iron Man.

Several things mark *Iron Man* as a different kind of superhero movie. The opening needle-drop of AC/DC's "Back in Black" announces that this is a film with a rock'n'roll heart, not concerned with corporate synergy (see: *Batman* + Prince; *Spider-Man* + Macy Gray) or musical trends (just about any nineties superhero flick). The Afghanistan setting and references to everyday pop culture totems like *Maxim* and *Forbes* ground it in the "real" world. Downey's arrogant, cavalier Tony is more flawed than any previous superhero alter ego. As Tony and Pepper, Downey and Paltrow imbue the action flick with screwball comedy energy.

And *Iron Man* is *plausible* to a degree that many other superhero movies hadn't attempted. If one could accept the tech and the attendant Marvel pseudoscience, then just about everything that happens makes sense on a human and narrative level.

Chapter XIII. The Year Marvel Broke

Considering the assaults on logic that had come before (not to repeat any names), this was revolutionary.

Most obviously, at least to comic book fans, was that *Iron Man* was made by people *who got it*. The movie revealed nearly every previous superhero attempt for what it was: a series of compromises by people with competing interests and ideas and, often, little or no familiarity with the source material. This wasn't Universal's *Iron Man* or Sony's or Fox's. This was Marvel's.

"We ended up landing a tone with *Iron Man* that became the formula moving forward," Favreau later said. "You want to mix great casting, stay true to the characters, a combined universe that would allow cross-pollination. And have humor and adherence to canon."[26]

As for that combined universe, the movie makes tentative, and some might say presumptuous, steps in world-building. It introduces Marvel Comics concepts and characters like the Ten Rings, War Machine and J.A.R.V.I.S. (a human in the comics, here Tony's AI program). It also introduces the character who would be the connective tissue in the studio's evolving plans.

"I'm here to talk to you about the Avengers initiative," S.H.I.E.L.D. head Nick Fury tells Tony in an end-credits scene, setting the table for the most profitable interconnected movie universe in history.

"I remember being very excited that the movie worked well enough that we could do this," Feige said over a decade later. "'We're gonna do the plan! This is going to be a big deal.' And the press did not treat it like a big deal. It was a footnote to an article about the success of the *Iron Man* opening weekend. And I went, 'Oh, I guess people don't get it yet.'"[27] Four days after *Iron Man* opened, Marvel announced production on five more movies, including a sequel, *Thor*, *The First Avenger: Captain America* (as it was originally titled), *The Avengers* and *Ant-Man*.

And then the studio almost blew it.

Production on *The Incredible Hulk* began soon after Marvel made its deal with Universal in January 2006. Working with producer Gale Anne Hurd (Ang Lee's *Hulk*, *The Punisher*), the studio hired Zak Penn to write a script. Penn, whose credits include *X2* and *Elektra*, had written an earlier Hulk script for Universal. It was decided that, instead of a reboot, the movie would pick up where the 2003 version left off.

"One thing we absolutely knew for certain was that we didn't want to start with Bruce Banner and how he becomes the Hulk," Hurd said.[28]

To ensure an approach different from Lee's, Marvel wanted an action director. Feige had been impressed by Louis Leterrier's *Unleashed*, a 2005 thriller with martial arts star Jet Li. "It was both poignant and action-packed," the Marvel VP said.[29]

With uncertainty around the prospects for *Iron Man*, which was then still in production stage, Marvel decision-makers on the East Coast were wary of taking more risks with its better-known property. Leterrier liked Mark Ruffalo for Bruce Banner, but Marvel wanted someone "more famous."[30] Edward Norton agreed on condition that he could be involved in all aspects of the production, including the script.

"To be honest, that was the only way I was going to do it," he said. Nominated for a Best Actor Oscar for *American History X* (1998), Norton was also a producer and director. "Over the years, I've had people come at me with comic book franchise films or things like that and I felt they were just woefully under-realized as scripts."[31]

As filming commenced, Norton and Leterrier and Marvel butted heads; actor and director wanted a "more nuanced" Hulk but the studio, perhaps recalling Lee's more-talky, less-smashy version, wanted a leaner, meaner green machine.[32] In the end, the studio got its way. Several scenes that Norton had contributed were cut.

Picking up after the events of 2003's *Hulk*, the movie begins with Bruce Banner living in the favelas of Rio de Janeiro, where he works at a bottling plant. In his off hours, he obsesses over a cure for his condition and practices yoga breathing techniques to stay calm. His old adversary (and father of his ex, Betty) General Ross gets wind of his location and sends a team, headed by gung-ho British Royal Marine Emil Blonsky, to bring in the errant scientist. Bruce Hulks out, escapes from Blonsky's forces and returns to the U.S. He gets a job at a pizzeria in the Virginia town where his old flame Betty teaches. Bruce searches for a cure while stalking his ex, who is dating a psychologist. Jazzed after his Hulk encounter, and with Ross' blessing, Blonsky injects himself with super-soldier serum for Round Two. Ross' forces track Banner to Betty's school and the newly enhanced Blonsky provokes Banner, who turns into the Hulk and smashes him. Bruce and Betty go on the lam to locate the mysterious Mr. Blue, a scientist who might have a cure for Banner's condition. They find him in New York and discover that he has been synthesizing the blood samples Bruce has been sending him. Blue injects Bruce with an antidote which will "only reverse each transformation." Blonsky and some soldiers break into the lab, taking the scientists by surprise, and capture Bruce. Blonsky, who already has gamma-irradiated blood, injects himself with some of the synthesized serum. "The mixture could be an abomination!" Mr. Blue tells him.

He is correct. Blonsky turns into a giant monster and rampages through the city. Bruce throws himself out of an army helicopter and emerges from a big hole in the street as the Hulk. A block-rattling battle ensues between the two pixilated giants. Hulk smashes and, following the fight, Bruce decamps to the woods of British Columbia, where he works on mastering his transformation process. An end-credits scene shows Tony Stark telling Ross that he's putting a team together.

The Incredible Hulk is faster paced than Lee's 2003 film. The origin is relegated to the opening credits, which helps speed things up. And this Hulk is a scarier, more fearsome version than Lee's. Again, he's mostly silent: his only two lines, voiced by original live-action Hulk Lou Ferrigno, are "Leave me alone!," delivered early on, and one during the climactic fight. "Any last words?" asks Blonsky, poised to deliver a killing blow. "Hulk smash!" our hero roars back.

But Blonsky and his monstrous alter ego (modeled after Hulk's warty frenemy from the comics, the Abomination) is a more standard nemesis than Bruce's father-turned-Absorbing Man. And the relationship between Norton's Bruce and Liv Tyler's Betty is less convincing.

Leterrier had mixed feelings about the final product. "The first half is really mine and the second half is the studio's expected *Hulk* movie—two giants kicking each other's ass," the director said in 2013.[33] Years later, he amended that to: "It starts as the movie I wanted to make. Then it becomes Edward's movie sometimes, in the too-self-serious middle, where you lose a little bit of the fun. At the end, you go back into a Marvel world with a bar fight between two monsters, which is what we wanted."[34]

The movie did okay but was no leftfield hit like *Iron Man*. Critics couldn't be faulted for wondering if the latter had been a fluke, beginner's luck.

Still, mission accomplished: The Hulk was back in the public eye and teed up for what the studio had begun referring to as—to differentiate it from the Marvel (Comics) Universe[35]—the Marvel Cinematic Universe.

Chapter XIV

Summer of the Superhero (and a Winter of Discontent)

> "He's like the shark in *Jaws*. The Joker cuts through the film, he's incredibly important, but he's not a guy with a backstory. He's a wild card."
> —Christopher Nolan[1]

Emboldened by the success of *Batman Begins*, Christopher Nolan aimed higher for the sequel. He said he wanted to "provide a new experience, stretch in all directions [and] stage the action and story on a grander scale, using an operatic sensibility."[2] The next *Batman* movie wouldn't just be an epic collision of good and evil, but the story of a city, like Michael Mann's 1995 crime thriller *Heat*.

On these terms, *The Dark Knight* delivers. It's a high-octane, sleek, lavishly budgeted monument to moviemaking.

Grown men and women have gone mad (not Joker mad, but still) trying to explain a Nolan plot. Suffice it to say that the Joker is on a crime spree. He breaks into a bank and steals mob money. District Attorney Harvey Dent is trying to put new mob leader Salvatore Maroni in jail with the help of assistant D.A. Rachel Dawes, now Dent's girlfriend, and James Gordon, now head of the Gotham Police Department's Major Crimes Unit. A Chinese businessman, Lau, steals the mob's remaining money. The Joker interrupts a mob meeting with an offer to kill Batman in exchange for half of the money. Bruce goes to Hong Kong and, as Batman, captures Lau and brings him back to the U.S. Lucius Fox shows Bruce some new gadgets and Bruce asks if his Batman outfit can be modified so that he is able to move his head. The Gotham Police Department throws the mob leaders in jail. The Joker kills a faux Batman (a copycat who wears a Batsuit and tries to fight crime) and warns that the killing will continue unless the real Batman reveals his identity and "turns himself in." The Joker kills the police commissioner and a judge.

Bruce holds a fundraiser for Harvey. The Joker crashes the party and threatens Rachel. Bruce dons his Batman outfit and confronts the Joker. The Joker announces that he's going to go after the mayor next. Gordon saves the mayor but is shot. Batman goes to a mob nightclub and beats up mobsters and tries to scare Maroni into telling him where the Joker is. Batman considers quitting, figuring that he's the problem. Harvey holds a press conference and says that he's Batman. The Joker attempts to nab Harvey from an armored police vehicle. Batman follows in the Tumbler and, after a lengthy car chase, comes face to grinning face with the Joker. Gordon arrests the Joker. While in custody, the Joker tells Batman that his men have captured Rachel and Harvey, who are in separate locations filled with oil drums that are rigged to explode simultaneously.

Batman leaves to save Rachel but the Joker has given him Harvey's location.

While Marvel was beginning to forge its mix of action and comedy, Christopher Nolan explored the darkest corners of the DC Comics universe with 2008's *The Dark Knight*. Heath Ledger won a posthumous Oscar for his portrayal of the fiend who needs no back story, the Joker. Warner Bros.

Batman saves Harvey but during their escape the D.A.'s face, which was doused in oil, catches fire. The Joker burns a pyramid of cash. Dressed as a Gotham General Hospital nurse, he visits Harvey, half of whose face is scarred. The Joker frees Harvey and blows up the hospital. Batman learns that the Joker has planted bombs on two ferries. One is populated by law-abiding Gothamites the other by criminals. Each group has been given

Chapter XIV. Summer of the Superhero (and a Winter of Discontent) 115

a detonator and the Joker tells them that they each have until midnight to blow up the other ferry before the people on the other ferry blow *them* up.

Harvey, driven mad by Rachel's death and his own disfigurement, kills some people and takes Gordon's family hostage. Batman finds the Joker in a tall office building and throws him out the window but then saves him. Gordon and Batman confront Harvey in another building elsewhere in Gotham. Harvey shoots Batman, Batman tackles Harvey and they both fall. Harvey dies and Batman agrees to take the blame for his crimes so that Harvey can become a symbol of hope.

The two-and-a-half-hour saga looks like the future of cinema. Nolan and his director of photography, Wally Pfister, shot the film using state-of-the-art technology, including nearly 30 minutes in 70mm IMAX. The chase between the Tumbler and then the Batpod and a Joker-driven 18-wheeler is among the most thrilling action sequences of the decade.

But no amount of technology can upstage Heath Ledger's Joker. The Australian actor's casting was controversial ("We were fucking pilloried for it," said Nolan's brother Jonathan, who co-wrote the script[3]) but his Clown Prince of Crime is a seething, malevolent force of evil. He has no backstory, or need for one. As he tells Batman, "You made me."

Most of the supporting cast members from *Batman Begins* return, with the exception of Katie Holmes; this time it's Maggie Gyllenhaal's thankless task to portray Rachel. Her character's off-screen death registers less than the murder of the *faux* Batman. As Harvey Dent and Two-Face, Aaron Eckhart has better makeup and dials down the mania from Tommy Lee Jones' turn in *Batman Forever*. The Gotham City politics are tiresome.

Released in July 2008, a month after *The Incredible Hulk*, *The Dark Knight* generated best across-the-board reviews yet for a superhero movie, perhaps because it was less a *Batman* movie than a Christopher Nolan film with a little Batman sprinkled in. It became the first superhero picture to make $1 billion and it received eight Academy Award nominations. When none of these were for Best Picture, the ensuing uproar prompted the Academy to expand the category from five titles to ten.

Ledger won in his category, Best Supporting Actor. Unfortunately, the 28-year-old actor died, from a combination of prescription drugs, six months before *The Dark Knight*'s release.[4] Nolan dedicated the film to Ledger and to Conway Wickliffe, a special effects technician killed in an accident during filming.

• • •

For many, the pure cinema of *The Dark Knight* set the bar higher for superhero movies. Woe to any that came after, especially those celebrating the genre's pulp-y roots. And the last two superhero-related flicks of 2008 did just that.

First, there was yet another *Punisher*. And for the first time, a woman was given the chance to direct a Marvel-based property.

Lexi Alexander, a German-born former World Kickboxing Champion, moved to Los Angeles at 19 and enrolled at UCLA for classes in acting, directing, producing and writing. She financed her education and living expenses by working as a stuntwoman specializing in martial arts. After making short films, including the Oscar-nominated *Johnny Flynton* (2003), she directed a feature, *Green Street Hooligans* (2005). Lionsgate, Marvel and producer Gale Anne Hurd had already gone through several writers and directors and lost star Thomas Jane when Alexander's agent passed along a script for a new movie featuring vengeful Frank Castle and an enemy from the comics, scarred gangster Jigsaw.

Alexander, who was unfamiliar with the skull-shirted vigilante, passed—twice. "Then my agent said, 'Look, you know they have a $35 million budget. It's a comic book film. They don't want it to be a sequel. You can make this your own film. You can reboot it, you can put something new on it.' So I said, 'All right, then send me the comic books.'"

The director found herself enjoying *Punisher Max*, a 2004 series written by Garth Ennis and published under Marvel's adult audience imprint. "I was like, shit, this is great. Why didn't anybody do *this*? So once I had confirmation from them that they really would let me do this with a new actor and a new look and a new feel to it, I was totally up for it." She signed on in June 2007 and hired Ray Stevenson, an Irish actor best known for his role in the BBC/HBO series *Rome*, to play the lead.

Alexander's *Punisher: War* Zone begins with the protagonist blasting his way through a mob boss' dinner party. One gangster, Billy Russotti, escapes. Frank follows Billy to a recycling plant and administers some rough justice via a glass-cutting machine. His face disfigured, Billy dubs himself "Jigsaw."

It turns out that one of Frank's victims was an undercover FBI agent, Nicky Donatelli. The agent's murder motivates the NYPD's Punisher Task Force to bring down Frank, who is five years into his career of rampant vigilantism. Even Frank, upon learning his victim's identity, questions whether to continue his quest for vengeance. His armorer, Microchip, assures him that yes, he should.

Jigsaw breaks into the home of the murdered agent with a four-man crew and holds his wife and daughter hostage. The Punisher kills two of Jigsaw's men and the police arrest the leader and his brother, Loony Bin Jim.

Jigsaw and Jim make a bargain with the police and walk. This time they kidnap Microchip and the Donatellis and take them to a hotel. Now working with two members of the task force, Frank invades the hotel. Jigsaw and Loony Bin Jim hold Microchip and Grace, the daughter, at gunpoint. Jigsaw gives Frank a choice: shoot Microchip and he'll let Grace go free. Frank shoots and kills Jim, Jigsaw shoots and kills Microchip, and Frank impales and kills Jigsaw.

Reviewers were shocked—shocked!—at the violence in the R-rated release, which hit theaters as Christmas shoppers began checking off their lists. But some viewers loved Alexander's over-the-top take on Marvel's favorite homicidal maniac: "THE BEST time I've had at the movies this year," wrote comedian-actor (and future Marvel star) Patton Oswalt.[5]

In perhaps the movie's most notorious scene, the Punisher uses a rocket launcher to take out a bad guy in the midst of a parkour routine. "It was such a blunt, un-subtle squashing out of the trendy, that its artlessness reached true art," Oswalt said years later. "Everyone in the theater—six people—gave it a standing ovation when I first saw it."[6]

The Monday after *Punisher: War Zone* opened, Alexander stopped hearing from her agents. For the next decade, she had trouble finding work. She began speaking out, on social media, against gender disparity. Directing gigs began to roll in, some on DC-based CW TV series like *Green Arrow* and *Supergirl*.

In 2015, she talked about the problems in getting her vision on-screen. Marvel co-produced *War Zone* with Lionsgate, which inherited the rights to Frank after merging with Artisan. "Marvel was an equal partner, but unfortunately when there were

Chapter XIV. Summer of the Superhero (and a Winter of Discontent)

creative decision conflicts, Marvel would let Lionsgate be the tie-breaker," she said. "I always regretted that I made a Marvel movie this way, because 99 percent of their notes were much better than the studio's and I was more in tune with them."[7]

And then came another comics-based, Christmas-time Lionsgate release, *The Spirit*.

Like Dick Tracy and the Shadow, the Spirit was a holdover from the era when fedoras were all the rage. Created by writer-artist Will Eisner during the late thirties, the Spirit was Denny Colt, a detective who emerges from suspended animation after being shot. He wears a rumpled blue suit, eye-mask and hat, and fights crime in Central City. With its fluid lines, chiaroscuro inking, innovative layouts and seductive femme fatales, Eisner's art jumped out of the Sunday funnies. The New York cartoonist quit the strip in 1952, but not before creating a body of work that influenced generations of artists and writers.

One of these was William Friedkin. In the seventies, the *Exorcist* director optioned the rights to Eisner's hero and hired Harlan Ellison to write the screenplay. According to the famously cantankerous fantasy author, the project fizzled following a screaming match in a Paris restaurant over a disagreement about Friedkin's 1977 thriller *Sorcerer*.[8]

In 1987, Warner Bros. Television co-produced a Spirit TV-movie. A campy, lo-fi adaptation, it depicts the Spirit's origin and includes many of the supporting characters from the strip. Sam Jones, star of Dino De Laurentiis' 1980 *Flash Gordon*, played the lead.

Batman producer Michael Uslan later optioned the rights and approached comics artist-writer Frank Miller about making a feature. Miller revered Eisner, who was a huge influence on his neo-noir sensibility. At a 2005 memorial for Eisner, Uslan recalled telling Miller, "Frank, Will was your mentor; you've got to write and direct this." Uslan continued, "And Frank looked at me like I was out of my mind. He said: 'Touch the work of the master? How could I do that?' About ten minutes later, he tapped me on my shoulder and said, 'I can't let anyone else touch it.'"[9]

Miller, who first rocked the comics world in the eighties with his *Daredevil* run and his Batman mini-series *The Dark Knight Returns*, had gone on to projects like the neo-noir series *Sin City* and the historical comic book *300*. When Uslan asked him to consider the Spirit, director Zach Snyder had just turned *300* into a feature film while Miller had finished co-directing, with Robert Rodriguez, a movie adaptation of *Sin City*. Both efforts were as stylized as Miller's comics; the artist's *The Spirit* shares in those films' visuals-first aesthetic.

Written and directed by Miller, *The Spirit* delves into the character's origin in a complex plot that also involves his arch-nemesis the Octopus; Denny Colt's girlfriend Ellen; her father, Police Commissioner Dolan, and several of Eisner's femme fatales: Plaster of Paris, Sand Saref, Silken Floss and Lorelei: Angel of Death. The latter four were played by Paz Vega, Eva Mendes, Scarlett Johansson and Jamie King, respectively. Unknown New York actor Gabriel Macht played the title character.

Like *Dick Tracy* and the 1990s *Batman*s, *The Spirit* exists in its own hermetically sealed world. It's also confusing as hell.

"To ask why anything happens in Frank Miller's sludgy, hyper-stylized adaptation of a fabled comic book series by Will Eisner may be an exercise in futility," wrote the *Times*' A.O. Scott.[10]

The Spirit was another nostalgia bomb, in both senses. As with *Dick Tracy*, *The Shadow* and *The Phantom*, the kids just weren't interested. The movie finished ninth on its opening weekend.

Chapter XV

Alternate Histories

> "It's my hope and my intent to shine a light on the current state of super-hero movies and what they mean to pop culture, and what they mean to people who enjoy them, and comic book fans."
>
> —Zach Snyder[1]

The trend in comics that began in the seventies with more violent characters like the Punisher and Wolverine reached its apotheosis in the mid-eighties. The popularity of Frank Miller's no-holds-barred approach in *Daredevil* and *The Dark Knight Returns* indicated that fans were ready to see more grown-up, or at least more violent and tortured, versions of their childhood heroes. British comics writer Alan Moore went one step further: he deconstructed some old archetypes, dressed them in new outfits, and explored the real-world ramifications of costumed vigilantes and superpowers. Moore called his project *Watchmen*.

The seeds of the series were sown in 1985, when DC bought the rights to superheroes from a line of B-grade comics—B-grade in paper and printing processes, if not creators—and asked Moore to have a go at them. Instead, the writer and a fellow Brit, artist Dave Gibbons, used the characters as models for their own team of dysfunctional, non-powered costumed crimefighters. Their 12-issue series *Watchmen* set comic shops ablaze and took root in the mainstream; in 2005, the collected 1986 series was the only graphic novel to make *Time*'s Top 100 All-Time Novels (1923 and 2005). The following year, Warner Bros. announced the inevitable: The studio would make a movie based on *Watchmen*.

But it was not going to be easy. Producers Lloyd Levin and Lawrence Gordon had been trying to make a film version since optioning the rights shortly after the comics' publication. Filmmaker Terry Gilliam, who had spent years attempting to adapt *Don Quixote*, famously called *Watchmen* "unfilmable." Zach Snyder agreed with Gilliam ... at first:

> [Warners] said, "Hey, we have this other graphic novel lying around, this thing called, uh, *Watchmen*? Do you know about that?" [*Laughter*] And I said, "Listen, here is the deal.... I don't want to make that, do I look stupid? Do I look like I would do that to myself? That's crazy talk. Don't ever mention or bring that up again." And then I thought about it and I thought, you know what? It's probably the coolest thing on the planet.... And I thought, if I don't do it, someone else will.[2]

The Connecticut-raised director had studied fine arts and broken into the film industry with a visceral remake of George Romero's zombie flick *Dawn of the Dead*. Snyder was finishing his adaptation of Frank Miller's *300* when he got the call.

Warner Bros. had a script by *X-Men* screenwriter and *Watchmen* fan David Hayter. "The only goal for me was to retain everything about it," Hayter said, "for the sake of the fans, to honor Alan Moore and do the story properly."[3] Hayter originally envisioned Moore's layered, complex epic as an HBO mini-series.

Snyder too wanted to stay true to Moore and Gibbons' work. His first version was three hours long. "Everyone wants it shorter, and I'm trying to help them," he said. "Warner Bros., they're my partners, and I want to give them a movie that they feel like they can get behind. But there's going to be a point where I'm going to be, 'Look guys, I can't cut that. It's not *Watchmen* anymore.'"

In its warts-and-all depiction of its heroes, *Watchmen* contains a sex scene between two of its main characters, an attempted rape, and the nude (and blue) Doctor Manhattan. This wasn't the Comics Code anymore.

Snyder lobbied for, and got, an R. "It's not *Fantastic Four*, it's got to be hard R, it's got to challenge everyone's ideas," he said. "When they say, 'You should be less sexy and less violent,' I say, 'But that's *Watchmen*.'"[4]

Snyder trimmed the movie to two hours and 40. And, following a delay caused by Fox, which claimed distribution rights due to decades of complicated legal entanglements, *Watchmen* opened in March 2009.

Set in an alternate history, *Watchmen* is part thought experiment, part mystery and part getting-the-band-back-together story. It's 1985, and Richard Nixon is still president due to the godlike Doctor Manhattan's help in achieving U.S. victory in Vietnam. But the superpowered being, a former atomic scientist with control over time and space, has gone missing and now the Soviet Union is threatening nuclear war. "Superheroes," in the form of costumed but non-superpowered vigilantes, are outlawed. And someone has begun killing them.

One of the first to go is the Comedian, a former member of a World War II–era team known as the Minutemen. Rorschach, once a member of a more recent crimefighting group called the Watchmen, investigates the older hero's death. His detective work leads him to a former villain, Moloch. When Moloch is killed, the police charge and imprison Rorschach, a sociopath in a trench coat, fedora and ever-changing ink-blot face mask.

Meanwhile, Doctor Manhattan's girlfriend Laurie Jupiter visits an old friend, Dan Dreiberg. Laurie and Dan are also former Watchmen. Before being imprisoned, Rorschach had warned Dan about the Comedian's murder and what it might mean for other ex-crimefighters. Laurie and Dan break their Silk Spectre II and Nite Owl costumes out of mothballs and free their compatriot. Realizing that another former Watchman, billionaire Adrian Veidt, aka Ozymandias, is behind the murders, Nite Owl and Rorschach journey to the killer's Antarctic retreat. But it's too late; Veidt's ultimate plan—to unite the U.S. and the Soviet Union by setting off nuclear explosions that will look like the handiwork of Doctor Manhattan, turning the god-like being into a common enemy—has already been accomplished. Millions have died.

And so ends the movie which, from its alternate timeline to the sex, violence and intertwining plots, follows the series as faithfully as possible in under three hours. Besides the omission of some subplots, the only major change is the finale. In the comics, Veidt explodes a giant alien squid, not reactors.

"The reason that the squid got taken out of the movie was so there'd be more Rorschach and a little bit more Manhattan," Snyder explained. "Because we did the math,

To this day, Zach Snyder's *Watchmen* (2009) remains the only sustained and more-or-less faithful adaptation of a superhero comic book storyline. From left: Matthew Goode as Ozymandias, Billy Crudup as Doctor Manhattan, Malin Åkerman as Silk Spectre II, Jackie Earle Haley as Rorschach, Patrick Wilson as Nite Owl II, and Jeffrey Dean Morgan as the Comedian. Warner Bros.

and we figured it took about 15 minutes to explain [the squid's appearance] correctly; otherwise, it's pretty crazy."[5] (Although, as ign.com's Jim Vejvoda has pointed out, the squid was an external threat. Mass destruction caused by "America's ultimate superweapon," Doctor Manhattan, would unite the rest of the world against the U.S.[6])

The adaptation finished first on its opening weekend, but attendance dropped off by nearly 68 percent the following week. Considering its risky subject matter and inside-inside-baseball heroes, *Watchmen* was never cut out to be summer blockbuster fare, at least not at this stage of the superhero movie game. Reviewers praised its visual audaciousness while bemoaning its self-seriousness and ham-fisted needle-drops (i.e., Bob Dylan's "The Times They Are A-Changin'").

Watchmen remains an anomaly, the first and so far only soup-to-nuts faithful, big-budget, big-screen adaptation of a superhero comic book storyline.

A decade after its release, *Watchmen* found a home at HBO, just like co-scripter Hayter had envisioned. However, this *Watchmen* was its own thing, a nine-episode mini-series set in the same world but with a different story and characters. Receiving the effusive praise that eluded the feature film version, it received 11 Emmys.

• • •

The next *X-Men* movie was a step back for the franchise, in both setting and quality.

Fox began developing what would become *X-Men Origins: Wolverine* in 2004, following the release of *X2: X-Men United*. To write the prequel, which would explore the early days of the most popular X-Man, the studio hired David Benioff. The future co-creator of HBO's *Game of Thrones* was hot at the time for work on various movies, including an adaptation of the novel *The Kite Runner*.

"He was beating down our door to write this movie because he's the most passionate Wolverine fan," returning star Hugh Jackman said. "He's followed all of the books since he was nine years old. For us, it's one of those rare combinations where you have a writer who has all these Oscar-winning directors wanting to work with him and he's like, 'I want to do Wolverine!'"[7]

Benioff found inspiration in a few storylines from the comics, including "Weapon X." This 1991 arc by writer-artist Barry Windsor-Smith explored Wolverine's time as the subject of a government genetic research project.[8]

In 2006, Jackman said that he and the studio had signed off on a revised version of Benioff's screenplay. "If you know about the history of *X-Men* movies, that's a revolution for us. We're a year away from shooting the film and we have the script. And, by the way, it is unbelievable."[9] The revised screenplay was by David Ayer, a former U.S. Navy submariner who specialized in action films such as *Training Day* and *The Fast and the Furious*.

But Jackman had spoken too soon. As the movie's late 2007 start of production neared, Fox abandoned its original concept of "a $70 million, almost R-rated, seventies revenge movie" (Fox VP of production–comics fan Jeff Katz)[10] for something more summer-friendly and with spinoff potential. Fox ordered the addition of two more mutants: Gambit, an X-Man with extreme card-throwing abilities, and Deadpool, a wisecracking mercenary.

Writers were still fixing the script when director Gavin Hood began filming. Hood had won the 2005 Best Foreign Language Film Oscar for *Tsotsi*, about a young street thug in the slums of Johannesburg who steals a car and discovers a baby in the back.

As production wore on, the South African director butted heads with Fox CEO Tom Rothman. According to a 2008 *Variety* article, Fox nearly fired Hood during filming, and put two backup directors on alert. Richard Donner—director of *Superman*, husband of *Wolverine* producer Lauren Shuler Donner—flew to the Australian set to smooth things over.[11] Donner himself had been on the receiving end of a director's oversight, during *Superman*.

X-Men Origins: Wolverine begins in the Canadian Northwest Territories in 1845, with a young Wolverine, aka James Howlett (Logan is the name he adopts later), discovering his mutant abilities. He and his half-brother Victor Creed, who has similar powers, spend the next century as soldiers. In 1973, military man William Stryker recruits the Canadian siblings for Team X, a group of mutants. Logan becomes estranged from his half-brother as Victor grows more violent. After a few missions, Logan leaves the team and settles down to life as a logger with girlfriend Kayla Silverfox.

Six years later, Stryker, now a major, warns him that someone is killing Team X members. Logan refuses to help Stryker, then finds Kayla's bloodied body in the woods. He realizes that Victor, who has gone full Sabretooth, is responsible and attacks his half-brother but loses the fight. Stryker convinces Logan to let Stryker's team reinforce his skeleton with adamantium so he can defeat his feral half-brother. But Logan overhears the major's plan to erase his memory and weaponize him. Wolverine escapes and goes to New Orleans to recruit Gambit, a mutant previously held in Stryker's facility at Three Mile Island. Gambit and Logan invade Stryker's HQ, where the major is holding several mutants hostage. Wolverine encounters one of his former Team X teammates,

Wade Wilson. Wilson's mouth has been sewn shut and he is now Deadpool: He has the powers of a "pool" of mutants, including Wolverine. After a fight atop a cooling tower, Logan decapitates Wade. Stryker shoots Wolverine with adamantium bullets, temporarily incapacitating him. Kayla, who is still alive but mortally wounded, uses the last of her powers to telepathically order Stryker to walk away and keep walking until his feet bleed.

Moviegoers bought tickets because it was Hugh Jackman as Wolverine and an *X-Men* movie, and *Origins* turned a profit. But reviewers uninterested in Logan's backstory saw no reason to care. And fans decried the picture's treatment of Deadpool, a favorite in the comics since his 1991 debut for his snide, fourth-wall–breaking comments. In *Origins*, he is rendered mute for the movie's second half and he's not in costume.

Ryan Reynolds, who played Deadpool, became interested in playing the character in 2004, either through a discussion with David S. Goyer (with whom the Canadian actor had worked on *Blade: Trinity*) or a reference in a comic where the character compares himself "to a cross between a Shar-Pei and Ryan Reynolds," or both.[12]

"It was a very frustrating experience," said Reynolds. When Fox offered him *Origins*, he said, "it was sort of like, 'Play Deadpool in this movie or we'll get someone else to.' And I just said, 'I'll do it, but it's the wrong version. Deadpool isn't correct in it.'"[13]

Between the new prequel and the listless but profitable *X3*, the franchise was losing some of its X factor. Producer Lauren Shuler Donner & Co. realized that, like Sony with Spider-Man and Fox with the Fantastic Four, a fresh spin was needed.

• • •

With just *X-Men Origins: Wolverine* and *Watchmen*, 2009 was a slow year for cinematic super-action. Behind the scenes, though, wheels were turning. Disney bought Marvel Entertainment, including Marvel Studios, for $4.24 billion. A month later, Warner Bros. announced the formation of DC Entertainment, a new company that would oversee the use of DC Comics properties in movies, TV shows, games and merchandise much as Superman Inc. had in the publisher's early days. The studio put Diane Nelson, a former brand manager for the Harry Potter franchise, in charge.

Marvel's first show pony under new management was *Iron Man 2*. In the spring 2010 release, weapons manufacturer Justin Hammer teams up with vengeance-seeking Russian physicist Ivan Vanko against Tony Stark. Both villains came from the comics, although Vanko is a mix of two characters, the Crimson Dynamo and Whiplash.[14] Whiplash became a certainty when Kevin Feige and his team saw Ryan Meinerding's concept art; hired by Jon Favreau for *Iron Man*, Meinerding was fast becoming one of Marvel's chief designers. On Robert Downey, Jr.'s, recommendation, the studio hired Justin Theroux to write the screenplay.[15] The two had worked together on the comedy *Tropic Thunder*.

"The film had a release date even before we started working on it, so we had to work fast," Theroux said in 2016.[16] The decision to fast-track the sequel came from Marvel's corporate headquarters in New York.[17]

One of the studio's lesser efforts, the sequel nonetheless boasts a superlative villain thanks to Mickey Rourke's performance as the unflappable Vanko/Whiplash, who is outfitted with a self-devised exoskeleton more powerful than Tony's Iron Man armor. Marvel Studios CGI reaches new heights in a scene where Tony dons his costume out of a suitcase before a showdown with Vanko at the Monaco Grand Prix. The relationship between Tony and Pepper Potts is developed further and, more importantly, another Avenger is introduced: Scarlet Johansson's Black Widow. The actress had liked *Iron Man* and, before meeting with Marvel, researched characters who might be a good fit. She came up with the Wasp, the Golden Age character Blonde Phantom, and Black Widow.[18]

Many superheroes had rotated through the Avengers ranks over the years, but the Widow had been there since early days. Stan Lee, Timely artist Don Rico and artist Don Heck conceived of her as Natasha Romanoff, a Russian superspy attempting to steal Stark technologies. She soon hooked up with another villain, Hawkeye, to fight the Avengers before eventually changing her ways. Marvel scooped the rights to the heroine back from Lionsgate in June 2006.

Following her live-action debut in *Iron Man 2*, Black Widow wouldn't be seen again for a couple of years. First, Marvel had to set up two more Avengers, Thor and Captain America.

The former debuted in 1962, in an anthology called *Journey into Mystery*. Stan Lee, his younger brother Larry Lieber, and Jack Kirby all had a hand in his creation, although it was the latter's interest in Norse mythology that fueled the stories once Thor transitioned to his own title. By the seventies, Thor was, like Daredevil and Iron Man, regarded as a B-lister. But an early eighties run by artist-writer Walter Simonson introduced new villains Malekith the Accursed and Surtur and a hero named Beta Ray Bill, and took the hero in unexpected directions, like transforming Thor into a frog. By 2006, when Marvel announced a *Thor* movie, he was being redefined in the comics by writer (and creator of the *Babylon 5* TV series). J. Michael Straczynski and artist Olivier Coipel.

Thor had made his live-action debut over two decades earlier, in the TV-movie *The Incredible Hulk Returns*, where he was portrayed by actor–fight choreographer Eric Kramer in a bargain-basement Viking outfit. In the early nineties, Lee and director Sam Raimi had made the rounds of studios, pitching a movie based on the Asgardian.

"It was thrilling to be with Stan Lee and hysterical the way that we had to explain who Thor was, and walking out of there going, 'They didn't get it! They think it's gonna be some Hercules movie or something!'" Raimi said.[19]

The Marvel crew too had some difficulties on how to approach the material. The magical realm of the Asgardians had to fit in with the hi-tech world of *Iron Man*, and believably lead to the two working together in *The Avengers*. In the early comics, Thor had a human alter ego, a crippled doctor named Don Blake who discovers a wooden stick that turns out to be the mystical hammer Mjölnir; Blake was dropped for the movie. Thor's love interest, a nurse named Jane Foster, became an astrophysicist as various writers, including *Rise of the Silver Surfer* scribe Don Payne, worked on the script. (Payne also wrote the 2006 romantic comedy *My Super Ex-Girlfriend*, about an average guy who breaks up with his superhero girlfriend, G-Girl. In its most memorable scene, G-Girl throws a live great white shark into her ex's apartment. Uma Thurman, *Batman and Robin*'s Poison Ivy, and Luke Wilson starred; Ivan Reitman directed.)

Several directors were considered before the studio settled on Kenneth Branagh. As a boy in Belfast, the actor-director had been fascinated by Thor's mythic adventures and quasi–Shakespearean language. He met with the studio's Kevin Feige and producer Craig Kyle. "All three of us agreed that men in tights, riding across rainbow bridges, in space, across nine realms, represented a unique moviemaking challenge," he said.[20]

Another challenge: ensuring that *Thor* worked on as a stand-alone movie while expanding the Marvel Cinematic Universe, an increasingly complicated proposition as the architects at Marvel began forming long-range plans.

Branagh and Marvel's search for their Thor led them to the director's co-star in the BBC series *Wallander*, Tom Hiddleston. But, thanks to a second audition tape, Australian actor Chris Hemsworth got the lead, and Hiddleston was cast as Thor's troublesome brother, Loki. Natalie Portman signed on as Jane and Branagh sold Oscar winner Anthony Hopkins on playing Odin, Thor's dad. This was to be a pivotal role, as the story's main conflict is between father and son.

Their rift begins after Thor goes on a rogue mission against the Frost Giants. For his arrogance, he is banished by Odin from their kingdom of Asgard to Midgard, i.e., Earth. Thor arrives in New Mexico in pursuit of his hammer Mjölnir and meets astrophysicists Jane Foster and Erik Selvig and their friend Darcy. After learning that a government agency, S.H.I.E.L.D., has erected a test facility around Mjölnir, Thor breaks into the compound. However, he finds that he can no longer lift the magical weapon; he is no longer worthy.

Thor's half-brother Loki, who was partly responsible for his exile, sends a mechanical monster to destroy him. With his powers at half-mast, Thor nevertheless defeats the monster, thus re-establishing his worthiness. The movie ends with a battle between Thor and Loki and the destruction of the Bifröst Bridge, a piece of cosmic infrastructure connecting Asgard and Earth. Not for the last time, Loki falls to his death.

Thor was Marvel's most ambitious project yet. Lavish Asgardian sets and costumes pay homage to artist Jack Kirby's zigzaggy geometrical designs. The New Mexico town where Thor gets to know his new friends, and fights Loki's monster, was built from scratch by Bo Welch (*Batman Returns*) and his crew.

The scenario of Thor in small-town America, and Chris Hemsworth's ability to find the humor n the Norse god's pomposity, grounded the movie, Marvel's most fantastical yet. And in Hiddleston's roguish Loki, the studio had a surprise break-out star.

• • •

After *X-Men Origins: Wolverine*, Fox scrapped plans for a similar prequel with Magneto. Instead, Lauren Shuler Donner and her fellow *X-Men* producers Bryan Singer (welcomed back to the fold following his Warner Bros./*Superman Returns* transgression) and Simon Kinberg collaged together elements from one script that was set in the early sixties and another that featured a younger set of mutants. Singer wrote a treatment using the Cuban Missile Crisis as a backdrop and then bailed out as director. The studio turned to Matthew Vaughn.

The English director had almost made *X3* before deciding he didn't want to spend time away from his family. More recently, he had co-wrote, -produced and -directed *Kick-Ass* (2010), a low-budget hit about non-superpowered heroes based on a comic by Mark Millar and John Romita, Jr. Vaughn's violent and profane R-rated satire of hero worship and fan culture starred Nicolas Cage but gained notoriety for a line delivered by 12-year-old Chloë Grace Moretz as preteen heroine Hit Girl: "Okay, you cunts, let's see what you can do now."

For what became *X-Men: First Class*, Vaughn brought in his *Kick-Ass* co-writer Jane Goldman. The former journalist and TV presenter wasn't sure how to categorize the assignment. "Reboot? Prequel? I think there's a sense that we couldn't purely be called a reboot in that we wouldn't want to go utterly against the canon of the trilogy," she said.[21]

The producers hired new actors to play younger versions of Charles Xavier, Erik Lehnsherr (Magneto), Mystique and Beast, and added new villains Sebastian Shaw and

Emma Frost. Both Shaw and Frost came from the same formative Chris Claremont-John Byrne 1977–80 run on *The Uncanny X-Men* that launched the Dark Phoenix Saga. The franchise would return to that run for at least two more movies.

X-Men: First Class opens with flashbacks to Charles and Erik's respective youths before leaping ahead to 1962 and Las Vegas, where CIA agent Moira MacTaggert discovers a nest of evil mutants, the Hellfire Club. Moira learns of the club's plan to start a nuclear war and warns Charles. Charles, who is graduating from Oxford, recruits Erik to help him stop the club, which is led by Sebastian Shaw, a former Nazi scientist who killed Erik's mother at Auschwitz. In the final battle between the X-Men and the Hellfire folk, Erik kills Shaw. Charles is injured by a stray bullet.

Unburdened with the baggage of the original trilogy and *Origins*, and devoid (mostly) of mutant vs. human rhetoric, *X-Men: First Class* was fast-paced and novel, a well-needed shot in the arm for the franchise. As Charles, Magneto and Mystique, James McAvoy, Michael Fassbender and Jennifer Lawrence brought fresh appeal to familiar characters. Interest was renewed and the mutants would, in one form or another, go on.

• • •

Following the release of *The Dark Knight*, Warner/DC Entertainment released two turkeys, one minor and one major.

Jonah Hex (2010) starred Josh Brolin as the title character, a supernatural Western hero created in 1971. First-time director Jimmy Hayward's 81-minute feature was vilified by critics and sank at the box office. Screenwriters Mark Neveldine and Brian Taylor went on to direct the 2011 *Ghost Rider* sequel *Spirit of Vengeance*.

Where *Jonah Hex* was a low-budget disaster based on a niche character, *Green Lantern* was a $200 million megabomb that tarnished one of DC's most popular and long-running heroes and stalled Ryan Reynolds' burgeoning superhero movie career.

Conceived in 1940 by Batman co-creator Bill Finger and artist Martin Nodell, the hero began as Alan Scott, a railroad engineer who finds a magic lantern and fashions a ring that allows him to create solid objects with his imagination. The hero faded in the fifties, but at decade's end DC editor Julius Schwartz revived the concept. Writer John Broome and artists Gil Kane and Sid Green kept the name and the powers but gave the Golden Age hero a new identity (jet pilot Hal Jordan), new costume and new origin (a dying alien recruits Jordan into an elite intergalactic space force, the Green Lantern Corps).

Using his ring and lantern, the new Green Lantern adventured in space, fought alongside DC's premier super-team the Justice League, and became a stalwart secondary character. But then an early seventies run by writer Denny O'Neill and artist Neal Adams in DC's *Green Lantern/Green Arrow* comic set readers abuzz with stories about drugs, racism, and other social ills. Like many other DC B-listers, his live-action debut came in two 1979 hour-long primetime NBC specials, *Legends of the Superheroes: The Roast* and *Legends of the Superheroes: The Challenge*. Produced by Hanna-Barbera, the studio behind the network's successful Saturday morning DC-based cartoon *Super Friends*, the specials featured a host of heroes and villains, most of whom had never been seen in live-action form: Green Lantern, the Flash, Black Canary, the Huntress, Hawkman, the Atom, Giganta, Sinestro, Solomon Grundy, Mordru and the Weather Wizard.

Familiar faces in the cast included Adam West, Burt Ward and Frank Gorshin, reprising their *Batman* TV series roles. Two comedy writers from Flip Wilson's variety show wrote the scripts and added some of their own characters: Ghetto Man (yup), Retired Man (formerly Scarlet Cyclone) and Hawkman's mom.

In *The Challenge*, the heroes face a series of traps concocted by the bad guys, each trap leading up to a skit. The following week, *The Tonight Show*'s Ed McMahon hosted *The Roast*, in which the villains from the previous entry returned to mock the heroes.

Both shows came in at the bottom of the ratings; *Challenge* at 58 out of the 59 programs that aired that week, *Roast* at 62 out of 63.[22] It would be nice to report that they are undiscovered gems waiting for their steel-encased Blu-ray moment but they're strictly for hardcore fans and nostalgia buffs. For proof, look no further than Green Lantern's big moment in *Challenge*, when the superhero comes across his mortal enemy Sinestro (comedian Charlie Callas) disguised as a fortune teller. It ends with Green Lantern reciting his oath ("In brightest day and darkest night/No evil shall escape my sight") and Callas in his gypsy dress and bells reciting "Mary Had a Little Lamb."

The idea for a *Green Lantern* feature had been brewing since 1997, when Warner Bros. exec Lorenzo di Bonaventura approached Kevin Smith about the idea. The writer-director–comics fan had just finished working on a script for the abandoned Tim Burton–Nicolas Cage project *Superman Lives*. According to Smith, "[Di Bonaventura] said, 'How about Green Lantern? Do you think Green Lantern would make a good movie?' I said, 'I guess under somebody else, but I'm just not a huge Green Lantern fan, and I don't think I'm the guy you want adapting it.'"[23]

Others took a shot—comedian-writer Robert Smigel wrote a script with comic actor Jack Black in mind[24]—but in 2007, Warner Bros. announced that TV writer-producer Greg Berlanti would direct and co-write. In early 2009, the studio replaced Berlanti with Martin Campbell, who had just made the James Bond reboot *Casino Royale*. A few months later, Ryan Reynolds agreed to play Green Lantern, his second superhero after Deadpool.

The 2011 movie begins on Earth with the crash-landing of Abin Sur. A member of the interplanetary Green Lantern Corps, Abin Sur was pursuing the evil entity Parallax. The dying alien's ring summons pilot Hal Jordan, whose arrogance has just caused the destruction of a multi-million-dollar experimental fighter jet and two drones, to the site of the crash. Upon finding Abin Sur, Hal accepts the ring and is transported to the planet Oa. There, he begins training with Green Lantern Corps members Sinestro and Kilowog, a porcine, drill-sergeant-like alien. Though unimpressed by the cocky Hal, they help the Earthman learn to use his ring, which he will need to stop Parallax from devouring his planet.

Back on Earth, xenobiologist Hector Hammond begins mutating after exposure to Parallax via the corpse of Abin Sur. His head elongates and he gains telekinetic and telepathic powers. Hal returns to Earth in time to stop a Hammond-controlled helicopter from killing a bunch of partygoers, including Hal's ex-girlfriend Carol Ferris. Parallax mentally orders Hector to kill Green Lantern, so Hector kidnaps Carol and brings her to the government facility where Abin Sur's body is kept. Hal rescues Carol as Parallax, a giant cloud, appears. Parallax consumes Hector. Carol fires missiles into the cloud. Green Lantern lures Parallax into the sun, destroying the alien and almost dying himself before members of the Green Lantern Corps arrive and return him to Earth. In a mid-credits scene, a power-mad look comes over Sinestro's face as he exchanges his Green Lantern Corps ring for a yellow one that harnesses fear.

The implied sequel was not to be. The uninspired, messy *Green Lantern* is an emerald-green eyesore with another silly, amorphous threat *à la* Galactus in *Fantastic Four: Rise of the Silver Surfer*. "You can't have a movie where, frankly, your bad guy is a cloud with a face on it," director Martin Campbell said in 2017. "You simply can't."[25]

The movie has one cutely subversive moment. After the helicopter rescue, Hal visits Carol (Blake Lively) as Green Lantern. He lands on her balcony in full costume and, acting as though they've never met, lowers his voice. "I didn't have a chance to say goodbye," he says. She buys this for approximately ten seconds before looking into his green bandit eye-mask and exclaiming, "Hal? *Hal*? Oh my God, *Hal?!*"

The movie is also notable for the first appearance of Amanda Waller (Angela Bassett), an all-purpose government agent *à la* Nick Fury, and for the North American film debut of Taika Waititi. The New Zealand actor-director, who had just made his Sundance debut with his indie feature *Boy*, plays Hal's friend Thomas Kalmaku. "I guess [they] had an opening for a role in the film for someone who wasn't, I don't know, not-white or not-black," Waititi said laughingly. "I don't know what they were thinking, to be honest. But I wasn't really gonna ask. I just said, 'Yes. I'll do it.'"[26]

A more promising future in superhero movies awaited both Waititi and Reynolds. Another Green Lantern, however, wouldn't be seen again until 2017's *Justice League*, and even then only from a distance and in a flashback.

• • •

For decades, Marvel's oldest working superhero couldn't get any respect. First, there was the 1944 *Captain America* serial, which ignored everything interesting about the character. In 1979, two TV-movies turned him into a seventies action figure. Over a decade later, what was to be his modern big-screen debut ran out of money. So the bar was low for Marvel's *Captain America: The First Avenger*.

The plan was to introduce Cap, who was one of the original Avengers in the comics, before the 2012 *Avengers* blockbuster, and build on the introduction, at the end of *Thor*, of cosmic doohickey the Tesseract. It took some brainstorming before Marvel head Kevin Feige and his team decided that not just some but all of the story should be set during Cap's World War II heyday. Fortunately, there was a director who had already made a period superhero period movie, Joe Johnston, the man behind 1991's *The Rocketeer*. He signed on.

As *First Avenger* opens, Nazi deep-science division Hydra has the Tesseract and is intending to use the alien power source to win the war. In the U.S., Steve Rogers is obsessed with fighting overseas, but the scrawny American is designated 4F. A mysterious doctor, Abraham Erskine, impressed with Steve's gung-ho attitude, helps him enlist. During training, Steve demonstrates his valor by throwing himself on what he thinks is a live grenade, prompting Erskine to make him the first subject of an experimental super-soldier serum. In a secret Brooklyn lab, Steve undergoes treatment and, following a round of blue lightning, emerges from a science chamber with a new, super-buff body. Just then, a Nazi assassin breaks into the lab and kills Erskine. Steve catches him but the remaining serum is destroyed in the process.

Itching to use his super-strength and other powers to fight the Germans, Steve is stymied as the Army sends him on publicity rounds as "the star-spangled man with a plan." While meeting troops in Europe near the front, Steve goes rogue. He dons a more practical costume, designed by Howard Stark, and rescues a battalion of soldiers, including his friend James "Bucky" Barnes. Cap heads a battalion behind enemy lines to destroy Hydra bases and he eventually comes face-to-red-skull with Johann Schmidt, head of the Nazi Science Division. Schmidt has taken some super-soldier serum as well, though his dose has stripped his head of muscle and flesh. The fight leads to Schmidt's plane, which contains bombs meant for the U.S. and the Tesseract. The Tesseract opens a wormhole which sucks Schmidt into space, then burns through the plane and falls into the ocean just before Cap crashes the plane into the Arctic. The film ends with Steve coming out of his deep freeze and realizing it is no longer 1945.

The movie was a hit with audiences and critics. Its World War II setting demonstrated Marvel's growing versatility. In the title role, Chris Evans, an outside choice for the lead because of his familiarity to moviegoers as another superhero, the Human Torch, is earnest without being corny. The Red Skull (Hugo Weaving) looks suitably frightening, but the ground-breaking effect was Steve Rogers in the "before" third of the movie, prior to his transformation. To achieve the "Skinny Steve" look, effects house Lola developed new technology that placed Evans' head atop a stand-in's bony body.

Thanks to its WWII setting, *First Avenger* was more of a stand-alone movie than the previous two Marvel films, although the Tesseract subplot and a present-day appearance by Nick Fury continued the universe-building.

Introduced in the end-credits scene of *Iron Man*, Fury was another Lee/Kirby creation. He began his comics career in the early sixties, as the head of a US Army Ranger unit called the Howling Commandos. Shortly after, Kirby and Lee remodelled him as a CIA agent and then a James-Bond-like spy with S.H.I.E.L.D. (Supreme Headquarters, International Espionage and Law-Enforcement Division). In 1998 the eyepatch-sporting, cigar-chomping tough guy made his live-action debut in an ill-regarded TV-movie, *Nick Fury: Agent of S.H.I.E.L.D.*, with David Hasselhoff in the title role (and a script by the ubiquitous David Goyer). Marvel cast Samuel L. Jackson as Fury following a reboot of the character as a Jackson lookalike in the 2002 comic book series *The Ultimates*.

First Avenger also introduces Peggy Carter (Hayley Atwell), a British secret agent, and Bucky Barnes (Sebastian Stan), Steve's childhood friend, make their screen debuts. Both would become recurring characters in the expanding MCU.

But *First Avenger*'s most lasting contribution to the Marvel Cinematic Universe was the hiring of the screenwriting team Stephen McFeely and Christopher Markus. The two had been talking about writing a superhero movie set in the past when, in 2008, *Iron Man* decimated the McFeely-Markus–penned *The Chronicles Narnia: Prince Caspian* at the box office. So they were all too ready to take on *The First Avenger*, an assignment that led to two Marvel movies the size and scope of which no one could yet imagine.

Chapter XVI

Avengers Assembled

> "If you listen to the characters I named that we are working on currently, and you put them all together, there's no coincidence that they might someday equal the Avengers."
> —Kevin Feige, San Diego Comic-Con, 2006[1]

The Avengers weren't Marvel's first super-team—that was the Fantastic Four. Nor were they the publisher's most—*The Uncanny X-Men*, and various spin-off titles, had been the company's top sellers since the early eighties. But it was the team that was about to become synonymous with Marvel.

For the previous five years, the studio had introduced the core members one by one and planted the seeds of a story that would unite them. But all of that planning could have fallen apart if the studio hadn't found the right uber-nerd for the job.

Equally at home with Shakespeare, Tolstoy and *Marvel Two-in-One*, Joss Whedon had made a career relishing in and subverting genre tropes. The writer-director developed, wrote and directed *Buffy the Vampire Slayer* and the spinoff *Angel* series, both horror-adjacent, while his series *Firefly* was a short-lived but much-loved homage to space opera in general and *Star Trek* in particular. And Whedon was a comic-book reader whose father had written the live-action Spidey Super Stories segments for the seventies kids' show *The Electric Company*.

In 2010, when the geek auteur confirmed rumors that he would direct *The Avengers*, comics fandom breathed a collective sigh of relief.

"They were one of the first books [I read], back when George Perez was drawing them," Whedon said, earning instant credibility by citing a favorite artist. "This is a big deal for me."[2]

Whedon was taking on a formidable task. *The Avengers* would include 13 major characters, including two (Thor and Captain America) whose movies hadn't yet been released when he began working on the project. The budget was $220 million, over five times the cost of his only feature, the $39 million *Firefly* spinoff *Serenity*.

He began by throwing out a script by Zak Penn to work on his own. His first draft included a major part for the Wasp, an early Avenger, and featured Zeke Stane, son of *Iron Man*'s Obadiah, as the villain. But Marvel wanted to focus on established characters, including Loki—set to debut in *Thor* before the release of *The Avengers*—as the antagonist. In the tradition of big-budget superhero moviemaking, Whedon was still working on the script when filming began in April 2011.

"There is a weird element of: They handed me one of the biggest movies of all time, and I'm making it up as I go," he said seven months later, towards the end of principal photography.[3]

In *Captain America: First Avenger*, Tony Stark's father Howard retrieves the Tesseract after it falls into the ocean. In *The Avengers*, the alien power source is in the hands of S.H.I.E.L.D. when Loki breaks into the organization's underground base. This theft of "the key to unlimited sustainable energy" prompts Nick Fury to make good on his threat to assemble the world's mightiest heroes: Iron Man, Captain America, Black Widow and the Hulk. Their first mission is to stop Loki from acquiring iridium, which he needs to control the Tesseract. They capture the rogue Asgardian in Stuttgart and are transporting him to the Helicarrier, S.H.I.E.L.D.'s aircraft-carrier-in-the-sky, when Thor attacks. After a superpowered contretemps between Iron Man, Captain America and Thor, the heroes agree to work together. But Loki's forces attack the Helicarrier and he escapes. With the help of hypnotized physicist Erik Selvig, Loki opens a sky-portal for extra-terrestrial warriors the Chitauri. The Avengers fight back the alien hordes, save New York from nuclear missiles, and overcome Thor's villainous sibling.

The studio's biggest and most action-packed movie yet was everything fans could have hoped for, a witty, fast-paced, high-stakes battle between good and evil. Each of the major and even minor players, including new addition Maria Hill (Cobie Smulders), has his or her moment. For the first time, Whedon lets Hulk be Hulk; here, he's by turns comic relief, scary monster and secret weapon, while Mark Ruffalo gives a warm yet simmering performance as Bruce Banner. The Battle of New York, as it's been dubbed, brings all the Avengers together after two hours of in-fighting and bickering for an epic comic-book–style slugfest. Then, in a moment that defines Marvel's no-idea-too-out-there credo, a wordless end-credits scene shows the superheroes eating shawarma. In true guerrilla filmmaking fashion, director and cast shot the late addition after the movie's world premiere in L.A.

Some might take exception to Whedon's tendency to drop pop-culture references (*Point Break*, Galaga and Legalos, to name a few) and his use of emerging superhero

An ***Avengers*** **movie wouldn't be complete without the Marvel super-team assembled for a group shot. From left: Scarlett Johansson as Black Widow, Chris Hemsworth as Thor, Chris Evans as Captain America, Jeremy Renner as Hawkeye, along with Iron Man and Hulk. Marvel Studios.**

movie tropes like sky portals, faceless enemy hordes and last-minute deployment of nuclear missiles. But these are minor quibbles in the face of *The Avengers*' deft mix of action, comedy, character development and gripping set-pieces.

Released in May 2012, almost four years to the day it was announced, *The Avengers* opened to the biggest weekend ever in North America and became the year's highest-grossing film. In 2000, with the release of *X-Men*, superhero movies had entered the mainstream. Now they *were* the mainstream.

...

Despite the lukewarm critical reception to *Spider-Man 3*, Sam Raimi and cast were on track to spin another tale. But, in January 2010, Sony announced that it was rebooting the franchise with a new director and cast.

"We had a deadline, and I couldn't get the story to work on a level that I wanted it to work," Raimi said. "I was very unhappy with *Spider-Man 3*, and I wanted to make *Spider-Man 4* to end on a very high note, the best *Spider-Man* of them all." He told the studio to go ahead with its reboot—"which it had been planning anyway," said the director.[4]

Sony wasted no time in announcing a return to, in the words of co-chair–producer Amy Pascal, "Peter's roots."[5] Nothing was mentioned about the need to release another *Spider-Man* movie within five years of *Spider-Man 3* lest the rights revert back to Marvel.[6]

Raimi's replacement was Marc Webb, director of the well-received 2009 romantic comedy *(500) Days of Summer*. Sony was looking for someone who could deliver "real world relationships," said co-producer Avi Arad. "Relationships that we believe in, that make us feel like we know what he feels like and relating to it."[7]

The new Peter Parker was Andrew Garfield. In July 2011, a year before the movie's release, the American-born English actor surprised San Diego Comic-Con attendees when he appeared in an ill-fitting, homemade-looking Spidey costume. "You have no idea what this means to me," Garfield told the assembled. "I've always wanted to come here as a fan, and here I am as a fan…. I *needed* Spidey in my life when I was a kid. He gave me hope."[8] The stunt endeared him to fans, and Garfield gave them hope that Sony could reinvigorate the franchise.

This being a reboot, the producers decided to regurgitate the origin. And they decided that the villain should be the Lizard, an old nemesis from the comics who had been set up in the Raimi trilogy; Welsh actor Rhys Ifans was given the role of the Lizard's human alter ego, Dr. Curt Connors, previously played by Dylan Baker. Instead of Mary Jane, the filmmakers decided on Gwen Stacy, Peter's university classmate in *Spider-Man 3*, as the love interest. Emma Stone replaced Bryce Dallas Howard as Gwen. Other supporting characters were also recast. Alvin Sargent, who worked on the Raimi trilogy, has a screenplay credit, as do James Vanderbilt (also credited with the story) and Steve Kloves. Vanderbilt had co-written *The Losers*, a movie based on a comic about a black ops team based on a comic published by DC under its Vertigo imprint; Kloves had written several *Harry Potter* movies.

The Amazing Spider-Man begins with a flashback to the Parker family home with Peter's parents forced to go on the run due to Dad's genetics experiments. Richard Parker has been working with geneticist Curt Connors at Oscorp, the dangerously eclectic R&D company owned and operated by generations of Green Goblins. Years later,

Peter is investigating the corporation's New York City labs when he is bitten by a genetically modified spider. He discovers that he has the usual unusual powers. After again failing to stop the murder of his Uncle Ben, he makes a costume and begins fighting crime. Meanwhile, Dr. Connors works on a serum that will regenerate limbs. Under pressure from his boss at Oscorp, he tests his serum, which he has finished with the help of Peter's father's research, on himself and turns into an insane giant lizard-man. The Lizard decides to turn everyone in New York into lizard-people. With Gwen's help, Spider-Man stops the scaly monster from carrying out his plan.

Thanks to some clever touches and the sparks between Garfield and Stone, the origin portion of the reboot feels fresher than it should, considering that the story had been told just a decade earlier. Action highlights include a cleverly staged fight scene between Spidey and the Lizard at Peter's high school, which also features one of the funniest cameos by Stan Lee, who had been appearing in Marvel movies since 1989's *The Trial of the Incredible Hulk*. Fans still losing sleep over his organic web-spinning abilities in the Raimi trilogy could rest assured that Peter was back to making his own web-shooters, as in the original comics.

The Amazing Spider-Man opened at #1, but its $65 million first weekend take was less than half of *Spider-Man 3*'s $151 million. The final box-office tally placed it last of the four Spider-movies.

Even so, Sony was committed. Not only did the studio put a sequel into production, but Pascal *et al.* began mapping out their own interconnected universe of movies based on ancillary Spider-Man characters.

Three weeks after *The Amazing Spider-Man*'s unveiling, Warner Bros. released the last of Christopher Nolan's Batman trilogy. Bigger, longer and even more ambitious than *The Dark Knight*, *The Dark Knight Rises* begins with a James Bond–like skyjacking and climaxes with a supervillain siege of Gotham. Nolan said that he was inspired by Charles Dickens' *A Tale of Two Cities*; the 1859 novel "just felt exactly the right thing for the world we were dealing with. What Dickens does in that book in terms of having all his characters come together in one unified story with all these thematic elements and all this great emotionalism and drama, it was exactly the tone we were looking for."[9]

Like the previous movie, *The Dark Knight Rises* was written by Nolan and his brother Jonathan, based on a story by Nolan and David S. Goyer. They added Bane and Catwoman to their *dramatis personae*. The former, ill-used in 1997's *Batman & Robin*, was rebooted as a brutal criminal mastermind, the latter as a jewel thief with a heart of gold and the smartest person in any room—outside of Bruce Wayne, of course—that she's in. To play Bane, English actor Tom Hardy wears a mouth-hugging mask and adopts a diaphragm-shredding voice and off-kilter cadence. As Catwoman, Anne Hathaway wears a *Batman* '66-ish skin-tight black catsuit with cat ears and eye mask. When the movie begins, she's attempting to steal Bruce's mother's pearl necklace at Wayne Manor while Bruce, still mourning the death of Rachel Dawes, hides from his own party.

From there, *The Dark Knight Rises*' plot becomes so convoluted that, even with exposition delivered every ten minutes, it's difficult to follow. There's a subplot involving a nuclear physicist and a clean energy fusion reactor, an attack on the Gotham City stock exchange, an exploding football field, the return of the League of Shadows, a young cop trying to find Batman, another cop who hates Batman, a Catwoman subplot with mobsters, a fight between Batman and Bane that ends with the villain breaking the hero's back, Bruce's miraculous recovery in a prison-pit in a foreign country, a sprinkling of Bane backstory, Bane's takeover of Gotham, the Scarecrow presiding over a kangaroo court, a businesswoman who is actually the daughter of Ra's al Ghul, and a third-act launch of a nuclear warhead. What isn't in this movie? Well, a sense of humor, for one thing. But that was nothing new.

The Dark Knight Rises received less praise than *The Dark Knight* but was generally viewed as a fitting denouement to the trilogy. And, like its predecessor, it surpassed $1 billion at the box office.

While *Rises* marked the end of one era, Warner Bros. prepared for the start of another. Since 2010, the studio had been developing a reboot of Superman that would, it was hoped, do for the film company and its DC catalogue what *Iron Man* had done for Marvel: lay the foundation for its own interconnected universe of movies.

Over in Marvel-land, the studio was bringing to a close the trilogy inaugurated by that ground-breaking movie and preparing to launch Phase Two of its film slate. *Iron Man 3* began taking shape in 2010, when the studio asked British writer Drew Pearce what a post–Battle-of-New-York Tony Stark might look like. Marvel had met with Pearce based on *No Heroics*, a comedic TV series he created depicting a modern-day Britain where superheroes were commonplace. Pearce submitted a treatment.

When Jon Favreau declined to direct, the studio turned to Shane Black at Robert Downey, Jr.'s, suggestion. Downey had worked with Black, who had made his bones as the writer of action flicks like *Lethal Weapon* and *Last Action Hero*, on the writer-director's *Kiss Kiss Bang Bang*. The 2005 neo-noir comedy barely made its $15 million budget back, but Downey later credited it with helping him nab the lead in *Iron Man*.

Black and Pearce got to work on the script. The studio told Black that it didn't want a repeat of what it saw as misfires in *Iron Man 2*. "*Iron Man 3* will not be another 'two men in iron suits fighting each other' film," Black promised. "Instead, it will be more like a Tom Clancy thriller, with Iron Man fighting real world villains."[10]

They drew on characters and ideas from a 2005–06 storyline by writer Warren Ellis and artist Adi Granov about a super-soldier formula called Extremis. But Black and Pearce ran into pushback from Marvel's East Coast–based decision-makers when they tried to make the villain a female scientist named Maya Hansen. Kids didn't buy female action figures, they were told. "We had to change the entire script because of toy-making," Black said. "Now, that's not [Kevin] Feige. That's Marvel corporate…. New York called and said, 'That's money out of our bank.'"[11]

They went back to the Mandarin, an old comics villain who had been tapped for the first *Iron Man*. Black and Pearce gave the character, a racist caricature in the comics, a twist: He turns out to be an English actor "whose Lear was the toast of Croydon" and is a smokescreen for the real bad guy, technocrat Aldrich Killian. Motivated by a social slight from over a decade earlier, Killian plans to defeat Tony, kill the president and install a puppet in the White House.

Anticipation for the first post–*Avengers* Marvel movie was high, and *Iron Man 3* opened to the second highest (after *The Avengers*) domestic opening of all time. Highlights of the 2013 release include the destruction of Tony's Malibu home and a PTSD-afflicted Tony stranded in Tennessee with a non-working Iron Man suit and only his own innate McGyver-ness to rely on—that, and a pre-adolescent sidekick named Harley. A mystery element involves Tony trying to discover the truth behind Extremis and the Mandarin. In another casting coup, Marvel talked Ben Kingsley into playing Trevor Slattery, the overconfident, dissolute actor fronting as the villain.

A month after *Iron Man 3*'s release, Warner Bros. got back into the game with its long-promised Superman reboot. *Man of Steel* grew out of a notion hatched by David S. Goyer and endorsed by Christopher Nolan: if Superman were to show up today, wouldn't the story be about first contact with an alien?[12]

After selling the studio on the idea, Nolan and his wife, producer Emma Thomas, approached Zach Snyder. Not one to shy away from an ambitious pop culture experiment that could only end in polarizing audiences and alienating critics, the director agreed.

"I've been a big fan of the character for a long time, he's definitely the king of all superheroes, he's the one," he said.[13]

According to *Vulture*, "knowledgeable insiders" said that Warner Bros. picked Snyder because the studio believed he could get it done, even though Goyer's script was "still a bit of a mess."[14] The studio was in a time-crunch because, in 2009—following a lawsuit filed by the estate of co-creator Jerry Siegel over rights to the character—a U.S. district court judge had ruled that another *Superman* movie had to be in production by 2011. If not, the Siegels could sue to recover lost revenue on an unproduced film.[15]

For his lead, Snyder signed Henry Cavill. The son of a British stockbroker, Cavill had played a brother-in-law of Henry VIII in Showtime's *The Tudors*. The director knew he'd found his Superman when the actor tried on one of Christopher Reeve's old costumes. "Henry put it on in this trailer," Snyder said. "And there's a version of this where he comes out and is like, 'I'm Superman!' and you're like, 'Okay, it's Halloween.' But Henry came out and even the crusty grips we hired for the test got quiet. Everybody was heart-attack serious. He had just the right energy. We were like, 'Oh, he's Superman. That's what Superman looks like.'"[16] Snyder cast Amy Adams as Lois Lane, Russell Crowe as Superman's dad Jor-El, and Michael Shannon as the main villain, General Zod. Goyer wrote the screenplay based on a treatment he wrote with Nolan.

The reboot kicks off with an extended Krypton sequence that pits Superman's dad Jor-El against Zod before the planet explodes. Skipping over Kal-El's arrival on Earth, the story picks up with the young hero as a twentysomething working on a fishing trawler. He leaves the boat to investigate a downed alien (Kryptonian) scout ship in the Arctic, where he meets Pulitzer Prize–winning reporter Lois Lane.

Zod and his crew escape their exile in the Phantom Zone and come to Earth to claim a genetics codex for artificially incubated Kryptonian babies that Kal-El/Clark/Superman carries in his genes thanks to Jor-El. Zod forces Clark and Lois to board his ship but they escape with the help of Jor-El who, though dead, reappears via Kryptonian science. On Earth, Clark dons his Superman outfit and fights two of Zod's warriors in Smallville. Zod sets up a "planet engine" to terraform Earth for his new race of Kryptonians. Superman destroys it and, in a final confrontation, kills Zod. The movie ends with Kal-El donning his Clark Kent guise and starting work at *The Daily Planet*.

If Bryan Singer's *Superman Returns* was an homage to the 1978 original, Snyder's take is a watch-it-burn rejection of just about everything that film stands for. With its bleak, apocalyptic and borderline nihilistic tone, *Man of Steel* is also a flat-out rejection of Marvel's action-comedy formula. Yet the movie's seriousness can't spackle over its innate silliness, like two dead dads (Crowe as Jor-El and Kevin Costner as Pa Kent in flashback) who pop every time things get hairy or Kal-El needs a pep talk by way of confusing allegory (for example, Pa Kent's infamous "hero cake" monologue). That said, the special effects are the best yet in a Superman film and the smackdown in Smallville has a bludgeoning, earth-shaking impact missing in previous superhero flicks. The movie's PG-13 violence reaches its zenith in the final battle between Zod and Superman. The mad Kryptonian general is about to use his heat vision to kill innocent Metropolitans when Superman snaps his neck.

"Full-stop, Superman doesn't kill," wrote comics writer Mark Waid.[17] Many agreed, but the precedent had been set at least as far back as *Superman II* when the hero nonchalantly tosses his now non-superpowered enemies off a platform, presumably to their deaths.

Reviewers were less than enthralled, though for more varied reasons, and *Man of Steel* didn't sustain its record-breaking opening-weekend. Nevertheless, Warner Bros. had too much riding on the reboot; it was intended to jump-start the studio's own series of billion-dollar DC-based films, or what would become known as the DC Extended Universe (DCEU). As the movie opened, Warner announced that Snyder and Goyer would return for a sequel. A month later, Snyder revealed to a Comic-Con audience that the sequel's foe would be none other than Batman.

Just over a month later, Fox released *The Wolverine*. After the underperforming *X-Men Origins* installment, producers Lauren Shuler Donner and Hutch Parker hired James Mangold for the follow-up. New York–born and -raised, the writer-director had studied under Czech director Milos Forman. Mangold's credits included *3:10 to Yuma*, an adaptation of an Elmore Leonard Western, and, perhaps more importantly, a 2001 period piece called *Kate & Leopold* that starred Hugh Jackman.

Mangold tapped Scott Frank to rewrite a script by two other writers, including Christopher McQuarrie (*The Usual Suspects*). Frank had won an Academy Award for his screenplay for another Leonard adaptation, the 1998 movie *Out of Sight*. Mangold told Frank that he wanted the movie to be similar in tone to *The Outlaw Josey Wales*, a 1976 Civil War–era Clint Eastwood Western about a vengeful Missouri farmer. Frank also cited "Old Man Logan," a 2008 storyline set in the distant future by writer Mark Millar and artist Steve McNiven, which the writer "just loved."[18] Frank was also intrigued by the idea of a powerless Logan. "When I came on *The Wolverine* ... I said to Jim, 'Let's write a movie about a guy who is invincible and self-healing who loses his power on page 20, and explore that,'" Frank said.[19]

The Wolverine plops Logan into an intergenerational feudal saga in modern-day Japan. Ichirō Yashida, whose life Logan saved during World War II, is dying of cancer. One of the richest and most powerful men in the country, he offers Logan a deal: let Yashida's doctor transfer the mutant's healing abilities to him so that the businessman can recover and Logan can live a normal life. Logan refuses. At Yashida's funeral, Yakuza gangsters try to kidnap the dead man's granddaughter, Mariko. Logan takes it upon himself to protect the protesting young woman who, at the reading of the will, stands to inherit her grandfather's empire. But Logan soon finds that he is losing his healing abilities. On their second attempt, the Yakuza captures Mariko. With Yukio, a young mutant with precognitive abilities and friend of the Ichirō clan, Logan discovers that Mariko's father Shingen is behind the kidnapping. He returns to the Ichirō estate and discovers a parasite in his body that is causing his loss of powers. After some self-surgery, he and Yukio follow Mariko's trail to Ichirō's compound in southern Japan where they fight and defeat Viper, the mutant who planted the parasite, and a giant suit of armor, the Silver Samurai, inhabited by a still-living Yashida.

Aside from Jackman and Famke Janssen's Jean Grey/Phoenix (or her ghost), the cast consists of characters new to the franchise. Mariko (model Tao Okamoto) originated in Chris Claremont and John Byrne's *Uncanny X-Men* run and Yukio (model-actress Rila Fukushima) in a 1982 *Wolverine* mini-series by Claremont and Frank Miller. Viper (Russian actress Svetlana Khodchenkova) dated back to a 1969 issue of *Captain America* by Jim Steranko, one of Marvel's most celebrated artists of that era. Steranko, who was also a magician, publisher and musician, and who claims to have invented the concept of the go-go dancer,[20] helped revitalize Nick Fury as a superspy.

The new faces and exotic set-pieces—including an action sequence atop a bullet train—and the theme of Logan as a ronin, a samurai without a master, represented a serious step up from *Origins*. But little did fans and moviegoers know that it was just an amuse bouche for Mangold and Frank's next dish.

• • •

Marvel wanted a second *Thor* movie, but Kenneth Branagh had had enough. "It was a long time [making the first film] and they were way too quick for me to get straight back into another," he said in 2015.[21]

Directorial duties eventually went to *Game of Thrones*' Alan Taylor. Don Payne, who had worked on the first *Thor*, wrote a draft of the screenplay before health problems took him away from the picture.

"When we started *Thor 2*, he was the guy we wanted because he was the one who brought the tone—the fun and the spark," executive producer Craig Kyle said.[22] (Payne passed away from bone cancer in March 2013, eight months before the movie's release; the end credits include a dedication to the late writer.) Christopher Yost, who had been part of a writers program set up by Marvel in 2009, stepped in. *First Avenger's* Christopher Markus and Stephen McFeely also took a pass at the script.

The initial villain for what became *Thor: The Dark World* was Hela, Goddess of Death (*The Mighty Thor* #150, 1968), but Marvel in New York again put the kibosh on the idea of a female big baddie. Instead, Malekith the Accursed, Ruler of the Dark Elves, got the green light.

But the *Thor* sequel had a release date before it had a compelling *raison d'etre*, as those involved came to realize. Following principal photography, the Marvel brain trust saw that the story didn't advance Thor's journey. After a huddle, the producers decided that a month of reshoots would be necessary to reshape the film.

The emergency surgery failed to shield Marvel from its worst reviews yet. In 2019, *Comicbookmovie.com* ranked *Thor: The Dark World* last out of the studio's movies released up to that point.[23]

That same year, an interviewer had to remind Irish actor Chris O'Dowd that he'd been in the film (playing a rival to Thor for Jane Foster's affections). "God, I forgot I was in that one until you just mentioned it," O'Dowd told *MTV News*. "I was like, 'Why is he talking to me about Marvel movies?'"[24]

Asked if he took issue with the criticisms about the movie, Christopher Markus said, "Listen, there are 22 movies [in the Marvel Cinematic Universe]. One's going to be first and one's going to be last. I think there's plenty of delightful things in it."[25]

Chapter XVII

A Raccoon and a Tree Walk into a Bar

> "It's kind of amazing, looking back on it, how much freedom I was given.... They said, basically, 'Here are the comics. Come up with a good story. Choose the characters you like, and we'll just keep playing with it.'"
> —Nicole Perlman, screenwriter, *Guardians of the Galaxy*[1]

Anthony and Joe Russo were known for their TV work, particularly on *Arrested Development* and *Community*. After seeing the latter's second-season finale, a spoof of spaghetti Westerns called "For a Few Paintballs More," Marvel's Kevin Feige called the Cleveland-raised brothers: "You guys should be directing action movies," he told them.[2] The Russos signed on to make the sequel to *Captain America* just before *The Avengers* opened.

Feige's instincts proved to be correct. Working from a script by *First Avenger* screenwriters Stephen McFeely and Christopher Markus, the Russos' Marvel debut barely lets the superhero stop for breath as he careens from one action-packed crisis to another.

Captain America: The Winter Soldier picks up after the Battle of New York. Nick Fury and S.H.I.E.L.D. have built three Helicarriers that, once aloft and linked to satellites, can detect and eliminate threats. Steve Rogers, aka Captain America, is not a fan of the idea of spying on American citizens. He's even more alarmed when an attempt on Nick Fury's life reveals that S.H.I.E.L.D. has been compromised.

Natasha Romanoff, aka Black Widow, now a S.H.I.E.L.D. operative, joins Steve in trying to uncover the conspiracy and identify an unstoppable killing machine with a bionic left arm. Cap discovers that the killer is his friend Bucky. Captured by Nazis while helping Steve behind enemy lines, Bucky became the subject of Arnim Zola's experiments and has been under Hydra control ever since.

Aiding Natasha and Cap in their battles are Sam Wilson, an Armed Forces vet who has mastered a flying exo-skeleton, and S.H.I.E.L.D. agent Maria Hill. They help Natasha destroy two of the Helicarriers while Steve fights Bucky on the third. After saving Cap's life, Bucky disappears.

A tight thriller with heaps of action, *Winter Soldier* features some of the most white-knuckle sequences yet in a Marvel movie, including Cap going *mano a mano* with the deadly fighter Batroc; an elevator-set melee between Cap and several Hydra agents; and a fight between Natasha, Steve and Bucky on the streets of Washington.

While the story draws on the 2005 "Winter Soldier" arc by writer Ed Brubaker and artist Steve Epting (co-scripter McFeely called it "the coolest run in Captain America in modern comics"[3]), the filmmakers looked to seventies conspiracy movies like *The*

Parallax View and *Three Days of the Condor* for its tone. Marvel and the Russos even talked *Condor* star Robert Redford into playing the corrupt head of S.H.I.E.L.D., Alexander Pierce. "Guys, I gotta be honest with you, I don't know what these movies are," Redford told the Marvel team. "But my grandkids love them."[4]

With its smart script and political undertones, and enough character development for viewers to invest in the outcome—including a scene in which Steve visits Peggy Carter (Hayley Atwell), now in her nineties, in the hospital—*Captain America: The Winter Soldier* escaped the sequel doldrums that had set in for Marvel on *Iron Man 2* and *Thor: The Dark World*. (McFeeley and Markus had a year to develop the script, an unusually long period in the superhero movie world.) Most of the universe-building was tucked away in the mid- and end credits scenes, but the real news was in the main credits: the team-up of the Russos and McFeeley and Markus.

• • •

When in doubt, add more villains.

For *The Amazing Spider-Man 2*, Sony's sequel to its reboot, this meant no fewer than three bad guys to plague Peter Parker. Electro and the Rhino hailed from yellowing issues of *Amazing Spider-Man*, while the pumpkin-throwing madman the Green Goblin was all too familiar to moviegoers.

The Rhino bookends *The Amazing Spider-Man 2*, which continues Peter's investigation into his parents' deaths. The main focus is on Electro, aka Max Dillon, a Spider-Man stan and electrical engineer who works at Oscorp Industries. One night at work, Max falls into a vat of genetically engineered eels, proving once again that the Green Goblin really needs to update his company's employee safety standards.

While Max is gaining dominion over electricity, Peter is dealing with typical Peter Parker problems. He's trying to follow Capt. Stacy's dying request at the end of the previous movie keeping his distance from Gwen, who is about to leave for Oxford. And Peter's only friend Harry Osborn, heir to the Osborn fortune and Oscorp, is dying of a deadly genetic disease.

Believing that a transfusion of Spider-Man's blood will help, Harry asks Peter to put him in touch with the superhero. Peter refuses, so Harry uses venom from Oscorp's genetically altered spiders. The venom transforms him into the Green Goblin and he dons his dad's armor.

Max has embraced his identity as a supervillain and is menacing the city's power grid. Gwen helps Spider-Man defeat Electro. The Green Goblin arrives and, seeing Gwen, realizes that Peter is Spider-Man. The Goblin grabs Gwen and flies her to the top of a tower. In the ensuing fight, Gwen falls to her death. Peter quits being Spider-Man. He changes his mind in time to fight the Rhino, an armored Russian bank robber.

Director Marc Webb's second *Spider-Man* has the benefit of not having to rehash the hero's origin. But the void is filled with too many subplots and villains; writers Alex Kurtzman and Roberto Orci (*Mission: Impossible III*, *Star Trek*), along with Jeff Pinkner, contribute a script that hits all the marks for franchise-building without offering a compelling story. Even the palpable Garfield-Stone heat and some clever uses of Spider-Man's powers can't make up for uninspired takes on Electro (Jamie Foxx), a sad sack who looks like a reject from a seventies post-apocalypse flick, and yet another Green Goblin (Dane Dehaan).

Despite unenthused moviegoers and yawning reviewers, Sony assigned the screenwriters to work on a sequel. But when star Andrew Garfield failed to show at a planned press event in Brazil to announce the third installment, the studio changed its mind, according to Sony emails hacked by North Korea.[5]

The 2014 hack was in retaliation for *The Interview*, a Seth Rogen-James Franco comedy about a plot to assassinate the country's leader, Kim Jong-Un. (Perhaps here would be the appropriate place to note that Rogen starred in a 2011 *Green Hornet* movie directed by Michel Gondry. Although perhaps the less said the better.) Among the other revelations: Sony and Marvel had been discussing the possibility of including Spider-Man in the Marvel Cinematic Universe.[6]

The next big superhero release was another sequel to a reboot, *X-Men: Days of Future Past*. After introducing younger versions of familiar characters in *X-Men: First Class*, Fox decided to stay in the retro lane but jump ahead to the seventies. *First Class* director Matthew Vaughn co-wrote the story, a loose adaptation of a storyline from the much-plundered Byrne-Claremont comics run, with writing partner Jane Goldman and *X-Men* producer Simon Kinberg. Kinberg wrote the script and original *X-Men* and *X2* helmer Bryan Singer returned to direct.

Opening in a dystopian future, *Days* finds several X-Men on the run from giant killer robots called Sentinels. They come up with a plan to send Wolverine's consciousness back to 1973, in time to prevent Mystique from assassinating anti-mutant scientist Boliver Trask. The reasoning is that the assassination prompts the government to pursue Trask's Sentinels program.

At Xavier's School for Gifted Youngsters, Wolverine convinces Charles and Beast that he's from the future and they agree to help him. They recruit super-fast Peter Maximoff, another mutant, and together they break Magneto out of his cell in the Pentagon.

After Richard Nixon okays the Sentinels program, Magneto decides to kill the president. At the White House, Mystique saves Nixon and his cabinet from Magneto. The president rescinds the program and Wolverine wakes up at Charles' mutant school to find everything has been set right.

If *First Class* didn't confuse the average moviegoer, *Days*' smorgasbord of old, new and new-old mutants surely did. Along with the previous film's younger versions of Charles, Magneto, Beast and Mystique, the film features the modern-era versions of Storm, Kitty Pryde/Shadowcat and Rogue, but long after events in *X3*. Evan Peters debuts as the mutant Quicksilver, a character who was making his second appearance in a movie that year; he is also glimpsed at the end of *The Winter Soldier* although, owing to rights issues, only Fox could call him by his superhero sobriquet (or refer to him as a "mutant"). Quicksilver gets the movie's standout effects showcase, a slow-motion display of his powers in a Pentagon kitchen.

Despite the scorecard required to keep track of who was who and when, *Days* built on the good will engendered by *First Class* and was embraced by audiences and critics. Along with *The Wolverine*, it marked the franchise's third superior effort in a row. Could it last? A post-credits scene introduced the team's next nemesis, the aptly named Apocalypse.

For moviegoers who wanted something more than new faces in familiar costumes, Marvel still had a few tricks up its sleeve.

The first incarnation of the Guardians of the Galaxy appeared in a 1969 try-out title and again briefly in some 1974 comics and intermittently throughout the rest of the decade. In 1990, the team starred in a new series that lasted for a few years, and in 2008 they reappeared in a revamped form. The new lineup included Star-Lord, a half-human spaceman; Rocket Raccoon, a cybernetically enhanced raccoon; Groot, a sentient tree;

Gamora, an alien assassin and adopted daughter of intergalactic warlord Thanos; and Drax the Destroyer, an enhanced human designed to combat Thanos. It was this team, created by writer Dan Abnett and artist Andy Lanning, that inspired Nicole Perlman.

Perlman was two years into her screenwriting career when she was accepted into Marvel's writers program. The studio set up the script incubator shortly after releasing *Iron Man* and *The Incredible Hulk* to bypass the standard Hollywood method of hiring a writer (or writers) and sending them away for six months to work on a screenplay. The program also gave the studio access to in-house script doctors and help in deciding which of its thousands of characters had headliner potential.

The studio gave Perlman a binder full of options. "There were other properties that were better known, but I was drawn to the science fiction tone of that one," she said. Perlman wrote a script based on the Abnett-Lanning team, not thinking the movie would get made since the Guardians weren't popular even amongst comics fans.

"But [at the studio] we were discussing, 'What would be the most off-the-wall thing we could do?'" said producer Jeremy Latcham, an early Marvel Studios hire. "'Let's go make a space opera. Let's just beat everyone to the punch and make space opera cool again.'"[7]

After talking to more than 30 directors, Marvel hired James Gunn. Like Joss Whedon, Gunn seems to have been genetically modified at Oscorp to make superhero movies. The Missouri-born and -raised auteur began his film career with Troma, a proudly down-market studio best known for horror-comedies like the *Toxic Avenger* series. One of Gunn's early screenplays was for 1997's *Tromeo and Juliet*. In 2002, he broke into the mainstream with his script for *Scooby-Doo*, and in 2004 he became the first screenwriter

James Gunn, writer-director of Marvel's *Guardians of the Galaxy* (2014), unlocked the pathos behind the mercurial Rocket Raccoon. Marvel Studios.

Chapter XVII. A Raccoon and a Tree Walk into a Bar

with two movies to top the box office in consecutive weeks, *Scooby-Doo 2: Monsters Unleashed* and *Dawn of the Dead*.

But Gunn also wrote and directed two low-budget independent superhero movies of his own. The first, *The Specials* (2000), is a parody with original characters like the Strobe, the Weevil and Ms. Indestructible. *Super* (2010) is about a man inspired to fight crime by a public-access TV hero called the Holy Avenger.

When Marvel first approached him about directing *Guardians*, Gunn was reluctant—mainly because of Rocket Raccoon. "It seemed to me like it was Bugs Bunny in the middle of the Avengers," he said. But while pondering Rocket, "I started thinking, 'If there were a raccoon in this movie and he was talking, *how* could he be talking?' It was really taking that idea and discovering it was a very sad, tragic story at the center of the *Guardians of the Galaxy*.'"[8]

Inspired by the image of a portable cassette player in Perlman's script, Gunn wrote a treatment and eventually rewrote the screenplay, adding characters, quips and seventies music cues. The director's love of AM radio pop informs the finished film. Redbone's funk jam "Come and Get Your Love" sets the tone early on, and the hits keep coming.

The movie begins as Peter Quill–Star-Lord steals an orb on the abandoned planet Morag. When he tries to sell the orb on planet Xander, he draws the attention of mercenaries Rocket Raccoon and Groot and the green-skinned assassin Gamora. All four run afoul of the local authorities and are imprisoned. There they meet Drax, and the quintet escapes with the orb. Upon learning that the orb holds the Power Stone, and that it's sought by Thanos, the newly formed Guardians determine to keep it out of the despot's hands.

As catchy and breezy as its soundtrack, *Guardians* cleaned up on its July 2014 opening weekend. More space opera and comedy than superhero movie, it was indeed a departure for Marvel. Chris Pratt, known for his work as the well-meaning but dim-witted Andy on the workplace sitcom *Parks and Recreation*, brings his comedic chops to Peter Quill, an ego-driven, insecure leader. Former pro wrestler Dave Bautista is the literal-minded Drax and Zoe Saldana plays the no-nonsense (especially if the nonsense is coming from Quill) Gamora, half-daughter of Thanos. Bradley Cooper and Vin Diesel voice Rocket and Groot, respectively. The movie also debuts Scottish actress Karen Gillan as Nebula, Gamora's half-sister, Josh Brolin (briefly) as Thanos, and Benicio del Toro as Taneleer Tivan, the Collector. In an end-credits scene, moviegoers are treated to a cameo by one of the Collector's former specimens: Marvel's first matinee idol, Howard the Duck. This time, though, he's all CGI.

"I wasn't hip with the Caucasian eyelids," Gunn said of the 1986 movie's duck suit. "That upset me. Because they had the puppet, and it was a duck, and instead of having feathery or white eyelids, he had Caucasian eyelids and it was creepy."[9]

Guardians became the third-highest-grossing film of the year. A Gunn-curated collection of pop gems became the first superhero movie soundtrack to reach #1 on the *Billboard* chart. In the right hands, it seemed, no Marvel character was too weird or obscure to connect with the filmgoing public. And there were many more where the Guardians came from.

Chapter XVIII

High Hopes

> "They said, 'We're interested in you for a role in *Ant-Man*,' and I actually laughed."
>
> —Evangeline Lilly[1]

Some weeks before *The Avengers* opened, Joss Whedon said that he thought a sequel to the film should be "smaller, more personal, more painful." It didn't quite work out that way. Well, maybe the "painful" part did.

"Why would I do this again?" Whedon quipped three years later, in the Blu-ray commentary for what became *Avengers: Age of Ultron*. "Because I wanted to make a new movie. A different *Avengers* movie … and tell it differently."

Ultron begins with the Avengers raiding a Hydra base to retrieve Loki's scepter. Back in New York, Tony Stark uses the scepter's power source, the Mind Stone, to advance an AI he has designed to act as "a suit of armor around the world." Instead, the AI attains consciousness, assimilates Tony's AI Girl Friday J.A.R.V.I.S., and attacks the Avengers. Thor destroys Ultron's robot body but his program survives and builds another. Ultron takes refuge in Sokovia, where he raises the capital city into the sky to use as a bomb, causing the extermination of humankind. The Avenges attack and defeat.

With more characters, more plot and more action, *Age of Ultron* seeks to improve upon the first, but something seems off, especially in some of the character moments, like a romantic interlude between Bruce Banner and Natasha Romanoff, and in the confusing climactic showdown in the elevated city.

Whedon delivers another quip- and gag-filled script, though, and the actors are more comfortable in their roles. In one of the movie's funniest scenes, the Avengers take turns trying to lift Mjölnir. And a fight between Iron Man in his "Hulkbuster" armor and the Hulk was just the kind of thing to send comics fans into a frenzy.

Introduced at the end of *Winter Soldier*, Wanda and Pietro Maximoff, aka the Scarlet Witch and not–Quicksilver (since Fox owned the rights to the name) are given major roles; Pietro sacrifices himself in the end. The movie also debuts the Vision, a boiled-lobster-red cyborg played by English actor Paul Bettany, the plummy voice of J.A.R.V.I.S. Ultron, played via motion-capture by James Spader, is the smoothest-talking killer robot in history (sorry, HAL 9000). Ulysses Klaue (Andy Serkis), an arms dealer with a supply of the in-demand energy-emitting metal vibranium, also makes his first appearance. All of the new characters dated back to sixties Marvel. Pepper Potts and Jane Foster—and Loki, for that matter—sit this one out.

The second most expensive film ever made up to that point, *Ultron* became Marvel's third movie—after *The Avengers* and *Iron Man 3*—to earn over a billion dollars.[2]

Chapter XVIII. High Hopes

Reviews were mixed, with critics about evenly divided on whether the sequel measured up to or surpassed the first.

Behind the scenes, *Ultron* marked the end of the honeymoon between Whedon and the studio. The two were at loggerheads over scenes that Marvel wanted to include to tie in with the next two movies. By the time *Ultron* opened in May 2015, the director had already announced his retirement from future instalments.

Despite the discord, Whedon said the sequel was "the best experience I'll ever have with a studio. And honestly, all of this is a ridiculous dream. But at the end of the day, you know, it is a Marvel film."[3]

As Edgar Wright was about to find out.

The British director had been working on a movie about Marvel's Ant-Man even before Marvel announced its intention to get into the film business. Artisan Entertainment still had the rights when Wright and his writing partner Joe Cornish signed on.

For decades, Stan Lee had been championing an *Ant-Man* flick. The Marvel writer-publisher "loved Ant-Man beyond all reason, and nobody ever gave a damn," Boaz Yakin said. Yakin, who wrote the 1989 *Punisher* movie for New World, recalled Lee trying to sell the idea to the studio. "He wanted an *Ant-Man* script in the worst way. I had been arguing against Ant-Man because, let's face it, he can shrink down, go through a keyhole, and look at secret papers in a desk drawer and that's it."[4]

Howard Stern was another true believer. In 2000, the radio host attempted to purchase the rights to the character. (Stern also spent years trying to convince studios to bankroll his own superhero movie project, *Fartman*.)

Wright, whose breakout zombie comedy *Shaun of the Dead* hadn't yet opened, knew the character, which was more than anyone outside of comics fandom could say. As a kid, he had two seminal Ant-Man comics: a reprint of 1962's *Tales to Astonish* #27, which featured the first appearance of original Ant-Man Hank Pym, and 1972's *Marvel Premiere* #47. The latter introduced Ant Man Version 2.0, petty thief Scott Lang.

"So it was funny that I had both those issues, and I particularly thought 'The Man in the Ant-Hill' [the first *Tales to Astonish* story] was something extremely odd and cool and it almost had a horror movie feel to it," Wright said.[5]

The director was still attached when the rights reverted to Marvel. The studio included the movie in its original 2005 slate.

Wright and Cornish continued to polish the script. Then, in late 2013, Marvel announced that Paul Rudd (*Anchorman*, *Knocked Up*) would play the lead. According to Kevin Feige, the idea of casting the comic actor was the director's. "When Edgar Wright came to us with the idea of Paul Rudd, we felt a huge sense of relief because the first step in creating any Marvel Studios film is finding the right star," he said.[6]

But in May 2014, Wright left the film. *The Hollywood Reporter*'s Kim Masters cited sources who said that Feige had ordered rewrites of Wright's script without the director's input.[7] Feige denied this: "[E]verything was aboveboard. Everything was done with everybody else's knowledge. There was a sense of 'We're going in this direction, you're staying in this direction—maybe it's best that we end as friends.'"[8]

Wright's decision to leave sent shock waves through the fanosphere. Thanks to *Shaun* and *Scott Pilgrim vs. the World*, a 2010 adaptation of a Canadian indie comic, his involvement had generated a lot of buzz. "I thought the script was not only the best script that Marvel had ever had, but the most Marvel script I'd read," said Joss Whedon, in an interview prior to the release of *Ultron*. "I had no interest in Ant-Man. [Then] I read the script, and was like, 'Of course! This is so good!'"[9]

"Edgar Wright's *Ant-Man* could have only been made in 2006," producer Brad Winderbaum said. "By the time we were making *Ant-Man*, however, we were in a post–*Guardians of the Galaxy* world. We were in a post–*Winter Soldier* world ... there's a universe outside a single film that can't be ignored."[10]

Two weeks after Wright left, Marvel announced his replacement. Peyton Reed had come close to directing *Guardians of the Galaxy* and, for Fox, *Fantastic Four*. He, too, was an Ant-Man fan, and had once drawn himself as the character in a flyer for his punk rock band Johnny Quest. Meanwhile, Rudd had started working on the script with *Anchorman* director–co-writer Adam McKay. They kept the heist elements from the earlier version, added the Quantum Realm, and emphasized the relationship between Scott and his daughter Cassie.

Evangeline Lilly, the *Lost* actress who signed on to play the female lead Hope van Dyne partially due to Wright's involvement, said that her fears were allayed when she saw the new screenplay. "I saw with my own eyes that Marvel had just pulled the script into their world," she said. "I mean, they've established a universe, and everyone has come to expect a certain aesthetic [and] a certain feel for Marvel films. And what Edgar was creating was much more in the Edgar Wright camp of films."[11]

In *Ant-Man*, Scott Lang is a thief who has just been released from jail and is attempting to go straight, at least partly so that he can maintain contact with Cassie, his pre-teen daughter. His friends Luis, Dave and Kurt talk him into doing another job based on a tip Luis got from his cousin Ernesto at a wine-tasting. Scott breaks into the house but all he finds to steal is a costume. He takes it home, tries it on and shrinks to the size of an insect. Alarmed, he tries to return the costume but is caught by the owner, scientist-inventor Hank Pym. Pym tells Scott that he needs his help in stealing another shrinking outfit, the Yellowjacket, from Darren Cross. Cross wants to sell the technology to Hydra. In the final showdown, Ant-Man and Yellowjacket duke it out in miniature amidst Cassie's toys.

Like *Guardians*, *Ant-Man* was another surprise, as much a comedy and heist film as a superhero movie. Michael Peña nearly steals the show as Luis, a storyteller who never met a tangent he didn't like, and Rudd and Lilly have screwball chemistry as Scott and Hope. Still and motion-picture macrophotography, used for the shrinking scenes, inject something visually fresh into the Marvel Cinematic Universe.

At the box office, *Ant-Man*'s July 2015 opening was the studio's second lowest, after 2008's *The Incredible Hulk*. But it still went to #1, making it the twelfth Marvel movie in a row to do so, and drew the largest share of families (28 percent) and women (32 percent) of any Marvel superhero title.[12] Even Lilly, the most skeptical of all observers, left the premiere a true believer: "I came out giddy. I usually don't see my films and come out feeling like that.... But with *Ant-Man*, I felt like a kid watching [the] movie."[13]

Wright may have left because his vision didn't jibe with the needs of Marvel's greater cinematic universe, but the studio's approach was also alienating to some filmmakers. Zach Snyder's *Man of Steel* could be seen as a rejection of the Marvel action-comedy formula, and so could Josh Trank's *Fantastic Four*.

Jeremy Slater had begun working on a screenplay for the Fox reboot with the director when *The Avengers* was released. "I kept saying, 'That should be our template, that's what audiences want to see!" said Slater, a comics fan. "And Josh just fucking hated every second of it."[14]

In auteur fashion, Trank seems to have seen the Fantastic Four reboot as a way to work out some demons. "The end of *Fantastic Four* was going to very organically set up the adventure and the weirdness and the fun," he said. "That would be the wish fulfillment of the sequel.... But the first movie was going to basically be the filmic version of how I saw myself all the time: the metaphor of these characters crawling out of Hell."[15]

Trank got the assignment in the wake of his debut feature *Chronicle*. In 2012, the L.A.-based 28-year-old became the youngest director to open at #1 when the movie, about a trio of Seattle teenagers who gain superpowers from an alien artifact, earned more than $126 million on a budget of $12 million.

20th Century–Fox, *Chronicle*'s distributor, had first-look rights to Trank's next project. Studio president Emma Watts apparently called the director and asked if he had any ideas for a *Fantastic Four* reboot. A fan of Canadian director David Cronenberg, Trank said he would play up the body-horror angle of suddenly having the powers to stretch around a doorway, erupt into flame and turn invisible, and of becoming a walking pile of orange bricks.

Fox had already hired *X-Men: First Class* writers Zack Stentz and Ashley Edward Miller to write a script. After signing on, Trank worked on his own with his *Chronicle* co-writer Slater. Slater left after six months.

As pre-production progressed, Trank courted controversy. He cast African-American Michael B. Jordan, with whom he'd worked on *Chronicle*, for traditionally white flameboy Johnny Storm. For Johnny's sister Susan Storm, aka Invisible Woman, he cast Caucasian Kate Mara, which led to some fancy retconning footwork; Trank's explanation for the racial difference was to say that Sue was adopted—from

(From left to right) Michael B. Jordan, Miles Teller, and Kate Mara portrayed the third live-action incarnation of Marvel's first family, along with a CGI Thing (trailing behind), in 2015's *Fantastic Four*. 20th Century–Fox.

Kosovo, no less—an invention that went against 55 years of Fantastic Four history. He also cast 5'7" Jamie Bell, who was best known as the lead in the 2000 movie *Billy Elliott*, as Ben Grimm. In the comics, the man who would be Thing was a street-smart tough guy built like a stevedore, or like Mike Chiklis, who played both Ben and his alter ego (in prosthetics) in the two earlier Fox *Fantastic Four* movies. But since this film's Thing would be CGI, Trank figured, what difference did it make?

It mattered to fans. Nor did Mara help when, before the movie's release, she told an interviewer that she had not read any of the comics, and that the director discouraged her from doing so.[16]

Simon Kinberg, one of the movie's producers, shrugged off concerns. "I actually think that this *Fantastic Four* movie is sort of a celebration of all the Fantastic Four comics that have preceded it," he said.[17] "Sort of" being the key words in that statement.

During and after filming, rumors spread of conflicts between Trank and star Miles Teller and Trank and Fox. On the eve of release, the director practically disowned his film.

"A year ago I had a fantastic version of this," he tweeted. "And it would've received great reviews. You'll probably never see it. That's reality, though."[18]

Following a comics reboot from the mid-oughts, Trank's *Fantastic Four* reimagines the group as teen prodigies working for the government-sponsored R&D group the Baxter Foundation. Reed Richards is a high school brainiac, Johnny Storm an engineer, his sister Sue a scientist, and Ben Grimm is Reed's best friend. The Foundation's sole project, it seems, is the Quantum Gate, a portal designed by Victor von Doom. Doom is the protégé of project head Franklin Storm, father of Sue and Johnny.

One night, Reed, Johnny, Ben and Victor take an unauthorized trip through the gate to another dimension dubbed Planet Zero. After Victor touches a green lava-like substance, the environment destabilizes. Meanwhile, Sue has realized that someone has breached the gate and rushes to the lab. She is able to bring everyone back except Victor before the gate explodes. Reed, Sue, Johnny and Ben discover their respective powers following the gate explosion and exposure to Planet Zero. A year later, Sue, Johnny and Ben are government operatives and Reed is a fugitive. With Sue's help, Ben brings Reed back to repair the gate. Victor, his science suit fused to his body, passes through the gate from Planet Zero and kills a couple of scientists. Reed, Sue, Johnny and Ben use the gate and confront their co-worker on Planet Zero. They fight, Doom dies, and the team returns.

It's hard to imagine a more fundamentally misguided attempt at a *Fantastic Four* movie. The main characters, teens played by actors in their late twenties, are self-pitying and morose. CGI Thing looks like a pile of Jenga pieces. Doctor Doom is mostly absent, and when he finally reappears, is less worrisome than a student loans collector. Even the Dollar Store 1994 version, for all its faults, is recognizably Fantastic Four. Those who had dismissed the lighthearted *Fantastic Four* flicks of the previous decade were sorry now. If there is a faster-paced, more action-oriented version that could be salvaged out of whatever was filmed, it's nowhere in evidence here.

"You made it ugly," Reed says when he sees the military rebuild of the Gate. The same can be said about Fox's *Fantastic Four* reboot.

Chapter XIX

Ask Not for Whom Dawns the Justice

"I think it's indicative of the way that *Batman v Superman* was received that its central tenet was sort of belittled and made fun of."—Zach Snyder[1]

"Everyone knows that the third movie is always the worst."
 —Jean Grey (Sophie Turner) in *X-Men: Apocalypse*

Two thousand sixteen turned out to be a banner one for superhero movies. Not only were more of the specimens released than in any year previous, and of more varied quality, but of more variety too, from the R-rated black humor of *Deadpool* to the black-light-and-lava-lamp mysticism of *Doctor Strange*.

Politically, a seismic shift had occurred, or at least been recognized, in the U.S. For the most part, Hollywood was still delivering Obama-era product, and the culture wars had yet to boil over. But two movies, perhaps inadvertently, reflected the polarization that was coming to define the country. In *Batman v Superman: Dawn of Justice*, Bruce Wayne, enraged at the devastation left in the wake of Superman's battle with Zod, decides to kill Superman. In *Captain America: Civil War*, Captain America and Iron Man clash over questions of accountability.

Both movies also shared a mandate to reboot icons and debut new possible franchise headliners. Comparatively, they demonstrated just how much Warner Bros. and Marvel were diverging in their respective approaches. Story-wise, stakes in both were relatively low, depending on how one felt about Henry Cavill's Superman and Sebastian Stan's Bucky Barnes.

When *Batman v Superman* begins, Bruce Wayne is a media-saturated anger missile growing more and more murderous while watching footage of Superman's devastating fight with Zod. Also wanting to kill Superman is Lex Luthor. He blackmails Superman to confront Batman in what he calls "the greatest gladiator match in the history of the world" by kidnapping both Lois Lane and Martha Kent, Clark's adoptive mother. In case Batman isn't up to the job, Lex—a tech billionaire—also accesses the alien technology in Zod's downed Kryptonian ship to create Doomsday, a being powerful enough to kill Superman.

Batman preps for the big fight. Superman flies to Gotham City and confronts Batman. Following a protracted and unrelenting battle, Batman, through methodical planning, gadgets and a supply of illicit kryptonite, gets the upper hand. He is about to deliver the killing blow when Superman asks him to save his mother Martha. Batman flashes back to the death of his own mother, also named Martha. Cue pearl necklace flashback. "Why did you say that name?" Batman bellows repeatedly before Lois shows up to explain.

Batman backs off. He teams up with Superman to fight Doomsday; Superman is killed in the battle.

There is more, much more, including Pulitzer Prize–winning reporter Lois Lane chasing a story in Africa; a meeting between Bruce, Clark and Lex at a LexCorp gala; Holly Hunter as a U.S. Senator; the bombing and destruction of a Congressional hearing; and Bruce Wayne training for his fight *Rocky*-style. The new DCEU Wonder Woman (Israeli actor-model Gal Gadot) debuts, appearing first as Diana at the Lex-Corp gala and later in costume to help fight Doomsday. *Batman v Superman* also crams in brief intros to Aquaman, the Flash and Cyborg—the rest of the Justice League in the next DCEU flick—and a whole new Batworld, complete with an all-terrain Batmobile and an ultramodern Batcave. Jeremy Irons is the new Alfred and Ben Affleck the new Bruce Wayne/Batman. Real-world figures Neil deGrasse Tyson and Nancy Grace comment on happenings in the fictional cities of Gotham and Metropolis.

If critics weren't fond of *Man of Steel*, they loathed return director Zach Snyder's sequel. "*Batman v Superman* is 153 minutes of a grown man whacking two dolls together,"[2] "*Batman v Superman* is a Failure on Every Single Level"[3] and "Every Single Thing That Is Wrong with *Batman v Superman: Dawn of Justice*"[4] were just the titles of some of the reviews.

Many took issue with the tentpole's bleak tone and seemingly random story events. Chris Terrio, who had worked with Ben Affleck on the Oscar-winning 2012 film *Argo*

DC Comics' two most iconic heroes clash in Zach Snyder's *Batman v Superman: Dawn of Justice*. Critics generally loathed the 2016 film, which featured a much-derided scene in which good guys Superman (Henry Cavill) and Batman (Ben Affleck) bond over their mothers' shared first name. Warner Bros.

and was brought in by the actor to polish David S. Goyer's script, blamed the studio for what, in the final cut, comes across as one big dick move on the part of Batman. "I was proud of the script when I completed it, but it turns out that when you remove the 30 minutes that give the characters motivation for the climax, the film just doesn't work.... So this house of cards that had been built in order to motivate this clash between America's two favorite heroes made no sense at all."[5] The extra footage was restored in a 2016 Ultimate Edition.

Outside of the film's merits, or lack thereof, controversy followed Snyder's depiction of Batman. This Caped Crusader brands criminals, a flourish that istantamount to a death sentence once they get to prison (never mind that a Batman brand would more likely be considered a badge of honor in the Gotham City underworld). But this was an old complaint; Batman had been killing bad guys in the movies since Burton's 1989 movie.

The loudest jeers were reserved for "the Martha moment," when Batman realizes that his and Superman's Earth mom have the same name. "If only Biggie and Tupac's moms had the same first name, they might still be here today," wrote the *Guardian*'s Dave Schilling.[6]

Snyder defended the scene. "Clearly I am a fan of, and am very interested in how 'Martha,' that concept is central to the film," he said in 2021. "I mean, it's 100 percent the lynchpin that holds the entire movie together.... I personally think it is this beautiful and incredibly symmetrical idea that completely finishes it as a concept."[7]

Notices were mostly positive for the leads, though, including Gal Gadot as Wonder Woman. Most polarizing was Jesse Eisenberg's portrayal of Luthor as an overcaffeinated tech guru; some reviewers thought the performance unwatchable while others felt the actor was the only one having any fun. The film's supporters maintained that at least Snyder was offering an alternative to the company that was becoming synonymous with the genre. "*Batman v Superman* is too smart for Marvel fans," stated a *New York Post* headline.[8]

Box office–wise, the highly anticipated, heavily hyped extravaganza opened big but crashed on subsequent weekends. The $250–300 million film fell short of the billion-dollar mark that Marvel was reaching on an almost monthly basis. If they hadn't worried after *Man of Steel*, Warners execs were fretting now; Snyder was contracted to make what was supposed to be the biggest DCEU movie yet, *Justice League*.

Released a month after *Batman v Superman*, *Captain America: Civil War* begins in Lagos, where Captain America, Black Widow, Wanda Maximoff and the Falcon are on a mission to stop Hydra from stealing a bioweapon. When the confrontation ends in a fatal explosion, the United Nations creates the Sokovia Accords. The Accords, which require that all "enhanced" humans, i.e., superheroes, register and answer to a collective governmental body, split the heroes into two camps: those for, led by a conscience-stricken Tony Stark, and against, led by independent-minded Steve Rogers.

Following another explosion, this one at a U.N. conference in Vienna, the two sides clash at Leipzig Airport. Iron Man wants to bring in the rogue Captain America but Cap escapes with Bucky Barnes, who has been framed for the explosion at the conference. The two fly to a Hydra facility in Siberia where they expect to see more enemy super-soldiers. Instead, they find Helmut Zemo, a Sokovian whose family was collateral damage in the Avengers' fight with Ultron. Iron Man follows his former teammate to Siberia where he is informed by Zemo that Barnes killed his (Tony's) parents. Iron Man and Captain America fight over Barnes' fate until Cap disables Tony's armor and leaves with his friend.

Released the same year as *Batman v Superman*, Marvel's *Captain America: Civil War* (2016) had some fun with the idea of superheroes pounding the crap out of each other. From left: Anthony Mackie as Falcon, Paul Rudd as Ant-Man, Jeremy Renner as Hawkeye, Chris Evans as Captain America, Elizabeth Olsen as Scarlet Witch, and Sebastian Stan as Winter Soldier. Marvel Studios.

Civil War is solid throughout. Its biggest contributions to the Marvel Cinematic Universe, besides the epic airport battle, are the introductions of Black Panther and Marvel's artisanal version of Spider-Man. The former appears early on, following the explosion at the conference, in a chase scene. Spidey makes his Marvel movie debut during the airport fight sequence, adding webslinging to what was already a grand-scale, meticulously choreographed smorgasbord of power-blasting, shield-throwing, flying and Ant-Man turning into Giant Man (it's a comics thing). As the Panther, the first black superhero in mainstream comics, Marvel cast Chadwick Boseman; the actor had portrayed baseball player Jackie Robinson in the 2013 biopic *42* and singer James Brown in 2014's *Get On Up*. Marvel announced the pick, along with a stand-alone *Black Panther* movie, in 2014. Due in part to the extended back-and-forth with Sony for permission to use Spider-Man, though, the studio didn't sign its Peter Parker, British stage actor Tom Holland, until a month into the Russos' filming of *Civil War*.

Conspicuous by their absence were Thor and the Hulk. "You put those guys in a fight, it's over quickly," said Christopher Markus, who wrote the script with Stephen McFeely. "It's like, 'Well, we have the Hulk on our side.' Oh, fine, then."[9]

Refreshingly, there was not a single CGI villain in sight—although this was the second *Captain America* movie in a row in which the hero risks everything for Bucky, a guy who, after 70 years as a murder machine under Hydra control, has killed countless people. Not only does Cap almost murder Tony to save him, but Bucky gets an all-expenses paid vacation in Wakanda and, after losing it in the fight with Iron Man, a new bionic arm.

Chapter XIX. Ask Not for Whom Dawns the Justice

Oh well. As far as controversial superhero movie plot points go, this was no Martha moment.

• • •

Where *Dawn of Justice* and *Civil War* tried to tackle big ideas, Fox's *Deadpool*—released in February, more than a month before *Justice*—was always going to be as serious as a rubber chicken.

Despite the negative reaction to the mercenary's mouthless incarnation in 2009's *X-Men Origins: Wolverine*, Fox continued to develop a stand-alone *Deadpool* movie. The studio hired a writing team, Rhett Reese and Paul Wernick, and a director, Tim Miller. A visual effects ace, Miller's credits included the title sequence for *Thor: The Dark World*, a fight scene in Edgar Wright's *Scott Pilgrim vs. the World* and a six-minute trailer for a DC-based video game. He had also directed some Iron Man cartoons commissioned by Marvel prior to the first movie's release, to prove to kids that the character wasn't a robot.

However, *Deadpool* hit a snag following *Green Lantern*. Ryan Reynolds, who had starred in the mega-bomb, had played Deadpool in *Origins* and was attached to the character's solo adventure. Suddenly, though, "it was impossible to get a Ryan Reynolds superhero movie off the ground," Wernick said.[10] His and Reese's R-rated *Deadpool* script, rife with profanity, nudity and decapitations, probably didn't help.

The feature had reached a dead end when, in August 2014, someone leaked animated test footage of a freeway fight scene.

At first, everyone thought Miller was behind the leak, Reynolds said. But after conducting his own investigation, the actor concluded that "the initial [leak] came from Fox… [S]omeone recorded the footage on their iPhone and then released it. And then once that happened, somebody hacked into Blur Studios [Miller's visual effects company] and got the original footage in high-res and put it online."[11]

Whatever the method, the escaped scenes excited fans and proved to Fox that there was an audience for a *Deadpool* movie. According to Wernick, *X-Men* producer Simon Kinberg "really jammed it through the Powers-That-Be at Fox,"[12] and also sold the studio on the idea of keeping the adult content. "Simon's sell to Fox on the R was that there is a hole in the marketplace, let's do something that Disney and Marvel can't do."[13]

Violence and profanity were unusual for the high-stakes, PG-13 world of superhero movies, but they are crucial ingredients in *Deadpool*, which is otherwise a standard origin story.

As the movie begins, special forces operative Wade Wilson is diagnosed with cancer. Approached by a mysterious stranger, Wade accepts the offer of a cure via an experimental serum. The serum gives Wade superhuman healing abilities (*à la* Wolverine) but leaves him with severe facial scarring (*à la* Two-Face). He attempts to track down Ajax, the guy who injected him with the serum, but Ajax kidnaps Wade's fiancée Vanessa. With help from a couple of X-Men, Colossus and Negasonic Teenage Warhead, Deadpool confronts Ajax and his henchmen in a S.H.I.E.L.D. scrapyard.

The Fox film was the closest yet by another studio to capturing the irreverent tone of Marvel. Some of the funniest scenes occur between Deadpool and Negasonic Teenage Warhead, a surly teen played by Brianna Hildebrand. "She only appeared in one issue of one comic," said Reese of the character. "But the name was so delightful that we were like, 'We've got to build a character just around that name.'"[14] Writer Grant Morrison named the character after a song by the American rock band Monster Magnet. The writers traded her original telepathic powers for those of an actual warhead after Miller received permission from Marvel to do so in exchange for the rights to another character, Ego the Living Planet, which Fox controlled.[15] Colossus, played by Daniel Cudmore in previous X-Men installments, is CGI.

More comic relief came courtesy comedian T.J. Miller as Weasel, Wade's best friend and a bartender at Sister Margaret's School for Wayward Children; Karan Soni as Dopinder, a cabbie who befriends the hero, and Leslie Uggams as Blind Al, Wade's septuagenarian roommate. Uggams had, as they say, a long and storied career that included but was not limited to working as chorus girl–dancer at Harlem's famed Cotton Club, performing at the Apollo Theatre, recording for MGM at the age of ten, hosting her own TV variety show, and starring in *Roots*. It goes without saying that *Deadpool* was her first R-rated superhero movie.

While *Deadpool* took a self-aware approach to the whole business of super-heroing, Fox's next *X-Men* flick was a return to extinction-level threats.

Released just a few months after *Deadpool*, *X-Men: Apocalypse* was the third period piece in a row for the franchise. This one was set in the eighties for what producer-screenwriter Simon Kinberg called "extra fun color."[16] Bryan Singer returned to direct a lineup of mutants that includes new, younger versions of Cyclops, Jean Grey and Nightcrawler alongside the younger versions of Charles Xavier, Mystique and Beast introduced in *Days of Future Past*.

This batch of new-original X-Men is still learning how to use their powers and work as a team. They are tested by En Sabah Nur, aka Apocalypse, an ancient mutant who once ruled Egypt. After emerging from a centuries-long slumber, he decides that he is not impressed with the modern world and he gathers four "horsemen"—a young Ororo Munroe (aka Storm), Magneto, Archangel (previously Angel, but now dark) and the telekinetic Psylocke—to help him destroy it. Storm and Magneto eventually turn on the evil mutant and help the X-Men hold him off, although it's up to Jean, whose powers are becoming stronger, to deliver the final blow.

The ninth *X-Men* movie (counting *Deadpool*) was pronounced "a franchise-killing disaster" by *Forbes*[17] and "the best superhero film of 2016" by *Mother Jones*.[18] More reviews sided with the former, citing problems such as an overreliance on CGI, the dullest villain (Oscar Isaac, almost unrecognizable in blue makeup and prosthetics) since Dark Elf ruler Malekith, too many subplots and not enough character development.

A year after *Apocalypse*'s release, co-producer Hutch Parker sounded a familiar excuse—an unfinished script—and an unfamiliar one: a franchise that wasn't keeping up with the times. "It's always dangerous if your script is evolving while you're shooting. Certainly, in hindsight, we all feel like the genre has been evolving aesthetically and tonally and that the film … felt sort of dated relative to an evolution you were seeing play out everywhere else."[19]

Controversially, the movie returns the franchise to Auschwitz for a scene in which Magneto destroys the death camp. The use of a real-life location of unspeakable horror to give weight to the first *X-Men* was questionable enough, but for some this was one Holocaust reference too many. "A moment of incredible, impressive tastelessness that's unfortunately aiming for utter self-seriousness," David Sims wrote in the *Atlantic*.[20] According to Jordan Zakarin at inverse.com, "Manufactured mass death is a given now, raising the stakes enough for the summoning of superheroes to be required. It's much different, and more viscerally upsetting, when a very real tragedy is exploited as a plot point to aid a big blue demon in a corporate production."[21]

Chapter XIX. Ask Not for Whom Dawns the Justice

And then there was the promotional campaign, which included a billboard showing Apocalypse choking Mystique. "There is a major problem when the men and women at 20th Century–Fox think casual violence against women is the way to market a film," said actress-activist Rose McGowan. "There is no context in the ad, just a woman getting strangled. The fact that no one flagged this is offensive and frankly, stupid."[22] The studio pulled the billboards and apologized.

Apocalypse didn't kill the franchise, but it marked the end of Bryan Singer's involvement. Reports of questionable behavior (along with accusations of sexual misconduct) had dogged the director for years. In a 2014 *Hollywood Reporter* story, Kim Masters wrote that Singer's behavior (which the director's attorney attributed to "back pain and neck surgery")[23] had contributed to *Superman Returns* going over-budget.

A 2018 *Hollywood Reporter* story mentioned that the director would arrive to the *Apocalypse* set unprepared and late.[24] Later, *Deadline.com* said that producers Parker, Kinberg *et al.* had to fill in on *Days of Future Past* and *Apocalypse* "whenever Singer would reportedly go AWOL from the set."[25] (A Singer rep denied the claim.[26])

In November, following *Apocalypse*'s lackluster performance, Fox confirmed that the director would not return for the next X-film.

• • •

While Zach Snyder readied *Justice League*, Warner Bros. prepared to release the third movie in its DC Extended Universe.

Like the Guardians of the Galaxy, the Suicide Squad was an offbeat choice for a big-budget feature. Unknown to all but dedicated comics readers, the team had gone through a few iterations. Unlike the Guardians, the Suicide Squad was made up entirely of supervillains.

The first version of the team debuted in a 1959 issue of the DC title *The Brave and the Bold*. A 1987 revival featured a rotating cast of baddies. In 2009, Warner added the property to its slate and hired Justin Marks, who had worked with David S. Goyer on an unproduced movie featuring DC's star archer Green Arrow, to write the script.

Five years of development later, the studio turned to writer-director David Ayer. Ayer specialized in R-rated action movies like *Training Day*, which he wrote, and *Fury*, a World War II tank drama that he wrote and directed. He had also worked on the script for *X-Men Origins: Wolverine*. Ayer threw out Marks' version and penned his own, keeping some characters and substituting others. The most radical addition was Harley Quinn, a charming sociopath who had debuted as the Joker's girlfriend in a 1992 episode of *Batman: The Animated Series* and had been added to the team in the comics in 2011. Co-creators Paul Dini and Bruce Timm were inspired, Dini told the *Washington Post*, by the villainous henchwomen from the *Batman* TV series and a "girl gone wrong," usually in Joker's gang, in the Batman comics of the forties.[27]

Ayer kept the action strictly PG, but it wasn't the director's penchant for ultra-violence that spooked the studio. It was the virulent critical reaction to *Batman v Superman*, released while *Suicide Squad* was in post-production, that spooked the suits. According to birthdeathmovies.com, Warner Bros. ordered reshoots to lighten the tone of Ayer's movie.[28] Ayer tweeted, "#SuicideSquad 'reshoots for humor' is silly. When a studio loves your movie and asks what else you want, go for it! #ThanksWB #moreaction #SuicideSquad" (@DavidAyerMovies, April 11, 2016). In May, the studio tested two versions—Ayer's and another "with more characters introduced early in the film and jazzed-up graphics," according to

The Hollywood Reporter. The audience preferred the former. In a joint statement before the finished product's release, Ayer and Warner production president Greg Silverman said, "This was an amazing experience. We did a lot of experimentation and collaboration along the way. But we are both very proud of the result. This is a David Ayer film, and Warners is proud to present it."[29]

Following the death of Superman, U.S. intelligence officer Amanda Waller gathers a team of supervillains to stop a sorceress, the Enchantress, from turning people into monsters and, with her brother Incubus, destroying mankind. Waller's un-magnificent seven consists of leader Rick Flag, "the finest special forces officer this nation has ever produced"; Deadshot, "the most wanted hitman in the world"; Captain Boomerang, an Australian who hurls boomerangs; El Diablo, a human flamethrower; Killer Croc, a reptile-man; Slipknot, a mercenary; and Harley Quinn, a mallet-wielding psycho. Waller has implanted each with a micro-explosive that, if they try to escape, will blow off their heads.

Expected to earn $125 million on its opening weekend, the $175 million supervillain flick corralled $133.7 million. But the reviews were as bad, if not worse, than those for *Batman v Superman*, and took aim at the movie's incomprehensible plot, uninteresting backstories, dull action scenes and lame villain. Some critics came to Ayer's defense, including Kevin Smith ("This flick as a whole had me smiling the whole time," the writer-director–comics fan wrote on his Facebook page[30]) and director Patty Jenkins. Jenkins was in post-production on *Wonder Woman* when she tweeted that *Suicide Squad* "was awesome. And NOT just because I'm in the DC world."[31]

The one bright spot, most agreed, was Margot Robbie's Harley Quinn. Robbie was an Australian actress whose breakout roles came in the glitzy high-finance movies *The Wolf of Wall Street* and *The Big Short*. Much as she had in the *Batman* cartoon, Harley steals every scene. "Robbie is genuinely terrific as Harley Quinn, earning the movie's best lines and nailing almost every one of them," wrote the *Atlantic*'s Christopher Orr in a review titled "*Suicide Squad* Is the Worst of the Worst."[32]

Other notables included Will Smith as Deadshot and Viola Davis as the second big-screen Waller, after Angela Bassett's turn in *Green Lantern*. (This was Smith's second superhero movie following 2008's *Hancock*, about an alcoholic former hero with superpowers. Based on an original 1996 script by Vy Vincent Ngo, it was released a couple of weeks before *The Dark Knight Rises*.) Ben Affleck's Batman and Ezra Miller's Flash, first glimpsed in *BvS*, make guest appearances, and Jared Leto debuts his version of the Joker. Leto's method of getting into character apparently included sending used condoms, anal beads, a live rat and a dead pig to his castmates.[33] Most of his scenes ended up on the cutting room floor.[34]

Looking back a year after the movie's release, Ayer said that there were things he would change, including making the Joker the main villain.[35]

Clearly, the studio would have to do some serious housecleaning if it wanted to see fewer stories with headlines like "From *Suicide Squad* to *Batman v Superman*, Why Are DC's Films So Bad?"[36] In December, Warner Bros. replaced production head Greg Silverman with Toby Emmerich. Silverman said that he left to pursue a "multifaceted new venture"[37]; *Variety* reported that it was due partly to the poor critical reception to *Batman v Superman* and *Suicide Squad*.[38]

• • •

When it came to attracting director interest for a Marvel project, one character levitated above all others: Doctor Strange.

Chapter XIX. Ask Not for Whom Dawns the Justice

The combination of Stan Lee's cod-mystical dialogue and artist Steve Ditko's proto-psychedelic images in the mage's sixties adventures had a profound impact on young readers that went beyond the antics of his more "science"-based (that is, Marvel science) brethren. The character fell in and out of fashion throughout the years, but artists and writers kept coming back to the sorcerer, and every half-decade or so saw a mini–Doctor Strange revival on the comics pages.

Filmmakers too were entranced by the possibilities. In 1986, eight years after CBS's TV-movie, Roger Corman's New World Pictures considered a feature film with a script by *Back to the Future* co-writer Bob Gale. At various times, Alex Cox, Wes Craven, David S. Goyer, Stephen Norrington, Guillermo del Toro and Neil Gaiman had expressed interest. When, in 2013, Kevin Feige confirmed that the good doctor was on the slate, the *Spider-Man* cartoon ringtones started going off at the Marvel offices.

"Marvel told me there were more directors vying for this job than any directing job they've ever had," said the man who ultimately triumphed, Scott Derrickson.[39]

Using his own money, Derrickson made a 90-minute presentation to sell Marvel on his qualifications. The presentation included an animated storyboard of a fight in a hospital between spirits on the astral plane inspired by the 2007 *Doctor Strange* storyline "The Oath." The director, who had worked mostly in horror (*The Exorcism of Emily Rose*, *Sinister*) also created concept art for "other sequences to give an example of what I wanted the visuals to be like, the kind of mind-trip visuals."[40]

Screenwriter Jon Spaihts was as enthusiastic as the director. One of his screenplays, for a sci-fi movie called *Passengers*, had ended up on a list of best unproduced scripts. He said that he discussed with Derrickson and Marvel whether they should tackle an origin story at all, "or whether perhaps to release [Doctor Strange] into the world fully formed and then sketch his backstory in on the fly. In the end, his origin story from the comics is so compelling that we found it undeniable."[41]

As in the comics, the movie Dr. Stephen Strange is a talented but arrogant neurosurgeon who, following a car accident, suffers nerve damage to his hands. Seeking a cure, he goes to Nepal, where he convinces the Sorcerer Supreme, aka the Ancient One, to take him on as an apprentice.

After training under the Ancient One and another Master of the Mystic Arts, Mordo, Doctor Strange is sent to New York to guard one of the three sanctums that protect Earth from the Dark Dimension. Kaecilius, a former apprentice of the Ancient One, uses pages he has stolen from a mystical text to contact the Dark Dimension's ruler, Dormammu, and makes a deal with the flame-headed entity to help him invade Earth in exchange for immortality. Kaecilius and his helpers attack the New York sanctum. Strange, wearing the Cloak of Levitation, fends them off, but is injured. After surgeon (and ex-girlfriend) Christine Palmer saves his life, he returns to the New York sanctum. In the Mirror Dimension, Kaecilius wounds the Ancient One, who has been drawing her power from the Dark Dimension. Strange and Mordo travel to Hong Kong and find the sanctum destroyed and its Master of the Mystic Arts, Wong, killed. Strange reverses time to save Wong and journeys to the Dark Dimension, where he creates a time loop that so frustrates Dormammu that the evil entity backs off, taking Kaecilius with him.

The movie brought magic into the Marvel universe via an array of spells, astral projections and various mystical doodads, i.e., the Eye of Agamotto. Marvel's teams of visual effects artists expanded the Marvel Cinematic Universe with the Mirror Dimension and the Dark Dimension. Many of the visuals paid tribute to the work of

Directing *Doctor Strange* (2016) was one of Marvel's most sought-after assignments. Besides boasting one of the publisher's best origin stories, the material's mystic elements offered new challenges for the studio's VFX wizards. From left: Tilda Swinton as The Ancient One and Benedict Cumberbatch as Dr. Stephen Strange. Marvel Studios.

the artists who had worked on the hero's four-color adventures, particularly that of Ditko. The movie ends not with a big fight but with a battle of wits between the hero and Dormammu.

Once again, Marvel enlisted A-list talent to bring the characters to life. Kevin Feige even pushed the movie's release date back to accommodate Benedict Cumberbatch, who led a cast that included Chiwetel Ejiofor (Mordo), Rachel McAdams (Christine Palmer), Mads Mikkelsen (Kaecilius) and Benedict Wong (Wong).

The most innovative (and controversial) casting choice was Tilda Swinton as the Ancient One, a venerable (and male) Asian mystic in the comics. "The Ancient One and Wong in the comics were 1960s Western stereotypes perpetuating the old Fu Manchu mentor to the white hero and Wong was the kung-fu manservant," Derrickson said. "What was I supposed to do with those?" On the other hand, he said, casting an Asian woman would play into the Dragon Lady stereotype—"the domineering mystical woman with a secret agenda."[42] This wasn't the otherworldly Swinton's first time playing a mystical being in a comic book movie; she played an angel in *Constantine*, a 2005 film starring Keanu Reeves in the title role and based on a DC/Vertigo character created by Alan Moore. The studio also changed the location of Stephen's journey to Nepal from Tibet so as to not alienate China.[43]

The Marvel Cinematic Universe building blocks include a mention of another of those powerful cosmic jewels that kept popping up, the Time Stone, and a mid-credit appearance by Thor. The studio was lining up all its ducks for its biggest event yet: a two-part sequel to *Age of Ultron*.

Chapter XX

Let the Amazons Have Some

"We have to get her right, we have to."
—Diane Nelson, Warner Bros. Brand Manager
for Superheroes, on Wonder Woman, 2013[1]

"We literally started with a laundry list of all the things that you've seen in the other five movies and tried to make sure we didn't do those again."
—Jonathan Goldstein, co-screenwriter,
Spider-Man: Homecoming[2]

Several superhero-milestones marked 2017. The first entry of the new year took the genre to new heights, and the last brought it to a disastrous low. In between, Wonder Woman—long neglected compared to her male counterparts, Batman and Superman, in the DC trinity—made her film debut, and fans finally got to see what Marvel could do with a *Spider-Man* movie.

As *Logan* begins, the year is 2029 and mutants are nearly extinct. One of the last, Wolverine is working as a driver in Texas to pay for meds required by Charles. Charles is suffering from dementia; during an episode, he lost control of his powers and caused an accident that left several people dead.

Logan is approached by a woman who offers him $50,000 to transport her and an 11-year-old, Laura, to North Dakota. He later finds the woman murdered and takes charge of the girl. Logan discovers that the woman was a nurse at a biotech corporation called Alkali-Transigen and that the girl was part of a program to engineer mutant killing machines. The company now wants to destroy Laura. Wolverine, Laura and Charles go on a road trip to North Dakota, pursued by a force sent by Alkali-Transigen.

Returning to the franchise after 2013's *The Wolverine*, director James Mangold and writer Scott Frank engineered the most adult superhero movie yet. *Logan* is a meditation on mortality, aging and home, while the R-rating allows the filmmakers to realistically depict the bloodletting that would result from Wolverine's—and, as it turns out, Laura's—steel claws.

Because, yes, Laura, aka X-23, is a mutant too, with Logan's genes and powers. Created in 2003 by Marvel producer Craig Kyle for the *X-Men: Evolution* cartoon, the young heroine is played with quiet eeriness by British-Spanish actress Dafne Keen. The director said, "If anyone could steal a movie from Hugh Jackman, it would be Dafne. She carries, all the time, a slight strangeness."[3]

Reviewers showered *Logan* with the kind of serious praise not seen for a superhero flick since *The Dark Knight*. The March 2017 release received a Academy Award nomination for Best Adapted Screenplay, a first for the genre.

Not everyone was convinced that the *X-Men* spinoff rose above its genre trappings.

As mutant X-23, 11-year-old Dafne Keen nearly steals *Logan* (2017) from co-star Hugh Jackman. Twentieth Century Studios.

"Now we have the problem that they tell us *Logan* is a great movie," actor Ethan Hawke told an interviewer. "Well, it's a great superhero movie. It still involves people in tights with metal coming out of their hands. It's not Bresson. It's not Bergman. But they talk about it like it is."[4]

Whether or not it was as ground-breaking as some believed, the third stand-alone *Wolverine* movie (and ninth in total to feature Logan) was a fitting send-off for both character and actor. When production on *Logan* began, Jackman announced that it would mark his last turn as the mutton-chopped Canadian warrior. Sixteen years earlier, the Australian had been the long-shot choice, a last-minute substitute for Dougray

Scott. Perhaps more than any other actor in a major superhero role, he had made it his own. Another Wolverine was unthinkable. At least for the foreseeable future.

• • •

In *Guardians of the Galaxy*, James Gunn showed his love for seventies pop and for humanizing the most outlandish characters he could find. For *Guardians of the Galaxy Vol. 2*, he returned to his record and comic book collections.

Along with ELO's "Mr. Blue Sky," he dug up Ego the Living Planet. Yet another creation from the prodigious imagination of Jack Kirby, Ego debuted in a 1966 issue of *The Mighty Thor*; Marvel pried him away from Fox, which had the rights, in return for allowing the makers of *Deadpool* to take liberties with Negasonic Teenage Warhead.

Other additions include Taserface, an old foe from the *Guardians* title, and Mantis, an antennaed empath created by writer Steve Englehart and artist Don Heck in the pages of *The Avengers*.

In true Gunn style, or true to the character of Rocket Raccoon, *Vol. 2* kicks off when the pugnacious procyonid steals a battery from the Sovereign, a genetically engineered "perfect" golden race. The Sovereign's High Priestess Ayesha had hired the Guardians to protect the valuable power source from an inter-dimensional monster in exchange for Gamora's half-sister Nebula. Discovering the theft, the Sovereign pursue the Guardians. But they're rescued by a mysterious figure who turns out to be the human manifestation of Ego the Living Planet—and Peter Quill's bio-dad.

Meanwhile, under contract with Ayesha, Yondu Udonta and his crew of Ravagers capture some of the Guardians, including Rocket and Groot. Udonta's crew, led by Taserface, mutinies against Udonta. Nebula travels to Ego to kill Gamora, whom she blames for her torture at the big purple mitts of Thanos, their adoptive father. Mantis, Ego's servant, informs Drax of her boss' plan to remake the universe in his image. Rocket and Groot arrive on Ego in time to help the rest of the Guardians travel into the center of Ego and blow up the brain at the planet's core.

Gunn, the sole screenwriter this time, balances the fun stuff with Peter Quill's father issues and Nebula's quest for vengeance. The humor wins. Rocket's mocking of Taserface for his name, Gamora and Quill's romcom bantering about their "unspoken thing," and naïve Mantis (French actress Pom Klementieff) trying to communicate with thick-headed Drax are more engaging than Peter's conflicts with Ego and Yondu, his mentor-stepdad. (In the movie's most dramatic moment, Michael Rooker's Yondu sacrifices himself to save Quill.) Karen Gillan's return performance as the intense Nebula solidifies the character as one of the Marvel Cinematic Universe's most fascinating creations, a troubled cyber-alien on edge.

Box office was stellar and reviews positive. Gunn was on track to make a third in the series when he heard cancellation's knock. In July, Fox News released nearly two dozen tweets that the director had posted between 2008 and 2011. The tweets made light of pedophilia and rape. Disney fired him from *Guardians 3*. Gunn apologized, calling his words "totally failed and unfortunate efforts to be provocative."[5]

In March 2019, the Mouse announced that, after multiple meetings between Gunn and company chairman Alan Horn, the director would return.[6] But moviegoers would have to wait for another round of seventies pop hits and wisecracking raccoons: Warner Bros. had already lured Gunn away with the opportunity to reboot the Suicide Squad.

But in comic-book movie time, that was still light-years away. In 2017, Warner was still in the throes of the Snyderverse, with the Zach Snyder–directed *Justice League* on the way and the Snyder-produced *Wonder Woman* dropping in June, a month after *Guardians 2*.

Getting the Amazon onto the screen in her first stand-alone feature was as challenging as the Amazon Games. Warner Bros. had been failing to launch since 1996, with names like Ivan Reitman, Joss Whedon and Sandra Bullock attached. A 2012 TV pilot never aired.

Adding to the pressure of bringing the world's most famous superheroine to the big screen was the fact that female-led superhero movies had an abysmal track record critically and commercially (see *Supergirl*, *Elektra* and *Catwoman*). Wonder Woman's household name status only ensured bums in seats on opening weekend.

The movie finally found its director in 2015. California-born and -raised Patty Jenkins made a splash in 2003 with her feature debut *Monster*, a drama about serial killer Aileen Wournos, and she had come close to making a superhero flick when she was in talks with Marvel about *Thor: The Dark World*. Jenkins came onto *Wonder Woman* with a lead, Gal Gadot, and script already in place. Snyder had cast Gadot, known to North American audiences for the *Fast and Furious* franchise, for *Batman v Superman* after seeing hundreds of applicants.

"The thing with Gal is that she's strong, she's beautiful, and she's a kind person, which is interesting, but fierce at the same time … [and] she really held her own with Ben [Affleck] in the screen test," Snyder said. "Ben was like, 'Whoa, that girl is something else!' That was a good sign, because Ben is very tough in the scene, and he's big and commanding."[7]

Director Patty Jenkins came onto 2017's *Wonder Woman* with the lead already cast. Gal Gadot was a former Miss Israel with Israeli army training experience and roles in the *Fast and Furious* franchise. Warner Bros.

Chapter XX. Let the Amazons Have Some

This being the world of superhero movies, even Gadot's casting came in for some pushback. Complaints ran from her body type (too skinny), her (lack of) filmography, and how the role should have gone to Beyoncé (!?). "There were a lot of comments about the size of my breasts," said the former Miss Israel, who had also served two years in the Israeli Defense Forces. "I realized we can't please everyone. In one interview, I did say, 'If you want it to really be true to the origin story, the [myth goes that] Amazons had only one breast; otherwise it would get in the way of the bow and arrow.' So!"[8]

Snyder had brainstormed the story with a couple of screenwriters, including Allan Heinberg. The latter's bona fides included an off–Broadway play, *The Amazon's Voice*, about a cartoonist assigned to modernize Wonder Woman, and a stalled CW Wonder Woman prequel series. They set the story during the World War I, not the second as in the comics, something that threw Jenkins at first. She came around to the idea that it might be interesting to "take a god with a moral compass and a moral belief system, and … drop them into this world, [where] there are questions about women's rights, about a mechanized war where you don't see who you are killing."[9]

Outside of the change in time period, the movie follows the beats of William Moulton Marston's origin. Diana is living at peace on Themyscira with her Amazon clan when American pilot Steve Trevor, pursued by Germans, crashes near the island. Diana saves him and concludes that she must venture to the world of men and stop the god Ares, who she believes is responsible for the war.

The fourth movie in the DC Extended Universe stopped the bleeding, review-wise. A straightforward superhero movie period piece, *Wonder Woman* is in line with the two Zach Snyder films that preceded it, but it has a lightness missing from *Man of Steel* and *Batman v Superman*. Gadot's Diana, a mix of fierce, compassionate warrior and headstrong, naïve island girl, has an easygoing chemistry with Chris Pine's Steve Trevor, and the stakes feel real, especially in the film's middle, when Diana is behind enemy lines with her own small but devoted cadre of mission specialists. These scenes (particularly when she first appears in costume, while crossing No Man's Land against enemy fire, and one in which she liberates a Belgian town) achieve the kind of bigger-than-life thrills that, at their best, only superhero movies can deliver.

The movie broke several box office records, including the biggest domestic opening of all time for a female director. *Wonder Woman* not only ended the DCEU freefall but ended the curse of the woman-fronted superhero movie. Perhaps all that had been needed was a committed director and decent script.

• • •

After wresting some control from Sony, then introducing Spider-Man in *Captain America: Civil War*, it was Marvel's turn to ask: What did the studio want to see in a Spidey movie?

One thing Kevin Feige and his team knew they *didn't* want was yet another radioactive, or bio-engineered, or GMO-treated spider origin story. "We are going to take it for granted that people know that, and the specifics," Feige said.

They also wanted a Spidey more like the comics version—"very, very funny and very, very witty when he's in that costume, swinging around. Not as a stand-up comedian, obviously, but as almost his nervous energy, bothering the criminals with banter as much as with his powers."[10]

And the studio wanted a younger lead.

Tobey Maguire and Andrew Garfield were 25 and 27 when they first played Peter Parker. At 19, Tom Holland was at least in the ballpark of high-school age. "I really wanted to see somebody cast who was very close to a high schooler's age," said *Civil War* director Joe Russo. "What was so valuable to me about the character, when I was a kid, is that he's a high schooler with this power and responsibility, and it makes him very distinct as a hero."[11]

To direct its first Spider-Man solo venture, Marvel hired Jon Watts. The Colorado filmmaker started out with short films and music videos, then made two indie features. Exec producer Jeremy Latcham brought Watt to the attention of co-producers Feige and Amy Pascal, now head of her own company but still involved in all things Spider-Man. They liked what Watts had done with a limited budget on the $5 million *Cop Car*, a 2015 thriller about two juvenile delinquents who hijack the abandoned title vehicle.[12] For its *Spider-Man* flick, Marvel handed the director a budget of $175 million, 35 times more than *Cop Car*. Watts, who had wanted to make a coming-of-age film, was enthused about the studio's idea of approaching the superhero flick like a John Hughes movie.

John Francis Daley and Jonathan Goldstein were among those who pitched for a chance to write the blockbuster. After they got the job, the team—who had written sitcoms and the comedies *Horrible Bosses* and *Vacation*—also asked what they did and didn't want to see. Ixnay on Raimi's "aerial ballet." "We were tired of seeing Spider-Man swinging through the skyscrapers of Manhattan and thought of environments for him to be in where he isn't as able to use his powers," Daley said.[13]

Out of a list of 40 possible villains, they chose the Vulture. The writers pitched the vintage baddie as a scavenger who collects tech left behind in the Battle of New York and the Avengers' fight with Ultron. "We were like, 'Yeah, this is cool. It feels MCU [Marvel Cinematic Universe]. It feels unique. It feels like you haven't seen it before,'" said co-producer Eric Hauserman Carroll, a New York film school grad and comics fan who joined Marvel during the production of *Thor*.[14]

Much of the movie, winkingly titled *Spider-Man: Homecoming*, feels fresh. Following the crisis caused by the Sokovia Accords, Tony Stark takes Peter under his wing. At first, the high schooler is over the moon at the attention from the celebrity billionaire superhero, but he soon realizes that Stark has simply put him on the proverbial shelf. While waiting for some action, he stumbles upon an ATM robbery in which the thieves are using "a reclaimed sub–Ultron arm straight from Sokovia." Peter tracks the weaponry to a scavenger crew led by Adrian Toomes, who has fashioned some extra-terrestrial tech into a flying suit. A final showdown between the two takes place on a beach near Coney Island, where Spidey saves the Vulture's life when the latter's suit explodes.

There are few if any missteps in *Homecoming*, but to be fair, Marvel had the benefit of learning from Sony's mistakes. It's fast, funny and contemporary while remaining true to the youthful spirit and energy of the comics, especially the early issues. One scene even pays tribute to one of the most iconic sequences in all of Marvel Comics history, courtesy Steve Ditko: Spidey, trapped under a mountain of rubble, summoning all of his willpower and strength to escape.

As Peter, Holland is a believably awkward high school student with a big secret. The Vulture, aka Toomes, was always an odd duck in the comics—a bald, geriatric-looking inventor in a feathery green onesie with wings. *Homecoming* reinvents him as a middle-aged small-businessman who wants to protect his income and family. In the ultimate in superhero meta casting, he is played by Michael Keaton—not only a former

Chapter XX. Let the Amazons Have Some

Batman but also the star of *Birdman*, a 2014 Best Picture winner about an actor who can't escape the shadow of an early superhero role.

The screenplay, credited to six people including Watts, Goldstein and Daley, keeps the fictional stakes relatively low; no one's out to destroy the world or turn everyone into lizards. As a small-time crook tells Toomes' men, "I need something to stick up somebody. I'm not trying to shoot them back in time."

Comic relief comes in the form of Jon Favreau's put-upon Happy Hogan, who is tasked by Tony with watching over Peter, the teaching staff of Midtown Tech (comedians Hannibal Burress and Martin Starr) and Ned, Peter's self-proclaimed guy-in-a-chair. Played by Filipino American actor Jacob Batalon, Ned is part of a multicultural roster of classmates that includes Zendaya as intellectual wallflower "MJ" Jones and Guatemalan American actor Tony Revolori as Flash Thompson. Watts said that he was inspired in his casting by an oral history of *Freaks and Geeks* and the TV series' creative team's willingness "to adapt their ideas of who the characters would be to [the kids they cast]," the director said.[15] (*Homecoming* co-writer Daly had been a cast member on the show.) Tony Stark and Iron Man appear a couple of times to save Peter's bacon, playing up the chemistry between Holland and Robert Downey, Jr., that had helped land Holland the job in auditions. Captain America cameos in a few high school PSAs.

Reviews were overwhelmingly positive, though some took issue with the hero's new hi-tech Stark-designed Spidersuit. But, as Pascal put it, "We've always had to believe that Peter Parker invented this suit on a Singer sewing machine.... Now we don't have to do that anymore."[16]

While set pieces like Peter saving his classmates while they're trapped in the Washington Monument deliver action in the mighty Marvel manner, the standout scene is a quiet one in which non-costumed Peter and Toomes realize that they are each other's costumed enemies.

The webslinger wasn't the only Marvel hero to get a major overhaul that year. For the third *Thor* movie, Kevin Feige & co. determined that a rethink was necessary after the disappointing *Dark World*. "There were two things we knew Thor had to do," executive producer Brad Winderbaum said. "One was to be a completely different person at the beginning and end of the movie. And two, embrace the sides of Chris Hemsworth that were underutilized in our movies before. Which is that he's not just a handsome, muscly guy. He's also a really funny guy."[17]

Winderbaum had liked the first two features by Taika Waititi. The Indigenous New Zealand director-actor-writer's 2010 coming-of-age film *Boy* was a Sundance Grand Jury Prize nominee, and his follow-up was the much-lauded mockumentary about vampire roommates, *What We Do in the Shadows*. He had also played Hal Jordan's guy-in-the-chair in 2011's *Green Lantern*. Waititi was working on his third feature, *Hunt for the Wilderpeople*, when he was asked to pitch for a *Thor* flick. He came up with a sizzle reel of clips from *Big Trouble in Little China*, a 1986 John Carpenter film about a truck driver battling sorcerers and demons in San Francisco's Chinatown, John Hughes' *Sixteen Candles, Superman*, and *Teenage Mutant Ninja Turtles*, and set to Led Zeppelin's Norse-mythologizing anthem "Immigrant Song."[18]

Waititi decided to ignore the previous movies as much as possible, and to ensure that Hemsworth's God of Thunder was the film's "coolest character."[19] This wouldn't be easy, considering that Thor's co-star was the Hulk. "It started off as, 'Could we put Hulk in there too?'" Winderbaum said. "Then as soon as that sparked ignited, [Hulk] was married to the plot."[20]

Gladiatorial combat between "work friends" Thor (Chris Hemsworth) and Hulk (Mark Ruffalo) is one of the highlights of Taika Waititi's *Thor: Ragnarok* (2017). Marvel Studios.

In *Thor: Ragnarok*, Thor encounters his "friend from work" on Sakaar, a planet that acts as a hub to various portals to other parts of the universe. Thor has been captured by Scrapper 142, a former member of an elite corps of Asgardian warriors called the Valkyrie, now employed by the Grandmaster. The flamboyant impresario and ruler of Sakaar hosts the Contest of Champions for gladiators from across the universe. Thor soon finds himself going head to head with Hulk, who had been captured while drifting in space in the Avengers' Quinjet after their fight with Ultron. The two make up and escape Sakaar with Scrapper 142, aka Valkyrie, and and return to Asgard to stop Thor's sister Hela from destroying the place.

Ragnarok was just the kick in the codpiece the Norse god needed. The combination of Waititi's anything-goes approach (encapsulated by a self-aggrandizing play staged by Loki in Asgard, with Matt Damon as Loki), Hemsworth's timing and Jeff Goldblum's quirky Grandmaster took the franchise to new realms. Advances in motion-capture technology, particularly in facial recognition, resulted in the most fully realized Ruffalo Hulk yet. Given the limited vocabulary of his early comics incarnation, he can't help but steal most of his scenes.

Tessa Thompson's hard-drinking Scrapper 142, based on a long-time, blonde-braided Marvel warrior known as Valkyrie, is another scene-stealer. With the casting of Thompson, Valkyrie became Marvel's first mixed-race female hero. Cate Blanchett plays Hela, the studio's first female big bad. Waititi himself voices Korg, an alien made out of rocks. Karl Urban plays Skurge, a turncoat Asgardian. This was the New Zealand actor's second superhero film after playing the lead in *Dredd* (2012), an underrated reboot of the dystopian future cop written by Alex Garland.

Ragnarok walloped the other *Thor*s in terms of reviews and box office. Marvel's outside-the-box hiring of Waititi had paid off.

Warner Bros., on the other hand, was about to take another nosedive following the brief bump of *Wonder Woman*.

After *Man of Steel* and *Batman v Superman*, the studio needed something to justify its trust in Zach Snyder. *Justice League* was supposed to be that movie, an *Avengers*-like tentpole that would unite DC's so-called Trinity (Batman, Superman, Wonder Woman, with Ben Affleck, Henry Cavill, and Gal Gadot returning to the roles) and launch three new characters who could be spun off into their own blockbusters: Aquaman, the Flash and Cyborg.

But the film was troubled from the start. Snyder had already begun filming when the reviews for *BvS* came in, prompting panic in the halls of Warner Bros.; some execs apparently suggested that president Greg Silverman remove the director.[21] Instead, studio chair and CEO Kevin Tsujihara assigned Geoff Johns, a comics writer who had risen to the rank of DC Entertainment creative chief, and Warner Bros. co-production head Jon Berg to watch over the movie. Said Berg, "My job was to try to mediate between a creator whose vision is instinctually dark and a studio that perceived, rightly or wrongly, that the fans wanted something lighter."[22]

Snyder wrapped in October 2016. The following January, he showed his cut to Tsujihara. The studio head was not happy; among the issues was the movie's length. After the two-hour–plus running time of Snyder's two previous DCEU slugfests, Tsujihara wanted something less butt-numbing.

Enter Joss Whedon. At first, the *Avengers* writer-director, who was developing a *Batgirl* movie for Warner at the time, was asked just to tinker with the script for reshoots. "I thought maybe he could write some cool scenes," Snyder said. "I thought that would be fun."[23]

Then, in March, tragedy struck when the director's daughter Autumn Snyder took her own life. In May, Snyder and his wife, producer Deborah Snyder, left the film and the studio passed it on to Whedon. Apparently, there was little question of pushing back the troubled production's November release date; in October of the previous year, AT&T and Warners announced an $85 billion plan to merge. According to *TheWrap*, an unnamed executive said that Tsujihara and Silverman's replacement Toby Emmerich "wanted to preserve their bonuses they would be paid before the merger," and were worried that if they pushed the movie, "their bonuses would have been pushed to the following year and they might not still be at the studio."[24]

In June, the success of *Wonder Woman* convinced studio execs that, in wanting to brighten *Justice League*'s corners, they were on the right track. According to a July 2017 *Variety* story, the Warner brass allocated $25 million for Whedon to finish the movie, which required an additional 55 days of production. Reshoots usually cost between six and ten million and last one or two weeks.[25] As the release date neared, producer Charles Roven said that Whedon shot 15 or 20 percent of the finished film.[26] Other reports put the percentage at nearer 75.

The story picks up two years after the death of Superman. Seeing an opportunity, Fourth World predator Steppenwolf invades Earth with his army of parademons, "nightmare creatures who feed on fear." Steppenwolf is a disciple of Darkseid, an even bigger bad (like, Thanos-level bad) who tried to conquer the planet thousands of years ago but was defeated by an alliance of Amazons, Atlanteans, "all the tribes of men" and a Green Lantern.

Steppenwolf aims to retrieve three Mother Boxes. When connected, the alien sources of energy will "form the Unity, an apocalyptic power that not only destroys worlds but transforms them into the primordial hellscape of Steppenwolf's birth world."

Bruce Wayne, who feels bad because he almost killed Superman before a nuclear missile and Doomsday finished the job, takes it upon himself to form a team of meta-humans. First up is Diana, whom he knows from Lex Luthor's party and the fight with Doomsday. He then recruits Barry Allen, aka the Flash, a young man with super-speed, and Arthur Curry, aka Aquaman, a trident-wielding amphibious being who controls the oceans. Diana follows up with Cyborg, an angry young half-man, half-robot who can fly, and control ATMs. Alerted to the threat of Steppenwolf, the team confronts the big armored alien and his winged insect brigade under an abandoned water station outside Metropolis. The fight ends in a draw and Steppenwolf gets away. Bruce suggests using a Mother Box that they've managed to hold onto, a "Genesis Chamber" in Zod's ship and energy generated by Barry to resurrect Superman. The plan works, but the revived Superman is confused and fights the League until Lois Lane arrives. Superman flies away and visits his mom while the other members of the Justice League take Bruce's Bat-troop carrier to a Russian village to stop Steppenwolf. Superman arrives in time to save the day.

But not the movie.

"The script is not interesting," wrote *Vanity Fair*'s Richard Lawson. "The costumes are not fun. The film is, plainly stated, terrible, and I'm sorry that everyone wasted their time and money making it—and that people are being asked to waste their time and money seeing it. I hate to be so blunt, but it simply must be said this time."[27]

"It's consistently embarrassing to watch, and features plot holes so yawningly vast they have a kind of Grand Canyon–like splendour: part of you wants to hang around to see what they look like at sunset," wrote the *Telegraph*'s Robbin Collin.[28]

Even Henry Cavill's redacted mustache, grown for a role in a *Mission: Impossible* movie (2018's *Fallout*) and still in place during reshoots, couldn't escape the negative attention. "The 10 Most Terrifying Shots of Superman's CGI Mouth in *Justice League* (Photos)" was the title of a *Wrap* piece. What worked in 1966 for Cesar Romero, his 'stache covered in white makeup as the Joker on *Batman*, didn't work here.

Chris Terrio, who co-wrote both *Batman v Superman* and *Justice League* (Whedon also receives a screenplay credit), saw the finished product a couple of weeks before release. "I immediately called my lawyer and said, 'I want to take my name off the film,'"[29] said the writer.

Criticism extended beyond plot deficiencies. Whedon took heat for his depiction of Wonder Woman; *CBR.com* complained about the number of "upskirt" shots in the movie and charged that Diana comes across as a nag.[30] A scene where the Flash falls on Wonder Woman, his face in her chest, was singled out for sexualizing the hero. (The same thing happens in Whedon's *Age of Ultron* with Bruce and Natasha.) A few years later, some cast members criticized the director for his on-set behavior.

Box office–wise, the $300 million movie had the worst opening of a DC film since *Green Lantern*. Coming after the cauterizing effects of *Wonder Woman*, *Justice League* was a calamity that ended the franchise begun with *Man of Steel*, and nearly kiboshed the DCEU completely. Ben Affleck tried developing a *Batman* movie for a couple of years before giving up. In 2020, a feud erupted between Ray Fisher (Cyborg) and Warner Bros. A *Flash* movie, delayed by the pandemic and star Ezra Miller's legal problems, kept getting pushed back to, finally, a 2023 release.

Faring even worse was the mightiest superhero of them all. Rebooted in *Man of Steel*, killed in *Batman v Superman*, and resurrected in *Justice League*, Superman all but disappeared.

Chapter XXI

Peak Superhero

> "In one way it's incredibly satisfying. In the other way it's nearly unbelievable from where we started. There were days when I wasn't sure we would be able to get *Iron Man* in theaters. There were days when I thought *Avengers* was a pipe dream. And there were days after *Avengers* where I thought, 'Well, where do we go?'"
>
> —Kevin Feige[1]

A decade after *Iron Man*, superhero movies ruled the box office.

In 2016 and 2017, the genre accounted for half of the year's ten top-grossing films. In 2018, four of the ten top-grossing movies were superhero releases, four if we include Pixar's *The Incredibles 2*, while *Venom* and *Aquaman* came in at 11 and 13, respectively. Marvel properties alone accounted for three studios' top earners: *Deadpool 2* was Fox's #1 box office performer, and *Avengers: Infinity War* and *Black Panther* were Disney's. *Venom* and *Spider-Man: Into the Spider-Verse*—an animated feature that would win the Best Animated Feature Oscar—were Sony's #2 and #5 top-grossing films. All told, 2018 saw the release of eight big-budget superhero flicks, compared to 2017's previous record of six.

The year began with the release of one of Marvel's most long-awaited projects, *Black Panther*. Announced in 2005 as part of the studio's first slate–wish-list, the movie starred Chadwick Boseman as the title character, a superhero who rules the African kingdom of Wakanda. The first black superhero in mainstream American comics, the Lee-Kirby creation had been on the minds of filmmakers at least as far back as 1992, when Wesley Snipes was in talks with Sony to play the character.

Marvel found the movie's director in early 2016. A comic book fan since childhood, Ryan Coogler had seen *Iron Man* on opening night. "Hearing they were making an *Iron Man* movie was kind of similar to hearing when they made *Blade*—it was like, 'They're making a movie about *him*?!'"[2] His previous movies included *Fruitvale Station*, a 2013 indie, and *Creed*, the seventh installment in the *Rocky* franchise. In both, he worked with actor Michael B. Jordan, the Human Torch in the 2015 *Fantastic Four* reboot.

For *Black Panther*, Coogler collaborated on the screenplay with Joe Robert Cole, an alumnus of Marvel's writers program. The studio's mandate for the film included a predominantly Black cast. And the Panther had to "look cool in the suit," Coogler said, quoting Feige.[3] For preparation, and to gather ideas, Coogler made his first visit to Africa, including South Africa, Kenya and Lesotho.

In *Black Panther*, T'Challa has become king of Wakanda following the death of his father in the explosion at the United Nations summit in Vienna engineered by Baron Zemo. But there's another contender for the throne: his long-missing and bloodthirsty cousin, Erik "Killmonger" Stevens. After successfully beating T'Challa in hand-to-hand combat, Killmonger becomes ruler, and it's up to the former king to reclaim his crown.

Helping the Panther are Shuri, T'Challa's younger sister and resident tech genius, and the fierce Okoy, head of the Dora Milaje, Wakanda's all-female special forces. Andy Serkis returned from *Age of Ultron* as happy-go-lucky arms dealer Ulysses Klaue.

The February release exceeded all expectations, breaking box office records and racking up the kind of too-good-to-be-a-superhero-movie praise generated by *The Dark Knight* and *Logan*. Cultural critics also weighed in, debating the film's significance, its messages about race and its vision of Africa. "The most political movie ever produced by Marvel Studios, both in its very existence—it's the most expensive movie to have ever starred an almost entirely black cast—and in the questions its story raises," wrote *Slate.com*'s Jamelle Bouie.[4] New York resident Frederick Joseph began a #blackpantherchallenge campaign to raise funds for kids from Harlem to see the movie.[5]

Along with its numerous accolades, including a *Rotten Tomatoes* approval rating of 97 percent—the highest-ever score for a superhero movie—Marvel's eighteenth release became the highest earner of the year in Canada and the U.S. and the second highest worldwide. In January 2019, it became the first superhero movie nominated for a Best Picture Academy Award. At the awards, costume designer Ruth Carter and production designer Hannah Beachler became the first African-Americans to win in their categories. As of this writing, *Black Panther* is the twelfth highest-grossing film of all time.

Chadwick Boseman was first cast as Black Panther for *Captain America: Civil War* (2016). The character was the first Black superhero in mainstream comics. Marvel Studios.

Two months later, the Panther was back—along with Spider-Man, Doctor Strange, the Guardians of the Galaxy and the Avengers—in *Avengers: Infinity War*.

The job of herding all these cats fell to the people who had put the most superheroes on screen to date, the screenwriting-directing teams behind *Captain America: Civil War*: Stephen McFeely and Christopher Markus and Joe and Anthony Russo.

McFeely and Markus began spitballing ideas for *Infinity War* and its sequel, *Endgame*, while the Russos were filming *Civil War*. The writing duo approached the task as though coming up with storylines for *What If?*, a seventies comic that revolved around fan-luring thought-experiments such as

"What If the Hulk Had the Brain of Bruce Banner?" "What If Jane Foster Had Found the Hammer of Thor?" and "What If the Original Marvel Bullpen Had Become the Fantastic Four?"

"Wouldn't it be interesting if Groot and Rocket and Thor went on a journey together?" McFeely said, discussing their process. "What kind of chemistry could you get from that?"[6]

They were writing for 40 characters. The Russos would visit them in their conference room at Marvel where the walls were covered in post-it notes. "They'd come in and go, 'That's insane!'" Markus said.[7] Two of the principals, Black Panther and Spider-Man, hadn't even been in a Marvel movie when the team began working on the script.

The pressure must have been intense. As Tara Bennett and Paul Terry noted in *The Story of Marvel Studios*, if the two-part saga was a failure, it would cast a pall on the movies that had come before. In the two months leading up to filming, the Russos spent almost all their time with the writers. "The thousands of people who work on that movie have to be able to read that script and know exactly what we want from them as a collaborator," Joe Russo said.[8] When Mark Ruffalo saw the number of speaking parts, he told the directors, "You guys have jumped the shark now, man."[9]

As *Infinity War* begins, Thanos has defeated Thor and everyone else on board the ship that rescued much of Asgard from Hela and Surtur. Thanos has come for the Space Stone, one of six Infinity Stones he needs to achieve his ultimate goal: the destruction of half of the population of the universe. In a last act of defiance, Asgardian Heimdall sends Hulk hurtling to Earth. After crashing into Doctor Strange's Greenwich Village HQ, he transforms into Bruce Banner and warns Stephen and Wong of the imminent arrival of Thanos' emissaries. He's just in time: Stephen manages to contact Iron Man before Thanos' second-in-command, a vicious alien named Ebony Maw, arrives in New York with his cronies to seize the Time Stone from Stephen's Eye of Agamotto. After spying the battle between Iron Man and Doctor Strange and Maw's forces from a city bus, Peter Parker joins in the melee as Spider-Man. Maw captures Stephen but Iron Man and Spider-Man stow away on the alien ship. After defeating the alien, the heroes make it their mission to stop Thanos from procuring any more Infinity Stones.

Elsewhere in space, Peter Quill and the Guardians come across the Asgardian rescue ship. With Thor, they try to stop Thanos from getting the Reality Stone from Taneleer Tivan, the Collector, but they're too late. Thor, Rocket and Groot fly to Nidavellir, a cosmic forge, so that Thor can get a new weapon.

Back on Earth, the rest of the Avengers realize that Thanos is going to return for the Mind Stone in Vision's head. They fly to Wakanda so T'Challa's sister Shuri can remove the stone. On Thanos' home world, Tony, Spidey, Doc Strange and the Guardians lay a trap. But Thanos is too strong for them and escapes to Earth, where he plucks the Mind Stone out of Vision's head. Donning the now-complete Infinity Gauntlet, Thanos snaps his fingers and wipes out half of all life in the universe.

Clocking in at just under three hours, *Infinity War* juggles dozens of characters, leaps from subplot to subplot, and ends on a supreme bummer. Yet the $321 million April release made more on its opening weekend than any other film up to that time, reached the $1 billion mark faster than any other, and grossed more than any other Marvel Cinematic Universe film before becoming the first superhero movie to make over $2 billion.[10]

The majority of the reviews were positive, praising the film's intertwined stories, narrative choices and humor. The negative reviews dissed its intertwined stories, narrative choices, and humor.

Eight months later, Marvel released the first trailer for the sequel, *Avengers: Endgame*.

• • •

One of *Deadpool 2*'s more inspired ideas was, to paraphrase new director David Leitch, an extended prank on the audience.[11] To help him fight Cable, a soldier from the future, the titular mercenary assembles a team. Ten minutes later, most of the team is dead.

But that comes after Wade Wilson witnesses the accidental murder of his girlfriend Vanessa and some X-Men–enabled hijinks.

After failing to kill one of his targets, Wade returns home to the apartment he shares with Vanessa. The two decide to start a family when the target breaks in. Vanessa is killed in the melee, sending Wade into a downward spiral. Unable to kill himself, he tries to join the X-Men. Along with Colossus and Negasonic Teenage Warhead, he goes on a mission to stop a young mutant named Russell, aka Firefist, from destroying his orphanage. After Deadpool kills a staff member for abusing the young mutants, he and Russell are arrested and taken to a prison for mutants. There, a time-traveling soldier from the future, Cable, tries to kill Russell, who would otherwise grow up to kill Cable's parents. Deadpool escapes and forms a team he dubs "X-Force" to stop Cable. Except for one member, the ultra-lucky Domino, the team is wiped out in an attempt to free Russell from a prison convoy. Russell frees another prisoner, Juggernaut, who rips Deadpool in half. While Wade recovers at Blind Al's, Cable offers to help him stop Russell from killing the orphanage headmaster, which in Cable's timeline marks the beginning of the mutant kid's future murderous rampage. At the orphanage, Colossus, Cable and Deadpool face off against Juggernaut and Russell. Deadpool is killed, then brought back to life by Cable and his time-traveling device.

The May release gave fans more of what had made *Deadpool* a success: violence, swearing and fourth-wall–breaking meta jokes. Two of the best come in the end-credits scenes. Using Cable's device to travel back in time, Deadpool (Ryan Reynolds, again) his mouthless *X-Men Origins: Wolverine* iteration and then, just after he finishes reading the last page of the *Green Lantern* script, Reynolds himself. "God damn, that's beautiful," the actor says before Deadpool puts a bullet into his forehead.

All of the original's supporting cast returned. The additions: New Zealand's Julian Dennison, the star of Taika Waititi's *Hunt for the Wilderpeople*, as Firefist and Josh Brolin as Cable. Both characters dated back to 1986 in the comics, but Firefist was a minor mutant while Cable was a fan-favorite with a complicated backstory.

"I challenge someone who hasn't read the comics to read Cable's Wikipedia page and explain it to me," said returning scripter Paul Wernick.

"It's impossible," said his writing partner, Rhett Reese.

"Impossible," said Wernick.[12]

Juggernaut, originally played by Vinnie Jones in *X3: The Last Stand*, is CGI.

Though generally well-received, the movie generated controversy with what some reviewers saw as the "fridging" of Vanessa, Deadpool's fiancée. Coined by comics writer Gail Simone, the term denotes the plot trope where a female character is killed off solely to motivate the (male) hero. (The term comes from a 1994 issue of *Green Lantern* in which the protagonist finds his murdered girlfriend in his fridge.) Of course, *Deadpool 2* wasn't the first movie, superhero or non-, to do this.

"It's Deadpool's movie, and you need to take everything away from him to humanize him," countered Leitch, who had marked his territory with the action flicks *John Wick* (2014) and *Atomic Blonde* (2017). "He can be grating and he can be sort of offensive and he can be all these things, but you need an emotional hook that grounds the movie that we can go on this journey with this character and experience Deadpool."[13] Simone herself said that the term didn't quite apply since Vanessa reappears (as a spiritual guide) in the film.

But this was a conversation that took place in the far corners of the Internet. *Deadpool 2* became the highest-grossing R-rated feature of all time, and the highest-grossing of the 11 X-Men films.

Vanessa notwithstanding, superhero movies in general were becoming a more level playing field for women. But for all its ground-breaking efforts, Marvel had yet to place a female superhero in a headlining role. That was about to change with the sequel to *Ant-Man*.

"It was really important when we announced this was going to be called *Ant-Man and the Wasp* that it really is—she's not a supporting character, she's a lead character with Paul [Rudd] in the movie," returning director Peyton Reed said.[14]

The character was one of Marvel's earliest superheroines. Debuting in 1963, she was originally Janet van Dyne, the crimefighting partner of first Ant-Man Hank Pym and a founding member of the Avengers. Known for her fashion sense as well as her crimefighting abilities, she appeared intermittently in the *Avengers* comic, and led the team for a period in the eighties. She was glimpsed briefly in the first *Ant-Man* movie and it's this sighting that sets off the events of the sequel.

While under house arrest for violating the Sokovia Accords by teaming up with Captain America and the Falcon against Iron Man, Scott Lang has a dream in which he sees Janet in the Quantum Realm. He tells Hank that he believes the scientist's wife is still alive. "We have to bring back Janet!" declares Hank. But he needs one more component to complete a tunnel to the microscopic universe. Meanwhile, a mysterious young woman who can phase through solid objects and a small-time criminal named Sonny Burch are trying to steal his technology.

Aware that it would be released in the shadow of the all-encompassing *Infinity War*, Reed kept the summer film manageable; the running time is a mere two hours, only a few new characters are introduced, and the stakes are relatively low—until the end.

The release of the *Avengers* movie two months previous presented a narrative challenge for Reed and Marvel, since the deaths of half of the planet's population had already taken place when moviegoers sat down to watch *Ant-Man and the Wasp*. The film addresses this with a mid-credits scene in which, after sending Scott through the quantum tunnel, Hank, Janet and Hope dissolve into dust, placing the movie's events as concurrent (or just before) Thanos' Snap.

• • •

With its hottest property on loan to Marvel, Sony returned to its scheme of a Spider-verse series of movies based on ancillary Spider-Man characters. After planning and scrapping films featuring Black Cat and the Sinister Six, the studio greenlit *Venom*, a solo adventure for the black alien goo last seen in *The Amazing Spider-Man 2*. Due to Sony's deal with Marvel, the movie would have to be Spider-Man–free.

The producers, including Amy Pascal and Avi Arad, decided to reboot the character. Jeff Pinkner (*Amazing Spider-Man 2*) and Scott Rosenberg (*Spider-Man*, uncredited) wrote a script with an Eddie Brock who was slightly more in keeping with his comics incarnation than the one Topher Grace played in *Amazing Spider-Man 2*; instead of a *Daily Bugle* photographer and rival to Peter Parker, the man who becomes Venom's host is a disgraced San Francisco investigative journalist. The movie also followed the evolution of the alien symbiote in the comics by giving Venom a voice and personality. In *Venom*, released in the fall of 2018, Tom Hardy plays both Brock and Venom, and it's the British actor's sniping duologue—tweaked by Hardy's collaborator Kelly Marcel—that gives the film what little flavor it has.

"When you think of *Venom*, you'll never be able to think of anyone but Tom Hardy sitting in that bathtub of lobsters," said Pascal, referring to a scene in which Brock immerses himself into a restaurant's lobster tank. "And once you saw Tom Hardy do this character, that's all you needed to know."[15]

And all you needed to see, agreed most critics. But their cries went unheard, or ignored, and moviegoers dutifully bought tickets; *Venom* went on to earn $885 million, more than the studio's two *Amazing Spider-Man*s. As it turned out, not having the web-slinger around was no big deal.

• • •

On November 12, 2018, Stan Lee passed away of heart failure. The co-creator of the Marvel Universe and an indefatigable champion of bringing (his) superheroes to the big screen was 95.

Lee was the last of the Big Three architects of the Marvel Universe to go. Artist-writer Jack Kirby, whose contributions to comics and popular culture cannot be overestimated, died at 76 in 1994, long before the man born Jacob Kurtzberg had a chance to see any of his explosive visual artistry transformed into pixels. Steve Ditko, who predeceased Lee by only a few months, did live long enough for his co-creations Spider-Man and Doctor Strange to become movies. But there is no record of the famously reclusive artist having seen any of them.

It's unlikely. As he wrote to a fan shortly before his death, "The one thing in doing comic books is that the past work is irrelevant. As a freelancer my focus is on—what next?"[16]

• • •

Aquaman was a joke.

He was a running gag on *Entourage*, an early oughts HBO series, where the main character was the star of an *Aquaman* movie. He was a joke to Will Beall, whom Warner Bros. hired to write a script based on the Justice Leaguer. "My agent calls and he goes, 'Fasten your seat belts, Will. Like, I got something lined up for you. I can't tell you what it is, can't tell you what it is.' I came home to my wife and I was like, 'They're giving me Batman.' [*Laughs*] I shit you not. I was stockpiling comics…. And then he sends me a text with a picture of Aquaman on it. And I was like, 'Oh, fuck.'"[17]

And, for years, the WASPy, seahorse-riding Atlantean was a joke to comics fans. Created by artist Paul Norris and DC editor Mort Weisinger in 1941, Aquaman was a Silver Age also-ran until, in 1959, writer Robert Bernstein and artist Ramona Fradon retconned the character and he became a member of the Justice League. He appeared on the *Super Friends* cartoon in the seventies and received a much-needed reinvention by writer Peter David in the nineties. A 2011 run by Geoff Johns, the DC Comics writer who had risen to the position of DC Entertainment exec, turned him into, in Kevin Smith's words, a "badass king of the seven seas."[18]

Warner Bros. had announced an *Aquaman* movie in 2014, after Zach Snyder hired Jason Momoa to play the part in *Batman v Superman* and *Justice League*. Snyder and his wife Deborah had seen the actor play the silent Khal Drogo in *Game of Thrones*. At 6'4" and dark-haired, the Pacific Islander looked nothing like the original blonde preppy from the comics. Still, Aquaman purists, if there were any, remained relatively quiet.

In June 2015, Warner hired horror franchise maven James Wan to direct the *Justice League* spinoff. He worked on a story with Beall and Johns and began filming with Momoa in the lead, Amber Heard as love interest Mera, former Watchman Patrick Wilson as the villainous Ocean Master, and former Green Goblin Willem Dafoe as Aquaman's mentor Vulko. In December 2018, *Aquaman* became the first DC movie released under Warner's new owner, AT&T.

The movie begins with a flashback to a meet-strange between lighthouse keeper Thomas Curry and Atlantean queen Atlanna. Their surf-and-turf romance results in the birth of a boy, Arthur Curry. Years later, the grown-up Arthur is recovering from helping the Justice League defeat Steppenwolf by dividing his time between drinking on land and fighting at sea. While saving a submarine crew from pirates, the father of one of the bad guys is killed. His son, also a pirate, swears revenge.

Meanwhile, Arthur's half-brother Orm has become the ruler of Atlantis. He wants to wage war on the surface-dwellers for the environmental degradation they have caused. To do this, he must conquer and unite the Seven Kingdoms and become Ocean Master. Mera, queen of the Kingdom of Xebel, and Vulko convince Arthur to try to stop Orm. A war between the kingdoms ends in a showdown between Arthur and Orm.

If nothing else, *Aquaman* is an impressive technical achievement, considering that 90 percent of the movie takes place underwater. For these scenes, Wan shot the actors in the studio, where they emulated swimming and treading water while suspended on rigs and lifts. The CGI artists added air bubbles, wavy hair and other details for the illusion of submerged action. Action set-pieces include a James Bondian rooftop chase in an Italian villa and a horror-movie–style attack on a storm-tossed boat by undersea monsters.

Unlike previous DCEU movies, *Aquaman* wasn't afraid to lean into the inherent campiness of its premise, of character names like Ocean Master, and of talking crustaceans. Audiences and critics approved of the new, goofier superhero take, and the movie became the first DC-based flick to crack the $1 billion mark since 2012's *The Dark Knight Rises*. Warner was coming to realize that, if it couldn't beat Marvel at its own game, the studio would have to forge a different path. Whatever that might look like.

Chapter XXII

Endgame

"Whether you like all of the 24 movies or not, the capital that Marvel built up allowed them to do things like make a movie starring a raccoon and a tree, right? You would've already had *Iron Man 4* if it was any other studio. But they decided, No, we're going to take chances on all these other things. To put a flag in the ground and say, We're going to end something and take characters off the table, is, I think, kind of daring, but selfishly it was really great for us."
—Stephen McFeely, co-writer, *Avengers: Endgame*[1]

"I don't believe that in the real world if you fell into a vat of acid you would turn white and have a smile and your hair would be green. So you start backwards-engineering these things and it becomes really interesting."
—Todd Phillips, director, *Joker*[2]

Two thousand eighteen was Peak Superhero, and 2019 wasn't far behind. The year saw the release of ten superhero movies, from the mega (*Avengers: Endgame*) to the modest (*Fast Color*).

In Marvel news, the studio released its first female-fronted movie, *Captain Marvel*; killed off Scarlett Johansson's Black Widow and Robert Downey, Jr.'s, Iron Man; and brought its Phase Three to a close. Parent company Disney acquired Fox, bringing home (in the minds of comics fans) X-Men, Deadpool and the Fantastic Four. To the horror of said fans, Marvel and Sony fell out, raising the possibility of another less-than-amazing Spider-Man.

Meanwhile, Warner Bros.' DC arm experienced an upswing. As the new year began, *Aquaman* was still aswim in box office returns. A few months later, the studio released its most lighthearted superhero effort—and, at the end of the year, its darkest. Both would be successes.

The first superhero movie to ring in the New Year was *Glass*. This was the third in a trilogy that began in 2000 with *Unbreakable*. Released in the shadow of *X-Men*, *Unbreakable* was a comparatively low-key original film with Bruce Willis as David Dunn, a security guard who discovers that he has superpowers, and Samuel L. Jackson as Elijah Price, aka "Mr. Glass," the owner of a comic-book art store. Written and directed by *The Sixth Sense*'s M. Night Shyamalan, *Unbreakable* eschews cowls and capes while exploring superhero tropes. Dunn reappeared briefly at the end of Shyamalan's 2016 movie *Split*, which introduced James McAvoy as the Beast, a madman with super-strength and 23 different personalities. *Glass* brings together both movies' main characters and puts them under the care of a psychiatrist (Sarah Paulson) who tries to convince them that they are deluded. While the first two in the trilogy earned mostly positive reviews, critics found the third entry to be a dull execution of a potentially interesting premise. All three were modestly budgeted (*Unbreakable*, at $75 million, was the most expensive) and made a profit.

Two months later, Marvel released *Captain Marvel*. For its first solo superheroine adventure, the studio decided to showcase a new character (foreshadowed in *Infinity War*) rather than an established one. They chose one of the most powerful in the Marvel Universe, one who has as convoluted a history as any in comics.

In a nutshell: The original Captain Marvel was the Fawcett Comics do-gooder who became the first big-screen superhero in the 1941 serial *Adventures of Captain Marvel*. In 1953, following a lawsuit from DC over perceived similarities to Superman, Fawcett retired the character. With the name in limbo, Stan Lee and artist Gene Colan introduced Marvel's own Captain Marvel—also male—in 1967. The following year, Marvel retconned its Captain Marvel as an alien from the technologically advanced Kree race. Around this time, writer Roy Thomas and Colan debuted a U.S. Army officer named Carol Danvers. Carol is caught in the explosion of a Kree device.

Nearly a decade later, Marvel brought Carol back in her own title, *Ms. Marvel*, with superpowers resulting from the explosion. In the eighties, Ms. Marvel appeared alongside the X-Men and Avengers and in the ensuing decades went through various incarnations, including one called Warbird.

Then in 2012, Marvel relaunched the character as Captain Marvel. Writer Kelly Sue DeConnick updated her by delving into her background as an Air Force pilot. It was this modern template that Marvel wanted to see adapted, but set in the nineties so that Carol's story wouldn't interfere with the continuity that begins with Ground Zero for the Marvel Cinematic Universe, the end of *Iron Man*.

Marvel announced the movie in 2014, assigned Nicole Perlman (*Guardians of the Galaxy*) and Meg LeFauve (Pixar's *Inside Out*) to write a script, and began to search for a director. Brie Larson, an Academy Award winner for her performance in the 2015 drama

Oscar winner Brie Larson played the title character in 2019's *Captain Marvel*, Marvel's first female-led feature. Marvel Studios.

Room, was announced as the lead at the 2016 San Diego Comic-Con. Finally, after a year of searching, the studio confirmed its choice for director(s): Anna Boden and Ryan Fleck, a duo who had made two well-received character dramas *Half Nelson* and *Mississippi Grind*.

When the movie opens, Carol is known as Vers, a member of the Kree Empire's Starforce. On a mission to rescue a colleague, she's captured by Skrulls, the shape-shifting enemy of the Kree. Vers escapes and crash-lands in a Los Angeles Blockbuster video store, circa 1995. The Skrulls pursue her as, aided by Nick Fury, she recovers her memories of her past as a fighter pilot on Earth. Talos, a Skrull, helps her realize that she has been betrayed by the Kree and her mentor, Yon-Rogg, and Carol turns against her former colleagues to save the Skrulls. A fight aboard an orbiting spacecraft leads to a final battle on Earth between Captain Marvel and Yon-Rogg.

The nineties setting inspires some fun fish-out-of-water gags, and Larson exudes power and control as the intergalactic warrior. But the story never quite takes off and the action scenes are less empowering than generic, even if one is set to No Doubt's "Just a Girl." Nevertheless, one month after its March release, *Captain Marvel* surpassed the $1 billion mark, making it the seventh Marvel Cinematic Universe movie to do so.

In April, Warner released its own Captain Marvel movie—this one called, for legal reasons, *Shazam!* Including the serial, a seventies Saturday morning TV series (also called *Shazam!*) that lasted three seasons, and an appearance in 1979's *Legends of the Superheroes* TV specials, this was the fourth live-action incarnation of the character. In the comics, DC—which had bought the rights to the Fawcett hero in 1972, two decades after putting a kibosh on his adventures via a lengthy lawsuit—had given the Big Red Cheese several makeovers. In one of these, a 1987 series, the superhero retains the mind of young alter ego Billy Batson. Prior to the reboot, Captain Marvel had always had his own personality, more or less.

This was the version that made it into movie theaters in 2018, with Broadway/TV star Zachary Levi as the superhero and 16-year-old Asher Angel as Billy Batson up against the hero's arch-nemesis, Dr. Sivana (Mark Strong). Although set in the DCEU, with nods to events from previous movies, the decidedly un-dark *Shazam!* seemed to be grounded in an entirely different universe. Box-office-wise it held its own, and on a budget that was half of the average superhero feature.

On the other end of the spectrum, a heavy metal reboot of *Hellboy* upped the horror elements of the comic book at the expense of the original movie's monster-movie charm.

The *Hellboy* franchise had stalled after a commercially and critically well-received 2008 sequel, *Hellboy II: The Golden Army*, again written and directed by Guillermo del Toro and starring Ron Perlman. As the years ticked by, Hellboy creator creator Mike Mignola started working on a story with screenwriter Andrew Cosby. According to Mignola, when it became clear that del Toro "didn't want to have anything to do with it, he wasn't going to direct,"[3] the producers hired a new director, Neil Marshall, and decided on a reboot. David Harbour, of the Netflix series *Stranger Things*, donned the horns.

Hellboy (2019) met a wall of resistance. It was less that the new version offered an R-rated (for violence) take on the character than the sacrilege of making a *Hellboy* movie without del Toro and Perlman. From the reception to the movie, one would think that the filmmakers set fire to del Toro's collection of monster-movie props. *Variety*'s Owen Gleiberman held the film up as an example of exactly what not to do when rebooting a franchise.[4]

Amidst all the blood, thunder and multimillion-dollar IPs, did the superhero movie space have room for a low-budget, independent, inclusive, original film? Set in a future drought-ridden American Midwest, *Fast Color* was about three generations of Black women grappling with their hereditary powers to transform matter—what they call their "abilities." Julia Hart, a former high school teacher with one other feature to her credit, directed from a screenplay she wrote with husband, *Lala Land* co-producer Jordan Horowitz. Aided by lead Gugu Mbatha-Ra, and with its unique take on the genre, the film received positive reviews and found a modest audience.

And then, a week after *Fast Color*'s April release, the superhero blockbuster returned with a vengeance. Even more sprawling than *Infinity War*, *Avengers: Endgame* made its predecessor look like a student art film.

"We'll take blame for the scale, because we were pushing for it," said co-director Joe Russo. "We were pushing to make it bigger, saying, 'Look, what you've done is an impressive narrative over ten years, and why shouldn't this involve every character?.'.. You can't really look back and go, 'Hey, remember the last time that somebody took 12 franchises and blended them together and told the movie with 60 lead characters?'... [T]here is no real template for it."[5]

Five years after Thanos murdered half of the universe, Scott Lang emerges from the Quantum Realm with the news that time travel is possible at the subatomic level. Tony Stark comes out of paradisical semi-retirement and helps Bruce Banner, who has evolved into a Hulk-Banner hybrid, build a time machine so that the Avengers can scoop up the Infinity Stones before Thanos. Avengers and friends separate, traveling to different places and times before returning to present-day Earth for a final, all-hands-on-deck showdown with Thanos and his army. In the course of the mission, two major characters, Natasha Romanoff and Tony Stark, are killed off. The fate of another, Gamora, is unknown.

In the climax of *Avengers: Endgame* (2019), Marvel's mightiest superheroines band together to keep the Infinity Gauntlet from the power-mad despot Thanos. From left: Gwyneth Paltrow as Pepper Potts, Tessa Thompson as Valkyrie, Elizabeth Olsen as Scarlet Witch, Brie Larson as Captain Marvel, Pom Klementieff as Mantis, and Letitia Wright as Suri. Marvel Studios.

The three-hour *Endgame* became the studio's biggest film and one of the highest-grossing of all time, second only to *Avatar*. Outside of the usual Marvel detractors, naysayers were few. Directors Anthony and Joe Russo, writers Christopher Markus and Stephen McFeely, and cast and crew had pulled off the next-to-impossible by bringing a decade's worth of movies to a narratively and emotionally satisfying conclusion. In an age when longform storytelling more often than not ended with viewers taking to Twitter in frustration, this was a Herculean feat.

In May, *Brightburn* journeyed to the darkside of superhero-dom with a horror-movie spin on a classic origin story—Superman's. After crashing to Earth, an alien child terrorizes his adoptive parents. Co-produced by *Guardians*' James Gunn and co-written by his cousin and brother, the R-rated, low-budget Sony–Screen Gems flick received mixed reviews and did okay at the box office.

In its portrait of an out-of-control super-powered being, the movie foreshadowed *Dark Phoenix*. This was Fox's second attempt, following 2006's *X-Men: The Last Stand*, at adapting one of the most famous storylines from X-Men comics. Producer-screenwriter–de facto mutant wrangler Simon Kinberg convinced the studio to let him write and direct a version of the story with the cast of the new timeline that had been created in *Days of Future Past*.

But the movie faced even more blowback than *Last Stand*. Fans who wanted to see a faithful adaptation of the space-set original saga were greeted with an earthbound story and a different villain, Vuk, the leader of an alien race who want to harness Jean Grey's Dark Phoenix power. As Vuk, Jessica Chastain delivers clunkers like, "Your emotions make you weak." Reviewers who couldn't care less about the original comics run found the movie pointless. Moviegoers who hadn't been paying attention to Fox's twisty X-Men continuity were confused by the death of a character, Jean, who had already died in a previous movie. With Mystique, Beast, and Nightcrawler all part of the team, the X-Men were beginning to resemble the Blue Mutant Group.

Not only was the tenth X-Men flick the first to fail to win its opening weekend (it lost to *The Secret Life of Pets 2*), but its eventual worldwide gross of $252 million made *Phoenix* the lowest-earning in the series.

If there was a bright spot for fans of Charles Xavier's gifted youngsters, it was that they were now back at the Mothership. A few months before the release of *Dark Phoenix*, Disney acquired Fox. Outside of *The New Mutants*, a spinoff being held back by the studio, this meant the end of the long-running but mercurial franchise. The mutants were Marvel's problem now.

Speaking of which, the studio had one more Phase Three release: *Spider-Man: Far from Home*.

The second Marvel-Sony co-production, *Far from Home* is both coda to *Endgame* and sequel to *Homecoming*. The world is still reeling from the death of Tony Stark when Peter Parker goes on a school trip to Europe, where he encounters Mysterio, a costumed oddball in globe-shaped headgear. Returning screenwriters Chris McKenna and Erik Sommers update the classic smoke-and-mirrors villain from the comics as Quentin Beck, a disgruntled former Stark Industries employee out to take the place of Iron Man through drones and holograms. Spider-Man defeats Beck, but the bad guy, played by Jake Gyllenhaal, has the last laugh; *Far from Home* ends with the *Daily Bugle*'s J. Jonah Jameson broadcasting a video that Beck recorded before his death in which he reveals that Peter is Spider-Man. "What the fu—" says Peter before the credits roll. It's the same

Chapter XXII. Endgame

last half-line uttered by Marisa Tomei's Aunt May in *Homecoming* when she sees her nephew in his Spider-Man costume.

Far from Home became Sony's most successful movie in its history, but this didn't stop the studio from coming to a stalemate with Marvel over a third Spidey co-production.

The year's final "superhero" movie, if it can be called that, was also 2019's biggest cinematic surprise. Director Todd Phillips' *Joker* is a character study that owes more to New York-set character studies like *Taxi Driver* and *King of Comedy* than any *Batman* movie. And, unlike Christopher Nolan's approach to the Joker in *The Dark Knight*, Phillips' is all about his backstory.

A party clown and aspiring comedian, Arthur Fleck lives with his mother in a grimy inner-city apartment. After he's attacked by juvenile delinquents and loses his job, he shoots two drunken businessmen in self-defense and a third as he attempts to flee. The newly minted vigilante becomes a hero to some, and these followers don clown masks in emulation. He appears on a late-night talk show hosted by Murray Franklin, who has been mocking Arthur's attempts at stand-up. During the show, Arthur shoots Murray and is arrested. Following a riot by followers of the unhinged killer, the police arrest Fleck.

Aside from references to Gotham City, Arkham Asylum and the Wayne family, *Joker* offers few indications that it's based on a comic book or has anything to do with a larger cinematic universe or mythos. Phillips admitted that he wanted to use a well-established character as a way to get his message, society's collective lack of empathy, across to a mass audience. "To get people to go to the theater, you have to do something that cuts through the fog," he said.[6]

Astonishingly for a movie about an insane comic book clown, *Joker* won the top prize at the 76th Venice International Film Festival, where it premiered. When the feature opened wide five weeks later, it reset the global box office record for an October release with $234 million, vanquishing *Venom*'s $207.4 million.[7]

Critics were divided. Was it "a cinematic masterpiece," as filmmaker Michael Moore called it,[8] or "the most disappointing film of the year," as per *The Guardian*'s Peter Bradshaw?[9]

Most praised Joaquin Phoenix for his lead performance; *New York Times*' dance critic Gia Kourlas even gave the actor kudos for Arthur's dance moves, which he demonstrates on a Bronx staircase. In a bit of meta-casting, Phillips cast Robert DeNiro as talk-show host Franklin; in Martin Scorsese's 1982 movie *King of Comedy*, DeNiro had played a struggling comedian who dreams of getting a break on a late-night talk show. *Comedy* director Scorsese, the most direct influence on *Joker*, pronounced Phillips' movie "fine."[10] The remark came after the director likened Marvel movies to "theme parks."

The $62 million flick passed the $1 billion mark, becoming only the second DC-related effort to do so (after *Aquaman*) and the highest-grossing R-rated film of all time. In January 2020, the most non–DC of all DC films received 11 Academy Award nominations.

Chapter XXIII

After the Snap

> "The biggest snub in my opinion, and I am actually even angry about this I am embarrassed to say, is the unforgivable omission of *Spider-Man: No Way Home*. How did it not get one of the ten nominations for Best Picture? Forget the fact that the movie made $750 million [in the U.S.] and is still going. This was a great movie. It wasn't in the Top 10 best movies of the year? There were three Spider-Men in it."
>
> —Jimmy Kimmel[1]

And then, like a rejected plot for a Thanos limited series, Covid-19 happened.

The real-world Snap upended studios' schedules in a monumental way. Movies scheduled for release in 2020 were shuffled into 2021 and beyond. But while theaters were shuttered, streaming services claimed eyeballs and introduced a new platform perfect for, say, watching four hours of outtakes from *Justice League*.

The last superhero film released before lockdown was a spinoff of *Suicide Squad*. *Birds of Prey (and the Fantabulous Emancipation of One Harley Quinn)* paired that movie's breakout star with other DC heroines (and antiheroines).

A Harley movie with Margot Robbie in the role was probably inevitable. Just about everyone who made it through *Suicide Squad* agreed that she was the best thing about the 2016 supervillain team flick, and even while working on the earlier movie the actress realized the character had legs. But she didn't think that the nutty girl clown should be on her own. "Harley needs friends," Robbie said.[2]

She started working on a story for what she called her "R-rated girl-gang movie" with Christina Hodson, screenwriter of the Transformers prequel *Bumblebee*. They added Huntress and Black Canary, both regulars of a comic series called *Birds of Prey*; Cassandra Cain, a Batgirl from the comics (Warner Bros. was saving the original Batgirl, Barbara Gordon, for her own movie); and Renee Montoya, a Gotham City police detective who, like Harley, was originally created for *Batman: The Animated Series*.

(This was not the first live-action version of *Birds of Prey*. A 2002–03 TV series lasted 13 episodes on the WB Network and featured Barbara Gordon, who has taken on a new identity as Oracle following a Joker-related injury that has left her paraplegic, as well as Huntress and Black Canary's daughter. Harley Quinn, portrayed by Mia Sara, was the main antagonist.)

Although responsible for the incident that sets Harley, and the movie, on its careening path, the heroine's ex was never considered. "We knew from Day One that we just wanted to do a Harley story with no Joker," Hodson said.[3]

Robbie and Hodson also decided to keep the story down-to-earth—no portals

Chapter XXIII. After the Snap

to other dimensions, no aliens trying to repopulate the Earth, no Mother Boxes, just a bunch of badass ladies fighting a crime syndicate run by Black Mask, a Batman adversary.

To direct, Robbie and her co-producers recruited Cathy Yan. A former *Wall Street Journal* reporter, Yan had made one feature, the low-budget dark comedy *Dead Pigs*, filmed in Shanghai. Born in China and raised in Virginia, she became the first Asian woman to direct an American superhero film.

Released in early February, and rated R for language and violence, *Birds of Prey* mixes bloodless mayhem with fourth-wall–breaking asides. The latter prompted some reviewers to compare the movie to *Deadpool*, although Harley was already speaking directly to the audience in early versions of Hodson's script, before *Deadpool*'s 2016 release.[4]

Reviews leaned towards the positive. *The Hollywood Reporter*'s Ciara Wardlow commended the effort as "one of the more cognizant and thorough deconstructions of the male gaze to hit recent mainstream cinema, particularly as it relates to the superhero genre…. *Birds of Prey* acknowledges the existence of this gaze and adamantly rejects it, providing an entertaining but still thoughtful alternative."[5]

On the other hand, *San Francisco Chronicle*'s Mick LaSalle wrote, "*Birds of Prey* … is just a terrible thing to inflict on audiences, who, after all, didn't hurt anyone and just hoped to have a nice time."[6]

The Harley vehicle never had a chance to let viewers decide, though, opening as it did just as theaters began shutting down. But by then, the movie's tepid opening had already taken the wind out of its sails. Yan later said that she didn't have as much control as she would have liked. But, as she told *Hollywood Reporter*, WarnerMedia (its new name under AT&T) deserved credit for sticking to the R and for allowing them to make something that was not a direct sequel to *Suicide Squad*.[7]

The only other DCEU movie released to theaters in 2020 was *Wonder Woman 1984*. Returning director Patty Jenkins had more of a hand in the sequel than the first and co-wrote the story and screenplay with comics writer–former DC Entertainment exec Geoff Johns. (Dave Callaham, who had made a pass at the *Ant-Man* script, also has a screenplay credit.) They set the sequel in the eighties because Jenkins "was really craving seeing Diana at the height of her most evolved, full-power, top of her game."[8] They added an old Wonder Woman nemesis, the Cheetah, and all-purpose DC rich guy Max Lord.

Although notionally set in the Snyder-verse, the movie marks a Technicolor departure in both tone and visuals from its predecessor. The story, which hinges on a wish-granting ancient crystal, is pure comic book–pulp. Diana doesn't want to fight Cheetah, who is the super-powered alter ego of her friend Barbara Minerva (*Saturday Night Live* and *Bridesmaid* actress Kirsten Wiig) and continually tries to talk her out of her destructive path. The Amazon Games, Diana's invisible plane and her Golden Eagle Armor make their cinematic debuts, and seventies Wonder Woman herself, Lynda Carter, appears in the mid-credits scene.

For those who care about such things, the movie largely dispenses with continuity. What has Wonder Woman been doing since the end of World War I? Has she been fighting bad guys? If not, why does she suddenly appear at a shopping mall in 1984? If so, where was she during World War II? During Vietnam? Does no one realize that Diana and Wonder Woman are the same person, or does everyone? It's hard to tell.

Bumped five times before its release, *Wonder Woman 1984* finally arrived in theaters and on streaming services on Christmas Day. It had the best opening since the start of the pandemic and was the most-watched straight-to-streaming title of the year.[9] But unenthusiastic reviews, not to fear of the virus, kept people at home, in front of the TV.

There, just a few months later, they could see Diana again. Just like viewers in 2017 who got a double-dose of the Amazon in *Wonder Woman* and *Justice League*, *Wonder Woman 1984* warmed fans up for her reappearance in March 2021, wielding a sword against big bad Steppenwolf in *Zach Snyder's Justice League*.

After two years of fan pressure, WarnerMedia had caved. The clamor for a director's cut of *Justice League* began almost immediately after the movie's release—and even before Snyder confirmed that such a thing existed. Fans took out ads, flew banners, bullied studio execs on social media, and signed a petition. (The 2018 change.org petition received 179,054 supporters; two years earlier, a petition to "boot Zach Snyder off of *Justice League*" garnered a paltry 18,101.) In February 2020, the studio agreed to give Snyder another $70 million to film new scenes and finish the special effects. Just over a year later, the new, longer and, some would say, improved version debuted in March 2021 on HBO Max.

As it turned out, streaming and quarantine were the perfect—perhaps only—conditions to take in the four-hour magnum opus. Stuck at home, viewers could indulge in lengthy Cyborg and Flash backstories and set-ups for DCEU movies that would never happen.

Controversy accompanied the release, but it had little to do with Snyder or the new material. A few months after WarnerMedia announced that it would #releasethesnydercut, actor Ray Fisher (Cyborg) tweeted about Joss Whedon's treatment of the cast and crew on *Justice League*. He called the replacement director's on-set behavior "gross, abusive, unprofessional, and completely unacceptable."[10] Later, he added that Whedon seemed to still be stuck on what he viewed as negative reaction to *Age of Ultron*.[11]

Buffy the Vampire Slayer Cast members chimed in with their own allegations of bullying. In November 2020, Whedon left *The Nevers*, a show he created for WarnerMedia-owned HBO. In a plot twist few Hollywood outsiders could have seen coming, Snyder, the former destroyer of childhood fantasies, was the hero, rescuing his artistic vision. Whedon, the genre savant, was the toxic one.

As mentioned, the new old *Justice League* set up movies that had been glimmers in Snyder's eye. But WarnerMedia had since shied away almost entirely from its original plan to create an interconnected universe to rival Marvel's. Now it was just throwing ideas against the wall to see what would stick.

For some reason, the powers-that-be hadn't given up on the Suicide Squad following the dismal performance of the team's 2016 cinematic debut. Instead, the studio handed James Gunn the keys to the supervillain clown car.

Once again, no character proved too silly to be unredeemable with a traumatic backstory and witty repartee. The *Guardians of the Galaxy* director looked into the deepest, silliest corners of the DC Universe, where he found polka-dot-flinging Polka-Dot Man and rat-whisperer Ratcatcher, both old Batman adversaries (although for his movie, Gunn created Ratcatcher 2, the daughter of the original); King Shark, an anthropomorphic man-eater; and Peacemaker, who is dedicated to peace at any price, including mass murder. The villain of the piece is Starro, a giant starfish from outer space who debuted along with the original Justice League in a 1960 comic.

While everything else crashed around her, Margot Robbie's Harley Quinn remained an anarchic delight in the DC Extended Universe. Here she is in James Gunn's 2021 reboot *The Suicide Squad*. Warner Bros.

Familiar faces include Viola Davis' Amanda Waller, again offering the choice of a more lenient sentence or exploding head, Robbie's Harley Quinn, and Joel Kinneman's Rick Flag. Idris Elba (Heimdall in the MCU) plays Bloodsport who, like Deadshot in the previous movie, is an assassin who cares only about his daughter.

WarnerMedia okayed an R rating this time, and Gunn obliged with an opening scene in which a B-team of Suicide Squaders is slaughtered—shades of the jerry-rigged team in *Deadpool 2*—and another in which Deadshot—er, Bloodsport—and Peacemaker (WWE wrestler John Cena) compete to see who can kill more freedom fighters. The violence was offset by Gunn's slyly subversive humor, like a record-breakingly brief boy-meets-girl, boy-gets-girl, girl-kills-boy romance between Harley and a dictator. In another scene, Rick Flag and Bloodshot, er, Bloodsport, contemplate rescuing Harley from the dictator's headquarters when she comes up behind them. "Hey, guys. What're you doing?" she asks.

Although it did well in streaming, *The Suicide Squad* did not make back its budget of $185 million, a heavy price tag for an R-rated film. The pandemic, confusion over the movie's relation to the previous flick, and a lack of major stars were blamed. But reviews were enthusiastic. The *Los Angeles Times*' Justin Lang caught the mood when he wrote, "After 2016's ugly, bludgeoning *Suicide Squad*, I couldn't imagine liking—and could barely stomach the idea of seeing—another movie called *Suicide Squad*. I'm delighted to be proven wrong."[12]

The star of another critical pinata, 2018's *Venom*, also found some redemption. In *Venom: Let There Be Carnage*, Eddie Brock and his head-chomping alien guest battle a meaner and more powerful head-chomping alien. Doubling down on the first movie's most enjoyable quality, the *Odd Couple*–style banter between Tom Hardy's Brock and his Venom, the plot about another evil symbiote called Carnage (played in human form by Woody Harrelson) came in a distant second to the jokes. New director Andy Serkis, aka Ulysses Klaue in the MCU, brought the action in at about 90 minutes, a length that did not go unnoticed, or unappreciated, by critics. *Carnage* became the seventh highest-grossing film of 2021.

• • •

With Phase Four on hold due to Covid, Marvel postponed all of its 2020 releases and concentrated on streaming series like *WandaVision* and *Loki*. Both tied in with the MCU, a cross-media storytelling venture that could be seen as the next step in the evolution of multi-platform storytelling or a new layer in the biggest Ponzi scheme in the history of entertainment. Take your pick.

One Marvel-related superhero flick did escape out into the wild, though.

Based on a team originating in a 1982 graphic novel, the X-Men spinoff *The New Mutants* had been delayed for two years. The idea for a film adaptation of the young, ethnically diverse team first arose in 2009, around the time of *X-Men Origins: Wolverine*. In 2014, director Josh Boone sold his take to franchise producer Simon Kinberg, describing his vision as "a full-fledged horror movie set within the X-Men universe."[13]

But the studio got cold feet, then changed its mind again when the R-rated horror flick *It* became a hit. *The New Mutants* that finally struggled into theaters—after a release date that changed four times—in August 2020 failed to scare up an audience or positive press, although some reviewers appreciated the movie's queer romance subplot.

That same month, Chadwick Boseman passed away. The *Black Panther* actor, 43, died of colon cancer, which he'd kept private. His death was a shock in what was already, by most metrics, a dreadful year.

It wasn't until halfway through 2021 that Marvel started to get its groove back with the release of *Black Widow*.

A stand-alone Widow venture had been in the offing since the 2017 filming of *Infinity War* but, since the Avenger sacrificed herself in *Endgame*, any movie would have to be set in the past. Marvel decided on the period just before the end of *Captain America: Civil War*, when Natasha becomes a fugitive following the implementation of the Sokovia Accords.

As with Margot Robbie and *Birds of Prey*, Scarlett Johansson took an active role in making the Widow's solo venture. She lobbied for Cate Shortland, an Australian director who had made three features, including 2012's *Lore*; Johansson called the movie, which follows a teenage girl's quest to lead her four younger siblings to safety in Germany as the Third Reich crumbles, "a masterpiece" and "a perfect film."[14]

By this point, the actor had played Natasha Romanoff in seven movies. She felt it was time to show more sides to the assassin. Cortland, she thought, could zero in on Natasha's vulnerability.

Black Widow takes a deep dive into Natasha's past, introducing her parents—well, the sleeper agents who masqueraded as her parents—and a sister figure, also a trained assassin. The movie excels in the small family moments, including a dinner-table scene that explores the simmering tensions between the two trained parent-assassins, David Harbour's doofus-y Red Guardian and Rachel Weisz's no-nonsense mom. In Florence

Pugh's Yelena Belova, Natasha's competitive younger sibling, Marvel had another breakout star.

Family—and diversity—was also center stage in *Shang-Chi and the Legend of the Ten Rings*. In Marvel's first film with an Asian lead, Canadian actor Simu Liu plays the title character, a hero who made his mark in a seventies title *The Hands of Shang-Chi: Master of Kung Fu*.

At the time, the series was both ground-breaking and relatively sophisticated. But Shang-Chi came with some baggage. For years, his main adversary was his father, Fu Manchu, the "yellow peril" character from a series of old pulp novels. Marvel had bought the rights to the Sax Rohmer creation and wanted its money's worth—although this begs the question: What made anyone at the publisher think that a pulp villain with a creepy mustache would convince 12-year-olds in 1974 to plunk down their hard-earned paper-carrier money for a comic book?

In *Ten Rings*, Shang-Chi is still fighting his father, but now his dad isn't the anti-Western mystic of the comics but Xu Wenwu, an immortal warlord and leader of a criminal organization. To stop Wenwu from destroying a magical village, Shang-Chi teams with his sister Xu Xialing.

The movie won praise for its action, particularly a fight scene on a bus, and the performances of Liu and veteran Hong Kong actor Tony Leung as Shang-Chi's father. Actor-rapper Awkwafina and Ben Kingsley provide comic relief as the protagonist's friend Katy and Trevor Slattery, the British actor who fronted as the Mandarin in *Iron Man 3*. Fan-service included the reappearance of the Abomination, last seen on-screen in 2008's *The Incredible Hulk*.

As with *Black Widow*'s Cate Shortland, Marvel found its *Ten Rings* director outside of franchise filmmaking. Destin Daniel Cretton had made the indie drama *Short Term 12*, based on his own experiences working in a group home for teenagers (and starring Captain Marvel Brie Larson in her first lead performance), and an adaptation of the memoir *The Glass Castle*.

Marvel's interest in hiring talent outside of mainstream film-making continued with the studio's pick for the helmer of *Eternals*, its next release. Chinese-born Chloé Zhao had made *The Rider*, a 2017 movie about a rodeo star whose career was cut short by an accident. That film, and Zhao's even more acclaimed follow-up *Nomadland*—a contemporary drama following a woman who lives in a trailer and crisscrosses the country in search of work—could not have been further removed from *Eternals*' source material, Jack Kirby's cosmic tales of alien gods on Earth.

But Zhao—a Japanese manga fan since childhood and an MCU fan for a decade—had been keen to work with the studio. "So, I put the word out there that I wanted to make a Marvel movie and the right project came to me."[15]

Shang-Chi and *Eternals* shared faddish roots—respectively, martial arts and visitations from space (i.e., *2001: A Space Odyssey*, Erich von Däniken's 1968 book *Chariots of the Gods? Unsolved Mysteries of the Past*). Both introduced a whole new set of characters into the Marvel Cinematic Universe, and both embraced diversity: *Eternals*' cast includes British-Asian Gemma Chan, Pakistani-American Kumail Nanjiani, and Mexican Salma Hayek. Phastos, played by Brian Tyree Henry, is the MCU's first openly gay superhero.

The cast was one of the film's most remarked-upon features in otherwise lukewarm reviews. A big chunk of the movie is about getting the band back together, and great swaths of exposition stop the two-and-a-half-hour movie in its tracks; one reviewer called its many info dumps "bafflingly incoherent nonsense."[16] The Deviants, the creatures threatening humanity, are standard-issue CGI videogame monsters. Weirdly, the Marvel heroes make references to DC's Batman and Superman.

More interesting are the conflicts between the team members. Ikaris, who reveals that he knew the real mission all along—to stop the Deviants from decimating the Earth's population so that the planet could give birth to a new celestial—becomes the team's nemesis. And the movie takes risks. Rather than helping to stop the Emergence, as it's called, Nanjiani's Kingo, the most likable Eternal, returns to his cozy life as a Bollywood star—and then doesn't come back for the final fight. The Eternals must also deal with one of their own, Thena (Angelina Jolie), who has lost her mind due to her immortality. Still, it's a movie few but the most hardcore Marvel-ites would want to sit through a second time.

Unlike, say, *Spider-Man: No Way Home*, a movie that inspired one Florida man, Ramiro Alanis, to part with his disposable income 292 times.

The third Marvel Spidey almost didn't happen. But, after months of negotiations that ended in a stalemate, Disney CEO Bob Iger and actor Tom Holland stepped in to help broker a deal with Sony and voila, Spidey could sleep soundly again, at least until the next corporate falling-out.

No Way Home opens whole new dimensions for the Marvel Cinematic Universe. In *Far from Home*, Mysterio claimed he was from another Earth, and introduced the concept of the multiverse. The new film expanded on the idea by bringing together three Peter Parkers—Tobey Maguire's, Andrew Garfield's and Tom Holland's—and pitting their Spider-Men against the villains from the Raimi trilogy and the *Amazing Spider-Man* franchise. (Sony's *Into the Spider-Verse* also brought together a bunch of Spider-characters from different universes, including a middle-aged Spider-Man, a porcine Spider-Ham, a Spider-Woman and a noir film detective–style version voiced by

If three Spider-Men weren't enough for a Best Picture Oscar, how many did the Academy need? From left: Tobey Maguire, Tom Holland, and Andrew Garfield as various incarnations of movie Spider-Men in *Spider-Man: No Way Home* (Marvel/Sony, 2021). Marvel Studios.

Nicolas Cage.) Seeing three Spider-Men suit up was nearly as much fun as watching the three Peters give each other pep talks. Even the most hardened, anti-superhero movie critic couldn't help but be somewhat charmed.

Coming when it did, as Covid restrictions began to lift after over a year of quarantine, the Spidey-fest delivered both the financial relief that theater owners needed and the escapist entertainment that pandemic-exhausted moviegoers craved. The film broke box office records in its first weekend and became the fourth movie in history to make $800 million domestically. Industry watchers, studios and theater owners credited *No Way Home* for bringing people back to the cinema.

Did *No Way Home* save the movies? Not quite. But it represented the possibilities still left in a genre that showed little evidence of slowing down.

Epilogue

As I write this, in the summer of 2023, the superhero movie is at a crossroads, or perhaps at a portal.

Marvel, undisputed master of the genre, has nevertheless racked up some the worst reviews of its existence. Warner Bros. Discovery has abandoned the previous regime's blueprint to rebuild from scratch. Sony is still trying to make its live-action Spider-Verse a thing while continuing to mine gold with its animated Spider-Verse.

In 2022, Marvel released *Doctor Strange in the Multiverse of Madness*, *Thor: Love and Thunder*, and *Black Panther: Wakanda Forever*. All three received mixed notices, although audiences and critics were more forgiving of the *Black Panther* sequel's flaws than Sam Raimi's horror-inflected take on the Sorcerer Supreme and Taika Waititi's lean into silliness with his sequel to *Thor: Ragnarok*.

The slightly downward trajectory—the aforementioned films still cleaned up at the box office—dipped substantially with *Ant-Man and the Wasp: Quantumania*. Opening in February 2023, the Phase Five kick-off opened big but, following some of the harshest brickbats yet hurled at a Marvel movie, fell off 69 percent in its second weekend. Many critics singled out what they saw as shoddy CGI, a surprising misstep from a studio that could, at the very least, be depended upon for eye-popping spectacle. It didn't help that several VFX artists began calling out the company for long hours, impossible deadlines, and unclear (or nonexistent) guidelines. The criticisms continued over other Marvel fare, including the streaming series *Secret Invasion* and its use of AI in the opening credits.

And, in a C-suite remarkable for its image of stability, a surprise shakeup set insiders' tongues wagging. In March 2023 Marvel fired Victoria Alonso, a producer with the studio since 2006, as its president of physical production. The reason given: that she had violated her noncompete clause by working on a non-Disney project. Meanwhile, well-compensated Disney CEO Bob Iger (and de facto Marvel head) became symbolic of one-percenter tone-deafness for comments about striking writers and actors.

The Writers Guild of America's strike was just a few days old when *Guardians of the Galaxy Vol. 3* appeared in theatres. Positive reviews followed the release, which many agreed was a fitting end to the trilogy—and writer/director James Gunn's involvement with Marvel, at least for the foreseeable future.

Because, in October 2022, Warner Bros. Discovery announced that it was putting the writer/director, along with producer Peter Safran, in charge of rebooting the entire DC Universe, both for film and TV. In hindsight, the decision to give the reigns over to a proven commodity like Gunn, and his seizing the opportunity to map out an entire fictional universe, is the most and least surprising development in the last decade of superhero movies.

The announcement came a few months after Warner Bros. Discovery CEO David Zaslav decided to bury another DCEU leftover, *Batgirl*. Competing narratives said that the decision was based on cost-cutting measures and/or because of early negative reaction.

Yet, like pieces of the exploded planet of Krypton, remnants of the DCEU continued to drift Earthwards. Just a few days prior to the Gunn announcement, Warner released *Black Adam*, a Dwayne "The Rock" Johnson–led vehicle that immediately took its place alongside *Batman v Superman*, *Justice League*, and *Suicide Squad* as one of the worst reviewed DC efforts of the last decade.

Following *Black Adam*, *Shazam! Fury of the Gods* failed to match the praise directed at 2019's *Shazam!* Though ballyhooed in some quarters as "finally, a good DC movie," *The Flash* bombed with critics and audiences. Even nostalgia-bait like a reappearance by Michael Keaton's Batman failed to put bums in seats. (Speaking of the Caped Crusader, Robert Pattinson became the eighth actor to play the character in 2022's *The Batman*, a lengthy, atmospheric non-DCEU piece that benefits hugely from Paul Dano's slyly creepy performance as the Riddler.) Another DCEU remainder, *Blue Beetle*—scheduled for an August 2023 release—is being positioned as the first character but not the first film of the new DC Universe.

And yet we are due for one last gasp of the also-ran multibillion-dollar cinematic universe: *Aquaman and the Lost Kingdom*. Breath is bated.

As for Sony, the nadir of its Spider-Verse offerings came with the April 2022 release of *Morbius*, which starred Jared Leto as the chalk-white seventies Marvel vampire. When ironic memes began appearing after the film's opening, Sony failed to read the room (and its *Rotten Tomato* rating) and rereleased it. The rerelease also bombed.

But just over a year later the studio bounced back with *Spider-Man: Across the Spider-Verse*. The sequel to the 2018 Oscar winner again hit all the Spidey pleasure-points, even with a cliff-hanger ending that some saw as a cheat.

Meanwhile, with a script by (among others) Seth Rogen and his writing partner Evan Goldberg, *Teenage Mutant Ninja Turtles: Mutant Mayhem*—the *seventh* entry in the series that began in 1990—garnered the best reviews in the series' history. Arguably, *TMNT* remains the longest-running superhero movie franchise of them all.

And so here we are, on the precipice of a new age. Can Marvel again collect all the Infinity Stones? Can Gunn and co. do justice to DC's Justice League? Can Sony weave the magic of its animated Spider-Verse into its live-action Spider-Verse?

Or is it too late? Have audiences wearied of two-hour-plus superpowered CGI slugfests? Has the genre exhausted itself of fresh ideas and concepts? Is this the beginning of the long-predicted Superhero Movie Apocalypse?

Maybe. But superhero movies have been on life support before. If anything, they've shown how resilient they can be. In some form or another, they'll be around for a while yet. Even if that form is only pizza-loving, anthropomorphized reptiles named after Italian Renaissance painters.

Chapter Notes

Note: All box office and budget numbers are from Box Office Mojo or The Numbers unless otherwise noted.

Chapter I

1. Martin Pasko, *The DC Vault* (Philadelphia: Running Press, 2008), 79.
2. Patricia Ellsworth Wilson, "Present at the Creation of Superman and the Mole-Men," *The Adventure Continues Magazine* #14, http://theages.superman.nu/adventures/mole-men.php.
3. Jerry Blake, "The Case of the Silly Pictures: Superman Versus Captain Marvel (With Republic in the Middle)," *The Files of Jerry Blake*, February 9, 2020, https://filesofjerryblake.com/2020/02/09/the-case-of-the-silly-pictures-superman-versus-captain-marvel-with-republic-in-the-middle/.
4. *Ibid.*
5. Quentin Tarantino, "I Escaped from Devil's Island," thenewbev.com, April 6, 2020, https://web.archive.org/web/20200819045813/https://thenewbev.com/tarantinos-reviews/i-escaped-from-devils-island/?fbclid=IwAR0yx6FYh_-ZmdfrQaysB_1Umh84GidHEIAGgX2w39u03g95JZ-4DSB92WY.
6. Bruce Scivally, *Billion Dollar Batman* (Wilmette: Henry Gray, 2011), Kindle, loc. 833.
7. Grant Morrison, *Supergods: What Masked Vigilantes, Miraculous Mutants, and a Sun God from Smallville Can Teach Us About Being Human* (New York: Random House, 2011).
8. Ian Smith, "Interesting photos of Batman and Robin c.1943," thevintagenews.com, March 18, 2016, https://www.thevintagenews.com/2016/03/18/interesting-photos-batman-robin-c-1943-2/.
9. Scivally, *Batman*, loc. 898.
10. Jim Harmon and Donald F. Glut, *The Great Movie Serials* (Abingdon: Routledge, 1973), 259.
11. Geoff Mayer, *Encyclopedia of American Film Serials* (Jefferson: McFarland, 2017), 28.
12. Raymond William Stedman, *Serials: Suspense and Drama by Installments* (Norman: University of Oklahoma Press, 1971), 128.
13. Associated Press, "Kirk Alyn, 88, the Superman to Leap Tall Buildings First," *New York Times*, March 20, 1999, https://www.nytimes.com/1999/03/20/arts/kirk-alyn-88-the-superman-to-leap-tall-buildings-first.html.
14. Les Daniels, *Superman: The Golden Age* (San Francisco: Chronicle Books, 1999), 81.
15. Harmon and Glut, *Serials*, 204.
16. Scivally, *Batman*, loc. 1361–2.
17. Larry Tye, *Superman: The High-Flying History of America's Most Enduring Hero* (New York: Random House, 2012), 88.
18. Pasko, *Vault*, 79.
19. Pop Goes the Culture TV, "Superman's Noel Neill talks about Phyllis Coates and Kirk Alyn (with Jack Larson) Part 4 of 7," video, https://www.youtube.com/watch?v=IU-0zIYY6EA.
20. Bruce Scivally, *Superman on Film, Television, Radio and Broadway* (Jefferson: McFarland, 2007), 47.
21. Tye, *Superman*, 142.
22. *Ibid.*, 146.
23. Scivally, *Superman*, 57.
24. Tye, *Superman*, 153.
25. Jason Hofius and George Khoury, *Age of TV Heroes Age of TV Heroes* (Raleigh: TwoMorrows, 2010), 36.

Chapter II

1. Kelly Konda, "UPDATED Batman 75: Did An ABC Executive's Visit to the Playboy Club in 1965 Really Inspire the Adam West Batman TV Series?" weminoredinfilm.com, June 9, 2014, https://weminoredinfilm.com/2014/06/09/batman-75-did-an-abc-executives-visit-to-the-playboy-club-in-1965-really-inspire-the-adam-west-batman-tv-series/.
2. Chuck Dixon, "'Known Super-Criminals Still at Large': Villainy in *Batman*," *Gotham City 14 Miles: 14 Essays on Why the 1960s Batman TV Series Matters*, ed. Jim Beard (Edwardsville: Sequart Research and Literacy Organization, 2010), 121–22.
3. Joel Eisner, *The Official Batman Bat Book* (Chicago: Contemporary Books, 1986), 6.
4. Mike Barnes, "Yale Udoff, 'Bad Timing' Screenwriter and 'Batman' TV Booster, Dies at 83," *Hollywood Reporter*, July 27, 2018, https://www.

hollywoodreporter.com/news/yale-udoff-dead-bad-timing-screenwriter-playwright-batman-tv-booster-was-83-1130421.

5. Jeremy Dauber, *American Comics* (New York: W.W. Norton, 2021), 178.

6. Alex M. Parker, "An Evening with Batman and Robin," ordinarytimes.com, June 16, 2021, https://ordinary-times.com/2021/06/16/an-evening-with-batman-and-robin/.

7. Lorenzo Semple, Jr., "Requiem for a cheeky 'Batman,'" *Variety*, July 9, 2008, https://variety.com/2008/film/markets-festivals/requiem-for-a-cheeky-batman-1117988712/.

8. Arlen Schumer, "The Real Comic Book Origins of The Batman '66 TV Series," denofgeek.com, January 12, 2016, https://www.denofgeek.com/comics/the-real-comic-book-origins-of-the-batman-66-tv-series/.

9. William Dozier, "RetroBites: TV's Original Batman (1966)," interview by CBC, n.d., https://youtu.be/bAnOWQqLi8I.

10. Semple Jr., "Requiem."

11. Eisner, *Official Batman*, 9.

12. Ibid.

13. Dozier, "RetroBites."

14. Eisner, *Official Batman*, 6.

15. "History," 1966 Batman Pages/66batmania.com, https://www.66batmania.com/bios/history/.

16. Staff, "Pow! Zap! It's Batman and Robin," *New York Times*, January 13, 1966, https://www.nytimes.com/1966/01/13/archives/tv-pow-zap-its-batman-and-robin-bob-kane-heroes-open-abcs-2d-season.html.

17. Don Page, "From the Archives: The Times' original 1966 review of 'Batman,'" *Los Angeles Times*, January 14, 1966, https://www.latimes.com/entertainment/arts/la-et-st-batman-tv-review-20170610-story.html.

18. Scivally, *Billion Dollar Batman*, loc. 2275.

19. Dixon, "Villainy," 138.

20. Scivally, citing "Short Cuts," *Daily Variety*, April 19, 1966, 11; Burt Ward, *Batman* DVD featurette.

21. Lee Meriwether, "Interview with Cast of Batman: The Movie," interview by Jean Boone, CBS, 1966, https://texasarchive.org/2008_00062.

22. Eisner, *Official Batman*, 59.

23. Ibid., 98.

24. "Barbara Gordon," Batman.fandom.com, https://batman.fandom.com/wiki/Barbara_Gordon#Silver_Age.

25. Walt Dutton, "Batgirl Jumps Into Crime Fight (Zowie!)," *Los Angeles Times*, August 1, 1967, D1, https://www.latimes.com/entertainment/herocomplex/la-et-hc-yvonne-craig-vincent-price-batgirl-20150819-story.html.

26. Maurice Mitchell, "Eartha Kitt, A Brief History of the First Black Catwoman," *The Geek Twins*, October 15, 2019, http://www.thegeektwins.com/2019/10/eartha-kitt-brief-history-of-first.html.

27. "Batgirl and the Batman Phenomenon," tvobscurities.com, June 16, 2018 (updated), https://www.tvobscurities.com/articles/batgirl/#cite9.

28. Eisner, *Official Batman*, 163.

29. Ibid., 11.

30. Hofius and Khoury, *Age of TV Heroes*, 57.

31. Eisner, *Official Batman*, 113.

32. Glen Weldon, *The Caped Crusade: Batman and the Rise of Nerd Culture* (New York: Simon & Schuster, 2016), 98.

33. Krista Smith, "Q&A: J.J. Abrams on Steven Spielberg's Influence in Super 8—and Where Leonard Nimoy Is Hidden," *Vanity Fair*, June 8, 2011, https://www.vanityfair.com/hollywood/2011/06/jj-abrams-super-8.

34. Hofius and Khoury, *Age*, 56.

Chapter III

1. Mark Rathwell, incrediblehulktvseries.com (page no longer available).

2. William Moulton Marston entry, *Psychology Wiki*, https://psychology.wikia.org/wiki/William_Moulton_Marston, n.d.

3. Stanley Ralph Ross, Chapt. 4, interview by Dan Pasternack, Television Academy Foundation, February 11, 1998, https://interviews.televisionacademy.com/interviews/stanley-ralph-ross?clip=chapter4#about.

4. Ibid.

5. Hofius and Khoury, *Age*, 75.

6. Ibid., 80.

7. Ibid.

8. Ibid., 86.

9. "Rounding up the ratings for 'the season,'" June 16, 1979, https://worldradiohistory.com/hd2/IDX-Business/Magazines/Archive-BC-IDX/79-OCR/BC-1979-06-18-OCR-Page-0056.pdf#search=%22rounding%20up%20the%20ratings%22.

10. Ellen Bry, Episode 148, *Comic Book Central*, October 8, 2016, https://www.iheart.com/podcast/966-comic-book-central-30547986/episode/episode-148-ellen-bry-51046577/.

11. Hofius and Khoury, *Age*, 100.

12. Ibid., 102.

13. Ibid., 133.

14. Ibid.

15. Alpha-Girl, "Interviews: Kenneth Johnson (Part 1 of 2)," *Pink Raygun*, June 2007, https://archive.li/20130411172733/http:/www.pinkraygun.com/2007/06/07/interviews-kenneth-johnson-part-1-of-2/.

16. Hofius and Khoury, *Age*, 134.

17. Todd Gilchrist, "Interview: Kenneth Johnson," *IGN*, July 28, 2006, updated May 17, 2012, https://www.ign.com/articles/2006/07/28/interview-kenneth-johnson.

18. Hofius and Khoury, *Age*, 116.

19. Ibid., 116–17.

20. Rathwell, *Incredible Hulk TV Series*, incrediblehulktvseries.com.

Chapter IV

1. Don Shay, "Richard Donner on Superman," *Cinefantastique* 8, no. 4, 1979, https://archive.org/details/CinefantastiqueVol08No4Summer1979/page/n11/mode/2up.
2. Barry M. Freiman, "One-on-One Interview with Producer Ilya Salkind," Superman Homepage, n.d., https://www.supermanhomepage.com/movies/movies.php?topic=interview-salkind.
3. Ibid.
4. Ibid.
5. Ibid.
6. Aljean Harmetz, "The Life and Exceedingly Hard Times of Superman," *New York Times*, June 14, 1981, https://www.nytimes.com/1981/06/14/movies/the-life-and-exceedingly-hard-times-of-superman.html.
7. Ilya Salkind, "Ilya Salkind discusses Mario Puzo at USC's School of Cinematic Arts," 2012, https://youtu.be/5XviWxJziMg.
8. Bryan Stroud, "Interview with Carmine Infantino—From Penciller to Publisher and Everywhere In Between," *Nerd Team 30*, December 6, 2017, https://www.nerdteam30.com/creator-conversations-retro/an-interview-with-carmine-infantino-from-penciller-to-publisher-and-everywhere-in-between.
9. Carmine Infantino 1999 shoot interview by David Armstrong, posted at Comic Book Historians, December 2022, https://www.youtube.com/watch?v=apzHCgcMf84.
10. Tye, *Superman*, 194.
11. Echostation, "Absolutely Brilliant Tom Mankiewicz Interview," *Superhero Hype*, November 25, 2006, https://forums.superherohype.com/threads/absolutely-brilliant-tom-mankiewicz-interview-new.257534/.
12. Adam Smith, "From the Archive: The Making of *Superman*," *Empire*, January 31, 2013, https://www.empireonline.com/movies/features/making-superman/.
13. Don Shewey, "Caught in the Act: New York Actors Face to Face," Chris Reeve Homepage, http://www.chrisreevehomepage.com/sp-caught_in_the_act.html.
14. Thomas Alexander, "Exclusive Interview: Margot Kidder on Superman, the firing of Richard Donner and appearing in the DC TV universe," *Hey U Guys*, August 31, 2016, https://www.heyuguys.com/exclusive-interview-margot-kidder-on-superman/.
15. Shay, "Donner."
16. Echostation, "Mankiewicz."
17. Shay, "Donner."
18. Freiman, "Salkind."
19. Shay, "Donner."
20. Jason Sacks, *American Comic Book Chronicles: The 1970s* (Raleigh: TwoMorrows, 2014), 171.
21. Harmetz, "Hard Times."
22. Roger Ebert, "Superman," December 15, 1978, https://www.rogerebert.com/reviews/superman.
23. Vincent Canby, "Screen: It's a Bird, It's a Plane, It's a Movie," *New York Times*, December 15, 1978, https://www.nytimes.com/1978/12/15/archives/screen-its-a-bird-its-a-plane-its-a-movie.html.
24. Shay, "Donner."

Chapter V

1. SciFiNow 80s SciFi Almanac 3rd Edition, https://archive.org/details/SciFiNow.80s.Sci-Fi.Almanac.3rd.Edition.2016.True.PDF/page/n41/mode/2up.
2. "A Look Back at Howard the Duck," *Media Archive*, September 16, 2019, https://www.youtube.com/watch?v=Drj3MN6sQPo&feature=youtu.be.
3. Richard Pryor on *The Tonight Show*, May 20, 1981, https://youtu.be/3jus-OaJV8E.
4. Freiman, "Salkind."
5. Stephen Schiff, "Movies," *Vanity Fair*, July 1983, https://archive.vanityfair.com/article/1983/7/movies.
6. Jake Rossen, *Superman Vs. Hollywood* (Chicago: Chicago Review Press, 2008), 149.
7. Dwight Jon Zimmerman, "Gloria Katz," *Comics Interview* #38, September 1986, 50–52.
8. Ibid.
9. Caseen Gaines, "'Howard the Duck': An Oral History," Decider.com, March 11, 2016, decider.com.
10. Ibid.
11. Dwight Jon Zimmerman, "Steve Gerber," *Comics Interview* #38, September 1986, 6–19.
12. Dave Kehr, "Unlovable duck makes 'Howard' an unlovable film," *Chicago Tribune*, July 31, 1986, https://www.chicagotribune.com/news/ct-xpm-1986-08-01-8602250309-story.html.
13. *Variety*, September 17, 1986, as per Bernard F. Dick, *City of Dreams: The Making and Remaking of Universal Pictures* (Lexington: University Press of Kentucky, 1997) 178 at https://books.google.ca.
14. Gaines, "'Oral History."
15. Rossen, *Superman*, 158.
16. Scivally, *Superman*, 103.
17. Rossen, *Superman vs. Hollywood*, 164.
18. Bart Mills, "And Now... Mighty 'Superman IV' To The Rescue," *Los Angeles Times*, January 2, 1987, https://web.archive.org/web/20131009030250/http://articles.latimes.com/1987-01-02/entertainment/ca-1647_1_superman-iv.
19. Will Harris, "Jon Cryer on Charlie Sheen's work ethic and correcting Gene Hackman," *AV Club*, May 9, 2013, https://tv.avclub.com/jon-cryer-on-charlie-sheen-s-work-ethic-and-correcting-1798238147.

Chapter VI

1. Nancy Griffin and Kim Masters, *Hit & Run* (New York: Simon & Schuster, 1996), 165.
2. Patrick A. Reed, "I Like Bats: Producer Michael Uslan Remembers Batman '89 and the Alternate Films That Could Have Been," *Comics Alliance*, June 30, 2014, https://comicsalliance.

com/michael-uslan-batman-89-anniversary-movie-interivew/.

3. Michael Uslan, *The Boy Who Loved Batman* (San Francisco: Chronicle Books, 2011), 177.

4. Byron Burton, "The Battle to Make Tim Burton's 'Batman,'" *Hollywood Reporter*, June 21, 2019, https://www.hollywoodreporter.com/heat-vision/batman-michael-keaton-vetoed-michelle-pfeiffer-role-1989-film-1220139.

5. Rahul Gupta, "Batman producer Michael Uslan on bringing caped crusader to the big screen, and franchise's iconic cast," firstpost.com, July 15, 2019, https://www.firstpost.com/entertainment/batman-producer-michael-uslan-on-bringing-caped-crusader-to-the-big-screen-and-franchises-iconic-cast-6990881.html.

6. Reed, "I Like Bats."

7. Liam Burke, *The Comic Book Film Adaptation: Exploring Modern Hollywood's Leading Genre* (Jackson: University Press of Mississippi, 2015), 144.

8. Uslan, *Boy*, 204.

9. Griffin and Masters, *Hit & Run*, 165.

10. Uslan, *Boy*, 199.

11. Bob Costas, "Tim Burton," *Later with Bob Costas*, June 3, 1992, https://www.youtube.com/watch?v=gyZqwZfFqMo.

12. Alan Jones, "Batman," *Cinefantastique* 20, no. 1 & 2, November 1989, 51, http://www.1989batman.com/2013/08/vintage-magazine-article.html.

13. Steve Englehart, *Back Issue* 1, no. 118, February 2020, 50.

14. Stephen Rebello, "Sam Hamm," *Cinefantastique* 20, no. 1 & 2, November 1989, 44, http://www.1989batman.com/2013/08/vintage-magazine-article.html.

15. Scivally, *Batman*, loc. 4109–10.

16. Jon Peters, "Rare 24-Minute 1989 'Batman' interview w/ producer Jon Peters [audio]," *Eyes on Cinema*, https://youtu.be/y4nZGOFG4zQ.

17. Griffin & Masters, *Hit & Run*, 167.

18. Reed, "I Like Bats."

19. Burton, "Battle."

20. Scivally, *Batman*, loc. 4560–61; Masters and Griffin, *Hit and Run*, 169.

21. Alan Jones, "Designing the Legend," *Cinefantastique* 20, no. 1 & 2, November 1989, 61, http://www.1989batman.com/2013/08/vintage-magazine-article.html.

22. Griffin and Masters, *Hit & Run*, 171.

23. Pat A. Broeske, "Brute Forces," *Washington Post*, December 25, 1988, https://www.washingtonpost.com/archive/lifestyle/style/1988/12/25/brute-forces/ec5a17ad-a3c0-4357-974b-1bb80a281df5/.

Chapter VII

1. "How Happy Meals Killed Tim Burton's Batman," *What Culture*, n.d., https://whatculture.com/film/how-happy-meals-killed-tim-burtons-batman-2?page=4.

2. *Ibid*.

3. Aaron Couch, "'Teenage Mutant Ninja Turtles': Untold Story of the Movie Every Studio in Hollywood Rejected," *Hollywood Reporter*, February 4, 2015, https://www.hollywoodreporter.com/features/teenage-mutant-ninja-turtles-untold-785653.

4. Sean Mitchell, "Shellshocked by Turtlemania: Movies: The box office sets records, but product tie-ins are 'bigger than the movie,'" *Los Angeles Times*, April 21, 1990, https://www.latimes.com/archives/la-xpm-1990-04-21-ca-1154-story.html.

5. Peter David, "The Perfect Superhero Movie of All Time," *Peter David*, November 5, 1990, http://www.peterdavid.net/archives/001287.html.

6. Steve Weintraub, "Sam Raimi Interview," *Collider*, October 21, 2007, https://collider.com/sam-raimi-interview/.

7. Don Kaye, "Darkman: Sam Raimi's First Superhero Movie Was a Twisted Horror Hybrid," *Den of Geek*, August 24, 2019, https://www.denofgeek.com/movies/darkman-sam-raimi-superhero-horror-movie/.

8. Jim O'Kane, Rocketeer Minute Talks with Joe Johnston—Day 1, *The Rocketeer Minute Podcast*, 2017, https://podcasts.apple.com/us/podcast/rocketeer-minute-talks-with-joe-johnston-day-1/id1223819252?i=1000450851759.

9. Jon B. Cooke, "Of Hollywood and Heroes: Rocketeer creator Dave Stevens on his life as an artist," *Comic Book Artist* 15, November 2001, https://twomorrows.com/comicbookartist/articles/15stevens.html.

10. Paul Rowlands, "Daniel Waters on 'Batman Returns,'" *Money Into Light*, 2016, http://www.money-into-light.com/2016/06/daniel-waters-on-batman-returns.html.

11. *Ibid*.

12. *Ibid*.

13. *Ibid*.

14. Steve Daly, "Unhappy 'Returns,'" *EW*, July 31, 1992, https://ew.com/article/1992/07/31/unhappy-returns/.

15. Rowlands, "Waters."

16. Donna Britt, "As 'Batman Returns,' Parents Cringe Again," *Washington Post*, June 19, 1992, https://www.washingtonpost.com/archive/local/1992/06/19/as-batman-returns-parents-cringe-again/e151bb5d-0beb-41e8-aab7-515370fa81e8/.

17. Kelly Konda, "Batman 75: How Batman Returns Pissed Off McDonald's & Cost Tim Burton His Job," *We Minored in Film*, December 26, 2014, https://weminoredinfilm.com/2014/12/26/batman-75-how-batman-returns-pissed-off-mcdonalds-cost-tim-burton-his-job/.

18. Britt, "Batman."

19. Pat H. Broeske and Anne Thompson, "Hawking 'Batman,'" *EW*, July 10, 1992, https://ew.com/article/1992/07/10/hawking-batman/.

Chapter VIII

1. Mark Rahner, "Marvel Studios CEO on 'Spider-Man 2,' other films," *Seattle Times*, June

27, 2004, https://www.webcitation.org/6Ory51h8I?url=http://seattletimes.com/html/entertainment/2001964388_avi27.html.
2. Howe, *Marvel*, 310.
3. Brian Cronin, "Comic Book Legends Revealed #567," *CBR*, March 18, 2016, https://www.cbr.com/comic-book-legends-revealed-567/.
4. Howe, *Marvel*, 311.
5. SFe, "The Punisher," *Time Out*, September 10, 2012, https://www.timeout.com/movies/the-punisher.
6. William S. Wilson, "The 'Never Got Made Files' #66: Cannon's Captain America (1984–7)," *Video Junkie*, July 22, 2011, http://www.videojunkie.org/2011/07/never-got-made-files-66-cannons-captain.html.
7. Josh Bell, "Chatting With Original 'Captain America' Director Albert Pyun," *Las Vegas Weekly*, June 29, 2011, https://lasvegasweekly.com/ae/film/2011/jun/29/chatting-original-captain-america-director-albert-/
8. Ibid.
9. Robert Ito, "Fantastic Faux!" *Los Angeles*, March 2005, https://books.google.ca.
10. Sergio Pereira, "15 Things Fans Didn't Know About the Disastrous 1994 Fantastic Four Movie," *Screen Rant*, January 13, 2018, https://screenrant.com/fantastic-four-1994-facts-trivia-secrets/.
11. Graham Flanagan, "The inside story behind the Marvel movie you were never supposed to see," *Business Insider*, March 18, 2017, March 19, 2018 (updated), https://www.businessinsider.com/marvel-fantastic-four-unreleased-movie-roger-corman-hollywood-comic-book-superhero-stan-lee-2017-3.
12. Ito, "Fantastic Faux!"
13. "2015 Interview with The Fantastic Four (1994) Director Oley Sassone," *Film Voltage*, April 2, 2014, https://youtu.be/6uW6Y50hMTw.
14. *Doomed! The Untold Story of Roger Corman's The Fantastic Four*, Marty Langford dir., 2016.
15. Ibid.
16. Leona Laurie, "Kat Green's Oral History of Roger Corman's THE FANTASTIC FOUR," *Geek Girl Authority*, October 26, 2017, https://www.geekgirlauthority.com/kat-greens-oral-history-roger-cormans-fantastic-four/.
17. Sassone, *Film Voltage*.
18. *Doomed!*
19. Devin Leonard, "Marvel Goes Hollywood," *Fortune*, May 23, 2007, https://archive.fortune.com/magazines/fortune/fortune_archive/2007/05/28/100034246/index2.htm.
20. Ito, "Fantastic Faux!"
21. Ibid.
22. Erin McCarthy, "18 Fascinating Facts About the Crow," *Mental Floss*, February 2, 2016, https://www.mentalfloss.com/article/74690/18-fascinating-facts-about-crow.
23. Robert Levine, "From the Beginning, 'The Crow' Had a Grim Side: Movies: James O'Barr's comic book might have adapted smoothly to the big screen, but it was spurred by personal tragedy." *Los Angeles Times*, May 30, 1994, https://www.latimes.com/archives/la-xpm-1994-05-30-ca-63961-story.html
24. Richard Harrington, "The Shadow of the Crow," *Washington Post*, May 15, 1994, https://www.washingtonpost.com/archive/lifestyle/style/1994/05/15/the-shadow-of-the-crow/5852ee0f-6e8c-4a40-9aef-55440dcbed53/.
25. Judy Brennan, "'Mask' Makes Dark Horse into Sure Bet for Spinoffs." *Los Angeles Times*, July 31, 1994, https://www.latimes.com/archives/la-xpm-1994-07-31-ca-21854-story.html.
26. Wren Graves, "Joker is the most profitable comic book movie of all time," *Consequence of Sound*, November 9, 2019, https://consequenceofsound.net/2019/11/joker-most-profitable-comic-book-movie/.
27. Brennan, "Spinoffs."
28. Roger Ebert, "Timecop," *RogerEbert.com*, September 16, 1994, https://www.rogerebert.com/reviews/timecop-1994.
29. Chris Nashawaty, "12 Underrated Movie Gems," *EW*, November 12, 2010, https://ew.com/gallery/12-underrated-movie-gems/.
30. Clark Collis, "'It was a war!' The crazy behind-the-scenes story of Tank Girl," *EW*, March 30, 2020, https://ew.com/movies/tank-girl-lori-petty-rachel-talalay/.
31. Keith Garcia, "Director Rachel Talalay Talks Tank Girl and a Career of Dreams and Nightmares," *Westword*, July 28, 2016, https://www.westword.com/arts/director-rachel-talalay-talks-tank-girl-and-a-career-of-dreams-and-nightmares-8140107.
32. http://www.sci-fi-online.com/Interview/02-11-22_AlanMartin.htm, circa 2009.
33. Collis, "'It was a war!'"
34. Ibid.
35. Ibid.
36. Ibid.
37. Ibid.
38. Jerilyn Jordan, "Lori Petty reflects on Tank Girl, Jennifer Lawrence, and that Game of Thrones coffee cup," *Metro Times*, May 15, 2019, https://www.metrotimes.com/detroit/lori-petty-reflects-on-tank-girl-jennifer-lawrence-and-that-game-of-thrones-coffee-cup/Content?oid=21657056.
39. Frederick Blichert, "We Caught Up with the Director of 'Tank Girl' to Talk 'Wonder Woman,'" *Vice*, June 14, 2017, https://www.vice.com/en_ca/article/j5xapb/we-caught-up-with-the-director-of-tank-girl-to-talk-wonder-woman.
40. Matt Edwards, "Is Barb Wire Actually an Overlooked '90s Masterpiece?" *Den of Geek*, July 9, 2015, https://www.denofgeek.com/movies/is-barb-wire-actually-an-overlooked-90s-masterpiece/.

Chapter IX

1. Noel Ransome, "Twenty Years Later, Joel Schumacher Is Very Sorry About 'Batman &

Robin," *Vice*, June 12, 2017, https://www.vice.com/en/article/xw8vpk/twenty-years-later-joel-schumacher-is-very-sorry-about-batman-and-robin.

2. Anita M. Busch, "Dark Knight Becomes 'Bat' Lite," *Variety*, May 1, 1995, https://variety.com/1995/more/news/dark-knight-becomes-bat-lite-99127245/.

3. *Ibid.*

4. Bernard Weinraub, "Visual Flair, A Hip Sensibility And a Past," *New York Times*, June 11, 1995, https://www.nytimes.com/1995/06/11/arts/film-visual-flair-a-hip-sensibility-and-a-past.html.

5. BatmAngelus, "Interview with Batman Forever's Janet Scott Batchler," *Batman Online*, September 3, 2011, https://www.batman-online.com/features/2011/9/3/interview-with-batman-forever-screenwriter-janet-scott-batchler.

6. *Ibid.*

7. Chris Begley, "Michael Keaton reveals the moment he knew 'Batman Forever' would suck," *Batman News* (quoting *Hollywood Reporter*'s Awards Chatter podcast), January 3, 2017, https://batman-news.com/2017/01/03/michael-keaton-knew-batman-forever-would-suck/.

8. Adam Starkey, "Michael Keaton turned down 'Batman Forever' after creative clash with director," *NME*, January 5, 2022, https://www.nme.com/news/film/michael-keaton-turned-down-batman-forever-creative-clash-director-3130730.

9. Josh Weiss, "New documentary reveals why Val Kilmer only played Batman one time: 'It's very isolating,'" syfy.com, August 16, 2021, https://www.syfy.com/syfy-wire/val-kilmer-documentary-batman-forever.

10. Ryan Parker, "Tommy Lee Jones Really Hated Working with Jim Carrey on 'Batman Forever,'" *Hollywood Reporter*, October 3, 2017, https://www.hollywoodreporter.com/movies/movie-news/tommy-lee-jones-hated-working-jim-carrey-batman-forever-1045176/.

11. BatmAngelus, "Batchler."

12. Weiss, "Documentary."

13. Ben Travis, "Tim Burton on Batman Forever's Nipple-Suit: 'Go F-- Yourself,'" Empire Online, July 6, 2022, *Empire Online*, https://www.empireonline.com/movies/news/tim-burton-on-batman-forever-nipple-suit-go-f-yourself/.

14. Scivally, *Billion Dollar Batman*, loc. 7972–73.

15. Weldon, *The Caped Crusade*, 208.

16. Desson Howe, "'Batman': Winged Defeat," *Washington Post*, June 20, 1997, https://www.washingtonpost.com/wp-srv/style/longterm/movies/review97/batmanandrobinhowe.htm?noredirect=on.

17. Janet Maslin, "Holy Iceberg! Dynamic Duo Vs. Mr. Freeze," *New York Times*, June 20, 1997, https://www.nytimes.com/1997/06/20/movies/holy-iceberg-dynamic-duo-vs-mr-freeze.html.

18. Sims and Uzumeri, "'Batman & Robin' (1997), Part One," https://comicsalliance.com/batman-and-robin-movie-review/.

19. Variety Staff, "'Bat' beats up B.O.," *Variety*, July 8, 1997, https://variety.com/1997/film/box-office/bat-beats-up-b-o-1116677093/.

20. Mark Kermode, *Hatchet Job: Love Movies, Hate Critics* (London: Pan Macmillan, 2013), https://books.google.ca.

21. Holthouse, "Todd McFarlane."

22. Joe Chidley, "Dawn of Spawn," *Maclean's*, August 11, 1997, https://archive.macleans.ca/article/1997/8/11/dawn-of-spawn.

23. Marla Matzer, "'Spawn' of a New Era : Studios Turning to Mix of Houses for Modest-Budget Effects Films," *Los Angeles Times*, August 6, 1997, https://www.latimes.com/archives/la-xpm-1997-aug-06-fi-19784-story.html.

24. Laura Miller, "Spawn," *Salon*, September 1, 1997, https://www.salon.com/1997/09/01/spawn/.

25. Aisha Harris, "One of Cinema's First Black Superheroes Is Not Who You Think It Is," *Slate.com*, January 15, 2018, https://slate.com/culture/2018/02/abar-the-first-black-superman-is-a-ridiculous-blaxploitation-film-worth-watching.html.

26. *Ibid.*

27. Warner Bros., "Steel Production Notes," 1997, https://web.archive.org/web/20080411223603/http://movies.warnerbros.com/steel/cmp/production.html.

28. Noel Ransome, "Twenty Years Later, 'Steel' Director Admits Shaq Was Probably a Bad Choice," *Vice*, August 14, 2017, https://www.vice.com/en/article/evvnwn/twenty-years-later-steel-director-admits-shaq-was-probably-a-bad-choice.

29. Ransome, "Twenty Years Later."

30. Variety Staff, "Marvel characters holding attraction for filmmakers," *Variety*, December 8, 1992, https://variety.com/1992/film/news/marvel-characters-holding-attraction-for-filmmakers-101955/.

31. Leah Greenblatt, "Blade oral history: Wesley Snipes and the cast look back at a modern cult classic," *EW*, July 16, 2018, https://ew.com/movies/2018/07/16/blade-oral-history-wesley-snipes/?utm_source=twitter.com&utm_medium=social&utm_campaign=social-button-sharing.

32. Noah R. Taylor, "TSC: David S. Goyer talks Blade, Batman, and Man of Steel," *That Shelf*, April 16, 2015, https://thatshelf.com/tsc-david-s-goyer-talks-blade-batman-and-man-of-steel/.

33. Reggie Ugwu, "'They Set Us Up to Fail': Black Directors of the '90s Speak Out," *New York Times*, July 3, 2019, https://www.nytimes.com/2019/07/03/movies/black-directors-1990s.html.

34. Mike De Luca, "La Magra," featurette, *Blade* DVD.

35. Staff, "Blade test screenings…," *Ain't It Cool News*, April 30, 1998, http://legacy.aintitcool.com/node/928.

36. Greenblatt, "Blade."

37. *Ibid.*

38. Devin Leonard, "Marvel Goes Hollywood,"

Fortune.com, May 23, 2007, https://archive.fortune.com/magazines/fortune/fortune_archive/2007/05/28/100034246/index2.htm.

Chapter X

1. Scott Chitwood, "X-Men's Sabretooth scares crap out of kid, Toronto set visit, Wolvie love triangle, new pics, & more," *IGN*, February 10, 2000, https://www.ign.com/articles/2000/02/10/x-mens-sabretooth-scares-crap-out-of-kid-toronto-set-visit-wolvie-love-triangle-new-pics-more.
2. Fred Schruers, "Spider's Man," *Los Angeles Times*, June 27, 2004, https://www.latimes.com/archives/la-xpm-2004-jun-27-ca-schruers27-story.html.
3. "Stan Lee," interview by Lisa Terrada, *Emmy TV Legends*, March 22, 2004, https://interviews.televisionacademy.com/interviews/stan-lee.
4. Gaile Robinson, "The X-Men Want the Night Too: Merchandising: The Marvel comic characters have conquered Saturday morning TV. Now they are heading for a bedroom near you," *Los Angeles Times*, October 27, 1993, https://www.latimes.com/archives/la-xpm-1993-10-27-vw-50316-story.html.
5. Roy Thomas, "The Kon-Tiki Statue Blowing Its Nose Was Our Favorite Scene! A Conversation between Gerry Conway and Roy Thomas," *Alter Ego* 3, no. 58, December 2010, https://issuu.com/twomorrows/docs/alterego58preview/2.
6. Tim Molloy, "Chris Claremont's Dream X-Men Movie: James Cameron, Kathryn Bigelow, and Bob Hoskins as Wolverine," *The Wrap*, March 25, 2012, https://www.thewrap.com/chris-claremonts-dream-x-men-movie-james-cameron-kathryn-bigelow-and-bob-hoskins-wolverine-3/.
7. Sean Elder, "Lauren Shuler Donner, Prolific 'X-Men' Producer, Has the Superpower of Tenacity," May 22, 2014, newsweek.com.
8. Adam Chitwood, "Bryan Singer Reflects on Making 'X-Men 1,' Talks Evolution of the Superhero Genre," February 2, 2016, collider.com.
9. Aaron Couch, "'X-Men' Screenwriter on Michael Jackson Lobbying for Prof. X and Hugh Jackman Casting Drama," *Hollywood Reporter*, March 2, 2017, https://www.hollywoodreporter.com/heat-vision/x-men-screenwriter-hugh-jackmans-wolverine-casting-drama-982045.
10. Matthew Aguilar, "Sony Once Turned Down The Opportunity To Buy Movie Rights To All Marvel Characters For Only $25 Million," Comicbook.com, February 15, 2018, https://comicbook.com/marvel/news/sony-turned-down-marvel-movie-rights-25-million/ (quoting Ben Fritz, Wall Street Journal).
11. Adam B. Vary, "'Spider-Man' at 20: How Sam Raimi and Sony Pictures Rescued the Superhero Genre and Changed Hollywood Forever," *Variety*, April 27, 2022, https://variety.com/2022/film/features/spider-man-2002-oral-history-sam-raimi-sony-pictures-1235240553/.
12. "Interview Sam Raimi 'Spider-Man,'" *Mister Cinema*, May 2002, https://youtu.be/eT6Xt6FgZYk.
13. Vary, "'Spider-Man' at 20."
14. Michael A. Hiltzik, "Untangling the Web," *Los Angeles Times*, March 24, 2004, https://web.archive.org/web/20160304100601/http://articles.latimes.com/2002/mar/24/magazine/tm-34460.
15. Vary, "'Spider-Man' at 20."
16. Kienyen Chen, "Director's Influence on Spider-Man (2002 Film)," Gradesaver.com, October 9, 2019, https://www.gradesaver.com/spider-man-2002-film/study-guide/directors-influence.
17. Vary, "'Spider-Man' at 20."
18. *Ibid.*

Chapter XI

1. Elvis Mitchell, "FILM; Ang Lee on Comic Books And Hulk as Hidden Dragon," *New York Times*, June 22, 2003, https://www.nytimes.com/2003/06/22/movies/film-ang-lee-on-comic-books-and-hulk-as-hidden-dragon.html.
2. Kuljit Mithra, "Interview with Mark Steven Johnson," *Man Without Fear*, March 2002, http://www.manwithoutfear.com/daredevil-interviews/Johnson.
3. Rob Worley, "Daredevil," *CBR*, August 7, 2002, https://www.cbr.com/313179-2/.
4. Scott Meslow, "Let's Revisit Daredevil, the Terrible Movie that Paved the Way to the Modern Superhero Blockbuster," *GQ*, February 14, 2018, https://www.gq.com/story/daredevil-15th-anniversary; Darren Franich, "How Ben Affleck's 'Daredevil' got all the right stuff wrong," EW.com, April 9, 2015, https://ew.com/article/2015/04/09/ben-affleck-daredevil-look-back/.
5. Variety Staff, "Marvel characters holding attraction for filmmakers," *Variety*, December 8, 1992, https://variety.com/1992/film/news/marvel-characters-holding-attraction-for-filmmakers-101955/.
6. Tad Friend, "Credit Grab," *New Yorker*, October 20, 2003, https://www.newyorker.com/magazine/2003/10/20/credit-grab.
7. Rob Worley, "Countdown to 'Hulk': Producers Avi Arad and Gale Anne Hurd talk," *CBR*, June 5, 2003, https://www.cbr.com/countdown-to-hulk-producers-avi-arad-and-gale-anne-hurd-talk/.
8. Moriarty, "Mr. Beaks Interviews Lloyd Levin and Larry Gordon!! HELLBOY Week Begins!!" *Ain't It Cool News*, March 29, 2004, http://legacy.aintitcool.com/node/17280.
9. A. Cydney Hayes, "Guillermo del Toro fought 7 years for Ron Perlman to star as Hellboy," *EW*, December 2, 2018, https://ew.com/tv/2018/12/02/guillermo-del-toro-fought-ron-perlman-hellboy-role/.
10. Michael Fleming, "Artisan deal a real Marvel," *Variety*, May 16, 2000, https://variety.com/2000/film/news/artisan-deal-a-real-marvel-1117781709/.
11. Harry Knowles, "The Punisher (2004)

review," *Ain't It Cool News*, April 13, 2004, http://legacy.aintitcool.com/node/17355.

12. Meredith Amdur, "Heroic Marvel gain," *Variety*, May 4, 2004, https://variety.com/2004/scene/news/heroic-marvel-gain-1117904309/.

13. Brannon Costello, editor, *Conversations with Michael Chabon* (Jackson: University Press of Mississippi, 2015), https://books.google.ca.

14. Paul Rowlands, "Daniel Waters On 'Batman Returns,'" *Money into Light*, June 2016, http://www.money-into-light.com/2016/06/daniel-waters-on-batman-returns.html.

15. Stax, "An Interview with Denise Di Novi," *IGN*, July 2, 2004, https://www.ign.com/articles/2004/07/02/an-interview-with-denise-di-novi.

16. "Halle Berry accepts her RAZZIE® Award," https://youtu.be/U-7s_yeQuDg.

17. Manohla Dargis, "Moral Conflict Plus a Hot Bod: What More Does a Girl Need?" *New York Times*, January 14, 2005, https://www.nytimes.com/2005/01/14/movies/moral-conflict-plus-a-hot-bod-what-more-does-a-girl-need.html#:~:text=Still%2C%20the%20need%20for%20new,and%20Raven%20Metzner%20%2D%2D%20as.

18. Rodney, "Director Talks About Why Elektra Failed," *The Movie Blog*, October17, 2005, http://www.themovieblog.com/2005/10/director-talks-about-why-elektra-failed/.

19. Pamela McClintock, "Marvel to prime pupils," *Variety*, March 1, 2005, https://variety.com/2005/film/markets-festivals/marvel-to-prime-pupils-1117918741/.

Chapter XII

1. Weldon, *The Caped Crusade*, 235.

2. William Keck, "'Begins' gets the TV hero's approval," *USA Today*, June 21, 2005, http://usatoday30.usatoday.com/life/movies/news/2005-06-21-batman-flashback_x.htm.

3. James Greenberg, "Rescuing Batman," *Los Angeles Times*, May 8, 2005, https://www.latimes.com/archives/la-xpm-2005-may-08-ca-batman8-story.html.

4. Ibid.

5. Mark Harrison, "The Batman Movies That Never Were," *Den of Geek*, September 25, 2018, https://www.denofgeek.com/movies/the-batman-movies-that-never-were/.

6. "David Goyer," *Nerdist*, October 24, 2015, http://nerdist.libsyn.com/david-goyer.

7. Cameron Bonomolo, "Marvel's Peyton Reed Describes His Unmade 'Fantastic Four' Movie Idea," January 14, 2019, https://comicbook.com/marvel/news/marvel-ant-man-director-peyton-reed-describes-unmade-fantastic-four-1960s-movie/.

8. Abbie Bernstein, Bryan Cairns, Tara DiLullo, Anthony Ferrante, and David Grove, *Fantastic 4: Making of the Movie* (London: Titan Books, 2005), 15.

9. Ibid., 22.

10. Ibid.

11. Contributor, "Michael Chiklis Gets Into 'The Thing' in The Fantastic Four," *Movieweb*, October 19, 2004, https://movieweb.com/michael-chiklis-gets-into-the-thing-in-the-fantastic-four/.

12. Scott Brown, "'Fantastic Four' has incredible trouble," *EW*, July 1, 2005, https://ew.com/article/2005/07/01/fantastic-four-has-incredible-trouble/.

13. Brad Brevet, "Tim Story On Directing the 'Fantastic Four,'" Comingsoon.net, July 7, 2005, https://www.comingsoon.net/movies/news/505997-interview_tim_story_on_directing_the_fantastic_four.

14. Steve Weintraub, "Frosty Interviews Nicolas Cage," *Collider*, December 3, 2006, https://collider.com/frosty-interviews-nicolas-cage/.

15. Ibid.

16. Weintraub, "Cage."

17. Annalee Newitz, "10 Reasons Why 'Ghost Rider' Kicks Your Burning Ass," *Wired*, February 27, 2007, https://www.wired.com/2007/02/10-reasons-why-2/.

18. Heather Newgen, "Spider-Man 3 Interviews: Director Sam Raimi," *Superhero Hype*, April 22, 2007, https://www.superherohype.com/features/93443-spider-man-3-interviews-director-sam-raimi#yod2D5WeFyCFzMDs.99.

19. Morrison, *Supergods*, 378.

Chapter XIII

1. Geoff Boucher, "'Iron Man' At 10: How One Film Set A Dominant Path For Marvel, Kevin Feige, Robert Downey Jr. & Jon Favreau," *Deadline*, July 19, 2018, https://deadline.com/2018/07/iron-man-10th-anniversary-marvel-robert-downey-jr-kevin-feige-jon-favreau-comic-con-1202428754/.

2. Robinson, "Marvel."

3. Tara Bennett and Paul Terry, *The Story of Marvel Studios* (New York: Abrams, 2021), 21.

4. Anita Busch, "Avi Arad Slams BusinessWeek's Marvel Story: 'I Have Given Up On Journalistic Integrity,'" *Deadline*, May 5, 2014, https://deadline.com/2014/05/avi-arad-slams-businessweek-marvel-story-email-724106/.

5. Joanna Robinson, "Marvel Looks Back at Iron Man—the Movie That Started It All," *Vanity Fair*, November 29, 2017, https://www.vanityfair.com/hollywood/2017/11/marvel-looks-back-at-iron-man-the-movie-that-started-it-all.

6. Bennett and Terry, *Marvel Studios*, 18.

7. Devin Leonard, "The Pow! Bang! Bam! Plan to Save Marvel, Starring B-List Heroes," Bloomberg.com, April 3, 2014, https://www.bloomberg.com/news/articles/2014-04-03/kevin-feige-marvels-superhero-at-running-movie-franchises#xj4y7vzkg.

8. Kim Masters, "Marvel Studios' Origin Secrets Revealed by Mysterious Founder: History Was 'Rewritten,'" *Hollywood Reporter*, May 5, 2016, https://www.hollywoodreporter.

com/features/marvel-studios-origin-secrets-revealed-889795.

9. Bennett and Terry, *Marvel Studios*, 23.

10. Dave Itzkoff, "How 'Avengers' Was Assembled, Before Marvel Was Mighty," *New York Times*, April 18, 2019, https://www.nytimes.com/2019/04/18/movies/avengers-endgame-robert-downey-jr.html?em_pos=small&emc=edit_fm_20190419&nl=movies-update&nl_art=12&nlid=36242812emc=edit_fm_20190419&ref=headline&te=1.

11. Bennett and Terry, *Marvel Studios*, 24.

12. Edward Douglas, "Exclusive: An In-Depth Iron Man Talk with Jon Favreau," *Superhero Hype*, April 29, 2009, https://www.superherohype.com/features/96427-exclusive-an-in-depth-iron-man-talk-with-jon-favreau#1xbmz064Gu456lxk.99.

13. Benjamin Svetkey, "'Lethal Weapon' Wunderkind (and Former Party Boy) Shane Black Is Back ... and Still Looking for Action," *Hollywood Reporter*, May 13, 2016, https://www.hollywoodreporter.com/features/lethal-weapon-wunderkind-party-boy-892186.

14. Itzkoff, "Avengers."

15. Douglas, "Favreau."

16. Moriarty, "AICN EXCLUSIVE!! IRON MAN Has Found Its Tony Stark!!" *Ain't It Cool News*, September 29, 2006, http://legacy.aintitcool.com/node/30225.

17. Scott Bowles, "First look: Downey forges a bond with 'Iron Man' role," *USA Today*, April 27, 2007, http://usatoday30.usatoday.com/life/movies/news/2007-04-26-iron-man_N.htm.

18. "Question-and-Answer: Iron Man Director Jon Favreau," *Comics Continuum*, March 3, 2008, http://www.comicscontinuum.com/stories/0803/03/jonfavreau.htm.

19. Aaron Couch, "What If Robert Downey Jr. Were Never Iron Man?" *Hollywood Reporter*, May 2, 2018, https://www.hollywoodreporter.com/heat-vision/iron-man-movie-happened-before-robert-downey-jr-1107846.

20. Rich Johnston, "Lying in the Gutters Volume 2 Column 156," *CBR*, May 5, 2008, https://www.cbr.com/264974-2/.

21. Shaun Manning, "I AM (writing) IRON MAN: The Screenwriters," *CBR*, May 2, 2008, https://www.cbr.com/i-am-writing-iron-man-the-screenwriters/.

22. Bennett and Terry, *The Story of Marvel Studios*, 34.

23. Eric Eisenberg, "Jeff Bridges Says Iron Man Was All Improv," *Cinema Blend*, December 1, 2009, https://www.cinemablend.com/new/Jeff-Bridges-Says-Iron-Man-Was-All-Improv-15937.html.

24. Douglas, "Favreau."

25. Boucher, "'Iron Man' at 10."

26. Robinson, "Marvel."

27. Itzkoff, "Avengers."

28. Cal Kemp, "Gale Anne Hurd Interview—The Incredible Hulk," *Collider*, June 16, 2008, https://collider.com/gale-anne-hurd-interview-the-incredible-hulk/.

29. Cal Kemp, "Kevin Feige Interview—THE INCREDIBLE HULK," *Collider*, June 17, 2008, https://www.webcitation.org/6EdxYvGLK?url=http://collider.com/entertainment/interviews/article.asp/aid/8236/tcid/1.

30. Mike Ryan, "Louis Leterrier, 'Now You See Me' Director, On The Problems With 'The Incredible Hulk' And 'Clash Of The Titans,'" *Huffington Post*, May 28, 2018, https://www.huffingtonpost.ca/entry/louis-leterrier-now-you-see-me_n_3333311?ri18n=true.

31. Total Film, "Edward Norton talks Incredible Hulk," *Games Radar*, March 7, 2008, https://www.gamesradar.com/edward-norton-talks-incredible-hulk/.

32. Gregory Kirschling, "New 'Hulk': behind-the-scenes drama," *EW*, April 17, 2008, https://ew.com/article/2008/04/17/new-hulk-behind-scenes-drama/.

33. Ryan, "Leterrier."

34. Bennett and Terry, *Marvel Studios*, 69.

35. *Ibid*.

Chapter XIV

1. Scott Brown, "Dark Knight Director Shuns Digital Effects for the Real Thing," *Wired*, June 23, 2008, https://www.wired.com/2008/06/ff-dark night/?currentPage=all.

2. Merrick, "Nolan Talks DARK KNIGHT Blu-Ray, A 100,000 Person Screening of The Film (Featuring Live Q & A w/ Nolan), TDK Sequel, And More!!" *Ain't It Cool News*, December 5, 2008, https://www.webcitation.org/5xLwpPIh8?url=http://www.aintitcool.com/node/39348.

3. Rebecca Ford, "Heroes of Horror, Sci-Fi and Supervillains: The Genre Roundtable," *Hollywood Reporter*, July 18, 2018, https://www.hollywoodreporter.com/features/fanboys-fangirls-are-loudest-voice-genre-roundtable-1127307.

4. "Dark Knight Dedicated to Ledger," *BBC*, June 27, 2008, http://news.bbc.co.uk/2/hi/entertainment/7477095.stm.

5. Maria Lewis, "Punisher: War Zone Director Lexi Alexander on the Curious Journey to Cult Status," *Gizmodo*, December 5, 2018, https://io9.gizmodo.com/punisher-war-zone-director-lexi-alexander-on-the-curio-1830877179.

6. Maria Lewis, "Looking back on the insane parkour rocket launcher scene from Punisher: War Zone," *Flicks*, December 20, 2018, https://www.flicks.co.nz/features/looking-back-on-the-insane-parkour-rocket-launcher-scene-from-punisher-war-zone/.

7. Kevin Jagernauth, "Lexi Alexander Says She Wishes Marvel Had Made Creative Decisions On 'Punisher: War Zone' Instead Of Lionsgate," *Indiewire*, March 20, 2015, https://www.indiewire.com/2015/03/lexi-alexander-says-she-wishes-marvel-had-made-creative-decisions-on-punisher-war-zone-instead-of-lionsgate-265858/.

8. Kiel Phegley, "Ellison Gets In 'The Spirit,'"

CBR, May 21, 2010, https://www.cbr.com/ellison-gets-in-the-spirit/.

9. Andy Webster, "Artist-Director Seeks the Spirit of 'The Spirit,'" *New York Times*, July 20, 2008, https://www.nytimes.com/2008/07/20/movies/20webs.html.

10. A.O. Scott, "Returned from the Dead, Ducking Villains and Vixens," *New York Times*, December 24, 2008, https://www.nytimes.com/2008/12/25/movies/25spir.html?ref=movies.

Chapter XV

1. "Zack Snyder Fan Q&A—Part II," *Watchmen Comic Movie*, February 14, 2008, http://www.watchmencomicmovie.com/021408-zack-snyder-watchmen-interview.php.

2. Robert Sanchez, "Exclusive Interview: Zack Snyder Is Kickin' Ass With 300 and Watchmen!" *IESB*, February 13, 2007, https://web.archive.org/web/20090215050330/http://iesb.net/index.php?option=com_content&task=view&id=1883&Itemid=99.

3. Steve Weintraub, "Exclusive: Screenwriters Alex Tse and David Hayter talk WATCHMEN," *Collider*, March 2, 2009, https://collider.com/exclusive-screenwriters-alex-tse-and-david-hayter-talk-watchmen/.

4. Steve Weintraub, "Director Zack Snyder on Set Interview—WATCHMEN," *Collider*, February 16, 2009, https://collider.com/director-zack-snyder-on-set-interview-watchmen/.

5. Larry Carroll, "Zack Snyder explains his key 'Watchmen' changes on 'Spoilers,'" MTV.com, February 20, 2009, http://www.mtv.com/news/1605542/zack-snyder-explains-his-key-watchmen-changes-on-spoilers/.

6. Jim Vejvoda, "Watchmen Review," IGN.com, March 5, 2009, https://www.ign.com/articles/2009/03/06/watchmen-review.

7. Alex Billington, "Hugh Jackman Praises Wolverine Screenwriter David Benioff," *First Showing*, AugUST 7, 2007, https://www.firstshowing.net/2007/hugh-jackman-praises-wolverine-screenwriter-david-benioff/.

8. Michael Fleming and Peter Gilstrap, "Fox says Hood good for 'Wolverine,'" *Variety*, July 19, 2007, https://variety.com/2007/film/markets-festivals/fox-says-hood-good-for-wolverine-2-1117968848/.

9. Coming Soon, "Hugh Jackman Talks Wolverine!" *MovieXplosion*, October 16, 2006, https://www.moviexplosion.com/xarchivesweek42-06us.html.

10. Arye Dworkin, "Revisiting the Strange Cinematic Debut of Deadpool," *Vulture*, May 18, 2018, https://www.vulture.com/2018/05/revisiting-the-strange-cinematic-debut-of-deadpool.html.

11. Tatiana Siegel, "Fox's not-so-hot summer at the movies," *Variety*, September 5, 2008, https://variety.com/2008/film/features/fox-s-not-so-hot-summer-at-the-movies-1117991696/.

12. Stax, "Goyer confirms Deadpool," Feb 26, 2004, *IGN*, https://www.ign.com/articles/2004/02/26/goyer-confirms-deadpool; Rob Keyes, "Ryan Reynolds Talks Deadpool & Spinoff Possibilities," *Screen Rant*, March 15, 2009, https://screenrant.com/ryan-reynolds-discusses-deadpool-character-spinoff/.

13. Oliver Gettell, "Ryan Reynolds: 'X-Men: Origins' was 'frustrating experience,'" *EW*, Feb 2, 2016, https://ew.com/article/2016/02/10/ryan-reynolds-explains-x-men-origins-role/.

14. Michael Fleming and Marc Graser, "Mickey Rourke set for 'Iron Man 2,'" *Variety*, March 11, 2009, https://variety.com/2009/film/markets-festivals/mickey-rourke-set-for-iron-man-2-1118001114/.

15. Bennett and Terry, *Marvel Studios*, 70.

16. Adrienne Tyler, "Justin Theroux Wasn't Sure About Avengers; Reflects on Iron Man 2 Shortcomings," *Screen Rant*, February 1, 2016, https://screenrant.com/iron-man-2-justin-theroux-avengers/.

17. Bennett and Terry, *Marvel Studios*, 111.

18. *Ibid.*, 81.

19. Jeff Goldsmith, "Raimi well-suited for fantastic feats," *Variety*, July 18, 2006, https://variety.com/2006/film/markets-festivals/raimi-well-suited-for-fantastic-feats-1200339581/.

20. Bennett and Terry *Marvel Studios*, 75.

21. "Jane Goldman Talks X-Men: First Class," *Empire*, June 1, 2011, https://youtu.be/KeqiYPHS6zo.

22. Robert Jay, "Legends of the Superheroes," *Television Obscurities*, January 16, 2009, tvobscurities.com.

23. Elston Gunn, "Elston Gunn interviews KEVIN SMITH," *Ain't It Cool News*, May 14, 2009, http://legacy.aintitcool.com/node/5942.

24. Larry Carroll, "Jack Black Green With Envy Over New Lantern," *MTV*, November 21, 2007, https://www.webcitation.org/5zx6iqpI3?url=http://moviesblog.mtv.com/2007/11/21/jack-black-green-with-envy-over-new-lantern/.

25. Fred Topel, "Green Lantern Director Admits 'It Just Did Not Work,'" *Wizard World*, October 4, 2017, https://wizardworld.com/wizard/how-martin-campbell-would-fix-green-lantern.

26. Andrew Moraitis, "Boytown," *Newshit*, August 20, 2010, https://www.webcitation.org/5zva8TdxT?url=http://newshit.com.au/content/movies/boytown.

Chapter XVI

1. Kevin Feige, "Comic-Con 2006—Kevin Feige teases The Avengers," https://youtu.be/x-iw7FN0t3E.

2. Greg Tito, "Joss Whedon Officially Directing The Avengers," *Escapist*, July 22, 2010, https://v1.escapistmagazine.com/news/view/102287-Joss-Whedon-Officially-Directing-The-Avengers.

3. *Ibid.*

4. Kyle Buchanan, "Sam Raimi on Oz, The Avengers, and Two Huge Movies He Never Made," *Vulture*, March 5, 2013, https://www.vulture.com/2013/03/sam-raimi-on-oz-and-two-huge-films-he-never-made.html.

5. Matt Goldberg, "Spider-Man 4 Dead; Sam Raimi, Tobey Maguire, and Cast Out; Reboot Set for Summer 2012," *Collider*, January 11, 2010, https://collider.com/spider-man-4-dead-sam-raimi-tobey-maguire-and-cast-out-reboot-set-for-summer-2012/.

6. Travis Clark, "Spider-Man's movie adventures have been a headache for Sony for over a decade, but the character is too valuable to compromise on," *Business Insider*, August 21, 2019, https://www.businessinsider.com/sonys-spider-man-deal-with-disney-and-marvel-studios-explained-2019-8.

7. Edward Douglas, "Exclusive: Talking with the Producers of The Amazing Spider-Man," *Superhero Hype*, July 2, 2012, https://www.superherohype.com/features/171409-exclusive-talking-with-the-producers-of-the-amazing-spider-man.

8. Andrew Garfield, "The Amazing Spider-Man—Andrew Garfield panel intro," HitFix, July 23, 2011, https://youtu.be/JMcyclphuNs.

9. Silas Lesnick, "Christopher Nolan on The Dark Knight Rises' Literary Inspiration," *Coming Soon*, July 8, 2012, https://www.comingsoon.net/movies/news/92305-christopher-nolan-on-the-dark-knight-rises-literary-inspiration.

10. Quint, "Shane Black talks direction of Iron Man 3 and whether or not to expect more Marvel cameos!," *Ain't It Cool News*, March 7, 2011, http://legacy.aintitcool.com/node/48768.

11. Mike Ryan, "Shane Black On 'The Nice Guys,' Mel Gibson, And Why A Female 'Iron Man 3' Villain's Gender Changed," *Uproxx*, May 6, 2016, https://uproxx.com/movies/shane-black-the-nice-guys-iron-man-3/.

12. Josh Wilding, "David S. Goyer: 'We're Approaching Man of Steel As If It Weren't A Comic Book Movie...' *Comic Book Movie*, January 28, 2013, https://www.comicbookmovie.com/superman/david-s-goyer-were-approaching-man-of-steel-as-if-it-werent-a-comic-book-movie-a73389#gs.bh7qe0.

13. Mike Fleming, Jr., "SCOOP: Zack Snyder Directing Superman," *Deadline*, October 4, 2010, https://deadline.com/2010/10/zack-snyder-directing-superman-72340/.

14. Matt Goldberg, "Why Warner Bros. Hired Zack Snyder to Direct SUPERMAN: THE MAN OF STEEL; Plus the Film's Logline Revealed?" *Collider*, October 5, 2010, https://collider.com/superman-the-man-of-steel-zack-snyder-warner-bros-logline/.

15. Dave McNary, "Warner Bros. wins 'Superman' case," *Variety*, July 8, 2009, https://variety.com/2009/film/markets-festivals/warner-bros-wins-superman-case-1118005806/.

16. James Hibberd, "Why Henry Cavill Basically Already Is James Bond," *Hollywood Reporter*, November 10, 2021, https://www.hollywoodreporter.com/feature/henry-cavill-interview-witcher-superman-1235044553/.

17. Mark Waid, "Man of Steel, Since You Asked," *Thrillbent*, June 14, 2013, http://thrillbent.com/blog/man-of-steel-since-you-asked/.

18. Christopher McKittrick, "Wolverine: Two Writers, One Character," *Creative Screenwriting*, August 12, 2013, https://www.creativescreenwriting.com/wolverine-two-writers-one-character/

19. Christopher McKittrick, "Myth vs. Man: James Mangold and Scott Frank on Logan," creativescreenwriting.com, March 3, 2017, https://www.creativescreenwriting.com/logan/.

20. Alex Grand, "The Steranko Experience: In His Own Words with Jim Steranko and Alex Grand," *Comic Book Historians*, 2020, https://youtu.be/MyLfgrsyL-g.

21. Stephen Galloway, "'Cinderella' Director Kenneth Branagh on Casting His Princess, Working With Marvel and His Dream Shakespeare Film," *Hollywood Reporter*, March 1, 2015, https://www.webcitation.org/6WjNRSMuC?url=http://www.hollywoodreporter.com/news/cinderella-director-kenneth-branagh-casting-778478?page=1&template=cap.

22. Bennett and Terry, *Marvel Studios*, 146.

23. Charlie Ridgely, "2019 ComicBook.com Staff Ranking of the Marvel Cinematic Universe," *Comic Book*, April 25, 2019, https://comicbook.com/marvel/news/marvel-mcu-rankings-comicbook-staff-avengers-week/#1.

24. Chris O'Dowd, MTV News, Twitter, https://twitter.com/MTVNEWS/status/1092886518413357056.

25. Sonaiya Kelley, "Avengers: Endgame' writers on Thor-Lebowski, Black Widow and reviving 'Agent Carter,'" *Los Angeles Times*, May 4, 2019, https://www.latimes.com/entertainment/movies/la-et-mn-avengers-endgame-writers-markus-mcfeely-20190504-story.html.

Chapter XVII

1. Adam B. Vary, "Meet The Woman Who Made History With Marvel's 'Guardians Of The Galaxy,'" *Buzzfeed*, July 30, 2014, https://www.buzzfeed.com/adambvary/guardians-of-the-galaxy-nicole-perlman.

2. Emily Yahr, "'Captain America 2' directors talk filming in D.C., casting Robert Redford and the movie's very timely politics," *Washington Post*, April 4, 2014, https://www.washingtonpost.com/news/arts-and-entertainment/wp/2014/04/04/captain-america-2-directors-talk-filming-in-d-c-casting-robert-redford-and-the-movies-very-timely-politics/.

3. Bennett and Terry, *Marvel Studios*, 146.

4. *Ibid.*

5. Michael Kennedy, "Why the Amazing

Spider-Man 3 Was Canceled," *Screen Rant*, December 31, 2021, https://screenrant.com/amazing-spiderman-3-canceled-reason-plans/.

6. Ben Fritz, "Sony, Marvel Discussed Spider-Man Movie Crossover," *Wall Street Journal*, December 9, 2014, https://blogs.wsj.com/speakeasy/2014/12/09/sony-marvel-discussed-spider-man-movie-crossover/.

7. Bennett and Terry, *Marvel Studios*, 108.

8. *Ibid.*, 171.

9. Kevin Polovny, "Here's How Much 'Guardians of the Galaxy' Director James Gunn Hates 'Howard the Duck' the Movie," *Yahoo! Entertainment*, March 21, 2017, https://www.yahoo.com/entertainment/heres-how-much-guardians-of-the-galaxy-director-james-gunn-hates-howard-the-duck-the-movie-184952922.html.

Chapter XVIII

1. Clark Collis, "Astonishing Amazing Alarming Acrobatic Audacious (but teeny-tiny) Adventures of Ant-Man," *EW*, January 8, 2015, https://www.webcitation.org/6VQyvILDF?url=http://www.ew.com/ew/static/longform/antman/desktop/.

2. Pamela McClintock, "Box Office Milestone: 'Avengers: Age of Ultron' Joins the Billion-Dollar Club," *Hollywood Reporter*, May 15, 2015, https://www.hollywoodreporter.com/news/box-office-milestone-avengers-age-795912.

3. Adam B. Vary, "Joss Whedon's Astonishing, Spine-Tingling, Soul-Crushing Marvel Adventure!" *Buzzfeed*, April 20, 2015, https://www.buzzfeednews.com/article/adambvary/joss-whedon-spine-tingling-soul-crushing-marvel-adventure.

4. Howe, *Untold Story*, 311.

5. William Martin, "Exclusive: Edgar Wright on Marvel's 'Ant-Man' movie," *Cultbox*, November 28, 2013, https://cultbox.co.uk/news/headlines/exclusive-edgar-wright-on-marvels-ant-man-movie.

6. Adam Chitwood, "Marvel Confirms Paul Rudd Will Lead Edgar Wright's ANT-MAN," *Collider*, December 19, 2013, https://collider.com/ant-man-paul-rudd/.

7. Kim Masters and Borys Kit, "Why 'Ant-Man' Director Edgar Wright Exited Marvel's Superhero Movie," Nick Romano, *Hollywood Reporter*, May 28, 2014, https://www.hollywoodreporter.com/news/why-ant-man-director-edgar-707374.

8. Clark Collis, "'Ant-Man': Paul Rudd was 'devastated' by the departure of Edgar Wright," *EW*, January 8, 2015, https://ew.com/article/2015/01/08/ant-man-paul-rudd-edgar-wright/.

9. Vary, "Joss Whedon."

10. Bennett and Terry, *Marvel Studios*, 235.

11. Adam B. Vary, "Evangeline Lilly Tried to Quit Acting, But Acting Would Not Quit Her," *Buzzfeed.com*, December 2, 2014, https://www.buzzfeed.com/adambvary/evangeline-lilly-ant-man-the-hobbit-squickerwonkers.

12. Pamela McClintock, "Box Office: 'Ant-Man' No. 1 With $58M; 'Trainwreck' Laughs to $30.2M," *Hollywood Reporter*, August 19, 2015, https://www.hollywoodreporter.com/news/box-office-ant-man-no-809752.

13. Bennett and Terry, *Marvel Studios*, 30.

14. *Ibid.*

15. Matt Patches, "The post-disaster artist," Polygon.com, May 5, 2020, https://www.polygon.com/2020/5/5/21246679/josh-trank-capone-interview-fantastic-four-chronicle.

16. *Ibid.*

17. TJ Dietsch, "'Fantastic Four' is a Celebration of 'Comics That Preceded It,' Simon Kinberg Says," *CBR*, July 24, 2014, https://www.cbr.com/fantastic-four-is-a-celebration-of-comics-that-preceded-it-simon-kinberg-says/.

18. Anthony Breznican, "'Fantastic Four' director Josh Trank disses his own movie," *EW*, August 7, 2015, https://ew.com/article/2015/08/07/fantastic-four-josh-trank-tweet/.

Chapter XIX

1. Massimiliano Orione, Davide Garelli, and Francesco Domaneschi, "Zach Snyder interview—Episode 1," *I Minutemen*, February 12, 2021, https://youtu.be/EIX-JWz71XE.

2. Lindy West, "Batman v Superman is 153 minutes of a grown man whacking two dolls together," *Guardian*, April 3, 2016, https://www.theguardian.com/commentisfree/2016/apr/03/batman-v-superman-grown-man-whacking-two-dolls-together-lindy-west.

3. Ben Dreyfuss, "'Batman v Superman' Is a Failure on Every Single Level," *Mother Jones*, March 25, 2016, https://www.motherjones.com/politics/2016/03/batman-v-superman-but-its-actually-glengarry-glen-ross-and-they-fight-over-the-good-leads/.

4. Dave Schilling, "Every single thing that is wrong with Batman v Superman: Dawn of Justice," *Guardian*, March 25, 2016, https://www.theguardian.com/film/2016/mar/25/review-batman-v-superman-dawn-of-justice.

5. Breznican, "Terrio."

6. Schilling, "Batman v Superman."

7. Orione, Garelli and Domaneschi, "Zach Snyder interview."

8. Kyle Smith, "'Batman v Superman' is too smart for Marvel fans," *New York Post*, March 30, 2016, https://nypost.com/2016/03/30/batman-v-superman-is-too-smart-for-marvel-fans/.

9. Anthony Breznican, "Spider-Man: 'Captain America: Civil War' role revealed," *EW*, December 3, 2015, https://ew.com/article/2015/12/03/spider-man-captain-america-civil-war/.

10. Jason Guerrasio, "The 'Deadpool' writers reveal everything you want to know about the sequel," *Business Insider*, January 14, 2017, https://www.businessinsider.com.au/deadpool-2-writers-reveal-sequel-plot-details-2017-1?r=DE&IR=T.

11. Jordan Zakarin, "Ryan Reynolds Explains How the Deadpool Movie Got Resurrected," *Yahoo! Entertainment*, February 3, 2015, https://www.yahoo.com/entertainment/ryan-reynolds-explains-how-the-deadpool-movie-got-109934676757.html.

12. Christopher McKittrick, "The Real Heroes: Reese and Wernick on Deadpool," *Creative Screenwriting*, February 15, 2016, https://creativescreenwriting.com/the-real-heroes-reese-and-wernick-on-deadpool/.

13. Guerrasio, "'Deadpool' writers."

14. Jordan Zakarin, "'Deadpool' Screenwriters Go Deep: X-Men Choices, De-powering Copycat, and All Those Sex Jokes," *Yahoo! Entertainment*, February 10, 2016, https://www.yahoo.com/entertainment/deadpool-screenwriters-go-deep-x-men-choices-184031515.html.

15. Jack Shepherd, "Deadpool and Guardians of the Galaxy Vol. 2 share a very interesting link," *Independent*, November 15, 2016, https://www.independent.co.uk/arts-entertainment/films/news/deadpool-guardians-of-the-galaxy-vol-2-ego-living-planet-negasonic-teenage-warhead-a7418271.html.

16. Christopher McKittrick, "The Consistent Link: Simon Kinberg on X-Men: Apocalypse," *Creative Screenwriting*, May 26, 2016, https://creativescreenwriting.com/the-consistent-link-simon-kinberg-on-x-men-apocalypse/.

17. Scott Mendelson, "'X-Men: Apocalypse' Review: It's A Franchise-Killing Disaster," *Forbes*, May 9, 2016, https://www.forbes.com/sites/scottmendelson/2016/05/09/review-x-men-apocalypse-is-franchise-killing-disaster/#2bf991743560.

18. Ben Dreyfus, "X-Men: Apocalypse" Is the Best Superhero Film of 2016," *Mother Jones*, May 9, 2016, https://www.motherjones.com/media/2016/05/yes-wolverine-is-in-x-men-apocalypse/.

19. Tim Stack, "Dark Phoenix team on what went wrong with X-Men: Apocalypse," *EW*, December 8, 2017, https://ew.com/movies.

20. David Sims, "X-Men: Apocalypse: A Calamitous Dud," *The Atlantic*, May 2016, https://www.theatlantic.com/entertainment/archive/2016/05/x-men-apocalypse-a-calamitous-dud/484457/.

21. Jordan Zakarin, "'X-Men: Apocalypse' destroys Auschwitz and it's really uncomfortable," *Inverse*, May 9, 2016, https://www.inverse.com/article/15398-x-men-apocalypse-destroys-auschwitz-and-it-s-really-uncomfortable.

22. Chris Gardner, "Rose McGowan Calls Out 'X-Men' Billboard That Shows Mystique Being Strangled," *Hollywood Reporter*, June 2, 2016, https://www.hollywoodreporter.com/rambling-reporter/rose-mcgowan-calls-x-men-898538.

23. Kim Masters, "Bryan Singer Sex Abuse Case: The Troubling History Behind the Accusations," *Hollywood Reporter*, April 30, 2014, https://www.hollywoodreporter.com/news/bryan-singer-sex-abuse-case-699833.

24. Kim Masters, "'How Many At-Bats Do You Get?': Why Fox Hired (Then Fired) Bryan Singer on 'Bohemian Rhapsody,'" *Hollywood Reporter*, October 31, 2018, https://www.hollywoodreporter.com/news/why-fox-hired-fired-bryan-singer-bohemian-rhapsody-1156527.

25. Anthony D'Alessandro, "'Dark Phoenix' Bound To Lose $100M+ After Worst Domestic Opening In 'X-Men' Series: Here's Why," *Deadline*, June 9, 2019, https://deadline.com/2019/06/dark-phoenix-bombs-at-the-box-office-reasons-why-1202629749/.

26. Zack Sharf, "Before the 'Bohemian Rhapsody' Mess, Bryan Singer Reportedly Went AWOL From 'X-Men' Movie Sets," *Indiewire*, June 10, 2019, https://www.indiewire.com/2019/06/bryan-singer-missing-xmen-sets-bohemian-rhapsody-1202148666/.

27. David Betancourt, "Harley Quinn of 'Suicide Squad' could be 2016's most popular movie character. How did she get started?" *Washington Post*, August 1, 2016, https://www.washingtonpost.com/news/comic-riffs/wp/2016/08/01/margot-robbies-harley-quinn-in-suicide-squad-could-be-2016s-most-popular-movie-character-how-did-she-get-started/.

28. Devin Faraci, "Suicide Squad Reshoots Bode Well for the DC Movieverse," Birthmoviesdeath.com, March 31, 2016, https://birthmoviesdeath.com/2016/03/31/suicide-squad-reshoots-bode-well-for-the-dc-movieverse.

29. Kim Masters, "'Suicide Squad's' Secret Drama: Rushed Production, Competing Cuts, High Anxiety," *Hollywood Reporter*, August 3, 2016, https://www.hollywoodreporter.com/heat-vision/suicide-squads-secret-drama-rushed-916693.

30. Andrew Dyce, "Kevin Smith Says Suicide Squad 'Does DC Proud,'" *Screen Rant*, August 4, 2016, screenrant.com.

31. Patty Jenkins, Twitter, *Screen Rant*, August 3, 2016, screenrant.com.

32. Christopher Orr, "Suicide Squad is the Worst of the Worst," *The Atlantic*, August 2016, https://www.theatlantic.com/entertainment/archive/2016/08/suicide-squad-review/494669/.

33. Joey Nolfi, "Suicide Squad: Jared Leto sent Will Smith anal beads and used condoms," *EW*, April 13, 2016, https://ew.com/article/2016/04/13/suicide-squad-jared-leto-will-smith-anal-beads-used-condoms/.

34. Ana Dumaraog, "Suicide Squad Director Says Most of Jared Leto's Work as Joker Hasn't Been Seen," *Screen Rant*, May 7, 2020, https://screenrant.com/suicide-squad-joker-deleted-scenes-footage-david-ayer/.

35. David Ayer, Twitter, Jan 21, 2017, Twitter.

36. Steve Rose, "From Suicide Squad to Batman v Superman, why are DC's films so bad?" *The Guardian*, August 3, 2016, https://www.theguardian.com/film/shortcuts/2016/aug/03/from-suicide-squad-to-batman-v-superman-why-dc-films-so-bad-zack-snyder.

37. Kim Masters, "Warner Bros. Regime Change: What's Behind Greg Silverman's Ouster," *Hollywood Reporter*, December 16, 2016, hollywoodreporter.com.
38. Brent Lang, "Toby Emmerich Named Warner Bros. Chief Content Officer, Greg Silverman Ousted," *Variety*, December 14, 2016, https://variety.com/2016/film/news/toby-emmerich-named-warner-bros-chief-content-officer-greg-silverman-ousted-1201942510/.
39. Steve Weintraub, "Scott Derrickson on What He Had to Do to Direct 'Doctor Strange,'" *Collider*, November 2, 2016, collider.com
40. Gary Collinson, "Marvel officially announces production is underway on Doctor Strange, synopsis released," *Flickering Myth*, November 24, 2015, https://www.flickeringmyth.com/2015/11/marvel-officially-announces-production-is-underway-on-doctor-strange-synopsis-released/.
41. Don Kaye, "Screenwriter Jon Spaihts: Doctor Strange Has the Best Origin Story," *Den of Geek*, November 5, 2016, https://www.denofgeek.com/comics/screenwriter-jon-spaihts-doctor-strange-has-the-best-origin-story/.
42. Stefan Kyriazis, "Doctor Strange director on 'whitewashing' Tilda Swinton: I didn't want a racist Fu Manchu," *Express*, October 27, 2016, https://www.express.co.uk/entertainment/films/725894/Doctor-Strange-whitewashing-Tilda-Swinton-Ancient-One-Wong-Scott-Derrickson.
43. *The Sunday Service #101*, podcast, April 17, 2016, https://doubletoasted.com/shows/4-17-16-the-sunday-service-live-500-pm-cst/.

Chapter XX

1. Borys Kit, "DC Entertainment Chief Reveals What's Next for Superman, Wonder Woman and 5 Superheroes Who Deserve Movies (Q&A)," *Hollywood Reporter*, July 17, 2013, https://www.hollywoodreporter.com/news/dc-chief-superman-wonder-woman-586081?page=2.
2. Christopher McKittrick, "No Cookie-Cutter One-Liners—Spider-Man: Homecoming," *Creative Screenwriting*, July 7, 2017, https://creativescreenwriting.com/spider-man/.
3. Josh Wilding, "Latest Official Color Image From LOGAN Puts The Spotlight On Wolverine And Professor X," *Comic Book Movie*, November 25, 2016, https://www.comicbookmovie.com/x-men/wolverine/the_wolverine/latest-official-color-image-from-logan-puts-the-spotlight-on-wolverine-and-professor-x-a147069#gs.b3lkxb.
4. Rory O'Connor, "Ethan Hawke on Dreaming of a Fourth 'Before' Film, Why He's Not Having a McConaughey Moment, and the Necessity of Film Festivals," thefilmstage.com, August 23, 2018, https://thefilmstage.com/ethan-hawke-on-dreaming-of-a-fourth-before-film-why-hes-not-having-a-mcconaughey-moment-and-the-necessity-of-film-festivals/.

5. Mike Fleming, Jr., "James Gunn Comments On Being Dropped By Marvel's 'Guardians Of The Galaxy' Franchise," *Deadline*, July 20, 2018, https://deadline.com/2018/07/james-gunn-responds-marvel-firing-guardians-of-the-galaxy-for-tweets-1202430535/.
6. Mike Fleming, Jr., "Disney Reinstates Director James Gunn For 'Guardians Of The Galaxy 3,'" *Deadline*, March 15, 2019, https://deadline.com/2019/03/james-gunn-reinstated-guardians-of-the-galaxy-3-disney-suicide-squad-2-indefensible-social-media-messages-1202576444/.
7. Gill Pringle, "Some Kind of Wonderful," *Film Ink*, January 5, 2016, https://www.filmink.com.au/some-kind-of-wonderful/.
8. Sara Vilkomerson, "Gal Gadot Is Wonder Woman: 'She Is Not Relying on a Man, and She's Not There Because of a Love Story,'" *Glamour*, May 7, 2016, https://www.glamour.com/story/gal-gadot-wonder-woman-cover-interview.
9. Nicole Sperling, "Wonder Woman filmmakers explain why they changed heroine's origin story," *EW*, May 30, 2017, https://ew.com/movies/2017/05/30/wonder-woman-world-war-i-setting/.
10. William Bibbiani, "Exclusive: Marvel's Spider-Man Reboot is NOT an Origin Story," *Mandatory*, April 11, 2015, https://www.mandatory.com/fun/845723-exclusive-marvels-spider-man-reboot-not-origin-story.
11. Chris Cabin, "'Captain America: Civil War' Directors on Landing Spider-Man, 'Infinity War' Shooting Schedule," *Collider*, January 14, 2016, https://collider.com/captain-america-civil-war-avengers-3-infinity-war-updates-russo-brothers/.
12. Ibid.
13. McKittrick, "No Cookie-Cutter One-Liners," Creative Screenwriting.
14. Peter Sciretta, "Spider-Man: Homecoming' Set Visit: Everything We Learned," *Slash Film*, April 3, 2017, https://www.slashfilm.com/spider-man-homecoming-set-visit/2/.
15. Bennett and Terry, *Marvel Studios*, 72.
16. Bennett and Terry, *Marvel Studios*, 73.
17. Ibid., 33.
18. Ibid., 34.
19. Aaron Couch, "Thor: Ragnarok' Writer on the Secret to Revitalizing a Franchise," *Hollywood Reporter*, November 2, 2017, https://www.hollywoodreporter.com/heat-vision/thor-ragnarok-writer-secret-revitalizing-a-franchise-1054023.
20. Ibid.
21. Umberto Gonzalez and Tim Molloy, "How 'Justice League' Became a 'Frankenstein,'" TheWrap.com, November 29, 2017, https://www.thewrap.com/justice-league-zack-snyder-batman-v-superman-wonder-woman/.
22. Anthony Breznican, "Justice League: The Shocking, Exhilarating, Heartbreaking True Story of #TheSnyderCut," *Vanity Fair*, February 22, 2021, https://www.vanityfair.com/hollywood/2021/02/the-true-story-of-justice-league-snyder-cut.

23. *Ibid.*
24. Gonzalez and Mollow, "Frankenstein."
25. Justin Kroll and Brent Lang, "'Justice League' Extensive Reshoots Causing Headaches for Star Schedules (EXCLUSIVE)," *Variety*, July 24, 2017, https://variety.com/2017/film/news/justice-league-reshoots-1202502433/.
26. Cooper Hood, "Justice League: Reportedly 15–20% Is from Joss Whedon's Reshoots," *Screen Rant*, November 13, 2017, https://screenrant.com/justice-league-joss-whedon-reshoots-amount/.
27. Richard Lawson, "Justice League Is a Big, Ugly Mess," *Vanity Fair*, November 15, 2017, https://www.vanityfair.com/hollywood/2017/11/justice-league-review.
28. Robbie Collin, "Justice League review: DC's superhero embarrassment is beyond saving," *Telegraph*, November 17, 2017, https://www.telegraph.co.uk/films/0/justice-league-review-dcs-superhero-embarrassment-beyond-saving/.
29. Breznican, "Terrio."
30. Nicole Mello, "10 Ways Wonder Woman Is Worse in Joss Whedon's Justice League," CBR.com, March 17, 2021, https://www.cbr.com/wonder-woman-worse-in-joss-whedon-justice-league/.

Chapter XXI

1. Kristopher Tapley, "Listen: Kevin Feige Reflects on Oscar Player 'Black Panther' and 10 Years of Marvel Studios," *Variety*, December 27, 2018, https://variety.com/2018/film/podcasts/playback-podcast-kevin-feige-black-panther-marvel-studios-1203095749/.
2. Bennett and Terry, *Marvel Studios*, 64.
3. *Ibid.*, 42.
4. Jamelle Bouie, "Black Panther Is a Marvel Movie Superpowered by Its Ideas," *Slate*, February 15, 2018, https://slate.com/culture/2018/02/black-panther-the-new-marvel-movie-reviewed.html.
5. Richy Rosario, "#BlackPantherChallenge Inspires Nationwide Initiative for Kids to Watch 'Black Panther,'" *Vibe*, January 18, 2018, https://www.vibe.com/2018/01/black-panther-challenge-gofundme.
6. Anthony Breznican, "How the Avengers: Endgame Writers Made Life-and-Death Decisions," *Vanity Fair*, November 20, 2019, vanityfair.com.
7. *Ibid.*
8. Bennett and Terry, *Marvel Studios*, 115.
9. *Ibid.*, 119.
10. Rebecca Rubin, "'Avengers: Infinity War' Officially Lands Biggest Box Office Opening of All Time," *Variety*, April 30, 2018, https://variety.com/2018/film/box-office/avengers-infinity-war-biggest-box-office-opening-ever-1202791751/.
11. Jack Giroux, "'Deadpool 2' Director David Leitch Discusses the X-Force Gag, Adding More Cable, and Embracing the Comic Book Aesthetic [Interview]," *Slash Film*, May 23, 2018, slashfilm.com.
12. Albert Ching, "Deadpool 2 Writers Break Down the (Many) Big Surprises in the Film," CBR.com, May 18, 2018, https://www.cbr.com/deadpool-2-spoilers-screenwriters-rhett-reese-paul-wernick-interview/.
13. Brandon Davis, "'Deadpool 2' Director Addresses Vanessa 'Fridging' Controversy," ComicBook.com, June 2, 2018, https://comicbook.com/marvel/news/deadpool-2-vanessa-fridging-director-dies/.
14. Aaron Couch, "'Ant-Man and the Wasp' Director on Wooing Michelle Pfeiffer and His Marvel Future," *Hollywood Reporter*, July 2, 2018, https://www.hollywoodreporter.com/heat-vision/ant-man-wasp-michelle-pfeiffer-had-be-convinced-join-1124434.
15. Erik Davis, "Tom Holland in 'Venom 2'? Producer Amy Pascal Offers Updates on the Future of the Spider-Verse," *Fandango*, June 20, 2019, https://www.fandango.com/movie-news/tom-holland-in-venom-2-producer-amy-pascal-offers-updates-on-the-future-of-the-spider-verse-753795.
16. Dan Gvozden, "Why Steve Ditko Didn't Look Back," *Hollywood Reporter*, July 9, 2018, https://www.hollywoodreporter.com/movies/movie-news/steve-ditko-fought-credit-spider-man-never-looked-back-1125706/.
17. Joe Deckelmeier, "Geoff Johns, David Leslie Johnson-McGoldrick & Will Beall Interview: Aquaman," *Screen Rant*, December 31, 2018, https://screenrant.com/aquaman-geoff-johns-will-beall-interview/.
18. Jax Motes, "Kevin Smith Sounds Off On Jason Momoa As Aquaman," ScienceFiction.com, June 25, 2014, https://sciencefiction.com/2014/06/25/kevin-smith-sounds-jason-momoa-aquaman/.

Chapter XXII

1. Breznican, "Avengers: Endgame Writers.".
2. Josh Rottenberg, "In 'Joker' the stakes are life and death, and comic book movies may never be the same," *Los Angeles Times*, August 28, 2019, https://web.archive.org/web/20190828143837/https://www.latimes.com/entertainment-arts/movies/story/2019-08-27/joker-todd-phillips-joaquin-phoenix.
3. Rosie Knight, "Mike Mignola talks killing Hellboy and resurrecting his world (exclusive)," nerdist.com, July 12, 2017, https://nerdist.com/article/mike-mignola-hellboy-movie-comics-exclusive-interview/.
4. Owen Gleiberman, "The Bombing of 'Hellboy': How the Blockbuster Mentality Can Be Its Own Worst Enemy," *Variety*, April 13, 2019, https://variety.com/2019/film/columns/hellboy-bombing-guillermo-del-toro-ron-perlman-david-harbour-1203188923/.
5. Joanna Robinson, "What RoboCop Has to Do with the Future of the Marvel Cinematic Universe,"

Vanity Fair, November 28, 2017, https://www.vanityfair.com/hollywood/2017/11/the-future-of-the-marvel-cinematic-universe-robocop.

6. "JOKER Movie full Q&A with Director Todd Phillips," *Making Your First Film Podcast*, January 18, 2020, https://youtu.be/gApESXfT9qc.

7. Anthony D'Alessandro, "Warner Bros' 'Joker' Final Number Grows To $96M, Setting Records For October, Todd Phillips, Joaquin Phoenix & Robert De Niro," *Deadline*, October 7, 2019, https://deadline.com/2019/10/joker-box-office-opening-weekend-1202752002/.

8. Michael Moore, "'Joker': Michael Moore Writes Tribute to Todd Phillips' 'Cinematic Masterpiece,'" *Variety*, December 18, 2019, https://variety.com/2019/film/awards/michael-moore-todd-phillips-joker-1203446280/.

9. Peter Bradshaw, "Joker review—the most disappointing film of the year," *Guardian*, October 3, 2019, https://www.theguardian.com/film/2019/oct/03/joker-review-joaquin-phoenix-todd-phillips.

10. Dave Itzkoff, "Martin Scorsese Is Letting Go," *New York Times*, January 2, 2020, https://www.nytimes.com/2020/01/02/movies/martin-scorsese-irishman.html.

Chapter XXIII

1. Louis Chilton, "Oscars 2022: Jimmy Kimmel slams Spider-Man: No Way Home's 'unforgivable' Best Picture snub," *Independent*, February 9, 2022, https://www.independent.co.uk/arts-entertainment/films/news/oscars-spider-man-no-way-home-kimmel-b2011179.html.

2. Hoai-Tran Bui, "Margot Robbie Pitched The Harley Quinn Movie As An 'R-Rated Girl Gang Film,'" slashfilm.com, May 9, 2018, https://www.slashfilm.com/558126/harley-quinn-movie-pitch-margot-robbie/?utm_campaign=cliphttps://www.slashfilm.com/558126/harley-quinn-movie-pitch-margot-robbie/.

3. Brian Davids, "How 'Birds of Prey' Writer Christina Hodson Crafted That Hair Tie Moment," *Hollywood Reporter*, February 11, 2020, https://www.hollywoodreporter.com/movies/movie-features/how-birds-prey-writer-christina-hodson-crafted-hair-tie-moment-1278778/.

4. Ibid.

5. Ciara Wardlow, "How 'Birds of Prey' Deconstructs the Male Gaze," *Hollywood Reporter*, February 8, 2020, https://www.hollywoodreporter.com/movies/movie-features/how-birds-prey-deconstructs-male-gaze-1277232/.

6. Mick LaSalle, "Review: Movies don't get any worse than 'Birds of Prey.' This is the bottom," *SF Chronicle*, February 5, 2020, https://datebook.sfchronicle.com/movies-tv/review-movies-dont-get-any-worse-than-birds-of-prey-this-is-the-bottom

7. Brian Davids, "'Bird of Prey' Filmmaker Cathy Yan Reflects on Box Office and Scene She Fought for," *Hollywood Reporter*, April 3, 2020, https://www.hollywoodreporter.com/movies/movie-news/bird-prey-director-cathy-yan-reflects-box-office-narratives-1288457/.

8. Patty Jenkins, "The Making of Wonder Woman 1984: Expanding the Wonder," *Wonder Woman: 1984* DVD.

9. Pamela McClintock, "'Wonder Woman 1984' Shows Promise for HBO Max, Audience Survey Finds," *Hollywood Reporter*, December 30, 2020, https://www.hollywoodreporter.com/movies/movie-news/wonder-woman-1984-shows-promise-for-hbo-max-audience-survey-finds-4109942/.

10. Ray Fisher, Twitter, July 1, 2020, https://web.archive.org/web/20210602191354/https://twitter.com/ray8fisher/status/1278362556214755329.

11. Anthony Breznican, "Justice League: The Untold Story of Cyborg and Deathstroke," *Vanity Fair*, March 12, 2021, https://www.vanityfair.com/hollywood/2021/03/ray-fisher-justice-league-joe-manganiello-batman-deathstroke-cyborg.

12. Justin Chang, "Review: James Gunn's 'The Suicide Squad' proves there's life after 'Suicide Squad,'" *Los Angeles Times*, July 28, 2021, https://www.latimes.com/entertainment-arts/movies/story/2021-07-28/the-suicide-squad-review-hbomax-margot-robbie-james-gunn.

13. Sara Vilkomerson, "The New Mutants details revealed: X-Men franchise goes horror," EW.com, May 25, 2017, https://ew.com/movies/2017/05/25/the-new-mutants-details-x-men-horror/.

14. Adam B. Vary, "Cate Shortland Turned Down Directing 'Black Widow.' So Scarlett Johansson Called Her on Zoom,'" *Variety*, 2021, https://variety.com/2021/film/news/cate-shortland-black-widow-scarlett-johansson-1235008158/.

15. Matt Donnelly, "Chloe Zhao and Barry Jenkins Discuss Authenticity, World-Building and Working on Billion-Dollar Disney IP," *Variety*, December15, 2020, https://variety.com/2020/film/news/chloe-zhao-barry-jenkins-nomadland-underground-eternals-lion-king-1234853986/.

16. Linda Marric, "Film review: Eternals," *The Jewish Chronicle*, October 24, 2021, https://www.thejc.com/culture/film/film-review-eternals-1.521860.

Bibliography

Books and Ebooks

Bennett, Tara, and Paul Terry. *The Story of Marvel Studios*. New York: Abrams, 2021.
Bernstein, Abbie, Bryan Cairns, Tara DiLullo, Anthony Ferrante, and David Grove. *Fantastic 4: Making of the Movie*. London: Titan Books, 2005.
Costello, Brannon, ed. *Conversations with Michael Chabon*. Jackson: University Press of Mississippi, 2015.
Daniels, Les. *Batman: The Complete History*. San Francisco: Chronicle Books, 1999.
Daniels, Les. *Superman: The Golden Age*. San Francisco: Chronicle Books, 1999.
Dick, Bernard. *City of Dreams: The Making and Remaking of Universal Pictures*. Lexington: University Press of Kentucky, 1997.
Dauber, Jeremy. *American Comics*. New York: W.W. Norton, 2021.
Dixon, Chuck. "'Known Super-Villains Still at Large': Villainy in Batman." *Gotham City 14 Miles: 14 Essays on Why the 1960s Batman TV Series Matters*, edited by Jim Beard. Edwardsville: Sequart Research and Literacy Organization, 2010.
Eisner, Joel. *The Official Batman Bat Book*. Chicago: Contemporary Books, 1986.
Fraga, Kristian, ed. *Tim Burton: Interviews*. Jackson: University Press of Mississippi, 2005.
Griffin, Nancy, and Kim Masters. *Hit & Run*. New York: Simon & Schuster, 1996.
Harmon, Jim, and Donald F. Glut. *The Great Movie Serials*. Abingdon: Routledge, 1973.
Hofius, Jason, and George Khoury. *Age of TV Heroes*. Raleigh: TwoMorrows, 2010.
Howe, Sean. *Marvel: The Untold Story*. New York: HarperCollins, 2012.
Hughes, David. *Comic Book Movies*. London: Virgin, 2012.
Kermode, Mark. *Hatchet Job: Love Movies, Hate Critics*. London: Pan Macmillan, 2013.
Kupperberg, Paul. "'Some Days You Just Can't Get Rid of a Bomb': The Legacy of Batman." In *Gotham City 14 Miles: 14 Essays on Why the 1960s Batman TV Series Matters*, edited by Jim Beard. Edwardsville: Sequart Research and Literacy Organization, 2010.
Mayer, Geoff. *Encyclopedia of American Film Serials*. Jefferson: McFarland, 2017.
Morrison, Grant. *Supergods: What Masked Vigilantes, Miraculous Mutants, and a Sun God from Smallville Can Teach Us About Being Human*. New York: Random House, 2011.
Muir, John Kenneth. *Wes Craven: The Art of Horror*. Jefferson: McFarland, 2004.
Pasko, Martin. *The DC Vault*. Philadelphia: Running Press, 2008.
Parish, John Robert. *Fiasco: A History of Hollywood's Iconic Flops*. Hoboken: John Wiley & Sons, 2007.
Raviv, Dan. *Comic Wars: How Two Tycoons Battled Over the Marvel Comics Empire—and Both Lost*. New York: Broadway Books, 2002.
Rossen, Jake. *Superman vs. Hollywood*. Chicago: Chicago Review Press, 2008.
Sacks, Jason, Keith Dallas, and Dave Dykema. *American Comic Book Chronicles: The 1970s*. Raleigh: TwoMorrows, 2014.
SciFiNow 80s SciFi Almanac 3rd Edition.2016. archive.org.
Scivally, Bruce. *Billion Dollar Batman*. Wilmette: Henry Gray, 2011. Kindle.
Scivally, Bruce. *Superman on Film, Television, Radio and Broadway*. Jefferson: McFarland, 2007.
Tye, Larry. *Superman: The High-Flying History of America's Most Enduring Hero*. New York: Random House, 2012.
Uslan, Michael. *Batman's Batman*. San Francisco: Red Lightning Books, 2022.
Uslan, Michael. *The Boy Who Loved Batman*. San Francisco: Chronicle Books, 2011.
Weldon, Glenn. *The Caped Crusade: Batman and the Rise of Nerd Culture*. New York: Simon & Schuster, 2016.

Podcasts

Bry, Ellen. *Comic Book Central*, Episode 148, October 8, 2016. https://www.iheart.com/podcast/966-comic-book-central-30547986/episode/episode-148-ellen-bry-51046577/.
Goyer, David. *Nerdist*, October 24, 2015. http://nerdist.libsyn.com/david-goyer.
Cargill, C. Robert. *The Sunday Service*, April 17, 2016. https://doubletoasted.com/shows/4-17-16-the-sunday-service-live-500-pm-cst/.
Johnston, Joe. "Rocketeer Minute Talks with Joe Johnston—Day 1." *Minute Podcast*, 2017. https://podcasts.apple.com/us/podcast/rocketeer-minute-talks-with-joe-johnston-day-1/id1223819252?i=1000450851759.
Lundgren, Dolph. *The Launchpad Podcast*, December 2019. https://soundcloud.com/user-7090288/dolph-lundgren.
Steranko, Jim. "The Steranko Experience: In His Own Words with Jim Steranko and Alex Grand." *Comic Book Historians*, 2020. https://youtu.be/MyLfgrsyL-g.

Social Media

Fisher, Ray. Twitter, July 1, 2020.
KiraHead. Reddit, 2019.
Ocasio-Cortez, Alexandria. Twitter, January 11, 2019.
Page, Ellen. Facebook, November 10, 2017.

Video Interviews

Berry, Halle. "Halle Berry accepts her RAZZIE® Award." February 26, 2005. https://youtu.be/U-7s_yeQuDg.
Burton, Tim. "Later with Bob Costas." June 3, 1992. https://www.youtube.com/watch?v=gyZqwZfFqMo.
Dozier, William. "RetroBites: TV's Original Batman (1966)." Interview by CBC, n.d. https://youtu.be/bAnOWQqLi8I.
Feige, Kevin. "Comic-Con 2006—Kevin Feige teases The Avengers." https://youtu.be/x-iw7FN0t3E.
Garfield, Andrew. "The Amazing Spider-Man—Andrew Garfield panel intro." HitFix, July 23, 2011. https://youtu.be/JMcyclphuNs.
Goldman, Jane. "Jane Goldman Talks X-Men: First Class." *Empire*, June 1, 2011. https://youtu.be/KeqiYPHS6zo.
Lee, Ang. "Ang Lee Interview (2003)." Interviewer Charlie Rose. https://youtu.be/P9x85neaftw.
Lee, Stan. Interview by Lisa Terrada for *Emmy TV Legends*, March 22, 2004. https://interviews.televisionacademy.com/interviews/stan-lee.
Meriwether, Lee. "Interview with Cast of Batman: The Movie." Interview by Jean Boone, CBS, 1966. https://texasarchive.org/2008_00062.
Neill, Noel. "Superman's Noel Neill talks about Phyllis Coates and Kirk Alyn (with Jack Larson) Part 4 of 7." Pop Goes the Culture TV. https://www.youtube.com/watch?v=IU-0zIYY6EA.
Peters, Jon. "Rare 24-Minute 1989 'Batman' interview w/ producer Jon Peters [audio]." Eyes On Cinema. https://youtu.be/y4nZGOFG4zQ.
Phillips, Todd. "JOKER Movie full Q&A with Director Todd Phillips." *Making Your First Film Podcast*, January 18, 2020. https://youtu.be/gApESXfT9qc.
Pinkner, Jeff. "The Mutuals Interviews—Jeff Pinkner." *Discussing Film*, December 11, 2018. https://youtu.be/o9ij2YOtc0E.
Pryor, Richard. *The Tonight Show*, May 20, 1981. https://youtu.be/3jus-OaJV8E.
Raimi, Sam. "Interview Sam Raimi 'Spider-Man.'" *Mister Cinema*, May 2002. https://youtu.be/eT6Xt6FgZYk.
Reynolds, Ryan. "Ryan Reynolds Says He Was 'Born' to Play Deadpool." *Lorraine*, May 14, 2018. https://youtu.be/ti04HoUg2gU.
Ross, Stanley Ralph. Chapt. 2, interview by Dan Pasternack, Television Academy Foundation, February 11, 1998. https://interviews.televisionacademy.com/interviews/stanley-ralph-ross?clip=chapter2#interview-clips.
Salkind, Ilya. "Ilya Salkind discusses Mario Puzo at USC's School of Cinematic Arts." 2012. https://youtu.be/5XviWxJziMg.
Sassone, Oley. "2015 Interview with The Fantastic Four (1994) Director Oley Sassone." *Film Voltage*, April 2, 2014. https://youtu.be/6uW6Y50hMTw.
Snyder, Zack. "I Minutemen interview Zach Snyder—Episode 1." February 12, 2021. https://youtu.be/EIX-JWz71XE.

Video Essays

HiTop Films. "Spider-Man: Homecoming is a Bad SPIDER-MAN Movie (Video Essay)." June 20, 2018. https://youtu.be/3Wn1uewM-aQ.

Films

Batman (featurette). Warner Bros., 2001.
Blade ("La Magra" featurette) DVD. New Line, 2014.
Captain America: Winter Soldier (commentary DVD). Marvel Studios, 2014.
Daredevil (commentary). 20th Century Fox, 2003.
Daredevil (DVD). "Beyond Hell's Kitchen: Making Daredevil." 20th Century Fox, 2003.
Doomed! The Untold Story of Roger Corman's The Fantastic Four. Dir. Marty Langford, 2016.
Howard the Duck (featurette). Universal, 2011.
Thor: Ragnarok (Blu-Ray). "Getting in Touch with Your Inner Thor." Marvel Studios, 2018.
Wonder Woman 1984 (DVD). "The Making of Wonder Woman 1984: Expanding the Wonder." Warner Bros., 2021.

Newspaper and Magazine Articles and Blog Posts

Aguilar, Matthew. "Sony Once Turned Down The Opportunity To Buy Movie Rights To All Marvel Characters For Only $25 Million." Comicbook.com, February 15, 2018. https://comicbook.com/marvel/news/sony-turned-down-marvel-movie-rights-25-million/ (quoting *Forbes*).

Alexander, Thomas. "Exclusive Interview: Margot Kidder on Superman, the firing of Richard Donner and appearing in the DC TV universe." *Hey U Guys*, August 31, 2016. https://www.heyuguys.com/exclusive-interview-margot-kidder-on-superman/.

Alpha-Girl. "Interviews: Kenneth Johnson (Part 1 of 2)." *Pink Raygun*, June 2007. https://archive.li/20130411172733/http://www.pinkraygun.com/2007/06/07/interviews-kenneth-johnson-part-1-of-2/.

Amdur, Meredith. "Heroic Marvel gain." *Variety*, May 4, 2004. https://variety.com/2004/scene/news/heroic-marvel-gain-1117904309/.

Andersen, Soren. "'Venom': Marvel's bad boy emerges in origin story that lacks bite." *Seattle Times*, October 4, 2018. https://www.seattletimes.com/entertainment/movies/venom-marvels-bad-boy-emerges-in-origin-story-that-lacks-bite/.

Armitage, Hugh. "Deadpool creator responds to rumours that X-Force movie is dead." *Digital Spy*, January 15, 2019. https://www.digitalspy.com/movies/a25900884/x-force-cancelled-deadpool-sequel-rob-liefeld/.

Associated Press. "Kirk Alyn, 88, the Superman to Leap Tall Buildings First." *New York Times*, March 20, 1999. https://www.nytimes.com/1999/03/20/arts/kirk-alyn-88-the-superman-to-leap-tall-buildings-first.html.

Bailey, Jason. "Second Glance: The Cheerfully Old-School 'The Rocketeer.'" *Flavorwire*, June 20, 2016. https://www.flavorwire.com/580784/second-glance-the-cheerfully-old-school-the-rocketeer.

"Barbara Gordon." Batman.fandom.com. https://batman.fandom.com/wiki/Barbara_Gordon#Silver_Age.

Barnes, Brooks. "With Fan at the Helm, Marvel Safely Steers Its Heroes to the Screen." *New York Times*, July 24, 2011. https://www.nytimes.com/2011/07/25/business/media/marvel-with-a-fan-at-the-helm-steers-its-heroes-to-the-screen.html?pagewanted=all.

Barnes, Mike. "Yale Udoff, 'Bad Timing' Screenwriter and 'Batman' TV Booster, Dies at 83." *Hollywood Reporter*, July 27, 2018. https://www.hollywoodreporter.com/news/yale-udoff-dead-bad-timing-screenwriter-playwright-batman-tv-booster-was-83-1130421.

"Batgirl and the Batman Phenomenon." *TV Obscurities*, June 11, 2003, updated June 16, 2018. https://www.tvobscurities.com/articles/batgirl/#cite9.

Batman Begins production notes. August 10, 2005. https://web.archive.org/web/20061028060305/http://www.cinemareview.com/production.asp?prodid=3003.

BatmAngelus. "Interview with Batman Forever's Janet Scott Batchler." *Batman Online*, September 3, 2011. https://www.batman-online.com/features/2011/9/3/interview-with-batman-forever-screenwriter-janet-scott-batchler.

Begley, Chris. "Michael Keaton reveals the moment he knew 'Batman Forever' would suck." *Batman News*, January 3, 2017. https://batman-news.com/2017/01/03/michael-keaton-knew-batman-forever-would-suck/.

Bell, Josh. "Chatting With Original 'Captain America' Director Albert Pyun." *Las Vegas Weekly*, June

29, 2011. https://lasvegasweekly.com/ae/film/2011/jun/29/chatting-original-captain-america-director-albert-/.

Betancourt, David. "Harley Quinn of 'Suicide Squad' could be 2016's most popular movie character. How did she get started?" *Washington Post*, August 1, 2016. https://www.washingtonpost.com/news/comic-riffs/wp/2016/08/01/margot-robbies-harley-quinn-in-suicide-squad-could-be-2016s-most-popular-movie-character-how-did-she-get-started/.

Bibbiani, William. "Exclusive: Marvel's Spider-Man Reboot is NOT an Origin Story." *Mandatory*, April 11, 2015. https://www.mandatory.com/fun/845723-exclusive-marvels-spider-man-reboot-not-origin-story.

Billington, Alex. "Hugh Jackman Praises Wolverine Screenwriter David Benioff." *First Showing*, August 7, 2007. https://www.firstshowing.net/2007/hugh-jackman-praises-wolverine-screenwriter-david-benioff/.

Blair, Dike. "Shadows On the Wall: Interview with James O'Barr." http://www.thing.net/~lilyvac/writing35.html.

Blake, Jerry. "The Case of the Silly Pictures: Superman Versus Captain Marvel (With Republic in the Middle)." *The Files of Jerry Blake*, February 9, 2020. https://filesofjerryblake.com/2020/02/09/the-case-of-the-silly-pictures-superman-versus-captain-marvel-with-republic-in-the-middle/.

Blichert, Frederick. "We Caught Up with the Director of 'Tank Girl' to Talk 'Wonder Woman.'" *Vice*, June 14, 2017. https://www.vice.com/en_ca/article/j5xapb/we-caught-up-with-the-director-of-tank-girl-to-talk-wonder-woman.

Bonomolo, Cameron. "Marvel's Peyton Reed Describes His Unmade 'Fantastic Four' Movie Idea." Comicbook.com, January 14, 2019. https://comicbook.com/marvel/news/marvel-ant-man-director-peyton-reed-describes-unmade-fantastic-four-1960s-movie/.

Boucher, Geoff. "'Iron Man' At 10: How One Film Set A Dominant Path For Marvel, Kevin Feige, Robert Downey, Jr. & Jon Favreau." *Deadline*, July 19, 2018. https://deadline.com/2018/07/iron-man-10th-anniversary-marvel-robert-downey-jr-kevin-feige-jon-favreau-comic-con-1202428754/.

Bouie, Jamelle. "Black Panther Is a Marvel Movie Superpowered by Its Ideas." *Slate*, February 15, 2018. https://slate.com/culture/2018/02/black-panther-the-new-marvel-movie-reviewed.html.

Bowles, Scott. "First look: Downey forges a bond with 'Iron Man' role." *USA Today*, April 27, 2007. http://usatoday30.usatoday.com/life/movies/news/2007-04-26-iron-man_N.htm.

Bradshaw, Peter. "Joker review—the most disappointing film of the year." *Guardian*, October 3, 2019. https://www.theguardian.com/film/2019/oct/03/joker-review-joaquin-phoenix-todd-phillips.

Brennan, Judy. "'Mask' Makes Dark Horse Into Sure Bet for Spinoffs." *Los Angeles Times*, July 31, 1994. https://www.latimes.com/archives/la-xpm-1994-07-31-ca-21854-story.html.

Brevet, Brad. "Tim Story On Directing the 'Fantastic Four.'" Comingsoon.net, July 7, 2005. https://www.comingsoon.net/movies/news/505997-interview_tim_story_on_directing_the_fantastic_four .

Breznican, Anthony. "'The Avengers': Your first look at the dream team!" *EW*, September 30, 2011. https://ew.com/article/2011/09/30/avengers-your-first-look-dream-team/.

Breznican, Anthony. "'Fantastic Four' director Josh Trank disses his own movie." *EW*, August 7, 2015. https://ew.com/article/2015/08/07/fantastic-four-josh-trank-tweet/.

Breznican, Anthony. "How the Avengers: Endgame Writers Made Life-and-Death Decisions." *Vanity Fair*, November 20, 2019. https://www.vanityfair.com/hollywood/2019/11/avengers-endgame-writers-alternate-storylines.

Breznican, Anthony. "Justice League Screenwriter Chris Terrio Is Super Pissed Off." *Vanity Fair*, April 8, 2021. https://www.vanityfair.com/hollywood/2021/04/chris-terrio-justice-league-batman-v-superman.

Breznican, Anthony. "Justice League: The Shocking, Exhilarating, Heartbreaking True Story of #TheSnyderCut." *Vanity Fair*, February 22, 2021. https://www.vanityfair.com/hollywood/2021/02/the-true-story-of-justice-league-snyder-cut.

Breznican, Breznican. "Justice League: The Untold Story of Cyborg and Deathstroke." *Vanity Fair*, March 12, 2021. https://www.vanityfair.com/hollywood/2021/03/ray-fisher-justice-league-joe-manganiello-batman-deathstroke-cyborg.

Breznican, Anthony. "Marvel Studios chief Kevin Feige on the future of Black Panther, Captain Marvel, X-Men—and beyond." EW.com, March 9, 2018. https://ew.com/movies/2018/03/09/marvel-studios-kevin-feige-mcu-future/.

Breznican, Anthony. "Spider-Man: 'Captain America: Civil War' role revealed." *EW*, December 3, 2015. https://ew.com/article/2015/12/03/spider-man-captain-america-civil-war/.

Breznican, Anthony. "Wonder Woman 1984 Director Patty Jenkins on Knowing When to Fight." *Vanity Fair*, March 25, 2020. https://www.vanityfair.com/hollywood/2020/03/wonder-woman-1984-director-patty-jenkins-on-knowing-when-to-fight.

Cronin, Brian. "Comic Book Legends Revealed #567." *CBR*, March 18, 2016. https://www.cbr.com/comic-book-legends-revealed-567/.

Britt, Donna. "As 'Batman Returns,' Parents Cringe Again." *Washington Post*, June 19, 1992. https://www.washingtonpost.com/archive/local/1992/06/19/as-batman-returns-parents-cringe-again/e151bb5d-0beb-41e8-aab7-515370fa81e8/.

Broeske, Pat H. "Brute Forces." *Washington Post*, December 25, 1988. https://www.washingtonpost.com/archive/lifestyle/style/1988/12/25/brute-forces/ec5a17ad-a3c0-4357-974b-1bb80a281df5/.

Broeske, Pat H., and Anne Thompson. "Hawking 'Batman.'" *EW*, July 10, 1992. https://ew.com/article/1992/07/10/hawking-batman/.

Brown, Scott. "Dark Knight Director Shuns Digital Effects For the Real Thing." *Wired*, June 23, 2008. https://www.wired.com/2008/06/ff-darknight/?currentPage=all.

Brown, Scott. "'Fantastic Four' has incredible trouble." *EW*, July 1, 2005. https://ew.com/article/2005/07/01/fantastic-four-has-incredible-trouble/.

Buchanan, Kyle. "Sam Raimi on Oz, The Avengers, and Two Huge Movies He Never Made." *Vulture*, March 5, 2013. https://www.vulture.com/2013/03/sam-raimi-on-oz-and-two-huge-films-he-never-made.html.

Buchanan, Kyle. "The Wolverine Is This Summer's Bechdel-Friendly Blockbuster." *Vulture*, July 29, 2013. https://www.vulture.com/2013/07/the-wolverine-movie-bechdel-test-female-characters.html.

Bui, Hoai-Tran. "Margot Robbie Pitched The Harley Quinn Movie As An 'R-Rated Girl Gang Film.'" slashfilm.com, May 9, 2018. https://www.slashfilm.com/558126/harley-quinn-movie-pitch-margot-robbie/?utm_campaign=cliphttps://www.slashfilm.com/558126/harley-quinn-movie-pitch-margot-robbie/.

Burton, Byron. "The Battle to Make Tim Burton's 'Batman.'" *Hollywood Reporter*, June 21, 2019. https://www.hollywoodreporter.com/heat-vision/batman-michael-keaton-vetoed-michelle-pfeiffer-role-1989-film-1220139.

Busch, Anita. "Avi Arad Slams BusinessWeek's Marvel Story: 'I Have Given Up On Journalistic Integrity.'" *Deadline*, May 5, 2014. https://deadline.com/2014/05/avi-arad-slams-businessweek-marvel-story-email-724106/.

Cabin, Chris. "'Captain America: Civil War' Directors on Landing Spider-Man, 'Infinity War' Shooting Schedule." *Collider*, January 14, 2016. https://collider.com/captain-america-civil-war-avengers-3-infinity-war-updates-russo-brothers/.

Canby, Vincent. "Screen: It's a Bird, It's a Plane, It's a Movie." *New York Times*, December 15, 1978. https://www.nytimes.com/1978/12/15/archives/screen-its-a-bird-its-a-plane-its-a-movie.html.

Carroll, Larry. "Jack Black Green With Envy Over New Lantern." *MTV*, November 21, 2007. https://www.webcitation.org/5zx6iqpI3?url=http://moviesblog.mtv.com/2007/11/21/jack-black-green-with-envy-over-new-lantern/.

Carroll, Larry. "Zach Snyder explains his key 'Watchmen' changes on 'Spoilers.'" MTV.com, February 20, 2009. http://www.mtv.com/news/1605542/zack-snyder-explains-his-key-watchmen-changes-on-spoilers/.

Cavanaugh, Patrick. "'Daredevil' and 'Ghost Rider' Director Still Proud of Early Marvel Films." *Comic Book*, February 28, 2019. https://comicbook.com/marvel/news/daredevil-ghost-rider-movies-mark-steven-johnson/.

Chang, Justin. "Review: James Gunn's 'The Suicide Squad' proves there's life after 'Suicide Squad.'" *Los Angeles Times*, July 28, 2021. https://www.latimes.com/entertainment-arts/movies/story/2021-07-28/the-suicide-squad-review-hbomax-margot-robbie-james-gunn.

Chen, Kienyen. "Director's Influence on Spider-Man (2002 Film)." Gradesaver.com, October 9, 2019. https://www.gradesaver.com/spider-man-2002-film/study-guide/directors-influence.

Chidley, Joe. "Dawn of Spawn." *Maclean's*, August 11, 1997. https://archive.macleans.ca/article/1997/8/11/dawn-of-spawn.

Chilton, Louis. "Oscars 2022: Jimmy Kimmel slams Spider-Man: No Way Home's 'unforgivable' Best Picture snub." *Independent*, February 2022. https://www.independent.co.uk/arts-entertainment/films/news/oscars-spider-man-no-way-home-kimmel-b2011179.html.

Ching, Albert. "Deadpool 2 Writers Break Down the (Many) Big Surprises in the Film." *CBR*, May 18, 2018. https://www.cbr.com/deadpool-2-spoilers-screenwriters-rhett-reese-paul-wernick-interview/.

Chitwood, Adam. "Bryan Singer Reflects on Making 'X-Men 1,' Talks Evolution of the Superhero Genre." *Collider*, February 2, 2016. collider.com.

Chitwood, Adam. "Marvel Confirms Paul Rudd Will Lead Edgar Wright's ANT-MAN." *Collider*, December 19, 2013. https://collider.com/ant-man-paul-rudd/.

Chitwood, Scott. "Superman Returns Set Visit—Part 4." *Superhero Hype*, May 4, 2006. https://www.superherohype.com/features/90885-superman-returns-set-visit-part-4#6ZkdK0sscWDxe1ij.99.

Chitwood, Scott. "X-Men's Sabretooth scares crap out of kid, Toronto set visit, Wolvie love triangle, new pics, & more." *IGN*, February 10, 2000. https://www.ign.com/articles/2000/02/10/x-mens-sabretooth-scares-crap-out-of-kid-toronto-set-visit-wolvie-love-triangle-new-pics-more.

"Christopher Nolan on Batman and Superman." *Superhero Hype*, June 4, 2010. https://www.superherohype.com/news/102090-christopher-nolan-on-batman-and-superman.

Clark, Travis. "Spider-Man's movie adventures have been a headache for Sony for over a decade, but the character is too valuable to compromise on." *Business Insider*, August 21, 2019. https://www.businessinsider.com/sonys-spider-man-deal-with-disney-and-marvel-studios-explained-2019-8.

Collin, Robbie. "Justice League review: DC's superhero embarrassment is beyond saving." *Telegraph*,

November 17, 2017. https://www.telegraph.co.uk/films/0/justice-league-review-dcs-superhero-embarrassment-beyond-saving/.

Collinson, Gary. "Marvel officially announces production is underway on Doctor Strange, synopsis released." *Flickering Myth*, November 24, 2015. https://www.flickeringmyth.com/2015/11/marvel-officially-announces-production-is-underway-on-doctor-strange-synopsis-released/.

Collis, Clark. "'Ant-Man': Paul Rudd was 'devastated' by the departure of Edgar Wright." *EW*, January 8, 2015. https://ew.com/article/2015/01/08/ant-man-paul-rudd-edgar-wright/.

Collis, Clark. "Astonishing Amazing Alarming Acrobatic Audacious (but teeny-tiny) Adventures of Ant-Man." *EW*, January 8, 2015. https://www.webcitation.org/6VQyvILDF?url=http://www.ew.com/ew/static/longform/antman/desktop/.

Collis, Clark. "Forging Iron Man: How director Jon Favreau launched the Marvel Cinematic Universe." *EW*, March 15, 2018. https://ew.com/movies/2018/03/15/iron-man-jon-favreau-marvel-cinematic-universe/.

Collis, Clark. "'It was a war!' The crazy behind-the-scenes story of Tank Girl." *EW*, March 30, 2020. https://ew.com/movies/tank-girl-lori-petty-rachel-talalay/.

Coming Soon. "Hugh Jackman Talks Wolverine!" *MovieXplosion*, October 16, 2006. https://www.moviexplosion.com/xarchivesweek42-06us.html.

Contributor. "Michael Chiklis Gets Into 'The Thing' in The Fantastic Four." *Movieweb*, October 19, 2004. https://movieweb.com/michael-chiklis-gets-into-the-thing-in-the-fantastic-four/.

Cooke, Jon B. "Of Hollywood and Heroes: Rocketeer creator Dave Stevens on his life as an artist." *Comic Book Artist* #15, November 2001. https://twomorrows.com/comicbookartist/articles/15stevens.html.

Couch, Aaron. "'Ant-Man and the Wasp' Director on Wooing Michelle Pfeiffer and His Marvel Future." *Hollywood Reporter*, July 2, 2018. https://www.hollywoodreporter.com/heat-vision/ant-man-wasp-michelle-pfeiffer-had-be-convinced-join-1124634.

Couch, Aaron. "'Dr. Strange': The Untold Story of the 1978 TV Movie Everyone 'Had Great Hopes For.'" *Hollywood Reporter*, November 1, 2016. https://www.hollywoodreporter.com/heat-vision/doctor-strange-untold-story-failed-1978-tv-movie-942728.

Couch, Aaron. "'Teenage Mutant Ninja Turtles': Untold Story of the Movie Every Studio in Hollywood Rejected." *Hollywood Reporter*, February 4, 2015. https://www.hollywoodreporter.com/features/teenage-mutant-ninja-turtles-untold-785653.

Couch, Aaron. "'Thor: Ragnarok' Writer on the Secret to Revitalizing a Franchise." *Hollywood Reporter*, November 2, 2017. https://www.hollywoodreporter.com/heat-vision/thor-ragnarok-writer-secret-revitalizing-a-franchise-1054023.

Couch, Aaron. "What If Robert Downey, Jr. Were Never Iron Man?" *Hollywood Reporter*, May 2, 2018. https://www.hollywoodreporter.com/heat-vision/iron-man-movie-happened-before-robert-downey-jr-1107846.

Cronin, Brian. "Comic Book Legends Revealed #567." *CBR*, March 18, 2016. https://www.cbr.com/comic-book-legends-revealed-567/.

D'Alessandro, Anthony. "'Dark Phoenix' Bound To Lose $100M+ After Worst Domestic Opening In 'X-Men' Series: Here's Why." *Deadline*, June 9, 2019. https://deadline.com/2019/06/dark-phoenix-bombs-at-the-box-office-reasons-why-1202629749/.

D'Alessandro, Anthony. "Warner Bros' 'Joker' Final Number Grows To $96M, Setting Records For October, Todd Phillips, Joaquin Phoenix & Robert De Niro." *Deadline*, October 7, 2019. https://deadline.com/2019/10/joker-box-office-opening-weekend-1202752002/.

Daly, Steve. "Unhappy 'Returns.'" *EW*, July 31, 1992. https://ew.com/article/1992/07/31/unhappy-returns/.

Daniell, Mark. "'Venom' review: Sony delivers the worst Marvel movie since 'Elektra.'" *Toronto Sun*, October 4, 2018. https://torontosun.com/entertainment/movies/venom-review-sony-delivers-the-worst-marvel-movie-since-elektra.

Dargis, Manohla. "Moral Conflict Plus a Hot Bod: What More Does a Girl Need?" *New York Times*, January 14, 2005. https://www.nytimes.com/2005/01/14/movies/moral-conflict-plus-a-hot-bod-what-more-does-a-girl-need.html#:~:text=Still%2C%20the%20need%20for%20new,and%20Raven%20Metzner%20%2D%2D%20as.

"Dark Knight Dedicated to Ledger." *BBC*, June 27, 2008. http://news.bbc.co.uk/2/hi/entertainment/7477095.stm.

David, Peter. "The Perfect Superhero Movie of All Time." Peter David, November 5, 1990. http://www.peter-david.net/archives/001287.html.

Davids, Brian. "'Bird of Prey' Filmmaker Cathy Yan Reflects on Box Office and Scene She Fought for." *Hollywood Reporter*, April 3, 2020. https://www.hollywoodreporter.com/movies/movie-news/bird-prey-director-cathy-yan-reflects-box-office-narratives-1288457/.

Davids, Brian. "How 'Birds of Prey' Writer Christina Hodson Crafted That Hair Tie Moment." *Hollywood Reporter*, February 11, 2020. https://www.hollywoodreporter.com/movies/movie-features/how-birds-prey-writer-christina-hodson-crafted-hair-tie-moment-1278778/.

Davis, Brandon. "'Deadpool 2' Director Addresses Vanessa 'Fridging' Controversy." ComicBook.com, June 2, 2018. https://comicbook.com/marvel/news/deadpool-2-vanessa-fridging-director-dies/.

Davis, Erik. "Tom Holland in 'Venom 2'? Producer Amy Pascal Offers Updates on the Future of the Spider-Verse." *Fandango*, June 20, 2019. https://www.fandango.com/movie-news/tom-holland-in-venom-2-producer-amy-pascal-offers-updates-on-the-future-of-the-spider-verse-753795.

Deckelmeier, Joe. "Geoff Johns, David Leslie Johnson-McGoldrick & Will Beall Interview: Aquaman." *Screen Rant*, December 31, 2018. https://screenrant.com/aquaman-geoff-johns-will-beall-interview/.

Dietsch, TJ. "'Fantastic Four' Isn't Based on Existing Comics, Kate Mara Says." *CBR*, July 15, 2014. https://www.cbr.com/fantastic-four-isnt-based-on-existing-comics-kate-mara-says/

Donnelly, Matt. "Chloe Zhao and Barry Jenkins Discuss Authenticity, World-Building and Working on Billion-Dollar Disney IP." *Variety*, December 15, 2020. https://variety.com/2020/film/news/chloe-zhao-barry-jenkins-nomadland-underground-eternals-lion-king-1234853986/.

Douglas, Edward. "Exclusive: An In-Depth Iron Man Talk with Jon Favreau." *Superhero Hype*, April 29, 2009. https://www.superherohype.com/features/96427-exclusive-an-in-depth-iron-man-talk-with-jon-favreau#1xbmz064Gu456lxk.99.

Douglas, Edward. "Exclusive: Talking with the Producers of The Amazing Spider-Man." *Superhero Hype*, July 2, 2012. https://www.superherohype.com/features/171409-exclusive-talking-with-the-producers-of-the-amazing-spider-man.

Dreyfuss, Ben. "'Batman v Superman' Is a Failure on Every Single Level." *Mother Jones*, March 25, 2016. https://www.motherjones.com/politics/2016/03/batman-v-superman-but-its-actually-glengarry-glen-ross-and-they-fight-over-the-good-leads/.

Dreyfus, Ben. "'X-Men: Apocalypse' Is the Best Superhero Film of 2016." *Mother Jones*, May 9, 2016. https://www.motherjones.com/media/2016/05/yes-wolverine-is-in-x-men-apocalypse/.

Dumaraog, Ana. "Suicide Squad Director Says Most Of Jared Leto's Work As Joker Hasn't Been Seen." *Screen Rant*, May 7, 2020. https://screenrant.com/suicide-squad-joker-deleted-scenes-footage-david-ayer/.

Dutton, Walt. "Batgirl Jumps Into Crime Fight (Zowie!)" *Los Angeles Times*, August 1, 1967, D1. https://www.latimes.com/entertainment/herocomplex/la-et-hc-yvonne-craig-vincent-price-batgirl-20150819-story.html.

Dworkin, Arye. "Revisiting the Strange Cinematic Debut of Deadpool." *Vulture*, May 18, 2018. https://www.vulture.com/2018/05/revisiting-the-strange-cinematic-debut-of-deadpool.html.

Dyce, Andrew. "Kevin Smith Says Suicide Squad 'Does DC Proud.'" *Screen Rant*, August 4, 2016. https://screenrant.com/suicide-squad-kevin-smith-review/.

Ebert, Roger. "Superman." RogerEbert.com, December 15, 1978. https://www.rogerebert.com/reviews/superman.

Ebert, Roger. "Timecop." RogerEbert.com, September 16, 1994. https://www.rogerebert.com/reviews/timecop-1994.

Echostation. "Absolutely Brilliant Tom Mankiewicz Interview New." *Superhero Hype*, November 2006. https://forums.superherohype.com/threads/absolutely-brilliant-tom-mankiewicz-interview-new.257534/.

Edwards, Matt. "Is Barb Wire Actually an Overlooked '90s Masterpiece?" *Den of Geek*, July 9, 2015. https://www.denofgeek.com/movies/is-barb-wire-actually-an-overlooked-90s-masterpiece/.

Eisenberg, Eric. "Jeff Bridges Says Iron Man Was All Improv." *Cinema Blend*, December 1, 2009. https://www.cinemablend.com/new/Jeff-Bridges-Says-Iron-Man-Was-All-Improv-15937.html.

Elder, Sean. "Lauren Shuler Donner, Prolific 'X-Men' Producer, Has the Superpower of Tenacity." *Newsweek*, May 22, 2014, newsweek.com.

"Ellen Bry, Spider man's new 'webmate.'" *Kokomo Tribune*, October 21, 1978. https://www.newspapers.com/clip/33303965/ellen-bry/.

Englehart, Steve. *Back Issue* 1, no. 118, February 2020.

"Episode 133: Danny Bilson and Paul De Meo." *Comic Book Central*, July 2, 2016. http://comicbookcentral.net/episode-133-danny-bilson-and-paul-de-meo/.

Evry, Max. "Tim Blake Nelson Talks Fantastic Four Reshoots." *Coming Soon*, April 24, 2015. https://www.comingsoon.net/movies/news/433773-tim-blake-nelson-talks-fantastic-four-reshoots#/slide/1.

Faraci, Devin. "Suicide Squad Reshoots Bode Well for the DC Movieverse." Birthmoviesdeath.com, March 31, 2016. https://birthmoviesdeath.com/2016/03/31/suicide-squad-reshoots-bode-well-for-the-dc-movieverse.

Flanagan, Graham. "The inside story behind the Marvel movie you were never supposed to see." *Business Insider*, March 18, 2017, March 19, 2018 (updated). https://www.businessinsider.com/marvel-fantastic-four-unreleased-movie-roger-corman-hollywood-comic-book-superhero-stan-lee-2017-3.

Fleming, Michael. "Artisan deal a real Marvel." *Variety*, May 16, 2000. https://variety.com/2000/film/news/artisan-deal-a-real-marvel-1117781709/.

Fleming, Michael, and Peter Gilstrap. "Fox says Hood good for 'Wolverine.'" *Variety*, July 19, 2007. https://variety.com/2007/film/markets-festivals/fox-says-hood-good-for-wolverine-2-1117968868/.

Fleming, Michael, and Marc Graser. "Mickey Rourke set for 'Iron Man 2.'" *Variety*, March 11, 2009. https://variety.com/2009/film/markets-festivals/mickey-rourke-set-for-iron-man-2-1118001114/.

Fleming, Mike, Jr. "Comic-Con Bombshell: WB Wants 'Batman V Superman' Scribe Chris

Terrio For 'Justice League.'" *Deadline*, July 25, 2014. https://deadline.com/2014/07/comic-con-batman-v-superman-chris-terrio-justice-league-809843/.
Fleming, Mike, Jr. "Disney Reinstates Director James Gunn For 'Guardians Of The Galaxy 3.'" *Deadline*, March 15, 2019. https://deadline.com/2019/03/james-gunn-reinstated-guardians-of-the-galaxy-3-disney-suicide-squad-2-indefensible-social-media-messages-1202576444/.
Fleming Mike, Jr. "James Gunn Comments On Being Dropped By Marvel's 'Guardians Of The Galaxy' Franchise." *Deadline*, July 20, 2018. https://deadline.com/2018/07/james-gunn-responds-marvel-firing-guardians-of-the-galaxy-for-tweets-1202430535/.
Fleming, Mike, Jr. "SCOOP: Zack Snyder Directing Superman." *Deadline*, October 4, 2010. https://deadline.com/2010/10/zack-snyder-directing-superman-72340/.
Ford, Rebecca. "Heroes of Horror, Sci-Fi and Supervillains: The Genre Roundtable." *Hollywood Reporter*, July 18, 2018. https://www.hollywoodreporter.com/features/fanboys-fangirls-are-loudest-voice-genre-roundtable-1127307.
Franich, Darren. "How Ben Affleck's 'Daredevil' got all the right stuff wrong." EW.com, April 9, 2015. https://ew.com/article/2015/04/09/ben-affleck-daredevil-look-back/.
Freiman, Barry M. "One-on-One Interview with Producer Ilya Salkind." Superman Homepage, n.d. https://www.supermanhomepage.com/movies/movies.php?topic=interview-salkind.
Friend, Tad. "Credit Grab." *New Yorker*, October 20, 2003. https://www.newyorker.com/magazine/2003/10/20/credit-grab.
Fritz, Ben. "Sony, Marvel Discussed Spider-Man Movie Crossover." *Wall Street Journal*, December 9, 2014. https://blogs.wsj.com/speakeasy/2014/12/09/sony-marvel-discussed-spider-man-movie-crossover/.
Gaines, Caseen. "'Howard the Duck': An Oral History." *Decider*, November 3, 2016. https://decider.com/2016/03/11/howard-the-duck-the-or.
Galloway, Stephen. "'Cinderella' Director Kenneth Branagh on Casting His Princess, Working With Marvel and His Dream Shakespeare Film." *Hollywood Reporter*, March 1, 2015. https://www.webcitation.org/6WjNRSMuC?url=http://www.hollywoodreporter.com/news/cinderella-director-kenneth-branagh-casting-778478?page=1&template=cap.
Garcia, Keith. "Director Rachel Talalay Talks Tank Girl and a Career of Dreams and Nightmares." July 28, 2016. https://www.westword.com/arts/director-rachel-talalay-talks-tank-girl-and-a-career-of-dreams-and-nightmares-8140107.
Gardner, Chris. "Rose McGowan Calls Out 'X-Men' Billboard That Shows Mystique Being Strangled." *Hollywood Reporter*, June 2, 2016. https://www.hollywoodreporter.com/rambling-reporter/rose-mcgowan-calls-x-men-898538.
Gettell, Oliver. "Ryan Reynolds: 'X-Men: Origins' was 'frustrating experience.'" *EW*, February 10, 2016. https://ew.com/article/2016/02/10/ryan-reynolds-explains-x-men-origins-role/.
Gilchrist, Todd. "Interview: Kenneth Johnson." *IGN*, July 28, 2006, May 17, 2012 (updated). https://www.ign.com/articles/2006/07/28/interview-kenneth-johnson.
Giroux, Jack. "'Deadpool 2' Director David Leitch Discusses the X-Force Gag, Adding More Cable, and Embracing the Comic Book Aesthetic [Interview]." *Slash Film*, May 23, 2018. https://www.slashfilm.com/deadpool-2-director-david-leitch-interview/2/.
Gleiberman, Owen. "The Bombing of 'Hellboy': How the Blockbuster Mentality Can Be Its Own Worst Enemy." *Variety*, April 13, 2019. https://variety.com/2019/film/columns/hellboy-bombing-guillermo-del-toro-ron-perlman-david-harbour-1203188923/.
Gleiberman, Owen. "Film Review: 'Spider-Man: Homecoming.'" *Variety*, June 29, 2017. https://variety.com/2017/film/reviews/spider-man-homecoming-review-tom-holland-1202481638/.
Goldberg, Matt. "SPIDER-MAN 4 Dead; Sam Raimi, Tobey Maguire, and Cast Out; Reboot Set for Summer 2012." *Collider*, January 11, 2010. https://collider.com/spider-man-4-dead-sam-raimi-tobey-maguire-and-cast-out-reboot-set-for-summer-2012/.
Goldberg, Matt. "Why Warner Bros. Hired Zack Snyder to Direct SUPERMAN: THE MAN OF STEEL; Plus the Film's Logline Revealed?" *Collider*, October 5, 2010. https://collider.com/superman-the-man-of-steel-zack-snyder-warner-bros-logline/.
Goldsmith, Jeff. "Raimi well-suited for fantastic feats." *Variety*, July 18, 2006. https://variety.com/2006/film/markets-festivals/raimi-well-suited-for-fantastic-feats-1200339581/.
Gonsalves, Rob. "The Spirit." Efilm Critic, September 23, 2010. https://www.efilmcritic.com/review.php?movie=17451&reviewer=416.
Gonzalez, Umberto, and Tim Molloy. "How 'Justice League' Became a 'Frankenstein.'" TheWrap.com, November 29, 2017. https://www.thewrap.com/justice-league-zack-snyder-batman-v-superman-wonder-woman/.
Graves, Wren. "Joker is the most profitable comic book movie of all time." *Consequence of Sound*, November 9, 2019. https://consequenceofsound.net/2019/11/joker-most-profitable-comic-book-movie/.
Greenberg, James. "Rescuing Batman." *Los Angeles Times*, May 8, 2005. https://www.latimes.com/archives/la-xpm-2005-may-08-ca-batman8-story.html.
Greenblatt, Leah. "Blade oral history: Wesley Snipes and the cast look back at a modern cult classic." *EW*,

July 16, 2018. https://ew.com/movies/2018/07/16/blade-oral-history-wesley-snipes/?utm_source=twitter.com&utm_medium=social&utm_campaign=social-button-sharing.

Guerrasio, Jason. "The 'Deadpool' writers reveal everything you want to know about the sequel." *Business Insider*, January 14, 2017. https://www.businessinsider.com.au/deadpool-2-writers-reveal-sequel-plot-details-2017-1?r=DE&IR=T.

Gunn, Elston. "Elston Gunn interviews KEVIN SMITH." *Ain't It Cool News*, May 14, 2009. http://legacy.aintitcool.com/node/5942.

Gupta, Rahul. "Batman producer Michael Uslan on bringing caped crusader to the big screen, and franchise's iconic cast." First Post, July 15, 2019. https://www.firstpost.com/entertainment/batman-producer-michael-uslan-on-bringing-caped-crusader-to-the-big-screen-and-franchises-iconic-cast-6990881.html.

Gvozden, Dan. "Why Steve Ditko Didn't Look Back." *Hollywood Reporter*, July 9 ,2018. https://www.hollywoodreporter.com/movies/movie-news/steve-ditko-fought-credit-spider-man-never-looked-back-1125706/.

Harmetz, Aljean. "The Life and Exceedingly Hard Times of Superman." *New York Times*, June 14, 1981. https://www.nytimes.com/1981/06/14/movies/the-life-and-exceedingly-hard-times-of-superman.html.

Harrington, Richard. "The Shadow of the Crow." *Washington Post*, May 15, 1994. https://www.washingtonpost.com/archive/lifestyle/style/1994/05/15/the-shadow-of-the-crow/5852ee0f-6e8c-4a40-9aef-55440dcbed53/.

Harris, Aisha. "One of Cinema's First Black Superheroes Is Not Who You Think It Is." *Slate*, January 15, 2018. https://slate.com/culture/2018/02/abar-the-first-black-superman-is-a-ridiculous-blaxploitation-film-worth-watching.html.

Harris, Will. "Jon Cryer on Charlie Sheen's work ethic and correcting Gene Hackman." *AV Club*, May 9, 2013. https://tv.avclub.com/jon-cryer-on-charlie-sheen-s-work-ethic-and-correcting-1798238147.

Harrison, Mark. "The Batman Movies That Never Were." *Den of Geek*, September 25, 2018. https://www.denofgeek.com/movies/the-batman-movies-that-never-were/.

Hayes, A. Cydney. "Guillermo del Toro fought 7 years for Ron Perlman to star as Hellboy." *EW*, December 2, 2018. https://ew.com/tv/2018/12/02/guillermo-del-toro-fought-ron-perlman-hellboy-role/.

Hiatt, Brian. "Rebecca Romijn-Stamos bares all about ''X2.'" *EW*, May 7, 2003. https://ew.com/article/2003/05/07/rebecca-romijn-stamos-bares-all-about-x2/.

Hibberd, James. "Why Henry Cavill Basically Already Is James Bond." *Hollywood Reporter*, November 10, 2021. https://www.hollywoodreporter.com/feature/henry-cavill-interview-witcher-superman-1235044553/.

Hiltzik, Michael A. "Studio rights to Spider-Man are Untangled." *Los Angeles Times*, March 2 1999. https://www.latimes.com/archives/la-xpm-1999-mar-02-fi-13115-story.html.

Hiltzik, Michael A. "Untangling the Web." *Los Angeles Times*, March 24, 2002. https://web.archive.org/web/20160304100601/http://articles.latimes.com/2002/mar/24/magazine/tm-34460.

History. 1966 Batman Pages. https://www.66batmania.com/bios/history/.

Holthouse, David. "The Devil and Todd McFarlane." *Phoenix New Times*, July 31, 1997. https://www.phoenixnewtimes.com/news/the-devil-and-todd-mcfarlane-6422808.

Hood, Cooper. "Justice League: Reportedly 15-20% Is From Joss Whedon's Reshoots." *Screen Rant*, November 13, 2017. https://screenrant.com/justice-league-joss-whedon-reshoots-amount/.

"How Happy Meals Killed Tim Burton's Batman." *What Culture*. https://whatculture.com/film/how-happy-meals-killed-tim-burtons-batman-2?page=4.

Howe, Desson. "'Batman': Winged Defeat." *Washington Post*, June 20, 1997. https://www.washingtonpost.com/wp-srv/style/longterm/movies/review97/batmanandrobinhowe.htm?noredirect=on.

Hughes, Mark. "Review: 'Batman V Superman' Triumphant." *Forbes*, March 22, 2016. https://www.forbes.com/sites/markhughes/2016/03/22/review-batman-v-superman-triumphant/#79e07265b265.

Hunt, Stacey Wilson. "'Spider-Man's' Laura Ziskin in Her Own Words." *Hollywood Reporter*, June 15, 2011. https://www.hollywoodreporter.com/news/spider-mans-laura-ziskin-her-202147.

Ito, Robert. "Fantastic Faux!" *Los Angeles*, March 2005. https://books.google.ca.

Itzkoff, Dave. "How 'Avengers' Was Assembled, Before Marvel Was Mighty." *New York Times*, April 18, 2019. https://www.nytimes.com/2019/04/18/movies/avengers-endgame-robert-downey-jr.html?em_pos=small&emc=edit_fm_20190419&nl=movies-update&nl_art=12&nlid=36242812emc=edit_fm_20190419&ref=headline&te=1.

Itzkoff, Dave. "Martin Scorsese Is Letting Go." *New York Times*, January 2, 2020. https://www.nytimes.com/2020/01/02/movies/martin-scorsese-irishman.html.

Jagernauth, Kevin. "Lexi Alexander Says She Wishes Marvel Had Made Creative Decisions On 'Punisher: War Zone' Instead Of Lionsgate." *Indiewire*, March 20, 2015. https://www.indiewire.com/2015/03/lexi-alexander-says-she-wishes-marvel-had-made-creative-decisions-on-punisher-war-zone-instead-of-lionsgate-265858/.

Jay, Robert. "Legends of the Superheroes." *TV Obscurities*, January 16, 2009. https://www.tvobscurities.com/2009/01/legends-of-the-superheroes/.

Johnston, Rich. "Fantastic Four Movie 'A Mess,' Goes To Reshoot, Louisiana Sets Being Rebuilt (UPDATE)." *Bleeding Cool*, January 15, 2015. https://bleedingcool.com/movies/fantastic-four-movie-mess-goes-reshoot-louisiana-sets-rebuilt/.
Johnston, Rich. "LYING IN THE GUTTERS VOLUME 2 COLUMN 156." *CBR*, May 5, 2008. https://www.cbr.com/264974-2/.
Jones, Alan. "Batman." *Cinefantastique* 20 No. 1 & 2, November 1989, 51. http://www.1989batman.com/2013/08/vintage-magazine-article.html.
Jones, Alan. "Designing the Legend." *Cinefantastique* 20 No. 1 & 2, November 1989. http://www.1989batman.com/2013/08/vintage-magazine-article.html.
Jordan, Jerilyn. "Lori Petty reflects on Tank Girl, Jennifer Lawrence, and that Game of Thrones coffee cup." *Metro Times*, May 15, 2019. https://www.metrotimes.com/detroit/lori-petty-reflects-on-tank-girl-jennifer-lawrence-and-that-game-of-thrones-coffee-cup/Content?oid=21657056.
Kael, Pauline. "Popeye (1980)." *The New Yorker*, January 5, 1981. Scrapsfromtheloft.com.
Kaye, Don. "Darkman: Sam Raimi's First Superhero Movie Was a Twisted Horror Hybrid." *Den of Geek*, August 24, 2019. https://www.denofgeek.com/movies/darkman-sam-raimi-superhero-horror-movie/.
Kaye, Don. "Neil Marshall on Hellboy Reboot: 'The Script Was Never Any Good.'" *Den of Geek*, May 17, 2021. https://www.denofgeek.com/movies/neil-marshall-hellboy-reboot-the-script-never-any-good/.
Kaye, Don. "Screenwriter Jon Spaihts: Doctor Strange Has the Best Origin Story." *Den of Geek*, November 5, 2016. https://www.denofgeek.com/comics/screenwriter-jon-spaihts-doctor-strange-has-the-best-origin-story/.
Keck, William. "Begins' gets the TV hero's approval." *USA Today*, June 21, 2005. http://usatoday30.usatoday.com/life/movies/news/2005-06-21-batman-flashback_x.htm
Kehr, Dave. "Pure Hackwork It's a Very Dull 'Blade' Indeed As Wesley Snipes Takes On the Undead." *New York Daily News*, August 21, 1998. https://www.nydailynews.com/archives/nydn-features/pure-hackwork-dull-blade-wesley-snipes-takes-undead-article-1.819050.
Kehr, Dave. "Unlovable Duck Makes 'Howard' an Unlovable Film." *Chicago Tribune*, August 1, 1986. https://www.chicagotribune.com/news/ct-xpm-1986-08-01-8602250309-story.html.
Kelley, Sonaiya. "Avengers: Endgame' writers on Thor-Lebowski, Black Widow and reviving 'Agent Carter.'" *Los Angeles Times*, May 4, 2019. https://www.latimes.com/entertainment/movies/la-et-mn-avengers-endgame-writers-markus-mcfeely-20190504-story.html.
Kemp, Cal. "Gale Anne Hurd Interview—THE INCREDIBLE HULK." *Collider*, June 16, 2008. https://www.webcitation.org/6EdwMPN77?url=http://collider.com/entertainment/interviews/article.asp/aid/8230/tcid/1.
Kemp, Cal. "Kevin Feige Interview—THE INCREDIBLE HULK." *Collider*, June 17, 2008. https://www.webcitation.org/6EdxYvGLK?url=http://collider.com/entertainment/interviews/article.asp/aid/8236/tcid/1.
Kennedy, Michael. "Why The Amazing Spider-Man 3 Was Canceled." *Screen Rant*, December 31, 2021. https://screenrant.com/amazing-spiderman-3-canceled-reason-plans/.
Keyes, Rob. "Ryan Reynolds Talks Deadpool & Spinoff Possibilities." *Screen Rant*, March 15, 2009. https://screenrant.com/ryan-reynolds-discusses-deadpool-character-spinoff/.
Kirschling, Gregory. "New 'Hulk': behind-the-scenes drama." *EW*, April 17, 2008. https://ew.com/article/2008/04/17/new-hulk-behind-scenes-drama/.
Kit, Borys. "DC Entertainment Chief Reveals What's Next for Superman, Wonder Woman and 5 Superheroes Who Deserve Movies (Q&A)." *Hollywood Reporter*, July 17, 2013. https://www.hollywoodreporter.com/news/dc-chief-superman-wonder-woman-586081?page=2.
Kit, Borys. "Did 'Deadpool' Director Tim Miller Leak the Test Footage That Launched a Franchise?" *Hollywood Reporter*, February 15, 2016. https://www.hollywoodreporter.com/heat-vision/did-deadpool-director-tim-miller-865307.
Kit, Borys, and Tatiana Siegel. "'Spider-Man' Finds Tom Holland to Star as New Web-Slinger." *Hollywood Reporter*, June 23, 2015. https://www.hollywoodreporter.com/heat-vision/spider-man-finds-tom-holland-794761.
Klady, Leonard. "Steel." *Variety*, August 18, 1997. https://variety.com/1997/film/reviews/steel-3-1117340064/.
Knight, Rosie. "Mike Mignola talks killing Hellboy and resurrecting his world (exclusive)." nerdist.com, July 12, 2017. https://nerdist.com/article/mike-mignola-hellboy-movie-comics-exclusive-interview/.
Knowles, Harry. "The Punisher (2004) review." *Ain't It Cool News*, April 13, 2004. http://legacy.aintitcool.com/node/17355.
Konda, Kelly. "Batman 75: How Batman Returns Pissed Off McDonald's & Cost Tim Burton His Job." *We Minored in Film*, December 26, 2014. https://weminoredinfilm.com/2014/12/26/batman-75-how-batman-returns-pissed-off-mcdonalds-cost-tim-burton-his-job/.
Konda, Kelly. "UPDATED Batman 75: Did An ABC Executive's Visit to the Playboy Club in 1965 Really Inspire the Adam West Batman TV Series?" *We Minored in Film*, June 9, 2014. https://weminoredinfilm.com/2014/06/09/batman-75-did-an-abc-executives-visit-to-the-playboy-club-in-1965-really-inspire-the-adam-west-batman-tv-series/.

Kourlas, Gia. "'Joker': A Dance Critic Reviews Joaquin Phoenix's Moves." *New York Times*, October 11, 2019. https://www.nytimes.com/2019/10/11/arts/dance/joaquin-phoenix-dancing-joker.html.

Krisis. "Marvel Horror of the 1970s—The $47 Most-Wanted Marvel Omnibus of 2017." *Crushing Krisis* (blog), May 17 2017. https://www.crushingkrisis.com/2017/05/marvel-horror-1970s-47-most-wanted-marvel-omnibus-2017/.

Kroll, Justin, and Brent Lang. "Justice League' Extensive Reshoots Causing Headaches for Star Schedules (EXCLUSIVE)." *Variety*, July 24, 2017. https://variety.com/2017/film/news/justice-league-reshoots-1202502433/.

Kyriazis, Stefan. "Doctor Strange director on 'whitewashing' Tilda Swinton: I didn't want a racist Fu Manchu." *Express*, October 27, 2016. https://www.express.co.uk/entertainment/films/725894/Doctor-Strange-whitewashing-Tilda-Swinton-Ancient-One-Wong-Scott-Derrickson.

Lang, Brent. "Spider-Man Will Stay in the Marvel Cinematic Universe." *Variety*, September 27, 2019. https://variety.com/2019/film/news/sony-marvel-tom-holland-spider-man-1203351489/.

Lang, Brent. "Toby Emmerich Named Warner Bros. Chief Content Officer, Greg Silverman Ousted." *Variety*, December 14, 2016. https://variety.com/2016/film/news/toby-emmerich-named-warner-bros-chief-content-officer-greg-silverman-ousted-1201942510/.

LaSalle, Mick. "Review: Movies don't get any worse than 'Birds of Prey' This is the bottom." *SF Chronicle*, February 5, 2020. https://datebook.sfchronicle.com/movies-tv/review-movies-dont-get-any-worse-than-birds-of-prey-this-is-the-bottom.

Laurie, Leona. "Kat Green's Oral History of Roger Corman's THE FANTASTIC FOUR." *Geek Girl Authority*, October 26, 2017. https://www.geekgirlauthority.com/kat-greens-oral-history-roger-cormans-fantastic-four/.

Lawson, Richard. "Justice League Is a Big, Ugly Mess." *Vanity Fair*, November 15, 2017. https://www.vanityfair.com/hollywood/2017/11/justice-league-review.

Leonard, Devin. "Marvel Goes Hollywood." *Fortune*, May 23, 2007. https://archive.fortune.com/magazines/fortune/fortune_archive/2007/05/28/100034246/index2.htm.

Leonard, Devin. "The Pow! Bang! Bam! Plan to Save Marvel, Starring B-List Heroes." Bloomberg.com, April 3, 2014. https://www.bloomberg.com/news/articles/2014-04-03/kevin-feige-marvels-superhero-at-running-movie-franchises#xj4y7vzkg.

Lesnick, Silas. "Christopher Nolan on The Dark Knight Rises' Literary Inspiration." *Coming Soon*, July 8, 2012. https://www.comingsoon.net/movies/news/92305-christopher-nolan-on-the-dark-knight-rises-literary-inspiration.

Lesnick, Silas. "James Gunn Confirmed to Direct and Rewrite Guardians of the Galaxy." Superherohype.com, September 18, 2012. https://www.superherohype.com/news/172755-james-gunn-confirmed-to-direct-and-rewrite-guardians-of-the-galaxy.

Levine, Robert. "From the Beginning, 'The Crow' Had a Grim Side : Movies: James O'Barr's comic book might have adapted smoothly to the big screen, but it was spurred by personal tragedy." *Los Angeles Times*, May 30, 1994. https://www.latimes.com/archives/la-xpm-1994-05-30-ca-63961-story.html.

Lewis, Maria. "Looking back on the insane parkour rocket launcher scene from Punisher: War Zone." *Flicks*, December 20, 2018. https://www.flicks.co.nz/features/looking-back-on-the-insane-parkour-rocket-launcher-scene-from-punisher-war-zone/.

Lewis, Maria. "Punisher: War Zone Director Lexi Alexander on the Curious Journey to Cult Status." *Gizmodo*, December 5, 2018. https://io9.gizmodo.com/punisher-war-zone-director-lexi-alexander-on-the-curio-1830877179.

"A Look Back at Howard the Duck." *Media Archive*, September 16, 2019. https://www.youtube.com/watch?v=Drj3MN6sQPo&feature=youtu.be.

Lyttelton, Oliver. "Review: 'Thor: The Dark World' The Most Deeply Flawed Marvel Movie Since 'Iron Man 2.'" *IndieWire*, November 8 2013. https://www.indiewire.com/2013/11/review-thor-the-dark-world-the-most-deeply-flawed-marvel-movie-since-iron-man-2-91982/.

Manning, Shaun. "I AM (writing) IRON MAN: The Screenwriters." *CBR*, May 2, 2008. https://www.cbr.com/i-am-writing-iron-man-the-screenwriters/.

Marric, Linda. "Film review: Eternals." *The Jewish Chronicle*, October 24, 2021. https://www.thejc.com/culture/film/film-review-eternals-1.521860.

Martin, William. "Exclusive: Edgar Wright on Marvel's 'Ant-Man' movie." *Cultbox*, November 28, 2013. https://cultbox.co.uk/news/headlines/exclusive-edgar-wright-on-marvels-ant-man-movie.

Maslin, Janet. "FILM REVIEW: BATMAN FOREVER; New Challenges for the Caped Crusader." *New York Times*, June 16, 1995. https://www.nytimes.com/1995/06/16/movies/film-review-batman-forever-new-challenges-for-the-caped-crusader.html.

Maslin, Janet. "Review/Film; Nonstop Action in 'Mutant Ninja Turtles.'" *New York Times*, March 30, 1990. https://www.nytimes.com/1990/03/30/movies/review-film-nonstop-action-in-mutant-ninja-turtles.html.

Masters, Kim. "Bryan Singer Sex Abuse Case: The Troubling History Behind the Accusations." *Hollywood Reporter*, April 30, 2014. https://www.hollywoodreporter.com/news/bryan-singer-sex-abuse-case-699828.

Masters, Kim. "'How Many At-Bats Do You Get?': Why Fox Hired (Then Fired) Bryan Singer on 'Bohemian Rhapsody.'" *Hollywood Reporter*, October 31, 2018. https://www.hollywoodreporter.com/news/why-fox-hired-fired-bryan-singer-bohemian-rhapsody-1156527.

Masters, Kim. "Marvel Studios' Origin Secrets Revealed by Mysterious Founder: History Was 'Rewritten.'" *Hollywood Reporter*, May 5, 2016. https://www.hollywoodreporter.com/features/marvel-studios-origin-secrets-revealed-889795.

Masters, Kim. "'Suicide Squad's Secret Drama: Rushed Production, Competing Cuts, High Anxiety." *Hollywood Reporter*, August 3, 2016. https://www.hollywoodreporter.com/heat-vision/suicide-squads-secret-drama-rushed-916693.

Masters, Kim. "Warner Bros. Regime Change: What's Behind Greg Silverman's Ouster." *Hollywood Reporter*, December 16, 2016. https://www.hollywoodreporter.com/news/warner-bros-regime-change-whats-behind-greg-silvermans-ouster-956749.

Masters, Kim, and Borys Kit. "Inside a 'Star Wars' Firing: 'Fantastic Four' Problems Led to Director Josh Trank's Ouster." *Hollywood Reporter*, May 1, 2015. https://www.hollywoodreporter.com/heat-vision/inside-a-star-wars-firing-792933.

Masters, Kim, and Kit Borys. "Why 'Ant-Man' Director Edgar Wright Exited Marvel's Superhero Movie." *Hollywood Reporter*, May 28, 2014. https://www.hollywoodreporter.com/news/why-ant-man-director-edgar-707374.

Matzer, Marla. "'Spawn' of a New Era: Studios Turning to Mix of Houses for Modest-Budget Effects Films." *Los Angeles Times*, August 6, 1997. https://www.latimes.com/archives/la-xpm-1997-aug-06-fi-19784-story.html.

McCarthy, Erin. "18 Fascinating Facts About The Crow." *Mental Floss*, February 2, 2016. https://www.mentalfloss.com/article/74690/18-fascinating-facts-about-crow.

McClintock, Pamela. "Box Office: 'Ant-Man' No. 1 With $58M; 'Trainwreck' Laughs to $30.2M." *Hollywood Reporter*, August 19, 2015. https://www.hollywoodreporter.com/news/box-office-ant-man-no-809752.

McClintock, Pamela. "Box Office Milestone: 'Avengers: Age of Ultron' Joins the Billion-Dollar Club," *Hollywood Reporter*, May 15, 2015. https://www.hollywoodreporter.com/news/box-office-milestone-avengers-age-795912.

McClintock, Pamela. "Marvel to prime pupils." *Variety*, March 1, 2005. https://variety.com/2005/film/markets-festivals/marvel-to-prime-pupils-1117918741/.

McClintock, Pamela. "'Wonder Woman 1984' Shows Promise for HBO Max, Audience Survey Finds." *Hollywood Reporter*, December 30, 2020. https://www.hollywoodreporter.com/movies/movie-news/wonder-woman-1984-shows-promise-for-hbo-max-audience-survey-finds-4109942/

McCluskey, Megan. "Ben Affleck Says He Hated Daredevil So Much He Decided to Play Batman." *Time*, December 14, 2016. https://time.com/4602028/ben-affleck-hated-daredevil/.

McKittrick, Christopher. "The Consistent Link: Simon Kinberg on X-Men: Apocalypse." *Creative Screenwriting*, May 26, 2016. https://creativescreenwriting.com/the-consistent-link-simon-kinberg-on-x-men-apocalypse/.

McKittrick, Christopher. "Myth vs. Man: James Mangold and Scott Frank on Logan." *Creative Screenwriting*, March 3 2017. https://www.creativescreenwriting.com/logan/.https://variety.com/2009/film/markets-festivals/warner-bros-wins-superman-case-1118005806/.

McKittrick, Christopher. "No Cookie-Cutter One-Liners—Spider-Man: Homecoming." *Creative Screenwriting*, July 7, 2017. https://creativescreenwriting.com/spider-man/.

McKittrick, Christopher. "The Real Heroes: Reese and Wernick on Deadpool." *Creative Screenwriting*, February 15, 2016. https://creativescreenwriting.com/the-real-heroes-reese-and-wernick-on-deadpool/.

McKittrick, Christopher. "Wolverine: Two Writers, One Character." *Creative Screenwriting*, August 12, 2013. https://www.creativescreenwriting.com/wolverine-two-writers-one-character/.

McNary, Dave. "Warner Bros. wins 'Superman' case." *Variety*, July 8, 2009.

Mello, Nicole. "10 Ways Wonder Woman Is Worse In Joss Whedon's Justice League." *CBR*, March 17, 2021. https://www.cbr.com/wonder-woman-worse-in-joss-whedon-justice-league/

Mendelson, Scott. "'X-Men: Apocalypse' Review: It's A Franchise-Killing Disaster." *Forbes*, May 9, 2016. https://www.forbes.com/sites/scottmendelson/2016/05/09/review-x-men-apocalypse-is-franchise-killing-disaster/#2bf991743560.

Merrick. "Nolan Talks DARK KNIGHT Blu-Ray, A 100,000 Person Screening Of The Film (Featuring Live Q & A w/ Nolan), TDK Sequel, And More!!" *Ain't It Cool News*, December 5, 2008. https://www.webcitation.org/5xLwpPIh8?url=http://www.aintitcool.com/node/39348.

Meslow, Scott. "Let's Revisit Daredevil, the Terrible Movie that Paved the Way to the Modern Superhero Blockbuster." *GQ*, February 14, 2018. https://www.gq.com/story/daredevil-15th-anniversary.

Miller, Laura. "Spawn." Salon.com, September 1, 1997. https://www.salon.com/1997/09/01/spawn/.

Mills, Bart. "And Now … Mighty 'Superman IV' To The Rescue." *Los Angeles Times*, January 2, 1987. https://web.archive.org/web/20131009030250/http://articles.latimes.com/1987-01-02/entertainment/ca-1647_1_superman-iv.

Mitchell, Elvis. "FILM; Ang Lee on Comic Books and Hulk as Hidden Dragon." *New York Times*, June 22,

2003. https://www.nytimes.com/2003/06/22/movies/film-ang-lee-on-comic-books-and-hulk-as-hidden-dragon.html.
Mitchell, Maurice. "Eartha Kitt, A Brief History of the First Black Catwoman." *The Geek Twins*, October 15, 2019. http://www.thegeektwins.com/2019/10/eartha-kitt-brief-history-of-first.html.
Mitchell, Sean. "Shellshocked by Turtlemania: Movies: The box office sets records, but product tie-ins are 'bigger than the movie.'" *Los Angeles Times*, April 21, 1990. https://www.latimes.com/archives/la-xpm-1990-04-21-ca-1154-story.html.
Mithra, Kuljit. "Interview with Mark Steven Johnson." *Man Without Fear*, March 2002. http://www.manwithoutfear.com/daredevil-interviews/Johnson.
Molloy, Tim. "Chris Claremont's Dream X-Men Movie: James Cameron, Kathryn Bigelow, and Bob Hoskins as Wolverine." *The Wrap*, March 25, 2012. https://www.thewrap.com/chris-claremonts-dream-x-men-movie-james-cameron-kathryn-bigelow-and-bob-hoskins-wolverine-3/.
Moore, Michael. "'Joker': Michael Moore Writes Tribute to Todd Phillips' 'Cinematic Masterpiece.'" *Variety*, December 18, 2019. https://variety.com/2019/film/awards/michael-moore-todd-phillips-joker-1203446280/.
Moraitis, Andrew. "Boytown." *Newshit*, August 20, 2010. https://www.webcitation.org/5zva8Tdx-T?url=http://newshit.com.au/content/movies/boytown.
Moriarty. "AICN EXCLUSIVE!! IRON MAN Has Found Its Tony Stark!!" *Ain't It Cool News*, September 29, 2006. http://legacy.aintitcool.com/node/30225.
Moriarty. "Mr. Beaks Interviews Lloyd Levin and Larry Gordon!! HELLBOY Week Begins!!" *Ain't It Cool News*, March 29, 2004. http://legacy.aintitcool.com/node/17280.
Motes, Jax. "Kevin Smith Sounds Off On Jason Momoa As Aquaman." *Science Fiction*, June 25, 2014. https://sciencefiction.com/2014/06/25/kevin-smith-sounds-jason-momoa-aquaman/.
Motes, Jax. "Warner Brothers And Screenwriter Chris Terrio Did Not Care For Geoff Johns' Rewrites Of 'Justice League.'" *Science Fiction*, June 12, 2018. https://sciencefiction.com/2018/06/12/warner-brothers-screenwriter-chris-terrio-not-care-geoff-johns-rewrites-justice-league/.
Nailbiter111. "Joss Whedon Rescued Thor: The Dark World With Rewrites." *Comic Book Movie*, September 18, 2013. https://www.comicbookmovie.com/thor/joss-whedon-rescued-thor-the-dark-world-with-rewrites-a87241#gs.bh8j5x.
Nashawatay, Chris. "12 Underrated Movie Gems." *EW*, November 12, 2010. https://ew.com/gallery/12-underrated-movie-gems/.
Newgen, Heather. "Spider-Man 3 Interviews: Director Sam Raimi." *Superhero Hype*, April 22, 2007. https://www.superherohype.com/features/93443-spider-man-3-interviews-director-sam-raimi.
Newitz, Annalee. "10 Reasons Why 'Ghost Rider' Kicks Your Burning Ass." *Wired*, February 27, 2007. https://www.wired.com/2007/02/10-reasons-why-2/.
Newman, Kim. "Teenage Mutant Ninja Turtles." *Monthly Film Bulletin*, December 1990. https://en.wikipedia.org/wiki/Teenage_Mutant_Ninja_Turtles_(1990_film).
Nolfi, Joey. "Suicide Squad: Jared Leto sent Will Smith anal beads and used condoms." *EW*, April 13, 2016. https://ew.com/article/2016/04/13/suicide-squad-jared-leto-will-smith-anal-beads-used-condoms/
O'Connor, Rory. "Ethan Hawke on Dreaming of a Fourth 'Before' Film, Why He's Not Having a McConaughey Moment, and the Necessity of Film Festivals." thefilmstage.com, August 23, 2018. https://thefilmstage.com/ethan-hawke-on-dreaming-of-a-fourth-before-film-why-hes-not-having-a-mcconaughey-moment-and-the-necessity-of-film-festivals/.
Orr, Christopher. "Suicide Squad is the Worst of the Worst." *The Atlantic*, August 2016. https://www.theatlantic.com/entertainment/archive/2016/08/suicide-squad-review/494669/.
O'Sullivan, Michael. "'Blade': Black, White and Red All Over." *Washington Post*, August 21, 1998. https://www.washingtonpost.com/wp-srv/style/movies/reviews/bladeosullivan.htm.
Page, Don. "From the Archives: The Times' original 1966 review of 'Batman,'" *Los Angeles Times*, January 14, 1966. https://www.latimes.com/entertainment/arts/la-et-st-batman-tv-review-20170610-story.html.
Parker, Alex M. "An Evening with Batman and Robin, ordinarytimes.com." June 16, 2021. https://ordinary-times.com/2021/06/16/an-evening-with-batman-and-robin/
Parker, Ryan. "Tommy Lee Jones Really Hated Working With Jim Carrey on 'Batman Forever.'" *Hollywood Reporter*, October 3, 2017. https://www.hollywoodreporter.com/heat-vision/tommy-lee-jones-hated-working-jim-carrey-batman-forever-1045176.
Patton, Joshua M. "Patty Jenkins Talks About How Superman Led Her to Take on Wonder Woman." comicyears.com, January 4, 2021. https://comicyears.com/comics/dc-comics/patty-jenkins-talks-about-how-superman-led-her-to-take-on-wonder-woman/.
Pereira, Sergio. "15 Things Fans Didn't Know About The Disastrous 1994 Fantastic Four Movie." *Screen Rant*, January 13, 2018. https://screenrant.com/fantastic-four-1994-facts-trivia-secrets/.
Phegley, Kiel. "Ellison Gets In 'The Spirit.'" *CBR*, May 21, 2010. https://www.cbr.com/ellison-gets-in-the-spirit/.
Polovny, Kevin. "Here's How Much 'Guardians of the Galaxy' Director James Gunn Hates 'Howard the Duck' the Movie." *Yahoo! Entertainment*, March 21, 2017. https://www.yahoo.com/entertainment/

heres-how-much-guardians-of-the-galaxy-director-james-gunn-hates-howard-the-duck-the-movie-184952922.html.

Pringle, Gill. "Some Kind of Wonderful." *Film Ink*, January 5, 2016. https://www.filmink.com.au/some-kind-of-wonderful/.

"QUESTION-AND-ANSWER: IRON MAN DIRECTOR JON FAVREAU." *Comics Continuum*, March 3, 2008. http://www.comicscontinuum.com/stories/0803/03/jonfavreau.htm.

Quint. "Shane Black talks direction of Iron Man 3 and whether or not to expect more Marvel cameos!" *Ain't It Cool News*, March 7, 2011. http://legacy.aintitcool.com/node/48768.

Raftery, Brian. "Virtuoso Action Director Lexi Alexander Fights Back Against Hollywood." *Wired*, August 1, 2017. https://www.wired.com/story/lexi-alexander-fights-back-against-hollywood/.

Rahner, Mark. "Marvel Studios CEO on 'Spider-Man 2,' other films." *Seattle Times*, June 27, 2004. https://www.webcitation.org/6Ory51h8I?url=http://seattletimes.com/html/entertainment/2001964388_avi27.html.

Ransome, Noel. "Twenty Years Later, Joel Schumacher Is Very Sorry About 'Batman & Robin.'" *Vice*, December 6, 2017. https://www.vice.com/en_ca/article/xw8vpk/twenty-years-later-joel-schumacher-is-very-sorry-about-batman-and-robin.

Ransome, Noel. "Twenty Years Later, 'Steel' Director Admits Shaq Was Probably a Bad Choice." *Vice*, August 14, 2017. https://www.vice.com/en_ca/article/evvnwn/twenty-years-later-steel-director-admits-shaq-was-probably-a-bad-choice.

Rathwell, Mark. incrediblehulktvseries.com (domain no longer available).

Rebello, Stephen. "Sam Hamm." *Cinefantastique* 20, No. 1 & 2, November 1989. http://www.1989batman.com/2013/08/vintage-magazine-article.html.

Reed, Patrick A. "I Like Bats: Producer Michael Uslan Remembers Batman '89 and the Alternate Films That Could Have Been." *Comics Alliance*, June 30, 2014. https://comicsalliance.com/michael-uslan-batman-89-anniversary-movie-interivew/.

Ridgely, Charlie. "2019 ComicBook.com Staff Ranking of the Marvel Cinematic Universe." *Comic Book*, April 25, 2019. https://comicbook.com/marvel/news/marvel-mcu-rankings-comicbook-staff-avengers-week/#1.

Robinson, Gaile. "The X-Men Want the Night Too : Merchandising: The Marvel comic characters have conquered Saturday morning TV. Now they are heading for a bedroom near you." *Los Angeles Times*, October 27, 1993. https://www.latimes.com/archives/la-xpm-1993-10-27-vw-50316-story.html.

Robinson, Joanna. "Joss Whedon on the Original Avengers Script: 'Pretend This Draft Never Happened.'" *Vanity Fair*, July 21, 2014. https://www.vanityfair.com/hollywood/2014/07/joss-whedon-first-avengers-script-disaster.

Robinson, Joanna. "Marvel Looks Back at Iron Man—the Movie That Started It All." *Vanity Fair*, November 29, 2017. https://www.vanityfair.com/hollywood/2017/11/marvel-looks-back-at-iron-man-the-movie-that-started-it-all.

Robinson, Joanna. "What RoboCop Has to Do with the Future of the Marvel Cinematic Universe." *Vanity Fair*, November 28, 2017. https://www.vanityfair.com/hollywood/2017/11/the-future-of-the-marvel-cinematic-universe-robocop.

Robinson, Tasha. "Captain America: The First Avenger." *AV Club*, July 21, 2011. https://film.avclub.com/captain-america-the-first-avenger-1798168981.

Rodney. "Director Talks About Why Elektra Failed." *The Movie Blog*, October 17, 2005. http://www.themovieblog.com/2005/10/director-talks-about-why-elektra-failed/.

Romano, Nick. "Edgar Wright explains how Ant-Man departure led to Baby Driver." *EW*, June 24, 2017. https://ew.com/movies/2017/06/24/edgar-wright-ant-man-marvel-baby-driver/.

Rosario, Richy. "#BlackPantherChallenge Inspires Nationwide Initiative For Kids To Watch 'Black Panther.'" *Vibe*, January 18, 2018. https://www.vibe.com/2018/01/black-panther-challenge-gofundme.

Rottenberg, Josh. "Director Josh Trank on the bumpy road to 'Fantastic Four': 'It's been nuts.'" *Los Angeles Times*, August 6, 2015. https://www.latimes.com/entertainment/herocomplex/la-et-hc-josh-trank-simon-kinberg-fantastic-four-20150806-story.html.

Rottenberg, Josh. "In 'Joker' the stakes are life and death, and comic book movies may never be the same." *Los Angeles Times*, August 28, 2019. https://web.archive.org/web/20190828143837/https://www.latimes.com/entertainment-arts/movies/story/2019-08-27/joker-todd-phillips-joaquin-phoenix.

Rottenberg, Josh. "Josh Trank sets the story straight on why he left 'Star Wars.'" *Los Angeles Times*, June 4, 2015. https://www.latimes.com/entertainment/herocomplex/la-et-hc-josh-trank-on-why-he-dropped-out-of-star-wars-20150603-story.html.

"Rounding up the ratings for 'the season.'" June 16, 1979. https://worldradiohistory.com/hd2/IDX-Business/Magazines/Archive-BC-IDX/79-OCR/BC-1979-06-18-OCR-Page-0056.pdf#search=%22rounding%20up%20the%20ratings%22.

Rowlands, Paul. "Daniel Waters On 'Batman Returns.'" *Money Into Light*, 2016. http://www.money-into-light.com/2016/06/daniel-waters-on-batman-returns.html.

Rubin, Rebecca. "'Avengers: Infinity War' Officially Lands Biggest Box Office Opening of All Time."

Variety, April 30, 2018. https://variety.com/2018/film/box-office/avengers-infinity-war-biggest-box-office-opening-ever-1202791751/.

Ryan, Mike. "Louis Leterrier, 'Now You See Me' Director, On The Problems With 'The Incredible Hulk' And 'Clash Of The Titans.'" *Huffington Post*, May 28, 2018. https://www.huffingtonpost.ca/entry/louis-leterrier-now-you-see-me_n_3333311?ri18n=true.

Ryan, Mike. "Shane Black On 'The Nice Guys,' Mel Gibson, And Why A Female 'Iron Man 3' Villain's Gender Changed." *Uproxx*, May 6, 2016. https://uproxx.com/movies/shane-black-the-nice-guys-iron-man-3/.

Sanchez, Robert. "Exclusive Interview: Zack Snyder Is Kickin' Ass With 300 and Watchmen!" *IESB*, February 13, 2007. https://web.archive.org/web/20090215050330/http:/iesb.net/index.php?option=com_content&task=view&id=1883&Itemid=99.

Schiff, Stephen. "Movies." *Vanity Fair*, July 1983. https://archive.vanityfair.com/article/1983/7/movies.

Schilling, Dave. "Every single thing that is wrong with Batman v Superman: Dawn of Justice." *Guardian*, March 25, 2016. https://www.theguardian.com/film/2016/mar/25/review-batman-v-superman-dawn-of-justice.

Schruers, Fred. "Spider's Man." *Los Angeles Times*, June 27, 2004. https://www.latimes.com/archives/la-xpm-2004-jun-27-ca-schruers27-story.html.

Schumer, Arlen. "The Real Comic Book Origins of The Batman '66 TV Series." denofgeek.com, January 12, 2016. https://www.denofgeek.com/comics/the-real-comic-book-origins-of-the-batman-66-tv-series/.

Sciretta, Peter. "'Spider-Man: Homecoming' Set Visit: Everything We Learned." *Slash Film*, April 3, 2017. https://www.slashfilm.com/spider-man-homecoming-set-visit/2/.

Scott, A.O. "Have Golden Locks, Seeking Hammer." *New York Times*, May 5, 2011. https://www.nytimes.com/2011/05/06/movies/thor-with-chris-hemsworth-review.html.

Scott, A.O. "Returned From the Dead, Ducking Villains and Vixens." *New York Times*, December 24, 2008. https://www.nytimes.com/2008/12/25/movies/25spir.html?ref=movies.

Semple, Lorenzo, Jr. "Requiem for a cheeky 'Batman,'" *Variety*, July 9 2008. https://variety.com/2008/film/markets-festivals/requiem-for-a-cheeky-batman-1117988712/.

SFe. "The Punisher." *Time Out*, September 10, 2012. https://www.timeout.com/movies/the-punisher.

Shaffer, R.L. "The Rocketeer Blu-ray Review." *IGN*, December 9, 2011, January 5, 2012 (updated). https://www.ign.com/articles/2011/12/09/the-rocketeer-blu-ray-review.

Sharf, Zack. "Before the 'Bohemian Rhapsody' Mess, Bryan Singer Reportedly Went AWOL From 'X-Men' Movie Sets." *Indiewire*, June 10, 2019. https://www.indiewire.com/2019/06/bryan-singer-missing-xmen-sets-bohemian-rhapsody-1202148666/.

Shay, Don. "Richard Donner on Superman." *Cinefantastique* 08, no 4, 1979. https://archive.org/details/CinefantastiqueVol08No4Summer1979/page/n11/mode/2up.

Shepherd, Jack. "Deadpool and Guardians of the Galaxy Vol. 2 share a very interesting link." *Independent*, November 15, 2016. https://www.independent.co.uk/arts-entertainment/films/news/deadpool-guardians-of-the-galaxy-vol-2-ego-living-planet-negasonic-teenage-warhead-a7418271.html.

Shewey, Don. "Caught in the Act: New York Actors Face to Face." Chris Reeve Homepage, n.d. http://www.chrisreevehomepage.com/sp-caught_in_the_act.html.

Shoard, Catherine. "Ant-Man review: diminishing returns for latest expansion of Marvel universe." *Guardian*, July 8, 2015. https://www.theguardian.com/film/2015/jul/08/ant-man-review-paul-rudd-michael-douglas.

Siegel, Tatiana. "Fox's not-so-hot summer at the movies." *Variety*, September 5, 2008. https://variety.com/2008/film/features/fox-s-not-so-hot-summer-at-the-movies-1117991696/.

Siegel, Tatiana. "How Martin Scorsese Paved the Way for 'Joker.'" *Hollywood Reporter*, October 9, 2016. https://www.hollywoodreporter.com/heat-vision/how-martin-scorsese-paved-way-joker-1246355.

Sims, Chris, and David Uzumeri. "'Batman & Robin' (1997), Part One." July 11, 2011. https://comicsalliance.com/batman-and-robin-movie-review/.

Sims, David. "X-Men: Apocalypse: A Calamitous Dud." *The Atlantic*, May 2016. https://www.theatlantic.com/entertainment/archive/2016/05/x-men-apocalypse-a-calamitous-dud/484457/.

Smith, Adam. "From the Archive: The Making of Superman." *Empire*, January 31, 2013. https://www.empireonline.com/movies/features/making-superman/.

Smith, Ian. "Interesting photos of Batman and Robin c.1943." thevintagenews.com, March 18 2016. https://www.thevintagenews.com/2016/03/18/interesting-photos-batman-robin-c-1943-2/.

Smith, Krista. "Q&A: J.J. Abrams on Steven Spielberg's Influence in Super 8—and Where Leonard Nimoy Is Hidden." *Vanity Fair*, June 8, 2011. https://www.vanityfair.com/hollywood/2011/06/jj-abrams-super-8.

Smith, Kyle. "'Batman v Superman' is too smart for Marvel fans." *New York Post*, March 30, 2016. https://nypost.com/2016/03/30/batman-v-superman-is-too-smart-for-marvel-fans/.

Sperling, Nicole. "Wonder Woman filmmakers explain why they changed heroine's origin story." *EW*, May 30, 2017. https://ew.com/movies/2017/05/30/wonder-woman-world-war-i-setting/.

Stack, Tim. "Dark Phoenix team on what went wrong with X-Men: Apocalypse." *EW*, December 8, 2017. https://ew.com/movies.

Stack, Tim. "Fantastic Four director Josh Trank promises huge multipower slugfest." *EW*, July 3,

2015. https://ew.com/article/2015/07/03/fantastic-four-josh-trank-slugfest/?hootPostID=1db44f-6cf4e7ccd9d0f3d902c89b72dc.

Stack, Tim. "Fantastic Four writer-producer Simon Kinberg defends film: 'I am proud of it. It's not a disaster.'" *EW*, August 3, 2015. https://ew.com/article/2015/08/03/fantastic-four-simon-kinberg-defends/.

Staff. "Blade test screenings…" *Ain't It Cool News*, April 30, 1998. http://legacy.aintitcool.com/node/928.

Staff. "Pow! Zap! It's Batman and Robin." *New York Times*, January 13, 1966. https://www.nytimes.com/1966/01/13/archives/tv-pow-zap-its-batman-and-robin-bob-kane-heroes-open-abcs-2d-season.html.

Starkey, Adam. "Michael Keaton reveals the moment he knew 'Batman Forever' would suck." *Batman News*, January 3, 2017. https://batman-news.com/2017/01/03/michael-keaton-knew-batman-forever-would-suck/.

Stax. "An Interview with Denise Di Novi." *IGN*, July 2, 2004. https://www.ign.com/articles/2004/07/02/an-interview-with-denise-di-novi.

Stax. "Goyer confirms Deadpool." *IGN*, February 26, 2004. https://www.ign.com/articles/2004/02/26/goyer-confirms-deadpool.

Stroud, Bryan. "Interview With Carmine Infantino—From Penciller to Publisher and Everywhere In Between." *Nerd Team 30*, December 6, 2017. https://www.nerdteam30.com/creator-conversations-retro/an-interview-with-carmine-infantino-from-penciller-to-publisher-and-everywhere-in-between.

Svetkey, Benjamin. "'Lethal Weapon' Wunderkind (and Former Party Boy) Shane Black Is Back … and Still Looking for Action." *Hollywood Reporter*, May 13, 2016. https://www.hollywoodreporter.com/features/lethal-weapon-wunderkind-party-boy-892186.

Tapley, Kristopher. "Listen: Kevin Feige Reflects on Oscar Player 'Black Panther' and 10 Years of Marvel Studios." *Variety*, December 27, 2018. https://variety.com/2018/film/podcasts/playback-podcast-kevin-feige-black-panther-marvel-studios-1203095749/.

Tarantino, Quentin. "I Escaped from Devil's Island." thenewbev.com, April 6, 2020. https://web.archive.org/web/20200819045813/https://thenewbev.com/tarantinos-reviews/i-escaped-from-devils-island/?fbclid=IwAR0yx6FYh_-ZmdfrQaysB_1Umh84GidHEIAGgX2w39u03g95JZ-4DSB92WY.

Tartaglione, Nancy. "'Doctor Strange' Crosses $600M WW; Now MCU's Biggest Single-Character Intro." *Deadline*, November 27, 2016. https://deadline.com/2016/11/doctor-strange-crosses-600-million-global-box-office-1201860255/.

Taylor, Noah R. "TSC: David S. Goyer talks Blade, Batman, and Man of Steel." *That Shelf*, April 16, 2015. https://thatshelf.com/tsc-david-s-goyer-talks-blade-batman-and-man-of-steel/.

Taylor-Foster, Kim. "EXCLUSIVE: Sony's Spider-Man Movies Happen in the 'Same Reality' as the MCU." *Fandom*, June 28, 2017. https://www.fandom.com/articles/exclusive-sonys-spider-man-movies-happen-in-the-same-reality-as-the-mcu.

Thomas, Roy. "The Kon-Tiki Statue Blowing Its Nose Was Our Favorite Scene! A Conversation between Gerry Conway and Roy Thomas." *Alter Ego* 58, December 2010. https://issuu.com/twomorrows/docs/alterego58preview/2.

Thompson, Anne. "Incredible Hulk: Setting the Record Straight." *Indiewire*, June 13, 2008. https://www.webcitation.org/6EdvMZv1t?url=http://blogs.indiewire.com/thompsononhollywood/incredible_hulk_setting_the_record_straight.

Tilly, Chris. "Jared Leto Unsure About Joker's Journey in Suicide Squad." *IGN*, August 5, 2016. https://www.ign.com/articles/2016/08/05/jared-leto-unsure-about-jokers-journey-in-suicide-squad.

Tilly, Chris. "Thor: The Dark World review." *IGN*, October 23, 2013. https://www.ign.com/articles/2013/10/23/thor-the-dark-world-review.

Tito, Greg. "Joss Whedon Officially Directing The Avengers." *Escapist*, July 22, 2010. https://v1.escapistmagazine.com/news/view/102287-Joss-Whedon-Officially-Directing-The-Avengers.

Topel, Fred. "Green Lantern Director Admits 'It Just Did Not Work.'" *Wizard World*, October 4, 2017. https://wizardworld.com/wizard/how-martin-campbell-would-fix-green-lantern.

Total Film. "Edward Norton talks Incredible Hulk." *Games Radar*, March 7, 2008. https://www.gamesradar.com/edward-norton-talks-incredible-hulk/.

"Toy Biz Inc., History." *Funding Universe*. http://www.fundinguniverse.com/company-histories/toy-biz-inc-history/.

Travis, Ben. "Tim Burton On Batman Forever's Nipple-Suit: 'Go F—— Yourself.'" *Empire Online*, July 6, 2022. https://www.empireonline.com/movies/news/tim-burton-on-batman-forever-nipple-suit-go-f-yourself/.

Tyler, Adrienne. "Justin Theroux Wasn't Sure About Avengers; Reflects On Iron Man 2 Shortcomings." *Screen Rant*, February 1, 2016. https://screenrant.com/iron-man-2-justin-theroux-avengers/.

Ugwu, Reggie. "'They Set Us Up to Fail': Black Directors of the '90s Speak Out." *New York Times*, July 3, 2019. https://www.nytimes.com/2019/07/03/movies/black-directors-1990s.html.

Van Gelder, Lawrence. "Fighting Forces of Evil With Endearing Smiles." *New York Times*, August 16, 1997. https://www.nytimes.com/1997/08/16/movies/fighting-forces-of-evil-with-endearing-smiles.html.

Variety Staff. "'Bat' beats up B.O." *Variety*, July 8, 1997. https://variety.com/1997/film/box-office/bat-beats-up-b-o-1116677093/.

Variety Staff. "Marvel characters holding attraction for filmmakers." *Variety*, December 8, 1992. https://variety.com/1992/film/news/marvel-characters-holding-attraction-for-filmmakers-101955/.

Vary, Adam B. "Cate Shortland Turned Down Directing 'Black Widow.' So Scarlett Johansson Called Her on Zoom.'" *Variety*, 2021. https://variety.com/2021/film/news/cate-shortland-black-widow-scarlett-johansson-1235008158/.

Vary, Adam B. "Evangeline Lilly Tried To Quit Acting, But Acting Would Not Quit Her." *Buzzfeed.com*, December 2, 2014. https://www.buzzfeed.com/adambvary/evangeline-lilly-ant-man-the-hobbit-squickerwonkers.

Vary, Adam B. "Joss Whedon's Astonishing, Spine-Tingling, Soul-Crushing Marvel Adventure!" *Buzzfeed*, April 20, 2015. https://www.buzzfeednews.com/article/adambvary/joss-whedon-spine-tingling-soul-crushing-marvel-adventure.

Vary, Adam B. "Meet The Woman Who Made History With Marvel's 'Guardians Of The Galaxy.'" *Buzzfeed*, July 30, 2014. https://www.buzzfeed.com/adambvary/guardians-of-the-galaxy-nicole-perlman.

Vary, Adam B. "'Spider-Man' at 20: How Sam Raimi and Sony Pictures Rescued the Superhero Genre and Changed Hollywood Forever." *Variety*, April 27, 2022. https://variety.com/2022/film/features/spider-man-2002-oral-history-sam-raimi-sony-pictures-1235240553/.

Vejvoda, Jim. "Spider-Man: Homecoming Review." *IGN*, June 29, 2017. https://www.ign.com/articles/2017/06/29/spider-man-homecoming-review

Vejvoda, Jim. "Watchmen Review." *IGN*, March 5, 2009. https://www.ign.com/articles/2009/03/06/watchmen-review.

Vilkomerson, Sara. "Gal Gadot Is Wonder Woman: 'She Is Not Relying on a Man, and She's Not There Because of a Love Story.'" *Glamour*, May 7, 2016. https://www.glamour.com/story/gal-gadot-wonder-woman-cover-interview.

Vilkomerson, Sara. "The New Mutants details revealed: X-Men franchise goes horror." *EW*, May 25, 2017. https://ew.com/movies/2017/05/25/the-new-mutants-details-x-men-horror/

Waid, Mark. "MAN OF STEEL, SINCE YOU ASKED." *Thrillbent*, June 14, 2013. http://thrillbent.com/blog/man-of-steel-since-you-asked/.

Wales, George. "X-Men: Apocalypse will be 'true birth of the X-Men.'" gamesradar.com, July 7, 2015. https://www.gamesradar.com/x-men-apocalypse-will-be-true-birth-x-men/.

Wardlow, Ciara. "How 'Birds of Prey' Deconstructs the Male Gaze." *Hollywood Reporter*, February 8, 2020. https://www.hollywoodreporter.com/movies/movie-features/how-birds-prey-deconstructs-male-gaze-1277232/.

Warner Bros. "Steel Production Notes." 1997. https://web.archive.org/web/20080411223603/http://movies.warnerbros.com/steel/cmp/production.html.

Webster, Andy. "Artist-Director Seeks the Spirit of 'The Spirit.'" *New York Times*, July 20, 2008. https://www.nytimes.com/2008/07/20/movies/20webs.html.

Weinraub, Bernard. "Visual Flair, A Hip Sensibility And a Past." *New York Times*, June 11, 1995. https://www.nytimes.com/1995/06/11/arts/film-visual-flair-a-hip-sensibility-and-a-past.html.

Weintraub, Steve. "Director Zack Snyder On Set Interview—WATCHMEN." *Collider*, February 16, 2009. https://collider.com/director-zack-snyder-on-set-interview-watchmen/.

Weintraub, Steve. "Exclusive: Screenwriters Alex Tse and David Hayter talk WATCHMEN." *Collider*, March 2, 2009. https://collider.com/exclusive-screenwriters-alex-tse-and-david-hayter-talk-watchmen/.

Weintraub, Steve. "Frosty Interviews Mark Steven Johnson." *Collider*, December 5, 2006. https://collider.com/frosty-interviews-mark-steven-johnson-the-writerdirector-of-ghost-rider/.

Weintraub, Steve. "Frosty Interviews Nicolas Cage." *Collider*, December 3, 2006. https://collider.com/frosty-interviews-nicolas-cage/.

Weintraub, Steve. "Sam Raimi Interview." *Collider*, October 21, 2007. https://collider.com/sam-raimi-interview/.

Weintraub, Steve. "Scott Derrickson on What He Had to Do to Direct 'Doctor Strange.'" *Collider*, November 2, 2016. https://collider.com/scott-derrickson-doctor-strange-interview/#images.

Weiss, Josh. "New documentary reveals why Val Kilmer only played Batman one time: 'It's very isolating.'" syfy.com, August 16, 2021. https://www.syfy.com/syfy-wire/val-kilmer-documentary-batman-forever.

West, Lindy. "Batman v Superman is 153 minutes of a grown man whacking two dolls together." *Guardian*, April 3, 2016. https://www.theguardian.com/commentisfree/2016/apr/03/batman-v-superman-grown-man-whacking-two-dolls-together-lindy-west.

White, Brett. "Quesada Reveals "Deadpool" Director's Role in Making 'Iron Man' Film." *CBR*, February 16, 2016. https://www.cbr.com/quesada-reveals-deadpool-directors-role-in-making-iron-man-film/.

Wilding, Josh. "David S. Goyer: "We're Approaching MAN OF STEEL As If It Weren't A Comic Book Movie..." *Comic Book Movie*, January 28, 2013. https://www.comicbookmovie.com/superman/david-s-goyer-were-approaching-man-of-steel-as-if-it-werent-a-comic-book-movie-a73389#gs.bh7qe0.

Wilding, Josh. "Latest Official Color Image From LOGAN Puts The Spotlight On Wolverine And Professor X." *Comic Book Movie*, November 25, 2016. https://www.comicbookmovie.com/x-men/wolverine/

the_wolverine/latest-official-color-image-from-logan-puts-the-spotlight-on-wolverine-and-professor-x-a147069#gs.b3lkxb.

William Moulton Marston. *Psychology Wiki*. https://psychology.wikia.org/wiki/William_Moulton_Marston.

Williams, Trey. "'Ant-Man and the Wasp' Director Peyton Reed Was Inspired by Elmore Leonard Crime Novels." *Wrap*, July 6, 2018. https://www.thewrap.com/ant-man-the-wasp-director-peyton-reed-marvel-gave-incredible-freedom/.

Wilson, Patricia Ellsworth. "Present at the Creation of Superman and the Mole-Men." *The Adventure Continues Magazine* #14, n.d. http://theages.superman.nu/adventures/mole-men.php.

Wilson, William S. "The 'Never Got Made Files' #66: Cannon's Captain America (1984-7)." *Video Junkie*, July 22, 2011. http://www.videojunkie.org/2011/07/never-got-made-files-66-cannons-captain.html.

Wolf, Jeanne. "'Blankman': Hero for the 'Hood." *Orlando Sentinel*, August 18, 1994. https://www.orlandosentinel.com/news/os-xpm-1994-08-18-9408180619-story.html.

"Wonder Woman: An Early Attempt." *TV Obscurities*, July 16, 2013, April 18, 2018 (updated). https://www.tvobscurities.com/articles/wonder_woman/#cite7.

Worley, Rob. "Countdown to 'Hulk': Producers Avi Arad and Gale Anne Hurd talk." *CBR*, June 5, 2003. https://www.cbr.com/countdown-to-hulk-producers-avi-arad-and-gale-anne-hurd-talk/.

Worley, Rob. "Daredevil." *CBR*, August 7, 2002. https://www.cbr.com/313179-2/.

Yahr, Emily. "'Captain America 2' directors talk filming in D.C., casting Robert Redford and the movie's very timely politics." *Washington Post*, April 4, 2014. https://www.washingtonpost.com/news/arts-and-entertainment/wp/2014/04/04/captain-america-2-directors-talk-filming-in-d-c-casting-robert-redford-and-the-movies-very-timely-politics/.

Yamato, Jen. "Kevin Feige on Avengers, Marvel Universe-Building, and the Legacy of Elektra." *Movie Line*, April 30, 2012. http://movieline.com/2012/04/30/kevin-feige-on-avengers-marvel-universe-building-and-the-legacy-of-elektra/.

"Zack Snyder Fan Q&A—Part II." *Watchmen Comic Movie*, February 14, 2008. http://www.watchmencomicmovie.com/021408-zack-snyder-watchmen-interview.php.

Zakarin, Jordan. "'Deadpool' Screenwriters Go Deep: X-Men Choices, De-powering Copycat, and All Those Sex Jokes." *Yahoo! Entertainment*, February 10, 2016. https://www.yahoo.com/entertainment/deadpool-screenwriters-go-deep-x-men-choices-184031515.html.

Zakarin, Jordan. "Ryan Reynolds Explains How the Deadpool Movie Got Resurrected." *Yahoo! Entertainment*, February 3, 2015. https://www.yahoo.com/entertainment/ryan-reynolds-explains-how-the-deadpool-movie-got-109934676757.html.

Zakarin, Jordan. "'X-Men: Apocalypse' destroys Auschwitz and it's really uncomfortable." *Inverse*, May 9, 2016. https://www.inverse.com/article/15398-x-men-apocalypse-destroys-auschwitz-and-it-s-really-uncomfortable.

Zimmerman, Dwight Jon. "Gloria Katz." *Comics Interview* #38, September 1986.

Zimmerman, Dwight Jon. "Steve Gerber." *Comics Interview* #38, September 1986.

Index

Numbers in **_bold italics_** indicate pages with illustrations

Abar, the First Black Superman 74–5
ABC 11, 12–7, 18, 20, 21, 22, 29
Abin Sur 126
Abnett, Dan 140
Abomination (Emil Blonksy) 28, 112, 185
Abrams, J.J. 19, 100
Ace the Bathound 13
Acheson, James 87
Action Comics 3, 5, 8, 39
Adams, Amy 134
Adams, Neal 33, 47, 69, 125
Adventures of Captain Marvel (serial) 5, 7–9, 34, 175
The Adventures of Superboy 11
The Adventures of Superman (radio show) 8, 10
Adventures of Superman (TV series) 10–1, 30
The Adventures of Superpup 11
Affleck, Ben 11, 86–8, 148, 154, 160, 166
Ain't It Cool News 77, 92, 108
Ajax 151
Åkerman, Malin **_120_**
Alanis, Ramiro 186
Alba, Jessica 98, **_99_**
Alexander, Lexi 115–6
al Ghul, Ra's 97, 133
Aliens 42, 89
Allen, Woody 73
Alonso, Victoria 108
Altman, Robert 36
Alyn, Kirk 8, 10–1
The Amazing Adventures of Kavalier & Clay 92
The Amazing Spider-Man (comic book) 60, 73, 79, 92, 138
The Amazing Spider-Man (film) 131–2
The Amazing Spider-Man (TV series) 24
The Amazing Spider-Man 2 138, 171–2
Ambrosia, Lorelei 38–9, 100
Ancient One 26, 155–6
Anderson, Pamela 67
Angel (Warren Worthington III) 100, 152
Angel, Asher 176
animatronics 41, 54, 67
Ant-Man 111, 143–4, 171
Ant-Man (Scott Lang) 91, 106, 143–4, 150, 171–2, 177
Ant-Man and the Wasp 171–2
Apocalypse 139, 152–3
Aquaman 172–4
Aquaman (Arthur Curry) 148, 165–6, 172–3
Arad, Avi 60, 62, 79, 89, 91, 95, 98, 101–2, 106–7, 131, 172
Archangel 152
Arclight 100
Archie Comics 53
Arctic World 57
Arkham Asylum 72, 179
Artisan Entertainment 91–2, 106, 116, 143
Asgard 124, 164, 169
Ashmore, Shawn 81
Astor, Tom 66
AT&T 173
The Atom 125
Atom Man vs. Superman 9
Atwell, Hayley 128
Atwill, Lionel 8
Auschwitz 80, 125, 152
Austin, William 7
The Avengers 25, 28, 79, 106–7, 109, 123, 127, 129–31, 142, 149, 164, 168–9, 171, 175, 177
The Avengers (comic book) 25, 159, 171
The Avengers (film) 111, 123, 129–31, 133, 142, 144, 165, 167
Avengers: Age of Ultron 142–3, 166, 168, 182
Avengers: Endgame 168, 170, 174, 177–8
Avengers: Infinity War 168–9, 171, 175
Awkwafina 185
Ayer, David 121, 153–4

Baker, Dylan 104, 131
Baldwin, Alec 55, 65
Bale, Christian 97
Bana, Eric 89
Bane 71–2, 132–3
Banner, David 86
Barb Wire 67
Barris, George 14
Barron, Steve 54
Barthelme, Donald 39
Barto, Pat 17
Basinger, Kim 49, 50
Bassett, Angela 127, 154
Bat-signal 9
Batalon, Jacob 163
Batboat 16–17
Batcave 7, 9, 12, 14, 18, 70, 96, 148
Batchler, Janet Scott 69–71
Batchler, Lee 69, 71
Batfilm Productions 46
Batgirl (Barbara Gordon) 17, 18, 180
Batgirl (Barbara Wilson) 71–2
Batgirl 165
Batman (Bruce Wayne) 5–7, 9, 11, 12–20, 46–52, 57–9, 69–73, 88, 96–7, 113–5, 132–3, 135, 147–9, 154, 157, 165–6, 172

225

Index

Batman (comic book) 13, 17, 153
Batman (film, 1966) 16, 17
Batman (film, 1989) 46–54, 56–9, 88, 97, 110
Batman (serial) 3, 5–8, 97
Batman (soundtrack) 65
Batman (TV series) 12–22, 24, 30, 34, 46, 48, 75, 125, 132, 153
Batman & Robin (film) 69–73, 96, 132
Batman and Robin (serial) 9, 49
Batman Begins 96–7, 105, 113
Batman Forever 68–71, 115
Batman Returns 43, 53, 57–9, 65, 69, 93–4
Batman: The Animated Series 96, 153–4, 180
Batman v Superman: Dawn of Justice 147–9, 151, 153–4, 160–1, 165–6, 173
Batmania 12, 16, 50
Batmobile 3, 6, 9, 14, 50, 148
Batroc 137
Batson, Billy 4, 5, 176
Battle of New York 130, 133, 137, 162
Batusi 14
Batwing 51
Bautista, Dave 141
Baxter, Anne 16
Beachler, Hannah 168
Beall, Will 172–3
Beast (Hank McCoy) 100, 124, 139, 152, 178
Beatty, Ned 34
Beatty, Warren 54
Beck, C.C. 4
Beckerman, Barry 47
Beetlejuice 48, 49, 57
Bell, Jamie 146
Belova, Yelena 184
Bendis, Brian Michael 109
Benioff, David 120–1
Bennet, Spencer Gordon 8, 9
Benton, Robert 31
Berg, Jon 165
Berlanti, Greg 126
Bernstein, Robert 172
Berry, Halle 81–2, 94
Bester, Alfred 31
Beta Ray Bill 123
Bettany, Paul 142
Big Boy Caprice 54
Bigelow, Kathryn 79
Bilson, Danny 56
The Bionic Woman 25, 26
Birdman 163
Birds of Prey (comic book) 180
Birds of Prey (TV series) 180
Birds of Prey (and the Fantabulous Emancipation of One Harley Quinn) 180
Birnbaum, Roger 48
Bixby, Bill 26, 89
Black, Jack 126
Black, Shane 108, 133
Black Canary 125, 180
Black Mask 180
Black Panther 76, 150, 167–8
Black Panther (T'Challa) 76, 82, 91, 106, 150, 167–9
Black Widow 184–5
Black Widow (Natasha Romanoff) 106, 123, 130, 137, 142, 149, 174, 177, 184–5
Blade 76–8
Blade 76–8, 85, 87, 167
Blade: Trinity 96, 122

Blade II 91
Blake, Don 123
Blake, Madge 13, 18
Blair, Selma 91
Blanchett, Cate 164
Blankman 74–5
Blind Al 152, 170
Bloodsport 183
Blue Öyster Cult 64
Boden, Anna 176
Bogart, Neil 47
Bond, James 19, 31, 47, 49, 126, 128, 132, 173
Bookworm 16
Boone, Josh 184
Boseman, Chadwick 150, 167, 184
Bosworth, Kate 101
Bowman, Rob 95
Bradstreet, Tim 91
Brainiac 38
Branagh, Kenneth 123–4, 136
Brando, Marlon 31–2, 38
Bratt, Benjamin 94
The Brave and the Bold 153
Bridges, Jeff 108, 110
Briggs, Peter 91
Brightburn 178
Brolin, Josh 125, 141, 170
Broome, John 13, 125
Brotherhood of Mutants 81, 88
Brown, Reb 28, 61
Brubaker, Ed 137
Brunner, Frank 26
Brutenholm, Prof. 91
Bry, Ellen 24
Buffy the Vampire Slayer 128, 182
Bullseye 86–8
Burch, Sonny 171
Burke, Nathaniel 75–6
Burton, Tim 48–52, 57–9, 69, 71, 101
Byrne, John 125, 136, 139

Cable 170
Cadence Industries 60
Cage, Luke 47, 76
Cage, Nicolas 101–2, 124
Caglione, John, Jr. 54
Cain, Cassandra 180
Caine, Michael 97
Calabrese, Jerry 95
Callaham, Dave 181
Calley, John 67, 82
Cameron, James 65, 76, 79–80, 83, 89, 98
Campbell, Bill 56
Campbell, Martin 126–7
Candy, Etta 22
Cannell, Stephen J. 29
Cannon Film Group 43–4, 61, 83
Captain America (comic book) 8, 28, 136
Captain America (film, 1990) 89
Captain America (serial) 7–8, 127
Captain America (Steve Rogers) 7, 23, 25, 28, 41, 61, 106, 123, 127–30, 137, 147, 149, 163
Captain America (TV movie) 28, 127
Captain America: Civil War 147, 149–51, 161, 168
Captain America: Death II Soon 28
Captain America: The First Avenger 111, 127–9, 137
Captain America: The Winter Soldier 137–9, 142, 144
Captain Boomerang 154

Index

Captain Marvel (Carol Danvers) 175
Captain Marvel (character, Fawcett/DC) 4–5, 175–6
Captain Marvel (comic book) 175–6
Captain Marvel (movie) 175
Captain Nice 16
Carolco Pictures 79
Carroll, Eric Hauserman 162
Carson, Johnny 38
Carter, Lynda 21–3, **22**, 181
Carr, Thomas 8, 9, 10
Carrey, Jim 65
Carter, Peggy 128, 138
Carter, Ruth 168
Casablanca 67
Casablanca Filmworks 47
Casablanca Records 47
Cash, Jim 54
cats 91, 94, 98
Catwoman (*Batman* TV series) 13, **15**, 16–8
Catwoman (film) 93–5, 132, 160
Catwoman (Patience Phillips) 94
Catwoman (Selina Kyle) 57–8, 70, 93
Cavill, Henry 134, 147; mustache, 166
CBC 13, 14
CBS 16, 22–4, 27, 28
Cena, John 183
CGI 41, 65, 73–4, 77, 81, 85, 89, 97–8, 101–2, 105, 108, 122, 152, 170, 173
Chabon, Michael 80, 92
Chan, Gemma 185
Chastain, Jessica 178
Cheetah (Barbara Minerva) 181
Chihara, Paul 27
Chiklis, Michael 98–9, 146
Chronicle 145
CIA 21, 22
Ciarfalio, Carl 63
Clancy, Tom 107, 133
Claremont, Chris 79, 125, 136, 139
Clifton, Elmer 8
Clooney, George 71, **72**
Coates, Phyllis 10
Cockrum, Dave 79
Coghlan, Frank, Jr. 5
Colan, Gene 76, 175
Cold War 98, 106
Cole, Joe Robert 167
Cole, Royal K. 9
Collector (Taneleer Tivan) 141, 169
Colossus 79, 100, 151–2, 170
Columbia 3–4, 6–9, 12, 60, 74, 76, 86
Collins, Anne 23
The Comedian 119
Comic Art Convention 47
Comics Code Authority 40, 76
Conan the Barbarian 64, 79
Conan the Destroyer 79
Condorman 36
Connelly, Jennifer 90
Connery, Sean 19, 49
Conway, Gerry 60, 79
Cook, Peter 40
Cooper, Aunt Harriet 13, 18
Constantine 156
Coogler, Ryan 167
Cooper, Bradley 141
Copiel, Olivier 123
Corman, Roger 60, 62–4, 89, 92
Cornish, Joe 143
Cosby, Andrew 176
Cop Car 162
Covid-19 180
Craig, Yvonne 17–8
Cramer, Douglas C. 20–2
Craven, Wes 47, 76
Cretton, Destin Daniel 185
Crimson Dynamo 122
Crisis on Infinite Earths 39
Croft, Douglas **6**, 7
Cronenberg, David 145
Crosby, Cathy Lee 20, 21
The Crow (comic book) 64
The Crow (Eric Draven) 64
The Crow (film) 64–5, 87
The Crow: City of Angels 76, 96
Crowe, Russell 134
Crudup, Billy **120**
Cryer, Jon 45
Cuban Missile Crisis 124
Cudmore, Daniel 152
Culp, Joseph 62
Cumberbatch, Benedict **156**
Cyborg (Victor Stone) 148, 165–6, 182
Cyclops (Scott Summers) 80–2, 88, 100, 153

Dafoe, Willem 83, 173
Daily Bugle 84–5, 92, 172, 178
Daily Planet 8, 33, 36, 38–9, 44, 101, 134
Daley, John Francis 162–3
Daly, Robert 69
Damon, Matt 164
Daredevil (comic book) 86–8, 117
Daredevil (film) 86–8, 93, 94–5, 101, 104, 107
Daredevil (Matt Murdock) 23, 86–7, 107, 123
Dark Horse 65–6, 90–1
The Dark Knight 56, 113–5, 125, 132–3, 157, 168, 179
The Dark Knight Returns 47, 69, 86, 117
The Dark Knight Rises 132, 173
Dark Phoenix 100, 136, 178; *see also* Jean Grey
Dark Phoenix 178
Darkman 53, 55–6, 82
Darkman (Peyton Westlake) 55
Darkman II: The Return of Durant 55
Darkseid 165
David, Peter 55–6, 173
Davis, Viola 154, 183
Dawes, Rachel 97, 113, 115, 132
Dawson, Kim 53
DC Comics 13, 19, 46–8, 53, 57, 60, 73, 75, 93, 101, 116, 118, 122, 125, 131, 133, 166, 172–3, 175, 179, 181
DC Entertainment 122, 165, 173
DC Extended Universe (DCEU) 135, 148–9, 153, 161, 165–6, 173, 176, 180, 182
DC Universe 182
Deadpool 147, 151–2, 159, 181
Deadpool (Wade Wilson) 91, 121–2, 126, 151–2, 170–1, 174
Deadpool 2 170–1, 183
Deadshot 154, 183
The Death of the Incredible Hulk 89
DeConnick, Kelly Sue 175
Dehaan, Dane 138
del Toro, Benicio 141
del Toro, Guillermo 90–1, 176
De Luca, Mike 76
De Meo, Paul 56

DeNiro, Robert 179
Dennison, Julian 170
Derrickson, Scott 155–6
DeSanto, Tom 80
D'Esposito, Louis 108
Detective Comics 47, 48
DeVito, Danny 57, 74
Diaz, Cameron 65
di Bonaventura, Lorenzo 126
Dick Tracy 53–4, 65, 68, 117
Dickerson, Ernest 76
Diesel, Vin 141
Dini, Paul 153
Di Novi, Denise 57, 93–4
Dippé, Mark A.Z. 74
Disney 48, 54, 56, 107, 122, 151, 159, 174, 178
Ditko, Steve 3, 23, 26–7, 102, 155–6, 162, 172
Dixon, Chuck 12
Doc Savage 68
Dr. Daka 6–7
Doctor Doom (Victor von Doom) 62–3, 98–100, 104–5, 146
Doctor Manhattan 119–20
Doctor Octopus (Otto Octavius) 83, 92–3
Doctor Sivana 5, 176
Doctor Strange (comic book) 155
Doctor Strange (film) 74, 76, 147, 155–6
Doctor Strange (Stephen Strange) 25–7, 47, 86, 106, 154–6, 168–9, 172
Doctor Strange (TV movie) 155
Dolby, Thomas 43
Domino 170
Donner, Lauren Shuler 79–80, 107, 121–2, 124, 135
Donner, Richard 30–5, 47, 80, 100–1, 121
Doomsday 147–8, 166
Dora Milaje 168
Dorf, Stephen 77
Dormammu 155–6
Dougherty, Michael 100
Douglas, Michael 69
Douglas, Sarah *37*
Downey, Robert, Jr. 108, **109**, 110, 122, 133, 163
Dozier, William 12–19, 64
Drake, Larry 55
Drax 140–1, 159
Dredd 164
Drexler, Doug 54
Ducard, Henri 97
Duncan, Michael Clarke 88
Dunn, David 174
Dunst, Kirsten 83, **84**, 85, 98
Durant, Robert 55
Dykstra, John 85

Easter eggs 93
Eastman, Kevin 53
Eastwood, Clint 60, 135
Ebony Maw 169
Eckhart, Aaron 115
Egghead 17
Ego the Living Planet 152, 159
Eichinger, Bernd 61–3, 98
Eisenberg, Jesse 149
Eisner, Will 64, 117
Ejiofor, Chiwetel 156
Elba, Idris 183
El Diablo 154
The Electric Company 24, 129

Electro (Max Dillon) 23, 24, 83, 138
Elektra 76, 94–5, 160
Elektra (Elektra Natchios) 86–8, 94–5
Elf 107
Ellis, Bret Easton 77, 108
Ellis, Warren 106, 133
Ellison, Harlan 117
Ellsworth, Whitney 3, 10–1
Ely, Ron 68
Emmerich, Toby 154, 165
The Enchantress 154
Englehart, Steve 26, 47–8, 159
English, John 8
Ennis, Garth 116
En Sabah Nur 152
Epps, Jack, Jr. 54
Epting, Steve 137
Erskine, Abraham 127
Eternals 185
Eternity 27
Evans, Chris 98–9, 128, **130**, **150**
Evel Knievel 101–2
An Evening with Batman and Robin 12
The Executioner 60

The Falcon (Sam Wilson) 149, 171
Falcone, Carmine 96
Falk, Lee 3, 67
The Fantastic Four 61–3, 97–100, 104–6, 129, 174
Fantastic Four 144–6, 167
The Fantastic Four (comic book) 23, 79, 97–8, 104, 146
The Fantastic Four (film, 1994) 61–4, 92, 97
The Fantastic Four (film, 2005) 97–100, 105, 119, 144
Fantastic Four: Rise of the Silver Surfer 104–5, 123, 126
Farrell, Colin 88
Fassbender, Michael 125
Fast Color 174, 177
Favreau, Jon 107–111, 122, 133, 163
Fawcett Comics 4–7, 175–6
Feiffer, Jules 36
Feige, Kevin 98, 106–7, 109, 111, 122–3, 127, 129, 133, 137, 143, 155–6, 161–3, 167
Fellini, Federico 23
Fergus, Mark 109
Ferrigno, Lou 25, **25**, 26, 89, 112
Ferris, Carol 126–7
Fields, Syd 79
Finger, Bill 5, 55, 125
Finn, Sarah 108
Firefist 170
Fishburne, Laurence 105
Fisher, Ray 166, 182
Fitzsimons, Charles B. 18
Flag, Rick 154, 183
The Flash 166
The Flash (Barry Allen) 125, 148, 154, 165–6, 182
Flashdance 47
Fleck, Arthur 179
Fleck, Ryan 176
Fleischer, Dave and Max 4, 10
Fleiss, Heidi 28
Flothow, Rudolph C. 8
Flugelheim Museum 50
Forman, Carol 9
Forman, Milos 135
Fortress of Solitude 36–7, 101
Foster, Jane 123–4, 136

Fourth World 165
Fox, Lucius 97, 113
Fox Kids Network 79
Fox News 159
Foxx, Jamie 138
Fradon, Ramona 172
France, Michael 89, 92, 98
Franco, Gianni 60–1
Franco, James 102, 139
Frank, Scott 135–6, 157
Frankfurt, Peter 77
Franklin, Murray 179
Frazetta, Frank 64
Freaks and Geeks 163
Freddy's Dead: The Final Nightmare 66
Freedman, Mark 53
Freeman, Morgan 97
fridging 170
Friedkin, William 117
Friedrich, Gary 101
Fries, Nora 72
From Hell 47
Frost, Deacon 77
Frost, Emma 125
Frost, Mark 98, 104
Frost Giants 124
Fu Manchu 156, 185
Fukishima, Rila 136
Furie, Sidney J. 44
Furst, Anton 49, 52, 57
Fury, Nick 106, 111, 127–8, 130, 136–7, 176

Gadot, Gal 148–9, **160**, 160–1
Gaines, Max 20
Galactus 104–5, 127
Gale, Ed 41
Gambit 121
Game of Thrones 121, 136, 173
Gamora 140, 141, 159, 177
Garfield, Andrew 131–2, 162
Garland, Alex 164
Garner, Jennifer 88, 94
Gerber, Steve 41–2
G-Girl 123
Ghost Rider (comic book) 101
Ghost Rider (film) 101–2
Ghost Rider (Johnny Blaze) 101–2
Ghost Rider: Spirit of Vengeance 125
Giant Man 150
Giant-Size Man-Thing 41
Gibbons, Dave 118–9
Gibson, Henry 22
Gibson, Walter B. 55
Giganta 125
Gillan, Karen 141, 159
Gilliam, Terry 118
Gish, Annabeth 76
Glass 174
Globus, Yoram 43–4
Golan, Menahem 43–4, 61
Goldblatt, Mark 60
Goldblum, Jeff 164
Golden Age 86, 125
Golden Harvest 53
Golden Raspberries 40, 42, 94
Goldman, Clint 74
Goldman, Jane 124, 139
Goldman, William 31

Goldsman, Akiva 71, 96
Goldstein, Jonathan 157, 162–3
Goode, Matthew **120**
Goodman, Daniel R. 24
Gordon, James 7, 9, 13, 16–8, 49, 71, 97, 113, 115
Gordon, Lawrence 65, 91, 118
Gorman, Gus 38–9, 100
Gorshin, Frank 13–9, 23, 75, 125
Gossett, Louis, Jr. 61
Gotham City 6, 17, 49, 50–2, 58, 71–3, 96–7, 115, 132, 147, 149, 179, 180
Gotham Plaza 57
Gothcard 72
Gough, Michael 49, 73
Gould, Chester 54
Goyer, David S. 76–7, 96, 101, 122, 128, 132, 134–5, 149, 153
Grace, Topher 172
Grandmaster 164
Granov, Adi 106, 109, 133
Grant, Maxwell 55
Grantray-Lawrence Animation 23
Greatest American Hero 29
Green, Kat 62
Green, Sid 125
Green Arrow 153
Green Goblin (Harry Osborn) 102–3, 138
Green Goblin (Norman Osborn) 83–5, 93
The Green Hornet (film) 139
The Green Hornet (TV series) 17, 64
Green Lantern (comic) 170
Green Lantern (film) 125–7, 151, 154, 163, 166, 170
Green Lantern (Hal Jordan) 125–7, 163
Green Lantern/Green Arrow 125
Greenway Productions 13
Grey, Jean 80–2, 100, 136, 147, 153, 178
Grissom, Carl 49, 50
Groot 139, 141, 159, 169
Gruffud, Ioan 98, 99
Grundy, Solomon 125
Guardians of the Galaxy 137, 139–41, 153, 159, 168
Guardians of the Galaxy (comic book) 139, 159
Guardians of the Galaxy (film) 137, 140–1, 144
Guardians of the Galaxy Vol. 2 159
Guber, Peter 46–7
Guinness, Alec 108
Gunn, James 140–1, 159, 178, 182
Gyllenhaal, Jake 178
Gyllenhaal, Maggie 115

Hackman, Gene 31, 34, 37–8, 44, 101
Haley, Jackie Earle 120
Hamilton, Guy 31
Hamilton, John 11
Hamilton, Neil 13
Hamm, Sam 48, 57
Hammer, Justin 122
Hammond, Hector 126
Hammond, Nicholas 24
Hancock 154
The Hands of Shang-Chi, Master of Kung Fu 185
Hanna-Barbera 125
Hansen, Maya 133
Happy Meals 59
Harbour, David 176, 184
Hardwicke, Catherine 67
Hardy, Tom 132, 172, 184
Harrelson, Woody 184

Harris, Dan 100
Harris, Rosemary 85
Harrison, Linda 20
Harrison, Sol 46
Hart, Julia 177
Hasselhoff, David 128
Hastings, Julie 55
Hathaway, Anne 132
Haupstein, Ilsa 91
Hawke, Ethan 158
Hawkeye 106, 123, **150**
Hawkman 125
Hayek, Salma 185
Hayter, David 80, 88–9, 119–20
Hayward, Jimmy 125
HBO 119–21, 172
HBO Max 182
Heard, Amber 173
Heat 113
Heathers 57
Heck, Don 106, 123, 159
Hedare, Laurel 94
Hefner, Hugh 12
Hefti, Neil 14
Heimdall 169, 183
Heinberg, Allan 161
Hela 136, 164, 169
Helicarriers 130, 137
Hellboy 90–1, 176
Hellboy (comic book) 90–1
Hellboy (film, 2004) 90–1, 105
Hellboy (film, 2019) 176
Hellboy II: The Golden Army 176
Hellfire Club 125
Hemingway, Mariel 45
Hemsworth, Chris 124, **130**, 163, **164**
Henry, Brian Tyree 185
Henry, Buck 16
Hensleigh, Jonathan 92
Herbeck, Bobby 53–4
Hero at Large 36
Hewlett, Jamie 66
Hickson, Julie 48
Hiddleston, Tom 124
Highlander 65
Hildebrand, Brianna 151
Hill, Maria 130, 137
Hillyer, Lambert 6
Hingle, Pat 49
Hit Girl 124
Hodson, Christina 180
Hoffman, Dustin 54
Hogan, Happy 163
Holland, Tom 150, 162, 186
Holmes, Katie 97, 115
Holocaust 152
Hood, Gavin 121
Hooten, Peter 27
Hopkins, Anthony 124
Horn, Alan 96, 159
Horowitz, Jordan 177
hot air balloons 37, 39
Howard, Bryce Dallas 104, 131
Howard, Robert E. 64
Howard the Duck 41–2, 90, 141
Howard the Duck (comic book) 41
Howard the Duck (movie) 36, 42–3, 53, 60, 78
Howe, Desson 73

Howling Commandos 128
Hughes, John 162–3
Hulk 86, 89–90, 92–3, 98, 107, 111
Hulk (Bruce Banner) 8, 23, 25–6, 28–9, 41, 75, 86, 89, 98, 106–7, 111–2, 130, 142, 150, 163–4, 169, 177
Hulkbuster 142
Human Torch (Johnny Storm) 62–3, 98–9, 104–5, 128, 145–6, 167
Hunt for the Wilderpeople 163, 170
Hunter, Holly 148
The Huntress 125, 180
Hurd, Gayle Anne 89, 91, 111, 115
Huyck, Willard 41–2
Hyde-White, Alex 62, **63**
Hydra 127, 137, 142, 144, 149–50

Iceman (Bobby Drake) 81, 88, 100
Ifans, Rhys 131
Iger, Bob 186
Image Comics 73
IMAX 115
The Incredible Hulk (comic book) 25, 41, 73
The Incredible Hulk (film) 107, 111, 140, 144
The Incredible Hulk (TV pilot) 26
The Incredible Hulk (TV series) 20, 28–9, 66, 86
The Incredible Hulk: Death in the Family 26
The Incredible Hulk Returns 89, 123
The Incredibles 98
Industrial Light & Magic 56, 74, 89
Infantino, Carmine 13, 17, 31
Infinity Gauntlet 169
Infinity Stones 169, 177
The Interview 139
Invisible Woman (Susan Storm) 62–4, 98–9, 104–5, 145–6
Iron Man (film) 106–12, 128–9, 133, 140, 167
Iron Man (Tony Stark) 23, 82, 106–12, 122–3, 130, 133–4, 142, 147, 149–51, 162–3, 169, 171, 174, 177–8
Iron Man 2 122–3, 133, 138
Iron Man 3 133–4
Irons, Jeremy 148
Isaac, Oscar 152
Isis 23
It's a Bird... It's a Plane... It's Superman 31

Jackman, Hugh 81–2, 121–2, 135, 157–8
Jackson, Michael 54
Jackson, Samuel L. 128, 174
Jameson, J. Jonah 24, 85, 92, 178
Jane, Thomas 91, 116
Janssen, Famke **81**, 82, 136
J.A.R.V.I.S. 111, 142
Jaws 113
Jenkins, Patty 154, 160–1, 181
Jenning, Walter 42
Jet Girl 66–7
Jigsaw 116
Jim Henson's Creature Shop 54
The Joan Rivers Show 57
Joker 6, 13, 16–8, 48, 50–1, 70, 113–5, 153–5, 166, 180
Joker 174, 179
Johansson, Scarlet 117, 123, **130**, 184
Johns, Geoff 165, 173, 181
Johnson, Kenneth 20, 25–6, 28, 75–6, 89
Johnson, Mark Steven 86–7, 101
Johnston, Joe 56–7, 127
Jolie, Angelina 186
Jonah Hex 125

Index

Jones, Doug 91, 105
Jones, Jeffrey 43
Jones, MJ 163
Jones, Quincy 75
Jones, Sam 117
Jones, Tommy Lee 70, 115
Jones, Vinnie 170
Jong-Un, Kim 139
Jordan, Michael B. 145, **145**, 167
Jor-El 33, 36, 134
Joseph, Frederic 168
Journey into Mystery 123
Judge Dredd 67
Juggernaut 100, 170
Justice League 125, 148, 165–6, 172–3, 182
Justice League 127, 149, 153, 160, 165, 173, 182

Kaecilius 155–6
Kahn, Jenette 48
Kamen, Robert Mark 60
Kane, Bob 3, 5, 9, 15, 55
Kane, Gil 125
Kant, Immanuel 39
Karnowski, Tom 61
Kato 64
Katz, Gloria 36, 41–2
Katzenberg, Jeffrey 56
Katzman, Sam 8–9
Keaton, Michael 49–52, 57, **58**, 70–1, 162
Keen, Dafne 157, **158**
Kellogg's 10
Kelly, Robert 81
Kent, Martha 33, 44, 147
Keslee 67–7
Khodchenkova, Svetlana 136
Kick-Ass 124
Kidder, Margot 32, **34**, 38, 101
Kidman, Nicole 71
Killer Croc 154
Killian, Aldrich 133
The Killing Joke 47
Killmonger 168
Kilmer, Val 70–1
Kilowog 126
Kimmel, Jimmy 180
Kinberg, Simon 98, 100, 124, 139, 146, 151–3, 178, 184
King of Comedy 179
King of the Rocket Men 56
King Shark 182
Kingpin (Wilson Fisk) 86–7
Kingsley, Ben 134, 185
Kinneman, Joel 183
Kinney National Services 30
Kirby, Jack 7, 23, 25, 28, 61, 79, 89, 104–6, 123–4, 128, 159, 167, 172, 185
Kiss Kiss Bang Bang 108, 133
Kitt, Eartha 18
Klaue, Ulysses 142, 168
Klementieff, Pom 159, **177**
Kloves, Steve 131
Knowles, Harry 92
Knox, Alexander 49, 50
Koepp, David 65, 83
Konner, Lawrence 44
Korg 164
Kowalski, Kitty 101
Kramer, Eric 123
Kree 175–6

Kreuger, Freddy 65
Kristofferson, Kris 77
Kroenen, Karl 91
Krypton 33, 36, 39–40, 134
kryptonite 8, 34, 38–9, 147
Kurtzman, Alex 138
Kusatsu, Clyde 27
Kyle, Craig 123, 136, 157

Ladd, Alan 66–7
Lady Deathstrike 88
Lady Tanaka 60
Laird, Peter 53
Lane, Lois 8, 10–1, 31–2, 34, 36–7, 39, 69, 101, 134, 147–8, 166
Lane, Margo 65
Lang, Cassie 144
Lang, Lana 11, 38–9
Langford, Marty 64
Lanning, Andy 140
Lansbury, Bruce 22, 23
Larson, Brie **175**–6, **177**
Last Action Hero 88, 133
Latcham, Jeremy 140, 162
Lawrence, Jennifer 125
Leachman, Cloris 22
The Leader 28
The League of Extraordinary Gentlemen 47
League of Shadows 97, 132
Lebental, Dan 108
Ledger, Heath **114**, 115
Lee, Ang 89–90, 107, 112
Lee, Bonni 48
Lee, Brandon 64
Lee, Bruce 17, 64
Lee, Christopher 28
Lee, Linda 40
Lee, Stan 23–6, 28, 31, 40, 79, 61–3, 86, 104–6, 123, 128, 132, 143, 155, 167, 172, 175
LeFauve, Meg 175
LeFay, Morgan 27
Legends of the Superheroes: The Challenge and *The Roast* 19, 125–6, 176
Leguizamo, John 74
Leibowitz, Jack 10
Leitch, David 170–1
Lemmon, Leonore 11
Lemon Popsicle 43
Leonard, Elmore 135
Lester, Richard 32, 36–9
Leterrier, Louis 111–2
Leto, Jared 154
Leung, Tony 185
Levi, Zachary 176
Levin, Lloyd 91, 118
Lewis, Darcy 124
LexCorp 148
Lieber, Larry 106, 123
Lilly, Evangeline 142, 144
Ling, Barbara 70
Lionsgate 61, 115–7, 123
Lippert Pictures 10
Liu, Simu 184
Live Entertainment 61
Lively, Blake 127
The Lizard (Dr. Curt Connors) 23, 93, 104, 131–2
Loesch, Margaret 79
Logan 80, 157, 168

Logan's Run 28
Loki 124, 129–30, 142, 164
Lone, John 65
Lone, Tom 94
Lord, Max 181
Lore 184
The Losers 131
Lothar 56
Love, Courtney 67
Lovecraft, H.P. 91
Lowery, Robert 9
Lowther, George 8
Luber, Bernard 10
Lucas, George 30, 41–2, 56, 74
Lundgren, Dolph 61
Luthor, Lex 9, 31, 33–4, 37, 44, 69, 101, 148–9, 166
Lydecker, Howard and Theodore 5

MacGregor-Scott, Peter 69
Macht, Gabriel 117
Mackie, Anthony **150**
MacTaggart, Moira 100, 125
Mad magazine 20
Madonna 54
Magneto (Erik Lehnsherr) 80–1, 88, 100, 124–5, 139, 152
Maguire, Tobey 83, *84*, 85, 162
Mahoney, Breathless 54
Maibaum, Richard 47
Maisel, David 107, 109
Malebolgia 74
Malekith the Accursed 123, 136, 152
Mamet, David 97
Man of Steel 134–5, 144, 148–9, 161, 165
Man-Thing 41, 47
Man-Thing 106
Mandarin (Trevor Slattery) 106, 109, 133–4, 185
Mangold, James 135–6, 157
Mankiewicz, Tom 31–3, 44, 47–8
Mann, Michael 113
Mannix, Toni 11
Manson, Marilyn 74
Mantis 159
Mara, Kate **145**, 146
Marcel, Kelly 172
Marks, Justin 153
Markus, Christopher 128, 136–8, 150, 168–9, 178
Maroni, Salvatore 113
Mars, Kenneth 22
Marsden, James 81–2
Marshall, Neil 176
Marston, William Moulton 20–1, 161
the Martha moment 149
Martin, Alan 66
Martinson, Leslie H. 16
Marvel Cinematic Universe 112, 123, 128, 139, 150, 155, 159, 162, 175–6
Marvel Comics 8, 23–4, 26–8, 33, 36, 40–3, 53, 60–4, 73, 75, 79, 81, 86, 92–3, 97, 100–1, 105, 107, 111, 115–7, 127, 129, 141–2, 154, 162, 171, 175
Marvel Enterprises 76–7, 89
Marvel Entertainment 79, 122
Marvel Premiere 143
Marvel Productions 79
Marvel Studios 24, 74, 76, 95, 98, 106–12, 115, 122–4, 127–9, 133–4, 136, 138–40, 142–3, 147, 149–52, 155–6, 159–62, 164, 167–9, 171, 173–4, 179, 184–5
The Marvel Super Heroes 23

Marvel Two-in-One 129
Marvel Universe 97, 112, 172, 175
Marvel writers program 136, 140, 167
The Mask (comic book) 65
The Mask (film) 65–6, 74
The Mask (Stanley Ipkiss) 65
Masters, Alicia 62–3
Maxwell, Robert 10
Mayerik, Val 41
Mbatha-Ra, Gugu 177
McAdams, Rachel 156
McAvoy, James 125, 174
McDonald's 58, 69
McDormand, Frances 55
McDowell, Malcolm 67
McElroy, Alan B. 74
McFarlane, Todd 73–4
McFeely, Stephen 128, 136–8, 150, 168–9, 174, 178
McGee, Jack 26
McGowan, Rose 153
McKay, Adam 144
McKellan, Ian 65, 81
McKenna, Chris 178
McLure, Mark 40
McMahon, Ed 126
McMahon, Julian 98
McNiven, Steve 135
McQuarrie, Christopher 135
Meinerding, Ryan 122
Melniker, Benjamin 46, 47
Menzies, Heather 28
Mephistopheles 102
Mera 173
Mer-Batman 13
Meredith, Burgess 16, 18
Meridian, Chase 69–70
Meriwether, Lee 16, 19
Merrill Lynch 106–7
Meteor Man 74
Metropolis 8, 33, 36–9, 148, 166
MGM/UA 46, 66, 82
The Mighty Thor 136, 159
Mignola, Mike 90, 176
Mikkelsen, Mads 156
Millar, Mark 124, 135
Miller, Ashley Edward 145
Miller, Ezra 154, 166
Miller, Frank 86, 88, 117, 136
Miller, Penelope Ann 65
Miller, Tim 151-2
Miller, T.J. 152
Mills, John 27
Minutemen 119
Miramax 64
Mission: Impossible (TV series) 22
Mission: Impossible 2 82
Mr. Blue 112
Mr. Fantastic (Reed Richards) 62–3, 98–9, 104–5, 146
Mr. Freeze 13, 71–2
Mister Mxyzptlk 38
Mr. Scarlet 7
Mr. Terrific 16
Mjölnir 123–4, 142
Mole Man 63
Molina, Alfred 93
Moloch 119
Momoa, Jason 173
Monroe, Marilyn 9

Monster Magnet 151
Montalban, Ricardo 21
Montoya, Renee 180
Moore, Alan 47, 91, 118–9, 156
Moore, Demi 40
Morag 141
Mordo 155–6
Mordru 125
Moretz, Chloë Grace 124
Morgan, Jeffrey Dean 120
Morrison, Grant 6, 105, 151
Mort the Dead Teenager 91
Most, Jeff 64
Mother Box 165–6
MS magazine 21
Ms. Marvel 175
Mulcahy, Russell 65
Mull, Martin 23
Murphy, Cillian 97
My Super Ex-Girlfriend 123
Mysterio (Quentin Beck) 23, 178, 186
Mysterious Doctor Satan 7
Mystery Men 91
Mystique (Raven Darkholme) 80–1, 88, 100, 124, 139, 152–3, 178

Nagy, Ivan 28
Naish, J. Carroll **6**, 7
Nameless One 27
Nanjiani, Kumail 185
Napier, Alan 13
Napier, Jack 50
National Allied Publications 3–5, 8–10, 13, 33, 44; see also DC
Nazis 7, 21–2, 56, 80, 91, 125, 127, 137
NBC 16, 19, 89
Nebula 141, 159
Neeson, Liam 53, 55, 97
Negasonic Teenage Warhead 151, 159, 170
Neill, Noel 8, 10
Nelson, Diane 122, 157
Nelson, Foggy 87, 107
Neveldine, Mark 125
Never Say Never Again 19, 49
Nevius, Crag J. 62, 98
The New Adventures of Wonder Woman 22–3
New Line Cinema 65, 74, 76–7, 106, 108
The New Mutants 178, 184
The New, Original Wonder Woman 21–22, 24, 66
New Regency 86, 95
New World Entertainment 60–2
New World Pictures 62, 89, 92, 143, 155
New York Comic Art Convention 47
Newman, David 31, 36–8, 40
Newman, Leslie 31, 36–8
Newmar, Julie **15**, 16–9
Ngo, Vy Vincent 154
Nicholson, Jack 48–50
Nick Fury: Agent of S.H.I.E.L.D. 128
Nightcrawler (Kurt Wagner) 79, 88, 100, 153, 178
Nilsson, Harry 36
Nite Owl II (Dan Dreiberg) 119
Nixon, Richard 119, 139
No Heroics 133
Nodell, Martin 125
Nolan, Christopher 88, 96–7, 113–5, 132, 134, 179
Nolan, Jonathan 115, 132
Nomadland 185

Non 36–7
Norrington, Stephen 77
Norris, Paul 172
Norton, Edward 111–2
Nuclear Man 44, 100

O'Barr, James 64
Ocean Master 173
Odell, David 40
Odin 124
O'Donnell, Chris 70–1, **72**
O'Dowd, Chris 136
Ogdru Jahad 91
O'Halloran, Jack **37**
O'Hara, Miles 13, 18
Okamoto, Tao 136
Okoy 168
Oldman, Gary 97
Olsen, Elizabeth **150**, **177**
Olsen, Jimmy 8, 40
Omegahedron 40
The Omen 31
O'Neal, Shaquille 75
O'Neill, Denny 47, 69, 125
Orci, Roberto 138
Oscorp 84, 93, 131–2, 138, 140
Ostby, Hawk 109
Oswalt, Patton 116
O'Toole, Annette 39
O'Toole, Peter 40
Otto, Barry 61
The Outlaw Josey Wales 135
Ozymandias (Adrian Veidt) 119

Pacino, Al 54, 70
Page, Bettie 56
Page, Linda 7
Palance, Jack 49
Paley, William 24
Palmer, Christine 155–6
Paltrow, Gwyneth 108, **177**
Paquin, Anna **81**, 82
Paradise Island (Themyscira) 21–2, 161
Parallax 126
The Parallax View 19, 138
Paramount 4, 8, 64, 67, 107
Parker, Ben 24, 84–5, 102, 104, 132
Parker, Bill 4
Parker, Hutch 135, 152–3
Parker, May 24, 84–5, 92–3, 102, 179
Parker, Richard 131
Pascal, Amy 82, 131–2, 162–3, 172
Patterson, Shirley 7
Paulin, Scott 61
Payne, Don 104, 123, 136
Peacemaker 182–3
Pearce, Drew 133
Pee-wee's Big Adventure 48
Peña, Michael 144
Pendleton, Don 60
Penguin (Oswald Cobblepot) 6, 13, 16, 18, 48, 57–8, 74
Penn, Zak 88, 95, 100, 111, 129
Pennyworth, Alfred 7, 13, 49, 71–3
Perez, George 129
Perlman, Nicole 137, 140–1, 175
Perlman, Ron 90–1, 176
Perlmutter, Ike 63, 107
Perrine, Valerie 34

Peter, H.G. 20
Peters, Evan 139
Peters, Jon 46
Petty, Lori 66–7
Pfeiffer, Michelle 57, *58*, 93
Pfister, Wally 115
The Phantom 3, 67–8
The Phantom 67–8, 117
Phantom Zone 9, 33, 36, 40, 134
Phillips, Arianne 67
Phillips, Todd 174, 179
Phoenix, Joaquin 179
Pierce, Alexander 138
Pillow, Mark 45
Pine, Chris 161
Pinewood Studios 49
Pinkner, Jeff 138, 172
Pitof 94
Pixar 98
Planet of the Apes 20
Playboy Club 12
Playboy magazine 12
Playboy Mansion 12
Playboy Theatre 12
Ploog, Mike 101
Plympton, George H. 9
Poison Ivy (Pamela Isley) 17, 71–2
Poland, Joseph F. 9
Polka-Dot Man 182
Popeye 3, 36
Popeye 36
Portman, Natalie 124
Potts, Pepper 108, 110, 123
Power Pack 106
Pratt, Chris 141
Pressman, Edward R. 64
Price, Elijah 174
Price, Frank 25, 43
Price, Vincent 17
Prince 50–1, 65, 110
Propper, Gary 53
prosthetics 61, 98, 152
Proyas, Alex 64
Pryor, Richard 38–9
Psylocke 152
Pugh, Florence 185
Pulitzer Prize 36, 92, 101, 134, 148
The Punisher (comic book) 60, 91
The Punisher (film, 1989) 60–1, 92, 143
The Punisher (film, 2004) 91–2, 106
The Punisher (Frank Castle) 60–1, 91–2, 115–6, 118
Punisher Max 116
Punisher: War Zone 115–6
Purcell, Dick 7–8
Puzo, Mario 31
Pym, Hank 143–4, 171
Pyun, Albert 61

Quantum Realm 144, 171, 177
Quesada, Joe 88
Quicksilver (Pietro Maximoff) 139, 142
Quinn, Harley 153–4, 180–1, 183

Radar Men from the Moon 56
Raiders of the Lost Ark 56
Raimi, Ivan 55
Raimi, Sam 55–6, 65, 79, 82–5, 92–3, 102–4, 123, 131
Rasputin, Grigori 91

Ratcatcher 182
Ratcatcher 2 182
Ratner, Brett 100
Ravagers 159
Red Guardian 184
Red Skull (Schmidt, Johann) 61, 127–8
Redford, Robert 138
Reed, Peyton 98, 144, 171
Reese, Rhett 151, 170
Reeve, Christopher 32, 34, *34*, 38, 40, 43–5, 49, 101, 134
Reeves, George 10, 11
Reeves, Keanu 156
Reitman, Ivan 160
Renner, Jeremy *130*, *150*
Rennie, Michael 17
Repp, Stafford 13
Republic 3–5, 7–8, 56
Resnais, Alain 23
Return of the Swamp Thing 47
Return to the Batcave 19
Revolori, Tony 163
Revolution Studios 91
Reynolds, Ryan 122, 125–7, 151, 170
Rhino 23, 138
Richardson, Mike 65
Rico, Don 123
Riddle, Nelson 16
Riddler (Edward Nygma) 13–19, 70, 75
The Rider 185
Ringwood, Bob 71
Ritter, John 36
Robbie, Margot 154, 180–1, *183*
Robbins, Tim 43
Robertson, Cliff 17, 85
Robertson, Robbie 24
Robin (Dick Grayson) 6, 9, 13, 15–6, 18, 48–9, 70–2
Robinson, Jerry 33
Rock, Kevin 62, 98
Rocket Raccoon 139, *140*, 141, 159, 169
The Rocketeer (comic book) 56, 91
The Rocketeer (film) 56–7, 68, 90, 127
Rodriguez, Richard 117
Rogen, Seth 139
Rogers, Marshall 47
Rogue 80–2, 100, 139
Romero, Cesar 16, 18, 166
Romita, John 93
Romita, John, Jr. 88, 124
Rooker, Michael 159
Roots 28, 152
Rorschach 119
Rosenberg, Scott 83, 172
Rosenthal, Mark 44
Ross, Betty 90, 112
Ross, Stanley Ralph 20–2
Ross, Thaddeus "Thunderbolt", General 90, 112
Rothman, Tom 121
Rourke, Mickey 122
Routh, Brandon 100
Roven, Charles 165
Rudd, Paul 143–4, *150*, 171
Ruffalo, Mark 26, 111, 130, 164, 169
Russell, Chuck 65
Russo, Anthony 137–8, 150, 168–9, 178
Russo, Joe 137–8, 150, 162, 168–9, 177, 178

Sabretooth (Victor Creed) 80–1, 121
Saint, Howard 92

The Saint 71
St. Cloud, Silver 48
St. Joseph, Ellis 17
Sakaar 164
Salinger, J.D. 61
Salinger, Matt 61
Salkind, Alexander and Ilya 30–5, 38–40, 43–4, 46, 47, 100
Salzman, David 75
San Diego Comic-Con 45, 129, 131, 135, 176
Sandman (Flint Marko) 17, 83, 102–4
Sapien, Abe 91, 105
Sarafian, Tedi 66
Sarecky, Barney A. 10
Sargent, Alvin 83, 92, 102, 131
Sassone, Oley 62
Scarecrow (Jonathan Crane) 97, 132
Scarlet Witch (Wanda Maximoff) 142, 149–50
Schamus, James 89
Scherick, Edgar 12
Schiff, Jack 13
Schiff, Stephen 39
Schumacher, Joel 69, 70–1, 73
Schwartz, Julius 13, 17, 125
Schwarzenegger, Arnold 71, 73, 88
Scorpion 23
Scorsese, Martin 179
Scott, Alan 125
Scott, Dougray 82
Scott Pilgrim vs. the World 143, 151
Seagren, Danny 24
Secord, Cliff 56
Seduction of the Innocent 10
Segar, E.C. 36
Selvig, Erik 124, 130
Semple, Lorenzo, Jr. 13, 15–6, 19
Sentinels 100, 139
Serkis, Andy 142, 168, 184
The Shadow 55, 65, 67–8, 83, 117
The Shadow (Lamont Cranston) 55, 65, 117
Shadowcat (Kitty Pryde) 100, 139
Shang-Chi 106, 185
Shang-Chi and the Legend of the Ten Rings 184
Shannon, Michael 134
Sharpe, Dave 5
Shaw, Sebastian 124–5
Shazam! 176
Sheen, Martin 74
Sheinberg, Sidney 43
Sherman, Liz 91
S.H.I.E.L.D. 111, 124, 128, 130, 137–8, 151
Shields, Brooke 40
The Shining 48
Shirley, John 64
Sholem, Lee 10
Shortland, Cate 184
Shreck, Max 58
Shuri 168–9
Shuster, Joe 3, 33, 44
Shyamalan, M. Night 174
Siegel, Jerry 3, 10, 33, 44, 134
Sikes, Mark 62
Silk Spectre II (Laurie Jupiter) 119
Silver Samurai (Yashida, Ichirō) 135
The Silver Surfer 104–5
Silverfox, Kyla 121–2
Silverman, Greg 154, 165
Silverstone, Alicia 71, **72**

Simmons, J.K. 85
Simon, Joe 7
Simone, Gail 170–1
Simonson, Walt 123
Sin City 117
Sinestro 125–7
Singer, Bryan 79–82, 88, 100–1, 124, 134, 139, 152–3
The Six Million Dollar Man 24–5, 28
Skrulls 176
Skurge 164
Slater, Helen 40, 44
Slater, Jeremy 144–5
Slipknot 154
Smalley, James 74
Smallville 38–9, 134–5
Smigel, Robert 126
Smith, Kevin 87, 126, 154, 173
Smith, Michael Bailey 62, 63
Smith, Rex 86
Smith, Will 154
Smulders, Cobie 130
Snipes, Wesley 76, 167
Snyder, Deborah 165, 173
Snyder, Zach 117, 118–20, 134–5, 144, 148–9, 153, 160–1, 165, 173, 182
Sokovia Accords 149, 162, 171, 184
Soldana, Zoe 141
Sommers, Erik 178
Son of the Mask 65
Sondheim, Stephen 54
Soni, Karan 152
Sony 56, 82, 91–2, 101, 104, 132, 138, 139, 150, 161–2, 167, 171, 174, 178–9, 186
Spacey, Kevin 101
Spader, James 142
Spaihts, Jon 155
Sparks, Susan "Sparky" 75–6
Spawn 73–4
Spawn (Al Simmons) 74
Spawn The Album 74
special effects 5, 9, 18, 34, 41–2, 44–5, 74, 97, 105, 128, 135, 139, 144, 155, 173, 182
The Specials 141
Spengler, Pierre 32
Spider Lady 8
Spider-Man (animated series) 23, 93, 102
Spider-Man (film) 76, 82–5, 87, 95, 110, 172
Spider-Man (Peter Parker) 8, 23–6, 61, 76, 78–9, 82–6, 92–3, 98, 102–3, 106, 131–2, 138–9, 150, 161–3, 168–9, 172, 178
Spider-Man (TV pilot) 24
Spider-Man: Far From Home 178–9, 186
Spider-Man: Homecoming 157, 161–3
Spider-Man: Into the Spider-Verse 167
Spider-Man: No Way Home 180, 186–7
Spider-Man 3 102–4, 131
Spider-Man 2 92–3, 102
Spidey Super Stories 24, 129
The Spirit (comic strip) 64
The Spirit (Denny Colt) 117
The Spirit (film) 117
The Spirit (TV movie) 117
Split 174
Stabb, Rebecca 62, **63**, 64
Stacy, George 103, 138
Stacy, Gwen 103, 131–2, 138
Stallone, Sylvester 67
Stalmaster, Lynn 32, 40

Index

Stamp, Terence *37*, 93, 95
Stan, Sebastian 128, 147, 150
Stane, Obadiah 108–110, 129
Stark, Howard 127, 129
Stark Industries 109–10, 178
Star-Lord (Peter Quill) 130, 141, 159, 169
Star Trek 10, 18, 21, 129, 142
Star Wars 19, 34, 41, 76, 107
Starro 182
Statue of Liberty 38, 44, 81
Steel 75–6
Steel Harbor 67
Steinem, Gloria 21
Stentz, Zach 145
Steppenwolf 165–6, 173, 182
Stephenson, Pamela 39
Steranko, James 136
Stern, Howard 143
Stevens, Dave 56
Stevenson, Ray 116
Stewart, Patrick 81
Stone, Emma 131–2, 138
Stone, Sharon 94
Storm (Ororo Munroe) 79–82, 100, 139, 152
Story, Tim 98, 100, 104–5
Straczynski, J. Michael 123
Strick, Wesley 57
Strong, Mark 176
Stryker, William 88, 121–2
Studio 54 73
Sub-Mariner 23
Suicide Squad 153–4, 159, 180
The Suicide Squad 182–3
Sullivan, Susan 26
Super 141
Super Friends 125, 173
Supergirl 39–40, 43–4, 47, 52, 95, 134, 160
Supergirl (Kara Zor-El) 39–40
Superman (comic book) 31, 75
Superman (film) 11, 30–36, 40, 48–9, 54, 80, 100, 121, 163
Superman (Kal-El; Clark Kent) 3, 5, 8, 12, 20, 30–9, 44, 46, 69, 75–6, 100–1, 134–5, 147–8, 154, 157, 165–6, 175
Superman (newspaper strip) 8, 10
Superman (serial) 8–9
Superman and the Mole-Men 3, 10
Superman IV: The Quest for Peace 44–5, 93
Superman Inc. 8, 122
Superman Lives 101, 126
Superman Returns 9, 100–1, 134, 153
Superman III 38–40
Superman II 35, 36–7, 39, 95, 100, 135
Superman II: The Donner Cut 38
Surtur 123, 169
Swamp Thing 55
Swamp Thing (Alec Holland) 29, 47
Swinton, Tilda *156*
Switzler, Beverly 42
Sylbert, Richard 54
Szwarc, Jeannot 40

Talalay, Rachel 66–7, 82
Talbot, Glenn 90
Talbot, Lyle 9
A Tale of Two Cities 132
Tales from the Crypt: Demon Knight 76
Tales of Suspense 106

Tales to Astonish 25, 143
Talos 176
Tank Girl 66–7, 82
Taserface 159
Taylor, Alan 136
Taylor, Brian 125
Team X 121
Teefy, Maureen 40
Teenage Mutant Ninja Turtles 53–5
Teenage Mutant Ninja Turtles (comic book) 53
Teenage Mutant Ninja Turtles (movie) 53–4, 65, 74, 163
Teller, Miles **145**, 146
Ten Rings 110–1
The Terminator 60, 66, 89
Terminator 2: Judgment Day 56
Terrio, Chris 148
Teschmacher, Eve 33, 37, 101
Tesseract 127–30
Thanos 140–1, 159, 169, 177
Theroux, Justin 122
The Thing (Ben Grimm) 62–3, 98–9, **145**–6
The Three Musketeers 32
Thomas, Emma 134
Thomas, Roy 79, 101, 175
Thompson, Flash 163
Thompson, Lea 43
Thompson, Tessa 164, **177**
Thor 23, 82, 123–4, 129–30, 136, 150, 156, 163–4, 169
Thor 111, 123–4, 127, 129
Thor: Ragnarok 163–4
Thor: The Dark World 136, 138, 151, 160, 163
Three Days of the Condor 138
300 117
Thurman, Uma 123
Timecop 65
Timely 8, 23, 28, 62, 123; see also Marvel Comics
Timm, Bruce 153
Tolkin, Michael 61, 89
Tolkin, Stephen 61, 89
Toad 80–1, 88, 100
Tomb of Dracula 76
Tomczeszyn, Lisa 95
Tomei, Marisa 179
The Tonight Show 38, 126
Touchstone Pictures 54, 56
Townsend, Robert 74
Toy Biz 76, 79, 107
Tracy, Dick 3, 12, 54–5, 117
Trank, Josh 144–6
Trask, Bolivar 139
Trevor, Steve 21–2, 161
Trevor, Steve, Jr. 22
The Trial of the Incredible Hulk 86, 89, 132
Troma 140
Tromeo and Juliet 140
Trueheart, Tess 54
Tsujihara, Kevin 165
Tumbler 97, 115
Turner, Sophie 147
20th Century-Fox 13–6, 79–80, 82, 86, 88, 98, 100, 105, 119–21, 135, 139, 144–5, 151–3, 159, 174, 178
20th Century-Fox Television 20
The Twilight Zone 10
Two-Face (Harvey Dent) 69–70, 113–5
Tyler, Liv 112
Tyler, Tom **4**, 5

Udoff, Yale 12
Uggams, Leslie 152
The Ultimates 128
Ultron 142, 149, 162, 164
Unbreakable 174–5
The Uncanny X-Men 79, 125, 129, 136, 178
Underwood, Jay 62, **63**
United Artists 46
United Nations 149, 167
Universal 3, 20, 25–8, 41, 43, 55, 65, 89, 107, 111
Unleashed 111
Urban, Karl 164
Urich, Ben 87
Ursa 36–37
USA Network 47
Uslan, Michael 19, 46–52, 117
The Usual Suspects 80

V for Vendetta 47
Vaccaro, Brenda 40
Vale, Vicki 9, 49–51, 57, 97
Valkyrie 164
Vallee, Rudy 18
Van Damme, Jean-Claude 61, 65, 76
Vanderbilt, James 131
van Dyne, Janet 171
Vanity Fair 39
Vanko, Ivan 122
Vaughn, Matthew 124, 139
Vaughn, Robert 39
Venom 171–2, 179, 183
Venom (Eddie Brock) 102–4, 172, 183–4
Venom: Let There Be Carnage 183–4
Vidocq 94
Violator 74
Viper 135–6
Vision 142, 169
Von Gunther, Baroness Paula 22
Vuk 178
Vulko 173
The Vulture (Adrian Toomes) 23, 162–3

Waggoner, Lyle 14, 19, 22
Waid, Mark 19, 135
Waititi, Taika 127, 163–4, 170
Wakanda 150, 167, 169
Walker, Andrew Kevin 80, 96
Walker, Ellie Wood 20
Waller, Amanda 127, 154, 183
Walter, Jessica 27
Wan, James 173
WandaVision 184
War Machine (James "Rhodey" Rhodes) 111
Warbird 175
Ward, Burt 14–16, 18, 19, 125
Warfield, David 44
Warfield, Lacy 44
Warner Bros. 19, 22, 30–5, 38, 40, 44, 46–50, 57, 69, 71, 93, 97, 100, 118–20, 126, 134–5, 147, 153–4, 159, 165–6, 172–3
Warner Bros. Records 52
Warner-DC Entertainment 125
WarnerMedia 181–2, 183–3
The Wasp (Hope van Dyne) 123, 129, 171
Watchmen 118–20
Watchmen (comic book) 47, 91, 118–9
Watchmen (movie) 118–20, 122
Waters, Daniel 53, 57, 93
Waters, John 66
Watson, Mary Jane 83–5, 92–3, 103–4, 131
Watts, Emma 145
Watts, Jon 162–3
Watts, Naomi 67
Waugh, Fred 24
Wayans, Damon 74–5
Wayne, Martha 147
Wayne Enterprises 70, 97
Wayne Manor 50, 70, 72, 132
Weasel 152
Weather Wizard 125
Weaving, Hugo 128
Webb, Marc 131, 138
Webster, Ross 38–9
Webster, Vera 38–9
Wein, Len 79
Weisinger, Mort 172
Weisz, Rachel 184
Welch, Bo 57, 124
Wenwu, Xu 185
Wernick, Paul 151, 170
Wertham, Fredric 10
West, Adam 14, **15**, 16, 18–9, 96, 125
What If? 168
Whedon, Joss 24, 129–31, 140, 142–3, 160, 165, 182
Whedon, Tom 24
Whiplash 122
White, Michael Jai 74
White, Perry 8, 11, 36, 38, 44, 101
White, Richard 101
White House 37, 133, 139
Wickliffe, Conway 115
Wiig, Kirsten 181
Williams, Robin 36
Williams, Steve 74
Williams, Van 17
Willis, Bruce 174
Wilson, Lewis **6**
Wilson, Patricia Ellsworth 3
Wilson, Patrick 120, 173
Winderbaum, Brad 108, 144, 163
Windsor-Smith, Barry 121
Winger, Debra 22
Winnipeg 7, 94
Winston, Stan 67
Winter, Ralph 98
Winter Soldier (James "Bucky" Barnes) 127–8, 137, 147, 149–50
The Witches of Eastwick 48
Witney, William 5
The Wizard 9
Wolfman, Marv 76
The Wolverine 135–6, 139, 157, 166
Wolverine (James Howlett; Logan) 79–82, 88, 118, 120–2, 135–6, 139, 151, 157–9
Wonder Woman (comic book) 21
Wonder Woman (Diana Prince) 18, 20–3, 25, 148–9, 157, 160–1, 166, 181–2
Wonder Woman (movie) 154, 157, 160–1, 165
Wonder Woman (TV pilot) 20–1
Wonder Woman 1984 181
Wong 27, 155–6, 169
Wong, Benedict 156
Woodrue, Jason 72
World Unity Festival 84
World War I 161
World War II 135

Wright, Edgar 143–4
Wright, Letitia *177*
Wright, N'Bushe 77
Wuhl, Robert 49
Wurst, David and Eric 62
Wynne, Jason 74

Xavier, Charles (Professor X) 80–1, 88, 100, 124–5, 130, 153, 157
Xavier's School for Gifted Youngsters 81, 139
X-Force 170
Xialing, Xu 185
X-Men 8, 23, 76, 78–81, 86, 100, 139, 153, 170, 174–5, 178
X-Men 79–82, 85, 87–9, 99, 107, 130, 152
X-Men: Apocalypse 147, 152–3
X-Men: Days of Future Past 139, 153, 178
X-Men: First Class 124–5, 139, 145
X-Men Origins: Wolverine 120–2, 135–6, 151, 153, 170
X-Men: The Animated Series 79
X-Men: The Last Stand (*X3*) 100, 123–4, 139, 170, 178
X2: X-Men United 88–9, 100, 120
X-23 157

Yakin, Boaz 60, 143
Yakuza 60, 135
Yan, Cathy 181
Yashida, Mariko 135–6
Yashida, Shingen 135
Yeh, Phil 33
Yellowjacket (Darren Cross) 144
Yinsen, Dr. Ho 110
Yondu Udonta 159
Yon-Rogg 176
York, Susannah 38
Yost, Christopher 136
Young, Sean 49, 57
Yuen, Cheung-Yan 87

Zach Snyder's Justice League 182
Zaltar 40
Zandar 141
Zane, Billy 67
Zappa, Frank 16
Zathura: A Space Adventure 107
Zebra Batman 13
Zelda the Great 16
Zemo, Baron Helmut 149, 167
Zendaya 163
Zhao, Chloé 185
Zod 36–7, 93, 95, 134–5, 147, 166
Zola, Arnim 137
Zorro 30